David Reede

Vacation Address.

17 Chantry Hurst, Epsom,

Surrey

Telephone Epsom 23146.

Urban History Yearbook 1980

Leicester University Press 1980

First published by Leicester University Press 1980

Printed and bound in Great Britain by Redwood Burn Limited, Trowbridge, Wiltshire and Royal Mills, Esher, Surrey, England

Designed by Arthur Lockwood

British Library Cataloguing in Publication Data

Urban history yearbook
  1980
  i. Cities and towns – History
  1. Reeder, David
  909'.09' 732   HT111
  ISBN 0–7185–6080–9
  ISSN 0306–0845

Contents

Editorial note

The purpose of the *Yearbook* is to provide a research tool and a forum of discussion for urban historians. The editors are particularly concerned to encourage the submission of articles. They would welcome contributions on methodological problems, wide-ranging bibliographical surveys, and discussions of major themes in urban history. Intending contributors should contact the general editor at the School of Education, University of Leicester, 21 University Road, Leicester.

The editors are indebted to Sydney Checkland, Lynn Lees and Daniel Roche, all of whom responded to invitations for articles. These and other articles in this issue emphasize the integrative function of urban history. They bring out relationships with the history of public policy, the study of social development, and the history of disease. The geographical range of these discussions takes in England, France, the U.S.A. and Japan. The issue also contains notes on the materials of urban history and a reflection on the main theme of last year concerning the fortunes of early modern towns.

There have been several changes in editorial responsibilities for this issue. Derek Fraser is now Reviews Editor, assisted by Peter Clark for the period before 1800. Of the two new members of the Board, David Cannadine had responsibility for the review of periodical articles and Martin Daunton for the reports on conferences. Joyce Ellis updated the register of research, and Diana Dixon and Anthony Sutcliffe compiled the bibliography as before.

The urban historian
and the political will

1

At the Leicester urban history conference in 1966 there was very little discussion of the relationship between public policy and urban history. There were some points at which linkages were implied, but these arose merely incidentally. There was no attempt to adopt public policy as a general perspective on urban development. Reciprocally, the planners paid no attention to the historians: Jim Dyos remarked that the largest part of 'research and policy making is taking place without reference to the historians'.[1] The picture has not greatly changed over the past 14 years. There have indeed been studies in which policy, its formation and limitations, have been implicit, but few in which they have played a central part.

It is an interesting conjecture why this divorce should have occurred. In part it was due to the prevailing idioms of study in the West. The early ecological/sociological framework of the Chicago school of urban research had given way to close economic analysis, but this did not lead to a policy orientation, for much of it was on neo-classical, market-determined lines. In consequence public policy, which by its nature is a force inhibiting and controlling spontaneous patterns, was given no real prominence. Nor have scholars in the collectivized economies produced an alternative frame of reference for urban history.

Has the time now come for a change of emphasis towards policy as a source of perspective? When one reflects how much of urban development over time and space has been subject to the political will, or even been the direct product of it, and how this tendency is increasing in our contemporary world, perhaps we should begin to test the policy perspective as an integrative point of view? Certainly if we wish to relate to the planners both in drawing upon and contributing to their thoughts, something of the sort is required.[2]

The present essay is an attempt to raise some of the considerations that are involved in using policy as an approach to urban history. Some general aspects of such a perspective are raised, and some special thought is given to the British case.

2

How may the city be envisaged from the point of view of public policy? We can perhaps start by identifying two notional types of city, the one the product of political will and the other the outcome of market decisions. But at once sub-categories begin to assert themselves.

The official city offers at least three types. There is the case in which the city is the expression of centralized policy in the most complete sense, its conception, site, shape and functions being determined by authority, where the city is an integral part of a system of rule, defence, government and exploitation of regional resources. The case of imperial China, so helpfully discussed by Skinner and Elvin and their colleagues,[3] and the cities of the Roman empire may be the most complete exemplifications of this. China has undergone great political discontinuity in recent years, but the new regime, like the old, is in a sense absolutist, taking to itself responsibility for its cities as for all principal aspects of its life; a continuity is therefore present. The artifact capitals of the world might provide a second subset, possibly including Madrid, St Petersburg,[4] Berlin, Canberra and Brazilia. The motivation for these has been various, including the desire by political masters to project the glory of the state and themselves in the form of a new city, attempts to separate politics and administration from the centre of business and from the immediate pressure of the urban crowd or mob, and the need to escape from the constraints present in an established city of high land values and an intricate tenure system. Third, and perhaps paradoxically, there are those cities launched by authority in order to improve the performance of the market economy by the provision of growth points: the British New Towns come into this group.

The second principal category of cities is concerned with those which have been the product of spontaneous market forces. A list of such might include Venice, Amsterdam, London, New York and Chicago, and the cities of north Britain which sprang out of the industrial revolution. Such a catalogue at once suggests diversity and the need for sub-categories.

The very attempt to present cases of the political versus the market-based city at once makes it clear that both, if considered in terms of the absolute exclusion of the other, are difficult, if not impossible, to exemplify. The most powerful political authority will find that a market sector will develop in order to supply and service the city, and will indeed help to generate taxable incomes. David Buck's study of the city of Tsinan shows how this hybridism could develop even in China.[5] The most free-enterprise city will require to structure itself politically in order to provide certain basic services, and in order to relate itself to other political entities. Venice and Amsterdam, the great examplars of pre-industrial trading initiative, produced powerful city oligarchies, partly in order to provide the political coherence necessary to meet the physical challenge of the Venetian lagoon or the North Sea by hydraulic control. Both, moreover, became the trading centres of great empires, by land and sea. In these cases political will was used to create market opportunity. By contrast, a location like that of Chicago made no such large-scale environmental control, with its political implications, necessary. The two influences of spontaneity and political will are always present. The interest lies in seeing what trend there is in the change of mixture in a given city over a chosen period, and why. This will involve a dual dynamic: the responses in terms of political organization and action within the city, and the changes in the nature and objectives of the state of which it is a component.

A wide array of questions at once presents itself. Will all the cities within a given state, or natural region, or system of markets, have a tendency to change their mix of market reliance and political action more or less in step with one another? Did the Mediterranean as seen by Braudel exhibit any such a unity of response? Did capital cities constitute a special case? Did one city take the lead over others, and thus assume a unique character *vis-à-vis* all the rest;[6] was there a tendency for the concentration of economic functions (as Kindleberger has argued in the case of financial facilities),[7] so that a single market metropolis arose, which might or might not be the political capital?

Pursuing our dichotomy of market spontaneity and political will a little further, are any generalizations possible with respect to the rationale governing the founding of cities, and their capacity to adjust either to initial errors or to changes in general circumstances? If the market is dominant in the formative phase of a city, a fairly lengthy process will be involved, because an atomistic set of decisions taken by individuals over time is necessary. Each decision is made in the light of an interpretation of preceding ones, as entrepreneurs perform their continuous exploration of profit potential. By these assumptions there can be no gross cumulative errors because of the continuous adjustment being made, partly by trial and error, but increasingly by foresight based upon experience. But this conclusion may be falsified. This may occur if specialization based on external economies reaches a high level, committing the city to a relatively narrow range of outputs, and is followed by a radical change in markets to be served; if the necessary adjustment to market demand cannot take place the city will shrink, become spatially incoherent and may even die if the state does not intervene. The market, in short, is not proof against error in town development.

On the other hand, if the founding decisions are political ones they may involve large and self-reinforcing errors from the outset, imposing costs both economic and social, and through them social and political tensions. A large and insensitive centralized state could generate a situation which becomes a heavy charge on the rest of the nation, thus exacerbating problems at that level. But even the autocratic will is sometimes capable of adjusting to the realities of circumstances, provided it is not too far cut off by its ideology from the reality of what is happening.

To give present-day immediacy to this duality of market versus collectivist-based cities it is necessary, of course, to think in terms of the cities of the 'Western' nations, including Britain, and those of the U.S.S.R., China and other collectivized states. At the discussion of urbanization at the Edinburgh International Economic History Conference in August 1978 this essential difference in parameters was present, but for the most part only by implication. There was, however, some suggestion that 'convergence' was taking place, that the problems of cities were universal, and that political structure was a secondary consideration. This idea has been about for some time in terms of large-scale industrial management. What legitimacy does it have in the planning and operation of cities?

Is it possible to assimilate the policy aspects of city development to a general theory of history? For Marxist scholars, city government, just like national government, is a weapon wielded by the ruling class for the exploitation of the ruled class. Presumably this must be true in terms both of the artifact city and the market-based one, though operating in very different ways. The question then becomes one of identifying the ruling class in any chosen historical context, and seeing how it projected its interest in terms of urban form. For more elliptical, pluralist historians, there is apparently no such single key. For one thing it omits much with respect to which exploitation is an insufficient explanation. The Chinese and Roman cities were part of the expansionist compulsion and the problems it generated of stabilization and coherence when land-mass empire had reached its limits, both in terms of internal stability and the pressures on the extended frontiers. The artifact capitals show too much variety to be explicable in the same terms, depending as each did upon the unique circumstances present in each state. The same is true of the market-based cities. Each had its own physical setting, its own access to resources, including water supply both as a human input and a medium on which to travel. Each such city responded in its own way to the challenges that derived basically from its environment.

Of course it is possible to say that the diversity of cities which lies outside any single historical theory is mere 'accident', and that we must look at a different level for the fundamental realities of 'essence'. But the dangers of this line of thought are obvious. Nevertheless the search for what might be 'essence' must go on. The first step is perhaps a form of categorization which allows us to group cities in a meaningful way, ordering them according to some common aspect of their experience that was cardinal to their responses.

3

How might British historians proceed in attempting an understanding of their own urban experience seen from the point of view of public policy? To do so requires a conceptualization appropriate to a family of cities developing within a market-based economy. Within such a context there would appear to be three principal roles for the city. The first is as a point of concentration for economic activity, especially in marketing and manufacture. The trading and manufacturing city will generate a pattern of power which, though related to the political, is in principle distinct from it and prior to it. Two elements of this have found their way into the literature, namely economic power in Marxist class terms (expressed in the form of the extraction of surplus value from the labour force by capitalists), and in territorial terms as relating to the manipulation by the towns of the terms of trade between themselves and the primary producers of the countryside. Of course, these aspects, especially the first, never disappear.

Second, there is the city as a unit of self-government. This is, indeed, what has defined a British city in law – it is a place with a corporate identity and a range of powers, both granted by the central government by charter. In this aspect policy will have to do with local concerns, ensuring the provision of streets, lighting, drainage, policing, markets, local courts and building regulations, all paid for out of the taxation of property within the city. Third, there is the city as a unit standing in relationship to national government. This link is a reciprocal one – the city will affect national government in outlook and action, and vice versa. The city will put pressure on government to extend its powers to act (including the authority to borrow). This will be done largely by promoting private Acts of Parliament for each such authorization. On the other hand the central government by Act and Order will push the cities into the acceptance of new responsibilities. In addition it may promote general programmes affecting all cities, especially through regional policy. In all these respects policy is seen as a departure from a norm provided by the market system.

With these three ways of regarding the city in mind (as a local economy with a wealth and power structure, as a political entity with its own initiatives, and as a component of a state), we can attempt an outline of the evolution of British cities in terms of political will. Within the present limits a high degree of simplification is necessary.

If we begin in the late eighteenth century the towns, where they had separate identities at all, were ruled by their corporations, often of long standing and usually highly oligarchic. They could perform their rudimentary civic functions without too much complaint from the burgesses; where they were in sufficiently serious default the government (by Act of Parliament) would appoint *ad hoc* bodies to perform particular tasks – the Improvement Commissioners. At the levels of city size then obtaining the State had as yet no general responsibilities it wished to impose on local government. Even so, the old corporations had by 1835 become indefensible: the Municipal Corporations Act of that year made them responsible to a more representative electorate (though still a small one). At the same time the powers of the civic corporations were now defined – the central government created conditions under which the old looseness concerning their scope could be done away with and civic powers made precise. Any action beyond the powers thus given had to be sought by private Act of Parliament.

Somewhat perversely it was the place in greatest need of reorganization, namely London, where the welter of jurisdictions lasted longest. This was because of the difficulty of remaking so vast a collection of people, with so many communities merged but not fused by the extension of the conurbation, and so many functions requiring to be discharged on a larger spatial scale giving birth to yet new organizational forms. By the later 1830s the government of London lay between the Corporation of the City and the city companies, seven boards of commissioners for sewers, almost 100 boards for lighting, paving and cleaning, about 170 assorted vestries, with the boards of guardians set up under the Poor Law Act of 1834, together with a miscellany of other authorities. All of this was compounded by the resistance of the City Corporation and some of its surrounding boroughs to proposals for rationalization. London, indeed, had not found a functional identity until the formation of the London County Council in 1888. But, though London responded less effectively to the organizational challenge than did the northern cities, it had, over the generations, a higher capacity for the continuous adaptation of its economic base; it might be argued that London, with its monopoly as the capital of 'national' functions, and its size as market, was in a sense parasitic upon the other cities.

Meanwhile two great urban problems were building up, namely housing and sanitation. The outlook of British governments of the day did not permit of an attack on housing shortage, but sanitation and health demanded it. For the first time, under the Public Health Act of 1848 the civic *polis* in England and Wales was placed under instruction from the centre to carry out certain functions in a prescribed manner, and was made accountable.[8]

There followed a long period over which no new general responsibility was imposed upon the cities. There were the Cross and Torrens Housing Acts, six of them between 1868 and 1890, but these were permissive, concerned mainly with slum clearance for health purposes, and so had little effect. But two important changes did take place. The new technology of the railway, with the profit opportunities it offered, forced a renovation of the transport infrastructure with profound effects on the cities.[9] The building of the railways was done by the market and not by state action, though to be sure state approval was necessary, and was given *ad hoc* in the form of an Act for each railway. Second, civic government became a supplier of services, each city acting independently: the cities became entrepreneurs in the fields of water, gas, electricity and tramways supply, doing so on as wide a range of formulae as suited their own needs and political configuration.[10] There were also attempts at inner city renewal from the 1860s and 1870s, as in Birmingham and Glasgow.[11]

This phase of city policy and action continued until after the First World War. It had two principal elements, namely the supply of environmental services such as sanitation and water, and the provision of certain public utilities. The central government had prescribed a minimal level of performance in the one function, and had authorized the second by private Acts of Parliament. Action had been mainly local, arising from the politics of each city. But a new age was about to begin. In it the central state would seek to operate in a much more fundamental way upon British cities. In so doing it would bring cities into the range of national policies in altogether new ways.

By 1919 the central government could no longer stand apart from the great national housing default. In that year by the Addison Act it imposed its second great duty on the cities, namely to build houses. It also provided a virtually open purse to the local authorities. Within a year it became apparent that a formula for the delimiting and sharing of financial responsibility between central and local government was required. Public sector housing thus became both one of the great links between central and civic government, and one of the most important ways in which local government could operate on the lives and conduct of the working classes at the domestic level within its jurisdiction. From 1930 the state had a second great impact on the cities, though this time an oblique one. By its programme of industrial restructuring (with the Bank of England in some sectors a proxy for the state) the central government undertook actions which had important effects on civic and regional economies, chiefly by rationalization schemes in shipbuilding and the cotton industry. There was also, with the Town Planning Act of 1909, the first tentative beginning of a governmental attempt to control the morphology of cities. But by 1939 it was clear that it was time for a national inquest on Britain's cities and the relationship of both local and central government: this the Barlow Commission undertook.

From 1945 came the age of Barlow. The Commission had reported in 1940 but the war made action impossible.[12] Government in post-war Britain was offered three related formulae. The one embodied a philosophy of the morphology of cities: it called for the imposition of a city shape, with urban sprawl contained by green belts, and with a great lowering of densities in the inner cities. The second was concerned with the regional distribution of employment and population, suggesting restraint on concentration in London and the South East and Birmingham and the West Midlands, and redevelopment in other parts of the country. Both of these sets of Barlow canons were adopted by government, so that central government sought to promote both a new city shape and a new national pattern of employment. To this the cities responded in a positive way, aware that it was time to seize hold upon their own shape and size, and to think in terms of a national distribution of jobs and people. There was a third Barlow proposal. It was that there should be a programme that combined the ideas of a new start and of growth points. This was to be done by the planning and construction of a system of New Towns. The necessary legislation came in the New Towns Act of 1946.[13] Within the market economy of Britain artifact towns were to be built, conceived and executed as acts of political will, carried through by appointed corporations. For the first time Britain began to think of towns in terms of *tabula rasa* first principles. Because at the start no towns existed, the democratic formula could not be used; only as their populations grew did a conflict between popular will and appointed corporations appear.

However, Barlow was overtaken by the second infrastructural transport revolution, brought on by the explosion of cars and lorries from the later 1950s. The remaking of the road system was moving up the scale of national priorities. Unlike the building of the railroads, this could not be left to the market. Moreovor the task was on such a scale that it required a rethinking of the philosophy of city shape as it affected very large communities. The demands of the motorway had to be superimposed on those of Barlow. Here a further close, intimate and sometimes difficult interplay between central and local government was called for. Things were helped along by innovative optimism. But there was a serious misjudgment of the relationship between the reduction of densities in the old inner cities and the employment needs of the New Towns, for in some cases the New Towns did not supply a simple receptacle for a cross-section of old town people; to some degree they creamed the labour force and left the inner cities with the unskilled and the aged.

In recent years the state, faced with problems of the general renewal of Britain's economic base added to those of inner city renewal, has set up new bodies to undertake action where both ministries and local authorities have been judged to be inadequate. The National Enterprise Board in England and the Scottish Development Agency represent an attempt to insert into the system of political government at the central and local levels a new kind of body, with a responsibility for sustaining business enterprises where this seems justified, and for locating and assisting new growth points in the form of new industrial ventures. In England the Department of the Environment is responsible for amenities; in Scotland the Scottish Development Agency has both growth point and amenity responsibilities; it is almost as if the Improvement Commissioners had returned! As in the past, the jurisdictional problem has inevitably arisen. Not surprisingly the elected councillors at the local level believe that it is they who should make decisions affecting their city-regions. They feel that their responsibilities have been encroached upon by corporatist, authoritarian bodies with no direct accountability to the community. But such bodies have been brought into being in order to provide more effective vehicles of action than those provided by local government.

4

The history of British cities exemplifies the principle of growth through market forces. It also provides one demonstration of the way in which it has proved necessary to augment and operate upon market responses by public policy in the interest of communal objectives. Action by central and local government has been of four principal kinds, namely providing facilities where the market has failed to do so, imposing upon firms social duties as well as making them meet a larger proportion of the social costs they have generated, and operating upon the morphology and economic bases of cities. In a sense, in the British case, there has been a fairly simple linear development, namely that with the increasing size and industrial and social sophistication of cities additional functions have required to be discharged by public will or enforced by it.

The general list of such functions is probably fairly similar for all those societies which have developed on market principles. But as between societies there is no inherent order in which these challenges will arise, nor any standard pattern which they will form, nor will they provoke any uniform political response. These will be different depending on the national experience, including the patterns of technology that are dominant at the time when major urban growth takes place, and the political configuration then prevailing. Each phase of technology will generate a certain kind of family of cities in a given context; this pattern as it encounters obsolescence will constitute the starting point for consideration of the policy challenge of the next generation. A political outlook, with attendant legislative and bureaucratic organization, will also have been passed on; this too may need to be renovated.

S. G. Checkland
Department of Economic History, University of Glasgow

Notes

1   H. J. Dyos (ed.), *The Study of Urban History* (1968), 4, 5.
2   For useful studies in today's terms see David H. McKay and Andrew W. Cox, *The Politics of Urban Change* (1979); Duncan Maclennan and John B. Parr (eds), *Regional Policy. Past Experience and New Directions* (1979); Gordon C. Cameron and Lowdon Wingo (eds), *Cities, Regions and Public Policy* (1973).
3   G. William Skinner (ed.), *The City in Late Imperial China* (Stanford, Cal., 1977); Mark Elvin and G. William Skinner (eds), *The Chinese City between Two Worlds* (Stanford, Cal., 1974).
4   See James H. Bater, *St. Petersburg. Industrialisation and Change* (1976).
5   David D. Buck, *Urban Change in China. Politics and Development in Tsinan, Shantung, 1890–1949* (Madison, Wisconsin, 1978).
6   See Mark Jefferson, 'The law of the primate city', *Geographical Review*, 29 (1939).
7   C. P. Kindleberger, 'The formation of financial centres. A study in corporative economic history', *Princeton Studies in International Finance*, xxxvi (Princeton, 1974).
8   Some of the absolutist states of the Continent, especially in the German lands, had extended their paternalistic philosophy to cover the health and physical well-being of the people; Prussia had a Board of Health in 1685. There were authors who produced entire systems of communal care, pronouncing a state duty to promote well-being, uninhibited by any fear of intrusion into the liberties of the individual. But the necessary bases in medical knowledge, social data and administrative machinery were lacking. The result was that the absolutist states, in spite of their difference in philosophy, did as Britain did; namely, left the matter to local community action until well into the nineteenth century. G. Rosen, *A History of Public Health* (New York, 1958).
9   J. R. Kellett, *The Impact of Railways on Victorian Cities* (1969).
10   J. R. Kellett, 'Municipal socialism, enterprise and trading in the Victorian city', *Urban History Yearbook* (1978).
11   C. M. Allan, 'The genesis of British urban development, with special reference to Glasgow'. *Economic History Review*, 2nd ser., 18 (1965).
12   *Royal Commission on the Distribution of the Industrial Population*, Cmd. 6153. (HMSO 1940).
13   Frank Schaffer, *The New Town Story* (1972); F. J. Osborn and A. Whittick, *The New Towns: The answer to megalopolis* (revised edn, 1969).

Urban history in France: achievements, tendencies and objectives

In the last ten years, a significant development in the study of urban history has allowed French historians to begin to consider some of the problems which have preoccupied their foreign colleagues, notably in Britain and the United States, for some time. The attraction of the town for the French historian is due, clearly enough, to two main factors. On the one hand, the town's growing dominance over the location of employment and population is bound to attract attention – in 1980 80 per cent of the population of France live in towns, exactly reversing the distribution of 200 years ago. On the other hand, this same distension of the town demands historical attention. It places the town at the centre of a very long-term development in which the urban criterion becomes increasingly dominant, defining a particularly appropriate field for the measurement of the linking mechanisms which regulate relationships between the different levels of social reality. Urbanity, in short, brings together the whole gamut of questions posed by the development of our system of civilization over the centuries. To reconstruct its history is to indulge in nostalgia for a past which appears all the richer in comparison with the drabness of our own day. It is also to dream of a city of the future, capable of reconciling community and social control, nature and culture. In France the history of towns is inseparable from a long process of examination which began with the humanist enthusiasm for the city, continued through the speculations of the Enlightenment and the tentative researches of nineteenth-century local antiquarians, and has recently been supplemented by the more precise discoveries of the urban historian.

Urban historiography is as old as the towns themselves; it was a necessity, a means of establishing the pedigree of their social conventions. From the earliest days of their emergence in the medieval West, the towns used history as a weapon against the lord, the bishop or abbot, and even against the king. To this end, archives were built up and texts were written which quite naturally were committed in character. Medieval communes preserved their muniments in closets or chests, the arrangement of which often symbolized the organization of history and the ordering of the world. In the sixteenth century the town of Orange purchased 14 closets. The first held the Bible and other religious texts. The second, which bore the inscription 'Moses' to evoke the myth of the founder-legislator, contained the charters and privileges of the town . . . And so on to the last closet, which they called 'Chaos', and which held a motley collection of documents and accounts. Each town would have a clutch of keys, shared between various magistrates, aldermen and consuls, to open the locks and bolts which protected their documentary treasures – six keys at Albi, 30 at Limoges. Bevies of archivists and clerks watched jealously over the precious heritage. In the seventeenth and eighteenth centuries a punctilious Crown went on to require the preparation of inventories and lists. Meanwhile, the town archivists went in constant fear of tax officials and dishonest historians. The whole point of the municipal authorities' passionate interest in legitimizing documents lay in the need to establish beyond all doubt the towns' ancient origins, and to proclaim their clear title to their privileges. Accounts, minutes, election records, and lists of officials and notables all contributed to the creation of an aggressive history which sought to establish the legitimacy of power. Urban jurisprudence drew its strength from this source, and in turn further extended its influence. Annals and chronicles – the Golden Book of Montbelliard, the Black Book of Angers, the Red Book of Toulouse – all bore witness to the rise of

the town, recorded key events, and founded traditions and customs. This instru-
mental history, the creation of industrious scriveners, was never forgotten; from
the reign of Louis XI until the Revolution it played its part in the disputes stirred
up by the efforts of the king's agents to exert their authority.

In the humanist and classicist periods, new motivations came to supplement
these early imperatives. On the one hand, those religious orders which took pride
in intellectual activity discovered in urban history an opportunity to produce
numerous learned writings. On the other, urban history offered the great lay
scholars an especially fertile field for original reflection. Both groups devoted
themselves to the celebration of urban civilization, expressed in the splendour of
its institutions, the grandeur of its social scene, and the pomp of its great city festivals, as we can see in the work of the Lyons Jesuit, Menestrier, and of Daniel Huet
at Caen.[1] Each town had its historian, while each house had its share of urban
tales. When the municipalities came under royal control, this inheritance became
a purely cultural echo of a lost independence. Furthermore, the development of
urban culture was accompanied by the rise of an extended network of learned
societies, maintained by the urban elites. The promotion of historical research was
the prime concern of these societies.[2] The creed of the Enlightenment scholar was
made up of love of scholarship, provincial patriotism, parochialism, and a philosophical justification of the progressive character of history. Between 1768 and
1778 Fevret de Fontette prepared a new edition of Father Lelong's historical
library, which had first appeared in 1719. With his associates, he listed more than
9000 works of relevance to the history of towns, four times Lelong's total of half a
century earlier. This bibliography deserves more thorough analysis than can be
undertaken here, but it is dominated by three modes of writing: first, studies of
urban origins, within which great monuments of erudition (such as Sauval and
Lebeuf for Paris) gradually come to replace the older, panegyrical tradition; then
archaeological and topographical descriptions; and third, urban pantheons composed of registers of great men.

For more than a century, from the Revolution until the end of the nineteenth
century, this tradition continued to flourish, as the abundant scholarly production
of a multitude of local researchers bears witness. Over 300 local and regional
societies, 117 of which were multi-purpose bodies of learning, were hard at work
producing proceedings, memoirs and bulletins. Issues and techniques of research
were diffused by regional and national congresses, the permanent *Congrès des
Sociétés Savantes* being founded in 1875.[3] A superficial examination of the
interests of these societies reveals that their main concern was with political
history. In their elucidation of conflicts between municipal and royal authority,
they reflected an urban patriotism which continued to hark back to the great days
of the League, the Fronde, and the Revolution. Next came studies of administrative institutions, in which jurisdictions, courts, collections and associations were
patiently listed. Finally, we note an interest in the history of personalities. Urban
elites are investigated, and family pedigrees and papers are analysed. Louis
Barbat's study of Châlons-sur-Marne is a good example. Barbat was a local
worthy of the Second Empire, a man of property, collector, scholar and denizen of
the archives. In his preface he clearly expressed the ideology which underlay the
work of countless local historians:

> The history of individual towns is less stirring than that of great empires, but for
> the local resident it has a powerful and incontestable attraction. To know
> everything that has happened on a piece of ground which one paces daily is to
> live amongst people who have long since passed on, surrounded by forgotten
> customs and demolished monuments. Local history provides the missing link
> which recreates the chain of tradition. It brings our ancestors back to life, link-
> ing the dead to the living and the living to those who are yet to come.[4]

In the work of Barbat and his fellow-historians, the town is a specially-favoured
stage on which a fragile conception of history acts out its role, redeemed then as

now by the aesthetic quality of its vision, its sense of a heritage which justifies the study of the past, and the catholicity of its interests.

Between the early twentieth century and the 1940s, a first wind of change began to ruffle the peaceful landscape of French urban studies. It came principally from the non-historical disciplines, first from sociology, and later from geography and town planning. Sociologists and jurists provided urban historians with models which have inspired them ever since. They have studied the relationship between urban growth and land values ever since M. Halbwachs published his first results in 1907.[5] Following M. Leroy's 1927 example, they have investigated urban legal systems.[6] Even more influential has been the geographical school of Vidal de la Blache, which created a monographic and genetic method for the study of urban space. This approach is reflected in R. Blanchard's study of Grenoble (1912), J. Levainville's of Rouen (1913), P. Arbos's of Clermont (1930), and A. Demangeon's of Paris (1933). Sustained until our own day, the investigations of French geographers have bequeathed an analytical system and an array of concepts (such as 'network' and 'function') which have been widely beneficial to urban history. Similarly, urban history owes a debt to the town planners, to Lavedan, Geddes and Giedion.[7] From them it drew its interest in the history of physical forms in their relationship with broad social changes. Urban historians now recognize that the urban complex is organized in accordance with the imperatives of changing technical levels, the impact of different time-series, and the interaction of social, economic and cultural elements which shape both the container and its content. Above all, historians no longer try to relate urban space to some ideal type which, because its disappearance was regretted, was often forcibly imposed on reality. Instead, they look for specific criteria of coherence, systems of social usages, and relationships between the different levels of the urban totality. However, the historians also had their own original contribution to make in this period, when they established the importance of economic and social structures. This theme ran throughout urban history from Henri Pirenne to Gaston Martin, and from Georges Lefebvre to Henri Sée.[8] Also worthy of mention here is the isolated, prophetic masterpiece of Gaston Roupnel on Dijon and its countryside.[9]

In this atmosphere the new specialism of social history was able, from the 1950s, to develop freely. In doing so, it drew attention to the value of new approaches to the more voluminous sources, and of the analysis of social and demographic structures. Both the explosion of social history and its failures have contributed to important revisions of historical problems which have now established the characteristics of the new urban history. The French branch of this new specialism is very much aware of foreign work and particularly of that of the Urban History Group, founded by H. J. Dyos at Leicester in the 1960s. From now on, the town can be the subject of specific historical study as long as certain earlier conceptions are set on one side. Eschewing the organicism which once brought geographers, historians and planners together in so cosy a relationship, and which generated such brilliant descriptions with their vocabulary drawn from anatomy or biology, urban history must rediscover a specifically social and economic explanation of urban evolution. Without giving way to the functionalism of the economists and the geographers, it must solve the double problem posed by the definition of urban functions according either to organic or to rationalist models. More important still, it has to establish the relationships between these functions. Finally, it has to dispel the billowing neo-positivist dream of an ultimate truth based on quantification and the use of computers, by showing that the town is something more than the sum of a number of forces. In this sense, as F. Bédarida has shown, recent research has been stimulated by the re-examination of the urban phenomenon from a dialectical, Marxist point of view. The importance of the study of contradictions between town and country has been re-emphasized, as has the need always to keep sight of the town's distinctive social struggles.[10] The analysis of urban problems cannot be reduced to the construction of an 'urban system' or the denunciation of some 'power' or other; instead, it must bring out the inherent contradictions which interact within the urban space, in their relationship with general processes.[11]

The very size of the modern town makes it a battlefield for conflicts between the uniformity of a totally organized space and the fragmentation produced by production relationships. In the words of Henri Lefebvre, the town is exploding and planners of every ideology are running around, trying to pick up the pieces. The historian is no more able than anyone else to reassemble the crushed fragments of urban traditions and urban spaces, but he can at least take part in the consideration of what ought now to be done. With his socio-cultural perception of the urban phenomenon, he can grasp the totality of the town as a social complex, the focal point of the encounter between individual and community, the locus of the development of interactions between material conditions and cultural factors, between norms and behaviour. In its houses and public buildings, its infrastructure, and its arrangement of space, the town gives shape to gestures and relationships. It is now, as it always has been, history in stone.[12] Indeed, we can see, in a number of recent public works and building projects, the emergence of certain new approaches. They all share a refusal to view the town as a neutral space, and a determination to rediscover the specific character of the relationship between people and space, through the analysis of the sites, locations and organizations generated by urban development.

'No town without people' is the watchword. Urban demographers have been at work for the last 20 years. They have encountered many difficulties, but the demographic features of the town are now coming to be widely appreciated. If the study of rural structures is more advanced, it is partly because of the bulk of the data; for a town of 20,000 people, between 150,000 and 180,000 instruments have to be processed.[13] For eighteenth-century Rouen, the historian has to master between 7000 and 8000 entries a year.[14] This sheer weight of numbers is exacerbated by the further problem of mobility. Within the town, movements from one parish to another are only to be expected, but movements from town to country upset all calculations of death, birth and fertility rates. At Lyons, between 1750 and 1774, less than half those born in the city are recorded as dying there. Finally, to complicate the analysis still further, the social heterogeneity of the population affects everything and often prevents the rudimentary calculations which rural demographic historians can almost always carry out. For all this, a number of specifically urban features have been established. In an exemplary monograph, published in 1969, Marcel Lachiver demonstrated the importance of mobility. Since then, M. Garden, J. C. Perrot, J. P. Bardet, Michel Terrisse, and A. Chamoux have confirmed, in their work on Lyons, Caen, Rouen, Marseilles, and Rheims, the influence of immigration, and of course of emigration as well, on very large towns.[15] We only have to remember that at Caen, between 1750 and 1775, 8000 people came in while another 6000 left. We now appreciate the unequal incidence of waves of high mortality in different age-groups, particularly where children are concerned. We also understand the specific characteristics of high birth rates among the masses. In short, the town unites several types of attitude towards demographic matters, the differences being directly related to social class. Contraception, as Louis Henry showed and M. Garden has confirmed, flourished among the elites, but with variations linked to cultural and religious allegiances and, perhaps even more, to those regional patterns from which the urban organism is never entirely free. The changes of the eighteenth and nineteenth centuries allow us to measure the ways in which the towns reacted, and adapted themselves, to the establishment of an industrial society. In an extremely diverse evolution, the methodology of the urban demographers brings out the influence of the local environment, an influence which can be tested most closely of all by the study of migration, by family reconstitution, and by the analysis of family life and social patterns. To measure family size, and to describe the specific structure of urban family units, leads on to the analysis of kinship links and networks. Here, the role of physical space reasserts itself, for urban anonymity conceals complex realities which can be detected, for instance, through acts of tutelage – a key source for the study of differentiated and localized social attitudes.[16] Mentality and biology form a whole range of different combinations from town to town and from class to class.

Beyond the physical measurement of urban populations, and the study of their renewal and patterns of behaviour, the whole of urban society is brought into consideration 'through the dynamic of the town, at once the creator and the product of that dynamic'.[17] Urban social history no doubt emerged from the study of socio-professional hierarchies, but it very soon began to oscillate between the classification of professions on the basis of the division of labour and the definition of social groups in class terms according to the mode of production. This debate ran the main part of its course between 1955 and 1970. With no solution possible, individual empiricism won easily, and as many classifications emerged as there were towns to study. But this left two conceptions of society facing each other, the one basing social analysis on the status commonly attached to each order and each function, the other using personal wealth and professional activity as the main criteria. The former attached particular importance to the definition of social groups through intermarriage and involved the prior study of family histories, supplemented by genealogies, before the study of aggregates at ward or town level was undertaken. Although quantitative analysis was not rejected, it was regarded as secondary to qualitative techniques. One product of this technique, for instance, was the dissection of Parisian society in the 1630s into nine strata or orders, and at least 35 estates or sub-strata.[18] The second conception, on the other hand, gave priority to the use of massive sources – tax rolls, notarial collections of marriage contracts and probate inventories, and registers – to effect the analysis of social groups defined on the basis of profession and wealth. In *Structures et relations sociales à Paris au milieu du XVIIIe siècle*, F. Furet and A. Daumard provided a sustained defence of the use of a socio-professional classification based on these criteria, while acknowledging the value of legal distinctions and drawing inspiration from the contemporary classifications of the INSEE (Institut national de la Statistique et des Etudes économiques).[19] In this way, they divided Parisian society into 13 categories based on professional distinctions moderated by status (the nobility being excluded) and position in the hierarchy of production (within a trade, journeymen were distinguished from masters, while simple traders were separated from merchants). For a time it seemed as though French historians of urban society could use notarial evidence to construct a hierarchy of categories and groups, and to provide both a measure of their homogeneity and diversity, and an appreciation of their mobility and the relationships between them. Large monographs began to appear in increasing numbers; A. Daumard studied the Parisian bourgeoisie in the first half of the nineteenth century, P. Deyon took their equivalents at Amiens in the seventeenth century, and M. Garden analysed the bourgeoisie of Lyons in the eighteenth.[20] In the end, however, the debate on orders and classes contributed to a general sterilization of research in urban social history, by formalizing a deadlock based on irreconcilable ideologies.[21]

The time has now come to reopen the file with an open mind, and in the spirit of healthy debate which the long-term study of urban social diversity requires. We know that no single matrix can be valid for all periods and all places. We have to accept a plurality of classifications, for a dual reason. On a theoretical level, first of all, social groups are, as Jean-Claude Perrot maintains,[22] both what they think they are and what they do not know they are. This means that there is no opposition at all between the use of old categories which past societies used to classify their own members, and social analysis based on our own scientific criteria. On the contrary, they are absolutely complementary. Indeed, the fact that a society can be viewed simultaneously through a variety of filters relating to distinctions of order, the hierarchy of personal wealth, and the distribution of economic functions, provides a fundamental justification for the study of urban history. No old classification can alone provide the key to a social structure; to reconstitute any social organization it is essential to combine the multiple categorizations which it applied to itself with the distinctions which quantitative analysis allows us to make. Information on wealth, position in the productive process, authority, and culture, must all be assembled within the urban space. Moreover, it must be considered not in snapshot fashion but in the context of an evolutionary development.

Within this methodology, three important lines of enquiry stand out. First, it is essential to follow the example of recent American studies by looking carefully at the phenomena of social mobility.[23] However, we need to look beyond the upward mobility of individuals and groups which has been the almost exclusive concern of historians up to now, by giving special attention to the opposite process of downward mobility and its attendant phenomena of withdrawal and marginalization. To this end, the analysis of the transmission of inheritances and their division over the generations helps us to detect, in respect of certain social groups, the ways in which social structures break up and re-form. The pre-industrial town brings us face to face with the problem of the origin of the marginals, that army of outsiders without which the industrial town could never have been created. Demographic studies of immigration and urban mortality, which perforce deal with this floating population, provide information of prime importance for the definition of zones of recruitment, and the reconstruction of the mechanisms of urban attraction and integration into the urban space.[24] Louis Chevalier pointed the way, in his work on Paris, more than 20 years ago,[25] and the historians of criminality and low-class social relations have gone on to accumulate a dossier of findings which deserve renewed consideration and emulation.[26]

The second area of interest is the confrontation, in the urban context, of power and knowledge. Who are the controllers of urban space, the technicians, engineers, architects, entrepreneurs, doctors, speculators, and property-owners both individual and institutional? Their relationships with space are the stuff of urban social history, and through them urban space can be reintegrated into the process of social production. Several of these groups have recently been examined: the members of the academies, whose views on urban design deserve further attention,[27] the royal engineers whose military and civil works affected the whole of urban France and whose activities call out for systematic listing,[28] and the architects.[29] The planning and equipment of the town need to be studied in the light of the conflicts between these different competences. New light can be shed on the urbanization process by studies of topography, circulation systems, typologies of itineraries and thoroughfares, trends in house rents, and building cycles in their relationships with economic cycles and demographic flows. J. C. Perrot has demonstrated that, at Caen, two cycles of urban transformation, very different in their dynamic and their spatial implications, were operating simultaneously. The one cycle was that of the development of the street-system, and it proceeded fully in step with economic development. The other was out of phase with the trade cycle, and mainly included river, port and quay improvements, works which looked to the future. The recognition of these cycles allows us to make sense of urban morphology even in cases where there was no serious divergence between the building and trade cycles as, for instance, at Rouen and in nineteenth-century Paris.[30] Also helpful in the elucidation of the evolution of urban planning over the centuries are disasters, man-made like the great fire of Rennes,[31] and natural like the Sicilian earthquake.[32] The ultimate objective, however, is to relate the intervention of participants in the social process to the physical products of planning and private building, to link building to occupation, and the provision of facilities to their use. In short, we must strive for a history of the habitat in which the dwelling and the public building are combined with their surroundings, both public and private. Hospitals, for instance – which on the eve of the Revolution had come to be regarded by doctors, scientists and those in authority as machines for curing people – provide a spatial reflection of sanitary policy. The idea of communal facilities was born at this time. Through inquiries, the dreams of urban designers, and the struggles of the doctors to master disease, all of which brought together a wide range of architectural and planning considerations, the hospital emerged as the definitive architectural model, as M. Foucault and his associates have demonstrated.[33] The same team of researchers, using a similar methodology to analyse Parisian spatial policy at the end of the *ancien régime*, was able to identify the impact of medical knowledge on the production of space in the French capital, a process which amounted to the generation of a new mode of planning which foreshadowed the rational methods of organization perfected in the industrial era.[34]

The third line of approach derives from the idea of urbanization as a social phenomenon. The whole range of varying perceptions of the town can be detected in alliances and conflicts, the short-lived phenomenon of the riot, and the age-old reflexes revealed in the routes taken by religious processions and festive gatherings.[35] Here, we are interested in the ways in which the individual viewed space, those about him, and himself. In the ceremonial of revolutionary France we note the adoption of new itineraries, centred on new landmarks, but we are also aware of 'the resistance which the towns put up to the despotism of Reason'. We can also throw light on the phenomena of solidarity, fidelity, and struggles between different groups and classes. The analysis can take account of social categories, relations between social groups, and intra-class movements, but it has to place all of them in a social perspective. Outstanding in this respect is Raison-Jourde's study of the Auvergnat community in nineteenth-century Paris. The author moves beyond the social history of a process of migration to classify patterns of behaviour and to analyse the day-to-day problems of the newcomers. Transplantation and acculturation are detected by a system of multiple filters – the stages of the journey, channels of movement, habitat, choice of marriage partner, diets, and styles of clothing. In this eminently social study, the problem of social success is discussed in association with the ways in which the immigrants experienced and mastered the urban space of Paris.[36] Also worthy of attention is the pattern of interventions in the creation of urban space. At Caen, J. C. Perrot was able to establish the varying attitudes in the circles of power towards the improvement of the town – the municipality, the army, the clergy and the speculators each had their view. At Rouen, J. P. Bardet emphasizes the immobility of a townscape which was scarcely affected by the predominantly utilitarian works undertaken on the fringes of the town by the municipality and the Intendants. Here, however, there was no population pressure. In a prophetic organization of urban space, rich and poor parishes were clearly separated as early as the beginning of the eighteenth century. Rent maps confirm this social segregation and the wide gap in life-styles between the fashionable centre, the mixed districts of north and west, and the proletarian areas of the east and the faubourgs.[37] Nantes, Bordeaux, Marseilles, and of course Paris, together with any number of other towns need to be looked at again in this perspective. Finally, we need to use the awareness generated by our analysis of material culture to improve our understanding of long-term changes in behaviour and mental attitudes.[38] All the spatial aspects of acts of solidarity and conflict must be traced, but we must go on to discover the comings and goings of daily life, and the spaces which contained them. Wards, parishes, streets, alleys, courtyards, staircases, landings, doors and passages were all the scenes of meetings, quarrels, flirtations and passionate encounters. Within them towndwellers sometimes helped each other out, or did each other down. For the Parisian the street was a place of special importance.[39] The judicial archives, when sensitively analysed, reveal a tempestuous world of sights, sounds and smells in which honest and dishonest beggars, rich and poor, workers and paupers, newcomers and old Parisian residents all came into contact. To observe street life is also to see social relationships acted out and to follow the gradual establishment of a new order. Urban authority acts to improve the street, to regularize its use, and to prepare the way for a new type of town. Thus, from mental perceptions to specific acts, a refined classification of cultural models remains the prime objective of the historian.

Behind this analysis of the intellectual and physical, collective and individual, construction of urban space, the historian constantly rediscovers a pattern of growth. Urban history, therefore, must never cease to take account of the various aspects of the fundamental process of urbanization. First of all, its effect on spatial organization has to be considered. If we examine the urban network over the European continent from the sixteenth to the twentieth century, we find that its features are too varied to be encompassed in a single explanation. They do not even allow us to produce a single, timeless definition of the urban phenomenon.[40] It still remains to draw up, systematically and comparatively, criteria of urbanity appropriate to each period, and to establish hierarchies of urban facilities and functions appropriate to these criteria, taking account of the population thresholds on which the urban networks were based. This work is well under way in respect of modern and contemporary Britain, but in France and other western countries it has hardly started. B. Lepetit is tackling the problem for the whole of France between 1750 and 1850, using statistical techniques adapted to the information which the sources of the time can provide.[41] At the provincial level, R. Favier is studying the urban network of the Dauphiné in a comprehensive perspective incorporating economic and cultural functions.[42] Jacques Dupaquier is demonstrating the feebleness of urbanization in the Paris area, dominated as it was by the influence of the capital itself.[43] More of these studies are needed. Moreover, the analysis of steps in the urban hierarchy must be related to the way in which we examine the organization of the various complex systems by which urban functions were distributed.

Administrative, legal and religious mechanisms induce flows of population, funds and commodities. Economic organization, the market, exchange and industry all induce further flows. We therefore have to find indicators which will reflect the relative contribution of these different factors to the development of the urban pattern. In the pre-industrial town, the list of principal functions and the role of property and trade must be analysed in a number of typical cases, taking account of growth and the social status of the corresponding groups – property-owners, rentiers, and administrators, employers and wage-earners. In the context of a social history of culture, demographic and cultural analyses prove to be complementary as, for instance, the study of the foundation of learned institutions in eighteenth-century France can demonstrate. These institutions did not develop everywhere, and their degree of success was even more uneven. Two-thirds of the towns with academies had over 20,000 inhabitants, and three-quarters of French urban centres with more than 20,000 inhabitants possessed an academy. Systems of flourishing learned societies grew up easily in the multi-functional metropoli of Bordeaux, Lyons, Montpellier, Nancy, Toulouse and Rouen, and in the constellation of regional capitals dominated by political functions (Metz, Besançon, Grenoble, Dijon) or economic ones (Marseilles, Orleans, Caen, La Rochelle). Below this level intellectual activity developed either slowly or with difficulty.[44] The same spatial and functional analysis is essential too for other cultural institutions such as the college and the masonic lodge, except of course that the existence of regional zones of culture, in which there is not always a clear distinction between urban and rural, has to be taken into account.[45]

Such an investigation into the functioning of urban systems implies the practicability of constructing a comprehensive listing of all flows (people, food and drink, other products, capital, power, and information), and assumes the importance of the hierarchical and complementary character of the relationships between them. Until the onset of industrialization, stable urban frameworks were to be found everywhere, and any variations in the flows almost always benefited the towns which were already in the strongest positions. In the modern period, it is only on the fringes of Europe that we find structural changes in the urban system when new systems of circulation are set up. As the study of demography has revealed, the most important changes were brought about by the great turning-points in the overall conjuncture. However, from the sixteenth century the big cities developed a better resistance to crises and conjunctural changes than smaller communities.

They were always able to adapt even to the disappearance of certain growth factors. At Lyons, for instance, silk manufacture took the place of long-distance trade, allowing migration flows to remain stable, while commerce actually expanded.[46] The town remained mistress of the situation because it added to its basic activities complementary ones which gradually developed their own dynamic. The maintenance of directive power made substitution possible.

This new approach to urban history, then, has two essential features. It aims to establish comparable series of a variety of indicators which will permit the perception of the various aspects of the urban phenomenon, economic flows, population movements, building and improvement cycles, and social and cultural stratification systems. Then, it relates all these features to a specific locality, where it reconstitutes the production, growth and various uses of urban space, and the links between the townscape and the cultural atmosphere out of which it grew.[47] It still remains to develop a historical method which can incorporate all these individual places, and the constellations in which they are grouped, on a comparative basis. And even further away, no doubt, lies the sophisticated economic and social model which will allow us to comprehend more than 1000 years of urban growth in a single conceptualization.

Daniel Roche
Sorbonne, Paris I

Notes

1 C. F. Menestrier, *Les Devoirs de la Ville de Lyon envers les Saints* (Lyon, 1659); *idem, L'Éloge historique de Lyon* (Lyon, 1669); *idem, L'Histoire civile et consulaire de Lyon* (Lyon, 1696); P. D. Huet, *Les Origines de la Ville de Caen* (Rouen, 1702).

2 D. Roche, *Le Siècle des Lumières en Province, Académies et Académiciens provinciaux, 1689–1789* (Paris – The Hague, 1978), and *idem,* 'L'histoire dans les activités des académies provinciales', in K. Hammer and J. Voss (eds), *Historische Forschung im 18 Jahrhundert* (Bonn, 1976).

3 R. de Lasteyrie and E. Lefebvre-Pontalis, *Bibliographie générale des Travaux historiques et archéologiques publiés par les Sociétés savantes de la France* (Paris, 1888); from 1909 this is complemented by *Répertoire bibliographique de l'Histoire de France*; finally P. Dollinger and P. Wolff, *Bibliographie d'Histoire des Villes de France* (1967), provided a convenient synthesis.

4 L. Barbat, *Histoire de la Ville de Châlons sur Marne et de ses Monuments depuis les Origines jusqu'à l'Époque actuelle* (Châlons, 1855).

5 M. Halbwachs, *Les Expropriations et les Prix des Terrains à Paris au début du XXe siècle* (Paris, 1907); see also: *idem, Classes sociales et Morphologie* (Paris, 1927); *idem, La Politique foncière des Municipalités* (1908), 177–98; *idem, Les Plans d'Extension et d'Aménagement de Paris avant le XIXe siècle* (1920), 199–224.

6 M. Leroy, *La Ville française* (Paris, 1927).

7 P. Lavedan, *Histoire de l'Urbanisme* (Paris, 1952), the synthesis of a quarter-century of research. See also M. Poète, *Histoire de Paris* (1924–31).

8 H. Pirenne, *Les Villes et les Institutions urbaines* (Paris, 1939); G. Martin, *Mantes au XVIIIe siècle, l'Ère des négriers* (Paris, 1931); G. Lefebvre, *Etudes orléanaises* (Paris, 1962) (most of the manuscript dates from before 1944); H. Sée, 'Saint-Malo à la veille de la Révolution', *Revue internationale d'Histoire du Droit* (1924); 'La population et la vie économique de Rennes vers le milieu du XVIIIe siècle', *Mémoires de la Société d'Histoire et d'Archéologie de Bretagne* (1923).

9 G. Roupnel, *La Ville et la Campagne dijonnaise au XVIIe siècle* (Paris, 1922) (2nd edn, 1955).

10 F. Bédarida, 'The growth of urban history in France: some methodological trends', in H. J. Dyos (ed.), *The Study of Urban History* (1968), 47–65.

11 H. Lefebvre, *La Pensée marxiste et la Ville* (Paris, 1972), 149–55.

12 J. C. Perrot, *Genèse d'une Ville moderne: Caen au XVIIIe siècle* (Paris – The Hague, 1975).

13 F. Lebrun, 'La démographie urbaine en France sous l'Ancien Régime: problèmes de

méthodes', *Actas de las i jornadas de metodologia aplicada de las Ciencias Historicas* (April, 1973), Santiago de Compostella (1976), 273–9.

14 J. P. Bardet, 'La démographie des villes de la modernité (XVIe–XVIIIe siècles)', *Annales de Démographie Historique* (1974), 101–26; M. Garden, 'La démographie des villes françaises du XVIIIe siècle', *Démographie Urbaine, XVe–XXe siècles* (Lyon, 1977).

15 M. Garden, *Lyon et les Lyonnais au XVIIIe siècle* (Paris, 1970); Perrot, *op. cit.* 152–65; J. P. Bardet, *Histoire de Rouen* (Toulouse, 1979), 218–26; M. Terrisse, 'La population de Marseille et de son terroir de 1694 à 1830' (Marseille, 1971), unpublished thesis; A. Chamoux, 'L'enfance abandonné à Reims à la fin du XVIIIe siècle', *Annales de Démographie Historique* (1973) 263–85; M. Lachiver, *La Population de Meulan du XVIIe siècle, 1600–1870* (Paris, 1969).

16 See the current work of M. Garden and Y. Lequin at Lyons.

17 L. Bergeron and M. Roncayolo, 'De la ville pré-industrielle à la ville industrielle', *Quaderni Storici* (1975), 827–76.

18 R. Mousnier, 'Problèmes de méthode dans l'étude des structures sociales des XVIe, XVIIe, XVIIIe siècles', *La Plume, la Faucille et le Marteau* (Paris, 1970); and *La Stratification sociale à Paris au XVIIe siècle; L'Échantillon de 1634, 1635, 1636* (Paris, 1976). *1635, 1636* (Paris, 1976).

19 Paris, 1961.

20 A. Daumard, *La Bourgeoisie parisienne de 1815 à 1848* (Paris – The Hague, 1969); P. Deyon, *Amiens Capitale provinciale, Étude sur la Société urbaine au XVIIe siècle* (Paris – The Hague, 1969); Garden, *Lyon, op. cit.*

21 D. Roche (ed.), *Histoire sociale, Sources et Méthodes* (Paris, 1967), and *idem, Ordres et Classes* (Paris – The Hague, 1971).

22 J. C. Perrot, 'Rapports sociaux et ville au XVIIIe siècle', *Annáles E.S.C.* (1968), 241–68.

23 S. Thernstrom and R. Sennett, *Nineteenth-century Cities: Essays in the new urban history* (New York, 1969).

24 We await the publication of J. P. Pousson's work on Bordeaux and immigration into Aquitaine. Meanwhile most of the urban and demographic studies cited here include relevant material. See also a study which, unfortunately, remains less well known in France than it merits, O. H. Hufton, *The Poor of Eighteenth Century France, 1750–1789* (1974).

25 L. Chevalier, *Classes laborieuses et Classes dangereuses à Paris pendant la première moitié du XIXe siècle* (Paris, 1958).

26 A. Abbiateci, F. Billacois, Y. Castan, P. Petrovitch, Y. Boncert, N. Castan, *Crimes et Criminalité en France 17e–18e siècle* (Paris, 1971); A. Farge, *Le Vol d'aliments à Paris au XVIIIe siècle* (Paris, 1974); 'Marginalité et criminalité à l'époque moderne', *Revue d'Histoire Moderne et Contemporaine* (1974).

27 Roche, *Siècle des Lumières en Province*, 374–6; Perrot, *Caen au XVIIIe siècle*, 553–600, 639–42, 882–906.

28 A. Blanchard, *Les Ingénieurs du Roi de Louis XIV à Louis XVI* (Montpellier, 1979).

29 B. Stoloff, *Rôle social et Fonction économique de l'Architecte français sous l'Ancien Régime* (Paris, n.d. [1978]).

30 'Une nouvelle Histoire des villes', *Annales, E.S.C.* (1975), 197.

31 C. Nières, *La Reconstruction d'une Ville au XVIIIe siècle, Rennes 1720–1760* (Paris, 1972).

32 *Urbanistique et Société Baroque, Premiers, Résultats d'une Recherche exploratoire sur la Sicile après le Séisme du 9 et 11 janvier 1693* (Paris, 1977).

33 M. Foucault, B. Barret-Kriegel, A. Thalamy, F. Beguin, B. Fortier, *Les Machines à Guérir, aux Origines de l'Hôpital moderne* (Paris, 1979).

34 B. Fortier (ed.), *La Politique de l'Espace parisien à la Fin de l'Ancien Régime* (Paris, 1975).

35 M. Ozouf, *La Fête Révolutionnaire, 1789–1799* (Paris, 1976).

36 F. Raison-Jourde, *La Colonie auvergnate de Paris au XIXe siècle* (Paris, 1976).

37 J. P. Bardet, *Histoire de Rouen* (Toulouse, 1979), 205–57.

38 D. Roche, R. Arnette, F. Ardellier, 'Inventaires après décès parisiens et culture matérielle', *Colloque de Strasbourg sur l'Utilisation des Archives notariales* (Strasbourg, 1979).

39 A. Farge, *Vivre dans la rue à Paris au XVIIIe siècle* (Paris, 1979).

40 D. Roche, 'Les armatures urbaines dans l'espace européen du XVIe au XIXe siècles', report presented at the third seminar of urban history, Maison des Sciences de l'Homme, Paris, 1977.

41 B. Lepetit, 'La croissance urbaine dans la France pré-industrielle: quelques méthodes d'analyse', *Recherches et Travaux de l'Institut d'Histoire Economique et sociale de l'Université de Paris I*, vii, December 1978, 1–19.

42 R. Favier, 'Une ville face au développement de la circulation au XVIIIe siècle: Vienne en Dauphiné', *Actes du 100e Congrès des Sociétés Savantes (Paris, 1975), Section d'Histoire Moderne et contemporaine* (Paris, 1977), 54–62.

43 J. Dupaquier, *La Population rurale du Bassin Parisien à l'époque de Louis XIV* (Paris, 1979).

44 Roche, *Siècle des Lumières en Province*, 75–96.

45 L. Bergeron and M. Roncayolo, *loc. cit.*, 851–2.

46 R. Gascon, *Grand commerce et vie urbaine au XVIe siècle, Lyon et ses marchands* (Paris – The Hague, 1967), M. Garden, *Lyon, op. cit.*

47 The value for urban history of these new approaches emerges from an examination of that massive series of urban biographies, still in progress, the *Collection Univers de la France et des pays francophones, série Histoire des Villes*. This enterprise alone would justify a full review article. So far, Rennes, Marseilles, Toulouse, Geneva, Angers, Lyons, Le Mans, Brussels, Brest, Nice, Grenoble, Lille-Roubaix-Tourcoing, Nantes, Nancy and Rouen have been studied. It would be useful to analyse, in respect of each of these 20 or so towns, the attention devoted to each period, the issues selected for examination, and the questionnaire. The preferences of the research teams responsible for each volume have produced massive divergences under all three heads.

Residential segregation in the American metropolis: concentration, dispersion and dominance*

Measuring residential segregation is a challenging and crucial task. Many important questions in urban history can be understood fully only after correctly assessing the importance and significance of the clustering patterns of different groups of urbanites. However, the extent to which and the ways in which various social classes, races, and ethnic groups congregated in the expanding industrial metropolis of nineteenth-century America form the subject of heated debates among historians. With large black ghettos now existing in all major cities, experts and lay citizens alike agree that Americans live in a 'separated society'.[1] In the first half of the twentieth century, metropolitan areas took the form of ghettoized central cities with white suburbs. With the transfer of many urban functions to suburban units, and the shift of America from a nation of urbanites to a nation of suburbanites, a complex pattern of suburban segregation also developed. The universal concern about the magnitude of today's segregation makes the historical debate intriguing. Was it once different? Was there a time when cities were integrated? At some time in the past, many believe, American cities were better places in which to live – hence we should strive to recover our lost community.

The argument that segregation increases over time carries a great deal of emotional import, regardless of its scholarly value. It goes roughly as follows: from the communities of the founding fathers to the walking cities of the latter part of the nineteenth century, no great specialization of land use, residential or otherwise, existed. Cities were spatially integrated. Many factors combined to change this and make current social divisions so visible in urban space: large-scale industrialization, the transformation of the walking city into a giant metropolis, the increased immigration of unskilled labour into the city (especially the massive migration of blacks from the south), and the development of outlying areas inhabited by the well-to-do. The increasing differentiation between residential areas was a process involving a redistribution of the population in the expanding metropolitan area.

The implications of the theory are particularly important in the area of race relations. Adherents insist that not only was the city of the past less segregated than the city of the present, but unlike today's blacks, still trapped in the ghetto, previous victims of segregation in the industrial metropolis found their way out of the ghetto. Thus the National Advisory Commission on Civil Disorders in 1968 reported:

> The later phases of Negro settlement and expansion in metropolitan areas diverge sharply from those typical of white immigrants. As the whites were absorbed by the large society, many left their predominantly ethnic neighborhoods and moved to outlying areas to obtain newer housing and better schools. Some scattered randomly over the suburban area. Others established new ethnic clusters in the suburbs, but even these rarely constituted solely members of a single ethnic group. As a result, most middle class neighborhoods – both in the suburbs and within central cities – have no distinctive ethnic character, except that they are white. Nowhere has the expansion of America's urban Negro population followed this pattern of dispersal.[2]

Such a statement assumes that white ethnic groups experienced at one point a

* I wish to thank Marjorie Spruill and Patricia R. Schroeder for their comments on the manuscript.

process of ghettoization at least temporarily similar to that of the blacks. Was this really the case? Before comparing the inability of blacks to leave the ghetto to the greater set of opportunities available to white minorities, we must know whether their ghettos were similar in the first place.

This paper focuses on the nature, degree and meaning of residential segregation during the 70 years from 1850 to 1920, the period of the creation of the modern metropolis. The last two generations of historians and sociologists have offered conflicting theories and accumulated much contradictory evidence. It is the purpose of this article to shed some light on the debate. It does not offer an exhaustive review but discusses what seem to be the most significant studies published on this aspect of American urban history. It is not a simple matter to identify clusters in the changing urban environment and to assess their meaning in the larger framework of the making of American society. Previous discussions of the industrial metropolis have misused the concepts of concentration and dispersion. They dealt only with obvious clusterings or obvious mixture, thus creating only two alternatives, the ghetto or the 'residential melting pot'. A more appropriate concept with which to measure segregation in the industrial metropolis is the concept of dominance. Measuring dominance is determining the threshold at which geographic concentration is significant for a group in an area.[3] Dominance is not determined by a rigid numerical criterion applicable in all instances but by the complex interplay of variables causing geographic concentration and dispersion. By integrating the more subtle forms of clustering found in the emerging ethnic city, the concept of dominance is useful for those who wish to grasp the complexity of the urban experience of immigrants in industrial America.

The traditional view of ethnic assimilation in American cities stresses concentration; it can be labelled the ghetto interpretation of American history. This view depicts immigrants to American cities as settling first in an area of confinement near the centre, and then dispersing throughout the city as their occupations, incomes, educational levels, and the composition of their families come to resemble those of the population as a whole. The theory was originally formulated at the University of Chicago by a group of sociologists who, under the leadership of R. Park, and including L. Wirth and E. Burgess, count among the fathers of urban sociology. The rich sociological image of the city divided into physical zones, each of them representing a step in the assimilation process of immigrants was presented as a universal phenomenon, applicable to all groups in the city. Wirth insisted that:

> The Jews drift into the ghetto . . . for the same reasons that the Italians live in Little Sicily, the Negroes in the black belt, and the Chinese in Chinatowns. The various areas that compose the urban community attract the type of population whose economic status and cultural tradition is more nearly adapted to the physical and social characteristics to be found in each. As each new increment is added to the population it does not at random locate itself just anywhere, but it brings about a resifting of the whole mass of human beings, resulting finally in the anchoring of each to a milieu that, if not most desirable, is at any rate least undesirable.[4]

Fifteen years after Burgess had formalized the model in a pilot study of Chicago, Cressey developed its most outstanding definition:

> Immigrant stocks follow a regular sequence of settlement in successive areas of increasing stability and status . . . An immigrant group on its arrival settles in a compact colony in a low rent industrial area usually located in the transitional zone near the center of the city . . . These congested areas of first settlement are characterized by the perpetuation of many European cultural traits. After some years of residence in such an area, the group is not so closely concentrated physically, there is less cultural solidarity, and more American standards of living

are adopted. Subsequent areas of settlement may develop in some cases, but the last stage in this series of movements is one of gradual dispersion through cosmopolitan residential districts. This diffusion marks the disintegration of the group and the absorption of the individuals into the general American population. The relative concentration or dispersion of various immigrant groups furnishes an excellent indication of the length of residence in the city and the general degree of assimilation which has taken place.[5]

The Chicago model suffered empirical weaknesses, pointed out by several critics over the years, but it remained unchallenged in its basic assumptions. Its great strength was consistency to an overall theory of assimilation into American society. Immigrants started at the bottom economically, and suffered from cultural and geographic isolation. With time, or from one generation to another, they improved their situation and became assimilated into an undefined middle-class America. The Chicago sociologists created this very attractive model of urban assimilation, in which the ecological, social, cultural, and eventually national levels of assimilation fit nicely. As Higham recently pointed out, Park's scheme of assimilation, very influential in casting the model, was

> an improved version of the classic American ideal of assimilation, now extended, as only a few radicals had done before, to include Negroes as well as immigrants. Park defined prejudice not as an exceptional or especially irrational phenomenon but simply as a kind of conservatism, a way of keeping what is strange and unfamiliar at a distance. Yet modern urban life inevitably throws people together . . . It widens their horizons while loosening their customary ties. In the long run assimilation usually occurs.[6]

It is no surprise that the Chicago model was so appealing to historians. Literary sources were filled with descriptions of the zone in transition, and sociological theory provided a guide for ordering the material. The zone in transition was visited by many social workers from the 1880s onward, who published accounts of their visits. They ran up and down the filthy stairways of crowded tenements, surveying the conditions of immigrant life, appalled by their findings. As their objective was to touch the sense of moral responsibility of the nation, they focused on the most extreme cases of poverty, overcrowding, and deterioration found in the ghetto. They were inspired by the social gospel, not by the credo of social science, and their surveys, although certainly accurate, were never serious attempts at representing the 'statistical' reality. Social workers described only the worst cases of deterioration. Jane Addams' story of the suicide of a talented craftsman, whose family was among those helped at Hull-House, is a good example:

> A Bohemian whose little girl attended classes at Hull-House, in one of his periodic drunken spells had literally almost choked her to death, and later had committed suicide when in delirium tremens. His poor wife . . . one day showed me a gold ring which her husband had made for their betrothal. It exhibited the most exquisite workmanship, and she said that although in the old country he had been a goldsmith, in America he had for twenty years shoveled coal in a furnace room of a large manufacturing plant . . . Why had we never been told? Why had our interest in the remarkable musical ability of his child, blinded us to the hidden artistic ability of the father?[7]

Such stories of deterioration, of personal decline, made up the raw material of Handlin's *The Uprooted*, the work which most forcefully promoted the ghetto interpretation of American history.[8]

In the 1960s, a very healthy reversal of historical scholarship began. The sociological model and its most dramatic and poetical historical adaptations were rejected. A new school of social historians, attempting to write history from the bottom up, took their questions directly to the archival records. They looked for the ghetto but they did not find it. On the contrary they discovered, or thought they discovered, a great mixing of people of all ethnic groups in the American metropolis. At first the criticism of the traditional model was mild. Nelli, studying Italians in Chicago, pointed out many of the oversimplifications of Cressey's succession–adaptation model.[9] However, he admitted that Cressey, if wrong in detail, was correct in the aggregate. Soon, however, there was more radical criticism. Thernstrom, whose studies of the relationship between geographic and social mobility have been very influential in the last ten years, made a very important contribution to the debate by pointing out the volatility of the American population.[10] The city was acting like an intelligent sieve, retaining the more successful but letting the poor go. The poor in turn wandered to other American cities, hoping for better days. According to this interpretation the ghetto, traditionally described as a zone of relative stability where immigrants stagnated and degenerated, was in fact the most fluid and volatile part of the city. At the same time Warner and Burke, using newly developed segregation indices, concluded that in most cities, concentration of the foreign-born did not exist at significant levels. The ghetto was an invention of the twentieth century, not a reality of the nineteenth. The authors clearly stated:

> Most foreign immigrants to American cities never lived in ghettos, and most immigrant ghettos that did exist were the product of the largest cities and the eastern and southern European immigrants of 1880–1940. Moreover, if a ghetto be defined as a place inhabited almost exclusively by one ethnic group, then only the caste isolated northern Negro has an extended tradition of ghetto living. Only the northern Negro has had a heavy preponderance of his group confined to a segregated quarter of the city . . . Chicago and New York ghetto literature should be read as pertaining to the special cases of the nation's largest and heaviest immigrant cities, not merely as large-scale versions of a common state of affairs.[11]

A few years later, Chudacoff combined 'geographic mobility' and 'spatial mixture' in his study of Omaha. He reached the conclusion that Omaha, from 1880 to 1920, the very period of arrivals of new immigrants and of the ghetto, was a 'typical' fluid and integrated medium-sized American city. Later Chudacoff, in a textbook on American urban history, generalized his own findings and included a number of others in this rapidly growing field.[12]

Should we take the revisionists' position seriously? And if so, are their conclusions as dramatic as they appear at first glance? Many Americans have been raised with the sense of an ethnic heritage, and attach certain value to this aspect of their identity as Americans. That the ethnic community was once clustered spatially, in the neighbourhoods of cities, is part of the story. If we are to say that this idea of the ethnic experience is only legend, that it has no root in reality, or in 'statistical' reality, one must be ready to support one's claim with considerable evidence. It is also important to explain how the concept of dispersion relates to the immigrant experience in general.

There are important points in the revisionists' position but also fatal weaknesses. On the positive side, I perceive three contributions. First, what was called ten years ago 'the new urban history' documented the great movement of the American population. As Katz recently put it: 'When Victorians sought a symbol of progress, they often chose the steam engine; had they wanted a metaphor for their cities, they could have found none more apt than the railroad station.'[13] Mobility studies, when seeking to understand the shift from 'ascribed' to 'achieved' status, worked out some of the relationships between geographic and social mobility; however, they failed to investigate sufficiently the ghetto interpretation of American history. In many ways 'new urban historians' have shared the liberal assimilationist positions of the Chicago sociologists. Thernstrom's subtitle *Poverty and Progress* could read *From Poverty to Progress* just as well.[14] But 'new urban historians' dismissed the importance of local spatial structures. While the Chicago sociologists were testing Park's theory that 'Physical distances are so frequently and so inevitably the indices of social distances',[15] historians did not recognize the importance of place in their fluid, volatile, and ascending society. They neglected to measure the impact of mobility on local institutions, and the workings of communities in the metropolis.

The second contribution has been to correct the Chicago model on the subject of the black ghetto. In the 1920s, Park, Burgess and Wirth had included the blacks in the succession of immigrants. It is clear now that the 'last of the immigrants' theory does not hold, that blacks have had a different experience in urban America. Many excellent studies describe the black ghetto taking shape, following a pattern of a 'tragic sameness'.[16] Indeed a pattern of enduring discrimination has been established in the spatial arrangement of the megalopolis. Yet the task of comparing the urban experience of blacks with that of the preceding white ethnic groups remains before us.

The third contribution of the revisionists has been to stress social class as a determining factor in the clustering patterns of the industrial metropolis. They suggest that the mixture of ethnic groups found in cities corresponded to a cluster of unskilled and semi-skilled workers. What was traditionally attributed to ethnic clustering could then be attributed to a broad grouping of similar classes. This is the point sociologist Herbert Gans made about the West End of Boston.[17] The 'peer group society' of the West End, Gans contended, was in fact a working-class area, labelled Italian only by force of habit. But his recognition of the peer group society came in the 1960s, 40 years after the closing of the doors. What about the 1890s or the early 1900s, when over 1,000,000 foreigners entered the country annually at Ellis Island?

These three important points were made by the revisionists, with varying degrees of analytical depth. No student of American urban history can now embark on a study of the spatial arrangement of the city without evaluating the impact of mobility, sorting out the different types of migrants, and working out the relationships between class and ethnicity. But the revisionists do not stop at this. We are told of the great mixing of people of all ethnic groups in the city. We are to believe that the ghetto is an invention of the twentieth century, and that the big city of the nineteenth century was 'a jumble of occupations, classes, shop, homes, immigrants, and native Americans'.[18] Should we conclude that the massive influx of newcomers to American cities did not really influence the shape of the city since all were dispersed equally throughout the urban area? And conversely, should we conclude that the process of assimilation of newcomers to American cities, and ultimately to the society as a whole, was unrelated to their settlement in the physical environment? Such are the implications of the revisionist argument if we take it too literally. Unfortunately the reader has to decide for himself the consequences of the mixed socio-spatial arrangement. For example, what are the consequences of residential dispersion on the institutional life of ethnic groups, traditionally organized around focal points, all spatially anchored: the church, the foreign language press, the labour agency, the fraternal organization, the singing society, the democratic boss? Did these institutions matter in the life of the majority of immigrants? If true, the dispersion theory brings about a revamping of all that we know about the expanding industrial metropolis, and the experience of immigrants. While the traditional ghetto model had integrated all of the aspects of the life of immigrants, including their assimilation into the society as a whole, the dispersion model remains descriptive. It does not offer any explanation theoretically relevant to the question of immigrant experience.

The revisionist position has left many historians confused. Some researchers have tried to find a compromise, a middle ground between the traditional model and the revision. In a recent study of the Irish in Detroit, Jo Ellen Vinyard successfully demonstrated that the Irish were better off in the Midwest than their compatriots who stayed in Boston, but she never said what was Irish about the Irish of Detroit.[19] Following the techniques of analysis promoted by Warner and Chudacoff, Vinyard found a rather thorough mixture of the Irish with other groups throughout the city. Yet she is uncertain as to how to interpret this finding, recognizing as she does the importance of the original Irish area, Corktown, its people, its architecture and its institutions. She fails to work out the relationships between the concentrated and the dispersed Irish, and the book wanders from model one to model two without ever deciding which one is right. Other recent work is also puzzling. Richard Wade, a noted urban historian, recently expressed the view of 'the mixture of people all the time', in an interview to the *Journal of Urban History*.[20] Wade's reference was to Chicago, the source of the ghetto interpretation of American history. Wade's judgment was based on a book since published, *The Slum and the Ghetto*, by Thomas Philpott.[21] The book is an especially interesting comparative treatment of black and white ethnic settlement patterns in a large American city, and correctly points out the unique kind of residential confinement of the blacks. Initially, Philpott seems to confirm the traditional model when describing the 'degrading' slums of late nineteenth-century Chicago. Unfortunately, he makes no attempt to estimate the proportion of immigrants living in such slum areas. Philpott then turns to the revisionists and describes the ethnic pattern of the slum as a 'melting pot'. The amazing thing is that Philpott's contention is not based on the analysis of new data, but on a new 'look' at the data assembled by the Chicago sociologists who had promoted the thesis of the ghetto. Who was right? Nobody. The sociologists, obsessed with the concept of the ghetto, forced everybody into it, even if there was only a pattern of slight dominance of a group in an area. In turn Philpott failed to recognize the importance of the concept of dominance, and thus failed to develop appropriate tools to measure it. The absence of concepts other than complete segregation or total mixture, and the absence of sensitive tools of measurement, led the author to conclude simply that there was a pattern of mixture.

If we are to come to a clearer understanding of residential segregation and its implications, we must have acceptable methods. To examine the urban environment and to divide it into homogeneous socio-spatial zones is a complex problem. While the highly impressionistic methods of Handlin must obviously be discarded, are the statistical methods used by the revisionists any more reliable?

Many problems must be considered in order to assess the relative degree of concentration of different groups. The general physical characteristics and the density pattern of the city must be understood in order to devise an appropriate strategy and develop units of analysis. American cities vary greatly at any time in size, shape and density. The unit chosen to measure concentration in a city like Detroit, which contained a maximum of 80 people per acre in 1880, may not be appropriate for Chicago, with some areas counting up to 400 people per acre, or New York, with quarters counting up to 600 people per acre. Usually a group dominated an area or several small areas within a larger region of the city, though members of other groups, related or not, lived there too. Two related aspects of spatial concentration must always be considered. The first concerns the proportion of people in one area that belongs to one ethnic group; this figure tells us how dominant a given group is in one area. The second concerns the proportion of an ethnic group membership in an area to the total population of that group in the city; this tells us how important a particular area is for the group, whether or not a large fraction of the group is living there. Often these two figures are related, yet they may differ substantially. For instance, it is conceivable that while a group may comprise only 20 per cent of any block in a region of the city, 90 per cent of this group might live in this region.

No attempts were made by the revisionists to define appropriate spatial units of measurement. As census data was available, already aggregated at the ward level, these scholars simply used city wards as a unit of analysis. The nineteenth-century electoral wards were very large, and their boundaries changed from one election to another. Often ward boundaries were changed precisely to divide ethnic neighbourhoods in order to weaken the ethnic vote. Thus wards in 1880 Detroit were long thin strips running north-south, dividing the German, Polish, and Irish neighbourhoods into two to four distinct wards. Such wards also contained varying amounts of uninhabited areas, and varying degrees of residential and non-residential land uses. They are hardly an ideal unit for measuring residential segregation, and it is no surprise that the use of them leads one to discover a miscellany of people.

The revisionists also relied on a single statistical index, the index of dissimilarity made popular by the Duncans in 1955.[22] Very popular for its great simplicity, 'the index of dissimilarity measures overall unevenness in the relative distribution of two populations'. In principle, 'It provides an easily interpretable measure varying from zero (no segregation – an even distribution) to 100 (maximum segregation – maximum displacement from an even distribution).' In fact a great deal of controversy persists in the sociological literature as to the true meaning of the index of dissimilarity, and its usefulness as an index of segregation. The index is commonly interpreted as a proportion of a minority group that would have to change its area of residence to achieve an even residential distribution. Thus a replacement index, an algebraic transformation of the dissimilarity index, is often computed to estimate the exchange of residents between areas. However, Massey recently demonstrated that under the assumption of equal sizes of the units, the index 'is correctly interpreted as the number of moves required to achieve evenness, expressed as a proportion of the number required if segregation was total',[23] and the index is the same whether we consider moves from the point of view of the majority or the minority. None of these complex problems of interpretation have entered the historical literature. Historians were content to use the simpler formula, and to use unwieldy and irregular spatial units. All too often they extended a formula originally conceived to handle a binomial distribution, the blacks and the whites, to a multinomial distribution, all the groups in the city, making it even more difficult to interpret the statistic. They were looking for concrete results: how much segregation of who and where? In fact they were bluffed by the apparent computational simplicity of a measure which gives only a very abstract notion of shift and replacement, with many strings attached to the interpretation. They had been rightly advised not to trust simple percentages and simple maps which can give fallacious images, but they did worse in their use – and misuse – of the index of dissimilarity.

Between extreme concentration and dispersion there are a great many nuances. Considering the many factors which play a role in urban location, it is much more reasonable to expect a complex pattern than a total integration or segregation. Dominance is a subtler and more useful concept than complete take-over. Instead of being clustered in one area only, a group may show a complicated pattern of scattered concentrations. In looking for past processes of settlement in the multi-ethnic industrial metropolis, the loose and somewhat imprecise concept of the neighbourhood – connoting relative concentration, relative cohesiveness, social interaction, and commonality of institutions – provides a better indication of the real patterns than does the more totalitarian concept of the ghetto.

Three studies have recently provided us with a balanced set of answers, forcefully rehabilitating the concept of the ethnic neighbourhood, but with a new perspective. In Philadelphia, where Warner had found no notable concentration of Irish and Germans in the 1850s, Hershberg and Burstein found a complex pattern:

> while the German immigrants were clustered, resulting in a distinct residential concentration, their area of the city was by no means a German area. The Irish were less clustered but tended to dominate their residential areas. Obviously neither group lived in ghettoes approaching the level of ethnic domination which can be observed in 20th century cities. However, the beginnings of an ethnic ghetto did exist, and these are found not among the clustered German immigrants, but rather among the more dispersed Irish immigrants. And while

many Irish immigrants displayed residential assimilation by living in areas which were characteristically native-white, the measure of relative clustering . . . suggests that yet another segment of the Irish immigrant group was increasingly residing in an Irish-dominated area.[24]

In turn, Conzen studying Milwaukee pointed to a similar complex pattern:

The pattern of immigrant settlement in Milwaukee implies a new twist to the conventional ghetto hypothesis. Milwaukee's two main immigrant groups were certainly segregated. For the great majority of Germans, particularly, residence involved minimal neighborhood contact with either natives or Irish. The new city permitted its major immigrant group to carve out an entire sector for itself, large enough to provide for internal variations in residential status. There was little sign among either Germans or Irish of the type of movement predicted by the classic ghetto hypothesis – movement from central receiving ghetto to more middle-class but still ethnically-defined fringe neighborhoods. In a city like Milwaukee, where primitive transportation placed a premium on central location, the newer immigrants developed the outer areas while the areas of first settlement improved in status as their residence gained greater security.[25]

And while Vinyard had concluded that Detroit in 1880 'was most characterized by the considerable geographic mix of classes and nationalities', my studies of the city at the same date led me to the opposite conclusion.[26] In fact there was a strong pattern of ethnic concentration in 1880 Detroit, especially in areas inhabited by four groups: Americans, Irish, Germans, and Poles; 37 per cent to 70 per cent of their populations were clustered in one area. There also existed a strong pattern of occupational clustering, especially in areas inhabited by low-status white-collar workers in the near centre and by skilled craftsmen on the East Side. Ethnic concentration, however, was numerically and spatially more important than occupational concentration. Despite some important interaction between occupation and ethnicity, such as German skilled craftsmen or American white-collar employees, areas of high ethnic concentration included all types of occupations, while areas of high occupational clustering, especially among white-collar employees, were inhabited by many different national groups. Finally both the more heavily populated and diversified central areas and the peripheral vacant areas showed remarkably little ethnic or occupational residential concentration.

These three studies were developed independently but they share a similar methodological concern. They adopted a unit of analysis considerably smaller than the ward (an artificial grid superimposed on the city plan in the case of Philadelphia and Milwaukee, a cluster of one city block augmented by two opposing frontages in the case of Detroit), and reorganized the census data according to these units. The three studies adopted refined statistical procedures, carefully reasoned and directly coupled with imaginative mapping techniques, permitting them to circumvent the concentrations spatially and to assess more accurately their importance. The index of relative clustering used for Philadelphia, the combination of gradient analysis and factor analysis used for Milwaukee, and the standardized chi-square index developed for the Detroit study, three refined tools for fine grain analysis, led the investigators not only to conclude upon a significant level of clustering, but also to explain it in the context of the particular city, and to distinguish the clustered population from the non-clustered population.

The great strength of the new studies mentioned so far is their ability to distinguish between members of an ethnic group which was spatially concentrated and of one which was dispersed. When such a distinction is made, it becomes possible to test the theory of increasing assimilation with residential integration. The extent to which the spatially concentrated members of an ethnic group differ from the others is a question of cardinal importance: is the sense of community best expressed within a spatial context? Does it survive without? The shift from spatial to non-spatial bonds is a complex one.[27] The Jews, for instance, have traditionally kept strong cultural ties, long after leaving the Yiddish-speaking streets of the Lower East Side. Other groups live with double standards. Andrew Greeley recently described the Irish-Americans in *That Most Distressful Nation* in the following terms:

> With the exception of the Jews, they have achieved the most remarkable success of any immigrant group, the only thing they have lost is their explicit sense of distinction as a group and their consciousness of a heritage – and, necessarily, any consciousness of goals for the future.

This did not happen abruptly but by a slow process of loosening of ancestral constraints, such as an early marriage, exogamy, and of course upward social mobility. But this did not happen without hard feelings; Greeley addresses society at large and says: 'You've tried to turn us into lower middle class WASPs and, damn it all, you haven't succeeded.' In turn, he addresses the Irish-Americans, reversing the terms: 'Why did you let them turn you into lower middle class WASPs?'[28] An ambiguous relationship exists between the members of a group who remain close to the core culture of the group, and those who do not. Does the geographic process of concentration and dispersion correspond to the socio-cultural shift of ethnic bonds to occupational bonds?

To put it maybe too schematically, members of ethnic groups could live in one of three types of areas in nineteenth-century urban America: in a neighbourhood dominated by their group, in an area of town where the population seemed to have been distributed at random, or in a neighbourhood dominated by another group. Many factors play a role in residential location; ethnicity is only one of them. Among other factors are the shifting locations of industries and other places of work; the expansion of urban services, such as sewers, roads, transportation; the availability of vacant land for building new neighbourhoods; and the quality and the price of the available housing stock. Considering the interaction between such factors and the continuous flow of people in and out of the city, it is quite normal to expect to find a significant proportion of members of an ethnic group residentially dispersed and an equally significant proportion residentially clustered on the basis of ethnic origin. What difference did it make to settle in a mixed or a clustered area? Some suggestions, derived from my analyses of Detroit – still in progress – may prove useful.

Ethnic neighbourhoods exemplified the characteristics of the group as a whole. If we take an indicator of cultural differences such as fertility levels, the neighbourhoods reflected accurately the fertility differentials between ethnic groups observed at the aggregate level for the group as a whole. For instance Polish, German, and Irish areas of Detroit had high fertility rates while Yankee clusters showed a lower degree of fertility. Other indicators of cultural cohesiveness such as endogamy and associational life work as well. How different were the ethnic populations living outside the ethnic neighbourhood, in areas where the population was – on the basis of our statistical indices – distributed at random? Preliminary analysis shows that on the basis of family composition, fertility, occupation, educational level, and other characteristics, these people resembled their group more than they did the population as a whole. Residential mixture was by no means a sure indication that the assimilation process had started. Only in the third case, with people holding minority status in an area dominated by a different group, was there a clear indication of a difference. In some instances, like the Poles or the Russian Jews in the German neighbourhood, the first settlers of a group were using another group's neighbourhood as a port of entry. In an opposite instance, the Germans or Irish who had settled in Yankee areas were marking the difference with their fellow countrymen. There, in the Yankee neighbourhoods of Detroit, the German and Irish heads of households tended to be white-collar workers, and the women had lower fertility rates, similar to that of Yankee women.

These preliminary remarks bring us back to our original questions. To be sure the revisionists were right to react against the oversimplifications of the disintegration-succession model. However, their conceptualization of the problem and their analytical tools were too primitive to allow them to define a viable alternative. They failed to recognize the importance of the concept of dominance and the interaction of dominance with randomness. It is in this complex pattern, well adapted to the realities of urban life, that the ethnic factor took on its significance, inside and outside the ethnic community. American cities were segregated in the nineteenth century as well as in twentieth. It is only the forms of segregation that have changed. The task before us is to explore this process of change. Only then will we be able to compare today's patterns of segregation with yesterday's.

Olivier Zunz
Department of History, University of Virginia

Notes

1 M. Danielson, *The Politics of Exclusion* (New York, 1976), 1.
2 *Report of the National Advisory Commission on Civil Disorders* (Washington, 1968), 119, quoted in Danielson, *op. cit.*, 7.
3 Theodore Hershberg defined 'dominance' as 'the proportion of an area's total population accounted for by a single group' in *The Philadelphia Social History Project: A methodological history* (Ph.D. dissertation, University of Stanford, August 1973), 293.
4 L. Wirth, *The Ghetto* (Chicago, 1928), 283.
5 P. F. Cressey, 'Population succession in Chicago: 1898–1930,' *American Journal of Sociology*, xliv, 1 (July 1938), 61.
6 J. Higham, *Send These to Me* (New York, 1975), 215.
7 J. Addams, *Twenty Years at Hull-House* (New York, 1911), 246–7.
8 O. Handlin, *The Uprooted* (Boston, 1951).
9 H. S. Nelli, *The Italians in Chicago, 1880–1930* (New York, 1970), 44.
10 S. Thernstrom, 'Reflections on the new urban history,' *Daedalus* (Spring 1971), 359–75, and S. Thernstrom and P. R. Knights, 'Men in motion, some data and speculations about urban population mobility in nineteenth-century America,' *Journal of Interdisciplinary History*, i (Autumn 1970), 7–35.
11 S. Bass Warner, Jr. and C. Burke, 'Cultural change and the ghetto,' *Journal of Contemporary History*, iv, 1 (1969), 173–87.
12 H. Chudacoff, *Mobile Americans: Residential and social mobility in Omaha, 1880–1920* (New York, 1972), and 'A new look at ethnic neighborhoods: residential dispersion and the concept of visibility in a medium-sized city,' *Journal of American History*, lx (1973), 76–93, and *The Evolution of American Urban Society* (Englewood Cliffs, N.J., 1975), 90–124.
13 M B. Katz, M. J. Doucet and Mark J. Stern, 'Migration and the social order in Erie County, New York: 1855,' *Journal of Interdisciplinary History*, viii, 4 (Spring 1978), 669.
14 S. Thernstrom, *The Other Bostonians* (Cambridge, Mass., 1973).
15 R. Park, 'The urban community as a spatial pattern and a moral order,' *Human Communities, The City and Human Ecology* (Glencoe, Ill., 1957), 177.
16 D. Goldfield, 'The Black Ghetto, "a tragic sameness",' *Journal of Urban History*, iii, 3 (May 1977), 361–9.
17 H. Gans, *The Urban Villagers* (Glencoe, Ill., 1962).
18 S. Bass Warner, Jr., *The Private City* (Philadelphia, 1968), 50.
19 J. Vinyard, *The Irish on the Urban Frontier: Nineteenth century Detroit* (New York, 1974), 174–5.
20 R. Wade, interviewed by B. Stave, in *Journal of Urban History*, iii, 2 (February 1977), 223.
21 T. L. Philpott, *The Slum and the Ghetto* (New York, 1978).
22 O. D. Duncan and B. Duncan, 'A methodological analysis of segregation indexes,' *American Sociological Review*, ii (April 1955), 210–17.
23 D. S. Massey, 'Measuring residential segregation using the index of dissimilarity: problems and interpretations', Office of Population Research, Princeton University, September 1978, 25.
24 A. N. Burstein, 'Patterns of segregation and the residential experience,' in T. Hershberg (ed.), *The Philadelphia Social History Project*, a special issue of *Historical Methods News-*

letter, ix, 2 and 3 (March–June 1976), 113. See also T. Hershberg, A. N. Burstein, E. L. Ericksen, S. Greenberg and W. L. Yancey, 'A tale of three cities: blacks and immigrants in Philadelphia: 1850–1880, 1930 and 1970' *Annals, AAPSS*, cdxli (January 1979), 55–81.

25 K. Conzen, *Immigrant Milwaukee, 1836–1860*, (Cambridge, Mass., 1976), 152.

26 O. Zunz, 'Detroit en 1880: espace et ségrégation,' *Annales E.S.C.*, xxxi, 1 (Janvier–Février 1977), 106–36, and 'The organization of the American city in the late 19th century, ethnic structure and spatial arrangement in Detroit,' *Journal of Urban History*, iii, 4 (Summer 1977), 443–66.

27 T. Bender, *Community and Social Change in America* (Rutgers, 1978).

28 A. Greeley, *That Most Distressful Nation* (Chicago, 1972), vii, viii, xxvi.

The study of social conflict
in English industrial towns

The problem of social conflict is central to the historiography of nineteenth-century cities. Since Friedrich Engels wrote his powerful indictment of social relations in English industrial towns, urban historians have told and retold tales of dramatic struggles between workers and their middle-class employers.[1] Whether seen from a Marxist or non-Marxist perspective, the standard books on social life in industrial towns abound with strikes, demonstrations, confrontations, and other more subtle signs of conflict. A. Temple Patterson and Malcolm Thomis depict the often tumultuous responses of Leicester and Nottingham framework knitters to their economic decline.[2] Accounts of urban Chartism regularly link workers' economic and social demands to strong middle-class disapproval and disavowal within a local context.[3] Books on the 1830s and 1840s are particularly rich in incidents of confrontation, but the growing literature on the late nineteenth century also emphasizes this theme. Gareth Stedman Jones places middle-class misconceptions and fears at the centre of his analysis of casual labour in London, and Robert Grey's discussion of Edinburgh artisans assumes the reality of class conflict as a determinant of urban social relations.[4] Nevertheless our understanding of divisions among urban social groups and of the relationships of one group to another remains primitive and unsatisfactory.

Our knowledge about urban social conflict comes primarily from studies of individual towns, which are deficient in comparisons stretching over time and over space. While political historians have produced major books comparing and contrasting cities of the industrial north and Midlands, social historians for the most part have failed to follow their lead.[5] Studies of Chartists that do not attempt to survey the entire movement usually concentrate on one city, and much recent work on violence and collective action displays a similar preoccupation with local studies. The contributions of John Foster, David Gadian, George Barnsby, and John Stevenson stand out for the rarity of their comparative approach.[6] In any case the mere act of comparison does not necessarily produce valuable results. Much depends on the choice both of the towns to be surveyed and of the variables to be studied.

The most common strategy for comparison has been narrow, focusing upon occupations and industries. The contrasts between heavy and light industry, or mining and mill towns, are standard categories that are frequently linked to differences in levels of urban conflict. Donald Read has argued, for example, that 'Birmingham and Sheffield were cities of political union; Manchester and Leeds were cities of social cleavage.'[7] He based his judgment upon the dissimilar consequences of production in small workshops and large factories. In a similar vein, Asa Briggs has linked the comparative appeal of Chartism to economic organization. He has argued that workers were more likely to join the movement in centres of collapsing industry or in new, single-industry towns. Manchester and Birmingham with their more complex occupational composition were 'less active' Chartist centres than nearby textile or metal-working areas.[8] Although John Foster's methods and concerns are far different from those of Read and Briggs, many of his arguments comparing Oldham, Northampton, and South Shields rest upon the implications of their differing economic bases. Class conflict and a radical workers' movement will arise, Foster has stated, where industrial structure hindered collaboration with the bourgeoisie and facilitated the social solidarity of a widely defined occupational group. The necessary work of a revolutionary vanguard to encourage militancy required a certain type of urban setting in which to flourish.[9] But however intriguing the results of comparisons carried out along the lines of Foster's inquiry might be, they will not yield widely generalizable results since they offer little basis upon which to judge the typicality of the cities involved. Other cotton-spinning towns may or may not have functioned like Oldham in the 1840s, but Foster does not tell us. If the towns did not, despite structural similarities, his analysis will not help us sort out the differences.

When occupational structure is made the basic element in a comparison among cities, it can reveal important differences in the nature of local skills, organization, and expectations. We need to know at a minimum how the local population is employed, what proportion are employers, shopkeepers, or professionals, and whether women work outside the home. Yet this knowledge does not take us very far because occupational structure is a static framework. Such categories distort and rigidify relationships that emerge primarily in the process of social events. In the words of Victor Turner, 'the social world is a world in becoming, not a world in being'.[10] Although some type of social structural analysis is necessary for a study of urban social conflict, it is not sufficient. It tells us nothing about how groups interact and about the other factors that shape social relations. It should be a starting point rather than a major focus of research.

Occupational categories are particularly deficient in providing material for analyses of change over time and of differences among towns with a similar technological base. Why, for example, should the incidence of food riots and attacks on employers' property have decreased so markedly in Leicester and Nottingham between the late eighteenth and late nineteenth century?[11] To give an answer based primarily upon the differences between factory and workshop production or upon the essential nature of the hosiery and lace industry would be unsatisfactory indeed. And why should early twentieth-century strike rates in Welsh coal mining areas be so much higher than those of mining settlements in north-eastern counties?[12] Structural arguments give little help in this case either. Hypotheses about differences in the levels of social conflict among towns should be constructed on a much wider base. In place of two or three towns the array of places surveyed should be widened to cover a region or ideally the entire country. In addition, the variables examined must be far more extensive than urban economic structure.

In fact, sources exist which permit a detailed mapping in time and space of the various types of conflict that took place in cities in the nineteenth and twentieth centuries. Strikes, riots, demonstrations and political meetings have been extensively recorded by newspapers and by government departments. These materials have been used effectively by historians of France in order to analyse the comparative incidence of conflict, but they have only begun to be exploited by scholars interested in England.[13] Newspaper accounts, although more difficult to use than the Home Office papers on disturbances, offer the advantage of being more complete in their coverage. Local newspapers, particularly after their rapid multiplication in the mid-nineteenth century, allow anyone with the patience to pore over their pages to compile detailed catalogues of political and social life in towns of all shapes and sizes. While ticklish questions of completeness and of the comparability of accounts have to be faced, the newspapers offer extensive information on both violent and nonviolent forms of conflict. By using a sample of provincial papers in order to avoid the possible regional biases of *The Times*, urban historians can investigate the distribution in time and space of selected types of events. And when one knows where certain conflicts were more frequent and more intense, it becomes possible to ask what sorts of similarities there were among towns of high social and political conflict. Changes over time as well as differences among regions and types of cities can be investigated. More important, the collection of data on a large group of cities puts comparison on a much more satisfactory basis than if only two or three cities are studied on the basis of a prior decision concerning their 'representativeness'.

A list of all strikes reported to the Board of Trade was compiled by the Labour Correspondent and printed in the parliamentary papers and later in the *Labour*

Gazette.[14] This set of data, which identifies strikes by their location and trade, offers a rich source for comparing local patterns of conflict between workers and employers in the late nineteenth century. Strikes can be classified not only by their size and duration but also by the issues involved and by results. When used in conjunction with other materials on labour relations, this strike data makes possible a detailed mapping of one of the most widespread forms of social conflict in late nineteenth-century Britain. Moreover, because the data is largely in numerical form, it can be used in combination with the census and other quantitative data on urban social and economic life. Statistical techniques, such as multiple regression analysis, can then be used in order to check possible links between strike rates and, for example, migration flows, urban death rates, wage levels, or the proportion of workers in low-skilled jobs. With such data, a wide variety of hypotheses can be tested.

When more information on the varying incidence of conflict in England is available, it will show that certain confrontations, notably food riots, became much less frequent after 1800–20 while other types, particularly strikes, became more common as the century progressed. In addition, collective action seems to have become over time less violent, more highly organized, and more extensively monitored and mediated by political institutions. Charles Tilly has convincingly identified and analysed the major changes that took place from the early nineteenth century in France in the forms, issues, and types of people involved in collective action;[15] Louise Tilly and Richard Tilly have found comparable transitions in Italian and German patterns of political protest.[16] A similar shift in the nature of collective activity occurred in English towns between the late eighteenth and later nineteenth century. For example, in Nottingham in the late eighteenth century the most common public conflicts were food riots and demonstrations by framework knitters. Crowds of men and women, artisans and labourers, rioted over food prices and food supplies in the market place. In bad times, framework knitters attacked employers' property and petitioned Parliament to legislate for minimum wages. Similar groups of people dunked local radicals in the pond, burned Tom Paine in effigy, and celebrated the arrival of military heroes in the town. There was an active street life that brought together neighbours in a regular cycle of events tied to economics and politics and often led to expressions of collective hostility or approval. By 1890 the food riots and attacks on employers had ceased. Instead, well-organized demonstrations were used to express opinions. Elections were peaceful affairs as supporters or opponents registered their feelings at meetings or in the ballot box rather than by public attacks. Workers, many organized into trade unions, turned to strikes as a way of resisting or pressuring employers. Many conflicts, however, had evolved formal means of settlement. Trade unions and employers worked out procedures for mediation and discussion of disputes that often eliminated direct confrontations. Conflicts over economic, political and social issues were for the most part expressed in ways that did not involve face-to-face encounters in the streets of Nottingham. Formal organizations had replaced crowds or groups of neighbours as the main participants in controversies.[17]

This transition in the forms of collective action affected the nature of urban social conflict in ways that are not reducible to the issue of class. Changes in urban social organization shifted the groups most actively involved in local affairs as well as the localities that were the scenes of conflict. As retail shops and more specialized buildings multiplied, the market place became less important a place for both meetings and riots. And changing form followed changing function: riots at the hustings disappeared as the suffrage widened and as political parties and pressure groups developed. While conflicts of interest did not disappear, they were expressed in different ways.

These changes in the forms of collective action can be analysed on several levels. In purely descriptive terms, it is clear that conflict between workers and employers became more highly organized over time. In the hosiery industry, for example, before the transition to factory production that took place in the third quarter of the nineteenth century, knitters worked at home. The small scale of the towns in which the knitters lived and their geographic concentration in one region meant, however, that it was easy for groups of workers to mount informal protests during bad times. City streets and the market place were the sites for collective actions, which were often directed toward the entire community. By the 1880s, the audience for joint actions had narrowed while the methods became more limited and formalized. Most of the male knitters and many of the female ones had joined unions and worked in factories. Disputes were referred first to local plant representatives, foremen and managers, and if that produced no resolution, to union officials, employers, and finally to a board of arbitration.[18] Strikes that went beyond a single plant were rare, a final resort when all other methods of resolution had failed. Confrontations between employer and employee occurred infrequently, if only because of the creation of layers of intermediaries, part of whose job consisted of deflecting or settling disputes.

It is easy to show that the methods of communication among workers and between workers and employers changed during the nineteenth century. A more important topic concerns the extent to which the aims and outlooks of each group shifted too. The work of anthropologists such as Victor Turner offers a possible approach to this problem. Turner has begun to apply his analyses of rituals and symbols to historical data.[19] Turner argues that social behaviour can best be understood through the models and metaphors present in an individual's conscious or unconscious mind. While the patterns of thought of any one person might be incomplete, those of the group constitute a structure guiding social action, which can be studied best in times of crisis – moments that Turner calls 'social dramas'. These 'social dramas' arise in situations when a social norm is breached, when they produce divisions along the lines of dominant social relationships. After a period of increasing tension and crisis, leading members of the social system attempt to mediate. Finally the crisis is resolved either by the reintegration of the disturbed group or by recognition of the legitimacy of the division.[20] Throughout this process, the verbal and nonverbal signs and symbols used by the participants can be studied for clues concerning the assumptions of the group. George Rudé's research on food riots offers a similar example of a historian seeking to reconstruct the mentality of an urban crowd in a time of crisis.[21] For Rudé, the relevant models and metaphors of the food rioters could be seen in their slogans, the targets of their actions, and in the forms of their demand. Alfred Young's work on Boston crowds in the 1770s is a similar search for deeper social patterns in street demonstrations.[22] A comparison between, for example, the assumptions and aims of hosiery strikers in the 1890s with those of their counterparts in early nineteenth-century knitters' protests would help to identify the differences in mentalities that accompanied changes in the forms of collective actions.

Once changes over time in the incidence and meaning of conflict are charted, historians can turn to the major differences in patterns of conflict that existed between high and low ranking places in a region's urban hierarchy. Because of the ways in which towns are interrelated, studies of conflict in cities need to extend beyond the urban boundary and to consider the ways in which central places of a higher order influence political and social relationships. Within any given region, towns act as a network for the exchange of people, information and services in a systematic way related to the size of settlements. While villages provide a few goods or services to a relatively small number of people residing in the immediate area, regional capitals like Manchester or Birmingham act as central places for a large territory extending beyond county boundaries; London's territory of influence and exchange crosses the national border. If the cities of a country are ranked according to size and functional complexity, systematic differences appear in the roles played within their regions by several different sorts of cities. Gilbert Rozman has developed a model of seven levels of central places, stretching from a national administrative centre through regional centres and down to market settlements with fewer than 3,000 people. In recent books he has applied the model with some success to China, Japan, Russia, England and France in the seventeenth and eighteenth centuries.[23] While his scheme is overly complex, its underlying principle is valuable for social historians. Peter Clark and Paul Slack have constructed for England between 1500 and 1700 a simpler, more useful, division of settlements into the four levels of national capital, regional capital, county town and market town.[24]

Either of these classifications can usefully be applied to the study of urban conflict because of the uneven distribution throughout the urban hierarchy of political activists, transportation and communication facilities, technology, police forces and other institutions shaping local conflicts. While the differences among types of towns changed during the nineteenth century, they did not disappear. Residents of towns with a low rank in the English urban hierarchy in 1900 still depended on their larger neighbours for newspapers, higher education, and legal services as they had in 1800 or 1700. Moreover, a town's place in the English urban hierarchy influenced the way in which political information spread to it and through it. London, regional capitals, and county towns were centres for the diffusion of information and for the meeting of dissidents of all sorts. Not only did the largest places have the highest numbers of printers and booksellers, but major movements such as Chartism, the campaign to repeal the Corn Laws, and efforts to reform Parliament in the 1790s, all originated in London or in a regional capital. As these movements grew, adherents visited places lower in the urban hierarchy and gathered new recruits. Chartism in Leicestershire spread from the county town to smaller market settlements and villages through the work of organizers based, for the most part, in Leicester.[25] George Barnsby's work on Warwickshire and the Black Country has shown that the unstamped press circulated in the region first from Birmingham and later from Wolverhampton. Owenite socialism found supporters in smaller Black Country towns only after leaders in Birmingham sent lecturers to Dudley and Wolverhampton and then later to less important settlements.[26] The process of building a socialist constituency travelled down the urban hierarchy. In the early 1890s the most active socialist clubs in the East Midlands were in Leicester and Nottingham. As late as 1906, the few socialists in Ashby de la Zouch or Shepshed had to travel to the county town to meet other like-minded people.[27] Both the resources and the freedom to organize were greater in larger towns. Even if the same proportion of the population were interested in a particular issue in both Leeds and Pudsey, the critical mass of people needed to form a group or to take some sort of public action was usually not present in the smaller place until a great deal of organizing work was done. The regional capitals and county towns with their active political life were the logical places to supply that organizing energy.

Differences in a town's position in a national urban hierarchy are also co-ordinated with certain institutional differences that shaped local conflicts during much of the nineteenth century. During the 1830s and 1840s, the structure of authority in regional capitals, county towns and most industrial cities with populations of more than 40,000 was qualitatively different from that of their smaller neighbours. This resulted from the limited spread during the early years of Victoria's reign of both municipal incorporation and city police forces. The Municipal Corporation Act granted borough status to 178 towns, giving their residents extensive political rights. Householders who paid their rates and met a year's residency requirement could vote in the yearly elections for local officials. While few citizens met the property requirements which limited candidacies for aldermen and town councillor, the nature of the borough franchise, the large number of minor offices, and the general right to attend vestry meetings brought the opportunity for political participation to a wide section of the male population. In addition, the right of larger towns to elect M.P.s made many boroughs the scene of election campaigns and polling which attracted the attention of many more citizens than those who had the franchise.[28] Derek Fraser has remarked that in the Victorian period, 'urban politics were a touchstone of urban society', and that 'political passion was a persistent although not continuous feature' of local administration and elections.[29] These statements could probably not be made of the non-incorporated towns administered by parochial or township authorities, court leets, boards of guardians, and perhaps an improvement commission.

In Lancashire, Yorkshire, and the East Midlands, incorporated status was reserved in the 1830s to the county towns, regional capitals, major ports (Leeds, York, Hull, Manchester, Liverpool, Preston, Leicester and Nottingham), and a few other places (Wigan, Bolton and Newark). In the 1840s only seven other cities in these regions were incorporated, most having over 40,000 people.[30] In northern manufacturing areas, the status of municipal borough was limited for the most part during the mid-nineteenth century to towns at the top levels of the urban hierarchy.

Just as the boroughs had a distinctive administrative structure that produced a more active political life during the first half of the nineteenth century, the structures of authority in incorporated towns differentiated them from other urban places. The Municipal Corporations Act gave boroughs the right to administer justice in a local civil and criminal court and also to appoint and to supervise a police force. As a result, the incorporated towns had several resident magistrates and in the North and East Midlands, boroughs with more than 40,000 residents had a local police force by 1850.[31] The medium-sized towns I have identified as the most militant places during the plug strikes of 1842 had neither a group of resident magistrates nor police during those conflicts. Instead, the administration of justice and decisions concerning riots and rioters often fell to outsiders, chiefly landowners and gentry, who were neither the employers nor the elected representatives of the population they controlled.[32] Moreover, during the 1840s the magistrates had to rely chiefly on the yeomanry and the army. There were no rural police in the West Riding in the 1840s; Leicestershire's and Nottinghamshire's rural forces were quite small at this time, and in Lancashire in 1846 about 400 constables were divided among 16 different areas outside Manchester.[33] As a result, the patrolling of the streets and the control of crowds in non-incorporated towns was carried out by outsiders who were generally disliked and possibly less tolerant of an urban crowd than a local police force would have been. Certainly in Leicester during the strikes and Chartist agitation of the 1830s and 1840s, the mutual familiarity of city officials and framework knitters meant that demonstrations and conflicts were carried out peacefully. Moreover, strikes were regularly averted by the intervention of town officials who mediated in an informal way in disputes between the knitters and their employers.

Institutional differences between the formerly incorporated and non-incorporated towns diminished after 1850. In any case, 13 more cities in Lancashire, Yorkshire, and the East Midlands received borough status between 1850 and 1880; by 1890 most towns of more than 20,000 people in these regions were incorporated, and smaller settlements had more complex forms of government to absorb political energies, as well as better police protection.[34] While the political life of large towns remained more sophisticated and, I suspect, more active than that of small towns, the difference in this regard was less marked in 1890 than in 1840.

Other institutional structures emerged, however, by the end of the 1890s to perpetuate differences between towns at different ranks of the urban hierarchy.

Relations between workers and their employers in the later nineteenth century were mediated by a series of organizations, which influenced the procedures of collective bargaining and the use of the strike. These associations – trade unions, trade councils, employers' organizations, and boards of conciliation – were widespread in the North and Midlands. Moreover, they were both stronger and better represented at the top than at the bottom of the urban hierarchy. Their incidence and diffusion illustrates the leading role played in labour relations by citizens of the largest towns.

Unionization in the hosiery, lace, cotton and various branches of the clothing trades began in the county towns and regional capitals of the Midlands and Lancashire. Organizations among framework knitters and lace workers in the period 1800 to 1850 originated for the most part in Leicester and Nottingham, and most of their members resided in the county town, despite the wide scattering of hosiery production throughout the East Midlands. Each county tended to have its own organizations which used the central town as a meeting place. Leicester and Nottingham price lists were the standards either to be adhered to or to be undercut for competitive advantage, and city workers regularly attempted to enforce their lists outside the town. The marketing and entrepreneurial roles of Leicester and Nottingham employers were paralleled by the attempted leadership of the hosiery labour force by workers from the county towns.[35]

In the cotton industry, the first trade societies appeared in Manchester, Stockport, and Oldham in the early 1790s. The Manchester union became the centre for a county-wide federation in 1810, in part by underwriting and organizing a major strike to bring county wage rates up to the Manchester level. Manchester spinners also led the movement for a general union in 1826 and initiated the National Association for the Protection of Labour in 1830. Early unions among the power loom weavers centred on the towns just below Manchester in the Lancashire urban hierarchy, in Oldham and in Preston, while Bolton workers assumed the leadership of the Lancashire Spinners Federation in the early 1840s.[36]

During the second half of the century, the primary role played by big city workers in organizing their fellows continued. The three main branches of the machine-made lace trade formed separate craft societies in 1851 centred on Nottingham; they amalgamated in 1874. By the 1860s they claimed the membership of virtually all Nottingham males employed in the industry, but they admitted that the union was weak everywhere else. Almost all unions for female lace workers and those in allied crafts existed only in the county town. Nottingham unionists regularly tried to organize branches in places such as Long Eaton, Bulwell and Beeston, but these lodges when created were weak and regularly collapsed. Some began as late as 1900.[37]

Midland hosiery unions were similarly centred on Leicester and on Nottingham. The Amalgamated Hosiery Union, organized in 1885, had its strongest branches in the county towns, despite the regular exodus of firms to country districts during the last quarter of the nineteenth century. In Leicestershire, hosiery unions in towns such as Hinckley, Loughborough and Earl Shilton came comparatively late, and members had to strike vigorously and repeatedly in the early 1890s to gain recognition by employers who earlier had broken several unions by firing members.[38]

Amalgamated cotton unions continued in the middle and later nineteenth century to be centred on the largest Lancashire cities. Manchester workers formed a general union of power loom weavers in 1840, and Blackburn weavers organized branches of their unions in neighbouring towns during the 1850s. An early spinners' amalgamation, the Association of Operative Cotton Spinners, Twiners, and Self-Acting Minders was based on Bolton; its most powerful members were the Manchester, Oldham, and Bolton societies. Although this organization collapsed in the late 1840s, it was succeeded by a new spinners' amalgamated union, which drew its main strength from Bolton and Oldham. Moreover, the Oldham union took the lead in labour affairs in its district and eventually broke away from the general union to form a separate district federation in 1880. Similarly, several of the amalgamated unions in the woollen industry centred on the bigger towns like Huddersfield and Bradford. Both the centrality of the larger cities and the greater size and wealth of their unions made their organizations the natural leaders in efforts to co-ordinate local societies.[39]

Another type of union was located disproportionately in the largest towns: independent trade societies for women. The localities where the Webbs reported separate female unions in the early 1890s were almost exclusively in London, large ports, regional capitals and the county towns: places like Liverpool, Leeds, Bristol and Manchester. Leicester had a union of women cigar makers, and the female lace workers in Nottingham were organized independently.[40]

The largest towns were also the places where co-operation among workers in different industries was most advanced. Trades councils, city organizations of union officials who acted as a local pressure group for labour interests, appeared first at the top ranks of the English urban hierarchy and then spread to other large and then medium-sized towns. The earliest such group was organized in Liverpool in 1848; it was then followed in the late 1850s and early 1860s by similar associations in London, Leeds, Manchester, Nottingham, Edinburgh, Glasgow and Sheffield. Shortly thereafter, workers in a variety of northern and Midland towns – Birmingham and Oldham among them – also organized local councils. During the 1870s and 1880s trades councils were to be found almost exclusively in the larger incorporated towns, but by the 1890s towns with fewer than 50,000 people such as Ashton or Dewsbury had acquired similar groups. The councils, while having little money or power, provided organizing energy for the entry of workers into local politics and for extending trade union standards. Most engaged in successful campaigns in the 1890s to get city authorities to adopt fair wages clauses in all town contracts, and their regular efforts to elect unionists to city councils, boards of guardians, and school boards produced a scattering of working-class officials in the boroughs. They also acted as organizers of the unskilled in towns as disparate as Barnsley, Derby, Sheffield, Walsall, and Halifax. Moreover, in a period when national negotiating machinery for labour disputes was in its infancy, the councils sponsored town boards of conciliation. By the early 1890s city arbitration boards, generally jointly organized by trades councils and chambers of commerce, had appeared in Leeds, Bradford, Halifax, Leicester, Dudley, Derby, and Wolverhampton.[41]

While the effects of trades councils and city arbitration boards in shaping local conflicts remain to be demonstrated, increased levels of workers' organizations are closely linked to propensity to strike.[42] Any study of urban social conflict needs therefore to include such institutions that served either as mediators or as representatives of the contending parties. While these groups can be seen as the products of class divisions, their independent shaping functions should be recognized.

Social conflicts, as well as social relationships more generally, are influenced by a series of structures much more extensive than those of either technology or the organization of a city's economy. The institutional complexity of a town and its place in a regional urban hierarchy exercise strong influences on local patterns of political and social activity. In addition, as Charles Tilly and others have shown, the forms of collective action change over time. Conflict in England, rather than increasing as capitalism developed, shifted its styles and probably became less violent and more frequently compromised. The largest towns, which were centres from which many radical ideas diffused, also acquired mediating institutions earliest. The net result, by late in the nineteenth century, was a sublimation of many conflicts in the capital, regional capitals, and county towns into nonviolent and often indirect forms. Although political and social consciousness was relatively high in these places, conflicts were controlled by a sophisticated political and institutional framework. Conversely in smaller cities and market towns, open conflicts could erupt much more easily, even though political consciousness was less advanced. The independent effects upon conflict of the urban hierarchy and of mediating institutions need to be recognized. While compatible with a Marxist model of class conflict, they are neither reducible to it nor deducible from it. Urban social history will gain in explanatory power to the extent that social historians widen their perspectives on the populations they observe.

Lynn Hollen Lees
University of Pennsylvania

Notes

1   Friedrich Engels, *The Condition of the Working Class in England* edited by W. O. Henderson and W. H. Chaloner (1958).
2   Alfred Temple Patterson, *Radical Leicester: A history of Leicester* (1954); Malcolm I. Thomis, *Politics and Society in Nottingham, 1785–1835* (New York, 1969).
3   Asa Briggs (ed.), *Chartist Studies* (1959).
4   Gareth Stedman Jones, *Outcast London: A study in the relationship between classes in Victorian society* (1971); Robert Q. Gray, *The Labour Aristocracy in Victorian Edinburgh* (1976).
5   E. P. Hennock, *Fit and Proper Persons: Ideal and reality in nineteenth-century urban government* (1973); Derek Fraser, *Urban Politics in Victorian England* (1976); François Vigier, 'Change and apathy; Liverpool and Manchester during the Industrial Revolution' (M. A. thesis, University of Cambridge, 1970).
6   John Foster, *Class Struggle and the Industrial Revolution: Early industrial capitalism in three English towns* (1974); D. S. Gadian, 'Class consciousness in Oldham and other northwest industrial towns, 1830–1850', *Historical Journal*, xxi (1978); George Barnsby, 'The Working Class Movement in the Black Country, 1815–1867' (University of Birmingham, M.A. thesis, 1965); John Stevenson, 'Food riots in England, 1792–1818', in R. Quinault and J. Stevenson (eds), *Popular Protest and Public Order: Six studies in British history, 1790–1820* (1974).
7   Donald Read, *The English Provinces, 1760–1960: A study in influence* (1964), 35.
8   Briggs, *op. cit.*, 3.
9   Foster, *op. cit.*, 121.
10 Victor Turner, *Dramas, Fields and Metaphors: Symbolic action in human society* (Ithaca, N.Y., and London, 1974), 24.
11 John F. Sutton, *The Datebook of Remarkable and Memorable Events Connected with Nottingham and Its Neighbourhood* (1895); *A Chronicle of Events in Leicester* (1890).
12 K. G. J. C. Knowles, *Strikes: A study in industrial conflict* (1952), 197.
13 Edward Shorter and Charles Tilly, *Strikes in France, 1830–1968* (1974); Charles Tilly, Louise Tilly and Richard Tilly, *The Rebellious Century, 1830–1960* (1975); Charles Tilly, 'Collective action in England and America, 1765–1775', in Richard Maxwell Brown and Don E. Fehrenbacher (eds), *Tradition, Conflict and Modernization: Perspectives on the American Revolution* (New York, 1977); R. A. Schweitzer, 'The study of contentious gatherings in early nineteenth century Great Britain', *Historical Methods*, xii (Summer 1979).
14 Labour Correspondent of the Board of Trade, 'Report on strikes and lockouts', P.P. 1890, LXVIII, 480–533; P.P. 1890–1, LXXVIII, 743–804; P.P. 1894, LXXXIII pt. 1, 594–660; P.P. 1895, XCII, 211; *The Labour Gazette*, 'Monthly lists of trade disputes', 1895–1911.
15 See Shorter and Tilly, *op. cit.*
16 Tilly, Tilly and Tilly, *op. cit.*; see also Charles Tilly, 'How protest modernized in France, 1845–1855', in William Aydelotte, Alan Bogue and Robert Fogel (eds), *The Dimensions of Quantitative Research in History* (Princeton, 1972), and Charles Tilly, 'Major forms of collective action in modern Europe', *Theory and Society*, ii (1976).
17 Sutton, *op. cit.*
18 Richard Gurnham, *Two Hundred Years: The hosiery unions, 1776–1976* (1976).
19 Victor Turner, *The Ritual Process: Structure and anti-structure* (Ithaca, N.Y., 1977).
20 Turner, *Dramas, Fields and Metaphors, op. cit.*, 35–41.
21 George Rudé, *The Crowd in History: A study of popular disturbances in France and England, 1730–1848* (New York and London, 1964), 214–36.
22 Alfred F. Young, *The Crowd and the Coming of the American Revolution: From ritual to rebellion in Boston, 1745–1776* (forthcoming).
23 Gilbert Rozman, *Urban Networks in Ch'ing China and Tokugawa Japan* (Princeton, 1973); idem, *Urban Networks in Russia, 1750–1800, and Premodern Periodization* (Princeton, 1976).
24 Peter Clark and Paul Slack, *English Towns in Transition, 1500–1700* (1976).
25 Patterson, *op. cit.*, 307.
26 Barnsby, *op. cit.*, 9–16, 74–94.
27 *The Pioneer*, ccxli (20 January 1906).
28 J. R. Somers Vine, *English Municipal Institutions, Their Growth and Development from 1835 to 1879 Statistically Illustrated* (1879), 11, 14–15.
29 Fraser, *op. cit.*, 10.
30 Vine, *op. cit.*, 52–9, 60–2.
31 'Abstract of a Return . . . of several cities and boroughs of Great Britain, their populations respectively, the number of police. . .', P.P. 1854 (C. 345), LIII, 509.
32 R. Quinault, 'The Warwickshire county magistracy and public order, c. 1830–1870', in

Quinault and Stevenson, *op. cit.*, 187–92.

33 'Abstract of a Return showing the Number of the Constabulary Force in each County or Division of a County in England and Wales', P.P. 1847, XLVII, 632–9.

34 Vine, *op. cit.*, 60–2; *The Census of England and Wales for 1891*, P.P. 1893–1894 (C. 6948), CIV, 160–75.

35 Gurnham, *op. cit.*, 6–16; Norman H. Cuthbert, *The Lace Makers' Society: A study of trade unionism in the British lace industry, 1760–1960* (1960), 10–19.

36 H. A. Turner, *Trade Union Growth, Structure and Policy: A comparative study of the cotton unions* (1962), 62–3, 66–7, 287–8.

37 Cuthbert, *op. cit.*, 31–2, 48, 54.

38 Gurnham, *op. cit.*, 26–8, 32–3, 50–6; Royal Commission on Labour, *Minutes of Evidence, Group C*, Vol. I, P.P. 1892 (C. 6708–III) XXXIV, 63.

39 H. A. Turner, *op. cit.*, 115–17, 122, 129–32, 144–6; Royal Commission on Labour, *Minutes of Evidence, Group C*, Vol. I, 18.

40 Webb Trade Union Collection, Series E, A-XLVII, British Library of Political and Economic Science.

41 Webb Trade Union Collection, Series E, A-IV.

42 Shorter and Tilly, *op. cit.*, 188.

Seaside holiday resorts in the United States and Britain: a review*

1

In the 1840s Henry Colman, an American agricultural expert travelling through Europe, described his visit to Tynemouth:

> It is much resorted to as a bathing place; for the English and Scotch indulge in this luxury much more than our northern people. They have a custom at which, perhaps, you may smile. They disrobe themselves either in boxes or in some nook on the shore, and then the ladies, and sometimes the men, in their bathing robes, are carried into the water by two women, and suddenly dropped, from an idea that to go in, walking, is apt to produce a rush of blood, which may be injurious. Is this not an amusing conceit?[1]

Tynemouth's bathing-houses did not turn out to be the resort's most popular feature for either the English or the Americans. Although water was prized in the nineteenth century for its life-enhancing properties by those who immersed themselves in it at water-cure establishments or imbibed it at the spas or in temperance circles, it was not the sea but the seaside which attracted thousands to the holiday towns. The pleasures of the pier or the promenade or the amusement park were more seductive than the healthy attractions of surf or sand or 'breathing the ozone'.

By the end of the nineteenth century, a distinct urban form had evolved along the Atlantic coast of the United States and near the large industrial areas in Britain. The popular seaside holiday resort provided residential accommodation for the middle and lower classes and more particularly, entertainment for the visitor on a day excursion from the city.*

A comparative study of mass resorts in England and the United States in the golden age 1870–1920 reveals some interesting contrasts. English historians have paid close and careful attention to class patterns in recreation.[2] Harold Perkin, for example, has studied the 'social tone' within and between north-western coastal resorts in the late Victorian period.[3] In both countries class bitterness was pervasive and wealthy city-dwellers sought exclusive vacation spots by the sea. Advances in transportation lowered costs and raised speeds and allowed the less affluent to take advantage of the increase in real wages and hours of leisure and emulate their social superiors. Hence, many seaside resorts near the large centres of population and reserved for the genteel passed into the hands of the lower and middle classes. Occasionally, as at Coney Island in the 1890s, the mass attractions all but submerged the genteel; often something of the former elite status continued, with 'posh' and 'popular' ends juxtaposed near the seafront promenade.

In addition to class animosity, the American promoters of the large seaside amusement parks faced problems of race and ethnicity which the English, with a

* Charles E. Funnell, *By the Beautiful Sea: The rise and high times of that great American resort, Atlantic City* (New York, 1975). xi + 199 pp. Plates. Illustrations. Bibliography. $12.95.
John F. Kasson, *Amusing the Million: Coney Island at the turn of the century* (New York, 1978). 120 pp. Plates. $12.50.
J. A. R. Pimlott, *The Englishman's Holiday: A social history* (1947, reprinted 1976). 318 pp. Plates. Illustrations, Bibliography. £5.50.
John K. Walton, *The Blackpool Landlady: A social history* (1978). x + 229 pp. Plates. Maps. £5.95.
James Walvin, *Beside the Seaside: A social history of the popular seaside holiday* (1978). 176 pp. Illustrations. Bibliography. £5.75.

more homogeneous population, did not have to confront. The amusements at Coney Island in which showmen like George C. Tilyou and Frederic Thompson invested millions of dollars were different not only in nature but also in function from those at the genteel resorts. That the Americans proved much more success- ful than their English counterparts in finding the right formula of escapism, archi- tectural splendour and mechanical thrills to please the mass urban public, is a tribute to their enterprise and shrewd business sense; by 1900 the pier and the promenade, once the glory of the seaside town, had lost much of their significance. Coney Island and not Blackpool became the symbol of the brash, vulgar but vital, resort in the early twentieth century.

2

In early nineteenth-century America, the seaside resorts catered for the wealthier classes. Newport, Rhode Island, and Nahant, Massachusetts, and Long Branch and Cape May on the New Jersey shore were smaller and usually less sophistica- ted versions of Brighton or Eastbourne. There, affluent Southerners escaped the steamy heat of their tidewater and piedmont plantations and joined the newly rich from the northern cities for their summer vacations. Saratoga Springs, in upstate New York and renowned for its medicinal mineral waters, set the model for the fashionable resort, whether beside the sea or the springs. In 1852 George Curtis described Saratoga as 'an oasis of repose in the desert of our American hurry', but noted that it was not the contemplation of the calm pastoral scene, or the delights of walking and physical exercise in what had been a quiet haven for invalids, which drew visitors. Most came for the entertainment in the elegant, luxury hotels, for the dancing, the soirées. 'Life is leisurely here', Curtis wrote; however, 'business is amusement'.[4]

Even in the 1850s the genteel resorts were beginning a slow decline. After the Civil War Saratoga's United States Hotel, Union Hall and Congress Hall did not quite maintain their former grand status. Newport lost some of its brilliant sparkle as the fashionable rich joined Henry James in search of cosmopolitan European capitals or went north to the quieter haunts of Maine's Bar Harbor, to Cape Cod or to second homes on Long Island.[5]

As the genteel resorts faded genteelly, newer ones serving a broader public arose. The most successful were within easy commuting distance from the great cities. Atlantic City began as a speculative real estate venture on the New Jersey coast in 1852 but for a generation the 60 miles which separated it from Philadelp- hia proved too severe a handicap for anything other than a slow and steady – and slowly and steadily profitable – growth. Coney Island was more fortunately situa- ted. A mere ten sea miles from Manhattan, it became closer to the Greater New York conurbation as Brooklyn swiftly expanded its boundaries into Long Island in the course of the century.[6]

In the early nineteenth century Coney Island was merely one of the many places which, like Rockaway Beach or Staten Island or the Elysian Fields in Hoboken, attracted crowds from New York City on Sunday excursions.[7] The very proximity to the metropolis made it within reach of many if not most of the inhabitants. One contemporary described Coney Island as offering the simple pleasures of escape:

> How many a poor jaded man, encrusted over with the rust of crowded rooms and confined 'business places' steps into the beating surf, and ere he is aware of it, feels like a happy shell-fish, that has lost a worn-out crustaceous covering and comes out literally rejoicing in a new birth, increased in capacity for life, and enlarged in size.[8]

There were a few squalid bath-houses, cheap taverns and sea-food eating places. George Foster, a contemporary journalist who delighted in exposing urban vice, thought the Island had a dubious reputation and equated the 'Coney Island busi- ness' with prostitution and immoral dancing-parties.[9] Most of the rich or respectable went elsewhere.

Restrictions on Sunday travel were difficult to enforce and strict sabbatarians lamented that the excursion traffic from New York City was already flourishing in the 1830s before the coming of the railroad. Indeed, as far as Coney Island's fortunes were concerned, Robert Fulton's adaptation of the steam engine to sea travel was possibly more important. Throughout the century the ferry service across the Hudson River was convenient, cheap and dependable. Of New York and the summer Sunday excursion, a magazine noted in 1882, 'the peculiar location of this city offers a more extended field for its development than that of any other in the country'.[10] Later, Coney Island benefited from the new Brooklyn Bridge built in 1883 and was well served by railroads, elevated railroads and electric trolley street-cars. A British observer commented, with some exaggeration, 'the whole railway system of America culminates there'.[11] By 1895 the trolley fare cost a mere nickel, and escape from the city was within the reach of even the poorest immigrant seamstress.

All resorts profited from better communications. In the 1830s the opening of the Saratoga and Schenectady Railroad had cut the travelling time from New York City by almost a third, to 17 hours. By the 1880s faster trains and rival companies brought Atlantic City within reach of Philadelphia in an hour and a half, and by 1900, in 50 minutes and perhaps more important, at a lower cost. In Britain, some resorts like Margate were already flourishing before the railway network which crisscrossed the country from the 1840s carried visitors of all classes to the seaside.[12] Elsewhere, as the temperance evangelical Thomas Cook and other entrepreneurs pioneered cheap railway excursions, new coastal resorts close to the urban and industrial areas of the North-West, the West Riding, the Midlands or the South-East appeared, or established ones were expanded and re-developed.

Access to transportation encouraged speculative development of the seaside resorts. As Funnell relates (chaps. 1 and 2), in Atlantic City in the 1870s the booster spirit flourished, and large land-owning corporations constructed large hotels, piers, amusement attractions and the famous Boardwalk. As a result, the permanent population increased almost five-fold between 1880 and 1900. A similar process was at work at Coney Island. Austin Corbin and other railroad and real estate magnates launched an ambitious plan to transform Coney's Manhattan Beach from an underdeveloped excursion spot into an exclusive resort for the wealthy with private railroad connections to the city. By the early 1880s the eastern end of the Island had palatial residential hotels and smart restaurants for the fashionable few (Kasson: 29–34). Two new and largely genteel resorts had been founded.

3

In the late nineteenth century some leading seaside resorts presented a curious spectacle. Within a town like Blackpool there might be a 'posh' area on the North Shore with hotels and landscaped parks, and a 'popular' section of fairground attractions catering for a wider and different range of interests some distance away. Walton (esp. chap. 2) gives an excellent example of how the competing claims of rate-payers and businessmen on Blackpool's town council determined the character of the resort.[113] However, this was not unique to the British resorts. At Coney, the cheap, exciting sideshows for the masses were still in an early stage of development but beginning to prosper under the corrupt regime of the local political boss John Y. MacKane and to encroach upon the smart hotels at Brighton Beach and Manhattan Beach. Like Blackpool, Atlantic City promoted the dual image of a resort offering sensational pleasures and quiet residential holidays (Funnell: chap. 4).

In the 1870s and 1880s entrepreneurs at both Coney Island and Atlantic City made extravagant claims to respectability. In the hope of attracting the upper classes they promoted the Englishness of the resort. Atlantic City boasted of being the 'American Brighton' and the 'Brighton of Philadelphia';[14] it had a magnificent Brighton Hotel and others with aristocratic-sounding names – a Marlborough-Blenheim Hotel, a Windsor Hotel, a Chalfonte Hotel, a Haddon Hall Hotel; Coney had its West Brighton and Brighton Beach, although the Prince Regent did not build its Ocean Pavilion (Kasson: 31–3).

However, the valiant attempts to attract the smart set which had once frequented Newport and Saratoga met with scant success. Instead of resorts comparable with England's finest, British visitors found the American Brightons, in their heyday of respectability, rather vulgar, more like Margate and Ramsgate.[15] Atlantic City's splendid new hotels were patronized by professionals and nouveaux riches and seldom by Philadelphia's social elite. The boarding-houses which catered for the less well-off were perhaps more typical accommodation. By the 1890s Austin Corbin's property speculation at Coney was only a limited success. The Island had become 'purely and wholly an excursion resort',[16] and unique in England and America in having almost no residential accommodation. The day-tripper reigned supreme, and other property developers turned their attention to providing for the many and not the genteel few.

The promoters of the seaside resorts had always claimed to cater for all tastes. Atlantic City wished to be thought 'a thoroughly democratic place' with no 'caste prejudice'. It was 'no uncommon sight', a guide-book announced in 1895, 'to see the children of millionaires and the little ones of laboring men riding happily on the merry-go-round at the same time and perhaps to find the parents fraternizing on the Switchback Railway'.[17] Journalists liked to think that Bertha, salesgirl at a Philadelphia department store, might associate on the Boardwalk with Mrs Hofheimer, her boss's wife.[18] Such dreams of social mobility and homogeneity, cherished values in a democratic republic, were dear to the age.

It may be that the American resorts were in fact much more successful than the British in attracting all save the upper classes. Funnell devotes a chapter (2) to the class of Atlantic City's clientele, but Kasson raises the question only briefly and indirectly; neither examines the shades and nuances of class feeling with the perception and sensitivity with which British historians have done. Certainly, contemporaries spoke of Coney Island as a melting pot of all Americans old and new where language and status were no barriers to a full and equal participation in pleasure. As early as 1878 *Harper's Monthly* reported that the cheap amusements at the Island attracted mixed crowds, respectable artisans, families of Germans, Jewish sewing-girls, as well as 'the genuine unadulterated hoodlum' and the 'showily dressed ebony couple.' A generation later, the *Century* rejoiced that the respectable middle classes also patronized the fairground attractions.[19]

In the United States, contact between the races was as troublesome an issue as contact between the classes, and a problem which luckily the English holiday towns could avoid. In 1919 the threat of black intrusion into the white bathing-areas on the shore of Lake Michigan provoked the bloody race riot in Chicago.[20] Whilst segregation was evident on Asbury Park's beachfront, Funnell (29–31) claims that the blacks who worked in the service trades in Atlantic City mixed freely with the white patrons. However, one of the contemporary descriptions he cites states the reverse. In 1908 blacks at Atlantic City relaxed on the 'negro pier' and had 'about a city block of the strand and Boardwalk for their very own'. It appears that racial lines were drawn almost as tightly at the seaside as in Philadelphia, from which the large majority of visitors had come.[21] Kasson does not even raise the question of racial prejudice. Blacks were a comparatively small percentage of New York's population before the First World War and perhaps their appearance at Coney Island posed no threat. Since at the time blacks as well as whites enjoyed the grotesque antics of blackface minstrels, they might not have found the entertainment offensive – perhaps not even the up-dated version of the coconut shy, the 'see-if-you-can-hit-the-nigger's-head' shooting gallery.

At the turn of the century, New York's more than a million Jews were far more numerous than London's or Manchester's immigrant population from Eastern

Europe. In the 1870s Corbin and the real estate developers of genteel Coney Island discriminated against Jewish guests in the new hotels.[22] Saratoga was celebrated for its anti-semitism and hotels are said to have posted placards, 'No Jews or Dogs admitted here'.[23] By the 1890s, the more affluent New York and Philadelphia Jews found some refuge from prejudice and established summer homes and synagogues on the Jersey shore at Long Branch, Asbury Park, Cape May, and Atlantic City.[24]

Nativist prejudice in the 1870s and 1880s seems to have been much more frequent in the private school, the country club and the elite hotel, and characteristic of upper-class attitudes to wealthy Jews. The less affluent and recent immigrant Jews in the Lower East side attended the Yiddish theatres, and on their annual holidays sought fresh air and entertainment in the 'borscht belt', the ethnic stronghold of boarding-houses and *kuchalanes* (self-catering bungalow colonies) in the Catskill and Adirondack mountains.[25] Whether they patronized these separate leisure institutions entirely by choice is by no means clear. Poor Jews must also have used the city's playgrounds and recreation piers and enjoyed Manhattan's Central Park or Brooklyn's Prospect Park in summer. The proprietors of Coney's amusement parks may not have made special provision for the sale of Kosher foods but they do not appear to have discriminated in any way against particular ethnic groups. By the 1920s migration into the Greater New York suburbs had made the Coney Island area more Jewish than Gentile, and many of the Jews resident nearby patronized the amusement parks.[26]

4

Between 1897 and 1904 three large amusement parks were constructed at Coney Island at the cost of at least $5,000,000 – Steeplechase, Luna Park and Dreamland. This was the 'New Coney Island' with lavish display and family entertainment replacing the former cheap and squalid sideshows. The mass public had their own extravagant version of what the genteel had had a generation before. Frederic Thompson, the estate promoter of Luna Park, announced the principles behind the 'amusement business': to 'manufacture' a carnival spirit and offer fast-moving 'elaborated child's play' in exotic but respectable surroundings and on no account attempt to educate.[27] Coney gave pride of place to the mechanical amusements which Atlantic City and the British resorts relegated to piers and promenades and in so doing attracted larger crowds than any other seaside resort in the world.

To a large extent, the mass resorts offered familiar urban pleasures in an unusual setting. New York's Bowery also had dance halls, vaudeville theatres, blackface minstrel acts, circuses and animal shows and exhibitions of human freaks and curiosities. P. T. Barnum had made a fortune with such attractions 50 years before. He had, however, advertised his shows to the middle classes as 'rational recreation', 'instructive' and educational. There were still some faint echoes of this in the 1890s when one amusement hall on Atlantic City's Boardwalk promoted its indifferent show as 'Refined, Instructive, Interesting, Amusing' (Funnell: 57). Most of the patrons, however, no longer seemed to care; they wanted action and excitement, what one observer described as 'a delirium of raw pleasure'.[28] The resorts supplied it on piers which jutted out into the sea where all the pleasures of New York or Philadelphia could be found uninterrupted by the normal occupational routine of urban life. In the music hall at the ocean end of Atlantic City's Steel Pier, the publicity brochure proclaimed, 'gay couples whirl in entrancing waltzes above the rolling waves of the big broad Atlantic', within sight if not sound of the sea.[29]

Coney Island attracted visitors with an architecture of fantasy and escape which gave even familiar pleasures an exotic allure.[30] Kasson (62–70) has a keen eye for its architectural qualities. The fairground buildings and sideshows which graced the 'popular' end of the Island before the destructive fires of 1893 and 1895 were comparatively modest, giving an appearance 'suggestive of a Western mining camp in its palmy days with a wonderful leaning towards the Moorish'.[31] The new

Steeplechase, Luna Park and Dreamland were far more extravagant. To complement the garish mechanical amusements there were Moorish minarets, Oriental temples and pagodas, skyscraper towers, classical frontages and fairytale gothic arches happily intermingled with lagoons, lakes and gondoliers. It was as if the set from D. W. Griffith's Bible epic *Intolerance* and the futuristic science fiction scene from a cover of Hugo Gernsback's *Amazing Stories* magazine were placed side by side.

The intention, explained Frederic Thompson, was to offer weary city dwellers from the tenement slums of the New York's East Side or West Side 'a different world – a dream world, perhaps a nightmare world – where all is bizarre and fantastic – crazier than the craziest part of Paris – gayer and more different from the every-day world'. Another described the architecture as 'rendering dull and petty the stately pleasure dome that Kubla Khan decreed in Xanadu'.[32] Several million electric light bulbs turned night into an eerie day. Many of the 'picture palaces', the early movie theatres, or the large department stores on Fifth Avenue and Forty-Second Street had the same ornate splendour and luxurious display to tempt the customer.[33] And, in keeping with the romantic surroundings, the camel and elephant rides at Luna Park or the donkey rides on the beach offered unusual means of locomotion even in the age of the horse. It was the appropriate setting for the visitor to choose the Trip to the Moon or be guided by an Eskimo on a submarine voyage to view the strange creatures of the deep.

Walton (42–50) devotes comparatively little attention in his otherwise excellent history of Blackpool's development as a tourist resort to its appeal for the visitor. There is little in Walton's description (chap. 4) of the attractions of other coastal resorts to indicate that the British pioneered in the technology of amusements. Even the kinetoscope, an early motion-picture projector and a standby of the penny arcades in the 1890s, was American. Blackpool's illuminations, its imitation Eiffel tower, its American fairground amusements and its copied American-style black-face minstrels, paled in comparison with the raucous splendour of Coney's Dreamland. Only the pleasure pier was an English innovation.

For what really distinguished the attractions of the mass seaside resorts, and of Coney in particular, from those of the large cities from which the visitors came, were the mechanical amusements. The Ferris Wheel, the roller coaster, the merry-go-round, the helter-skelter, the water slide and the centrifugal 'Human Whirl-pool' and a dozen other variations offered exhilarating movement. These amusements were not so dissimilar to the elevated railroads or the street cars on which people travelled to their dull weekday jobs except that they moved in an unproductive direction and usually beyond the passenger's control.[34]

Most middle-class commentators found this taste in pleasures profoundly puzzling. As early as 1882 a British observer remarked that at Coney Island, 'the inhabitants of New York appear to take delight in iron, steam, and machinery', and assemble for pleasure in dense crowds; their work and their play, he thought, seemed almost one and the same.[35] City-dwellers, a writer in the *Atlantic Monthly* reported in 1907, sought 'an artificial distraction for an artificial life'. 'What more ludicrous and what more sad', he noted, 'than the spectacle of hordes of people rushing to the ocean-side to escape the city's din and crowds and nervous strain, and, once within sight and sound of the waves, courting worse din, denser crowds, and an infinitely more devastating nervous strain inside an enclosure where the ocean cannot possibly be seen?'[36]

One reason for Coney Island's appeal, Kasson argues, was that it offered 'a moral holiday for all who entered its gates', a 'respite from . . . formal, highly regulated social situations' (50, 44). In function, the seaside amusements were similar to the carnival of fools or charivari of the pre-industrial and early industrial age described by historians such as Edward Thompson and Peter Burke in Britain and Alfred Young and Nathalie Zemon Davis in the United States.[37] On the helter-skelter or the Ferris Wheel joy-riders briefly forgot the conventional restraints of work and the world and ignored the prudential virtues of thrift and sobriety.[38]

Resorts offered another kind of vicarious pleasure; the less affluent holiday-makers could emulate the behaviour of their social superiors, even if they could not always imitate their style of dress and accommodation.[39] Atlantic City's seven-mile long Boardwalk offered the illusion of social levelling. Observers spoke of the 'ultra-, almost-, and near-swell' being thrown promiscuously together.[40] Even day-excursion visitors might see and be seen on the promenade, and the pier or the beach serve as their gathering-points, like the assembly rooms at the traditional spa towns.

If the period before the First World War did see a revolution in manners and morals,[41] then the resort both challenged and reaffirmed traditional sex roles in a time of change. In a limited way, the very anonymity of the pier and promenade allowed freer mixing between the sexes. The young woman who flirted with her beau seems to have been a phenomenon of the amusement park.[42] In both Britain and America, with postcards of scenic views and groups of joyful holiday-makers on the beach, there were some of women in modestly alluring poses, suntanned in the few areas exposed, and sometimes with mild *double entendres* in the messages of greeting.[43] However, there was no American equivalent of the typical Blackpool comic postcard of the red-faced, middle-aged, buxom virago intimidating the thin, weak and balding male. Perhaps the American male was made of sterner stuff – or liked to think he was.

5

The American seaside resorts gradually lost their appeal in the twentieth century. After a series of major fires in 1907, 1911 and 1949 which levelled much of the grand amusement parks, Coney Island did not recover its former glory and became part of Brooklyn's expanding urban squalor.[44] From 1921 Atlantic City hosted the tawdry annual spectacle of the Miss America contest and residential visitors tended to go elsewhere. Since the 1950s the new theme parks, typified by Disney-land outside Los Angeles and Walt Disney World in Orlando, Florida, have out-shone Atlantic City and Coney Island in both size and style.

In Britain after the Second World War, seaside holiday camps set a new trend (Pimlott: 246–54, 276–83; Walvin: chaps. 8, 9). Billy Butlin's camps offered accom-modation in family chalets not unlike the Catskill *kuchalanes* but with a central army-style mess, with Redcoat guides to jolly along the 'lads' and 'lasses' to join in the traditional entertainment for the older generation or pop music for the younger members; the camps were, however, self-contained and isolated from the resorts in which they were located. Blackpool struggled valiantly and successfully to retain its loyal visitors against the competition of cheap package tours to Spain's Costa del Sol.

Despite the relative decline of the seaside resort in the last 30 years, what seems most striking is the remarkable loyalty of the British lower and middle classes to the pier and promenade at holiday time. It may be largely a question of geography, for, even with aircraft and automobiles, the majority of Americans live further from the coast. Much more research needs to be done into the changing fortunes of the hundreds of smaller and minor resorts along the Atlantic coast, from Maine's tiny inlets, Massachusett's Cape Cod, Asbury Park, and to the south, Delaware's Rehoboth Beach, Maryland's Ocean City, Virginia Beach and South Carolina's Myrtle Beach. In time each major city had its version of the Coney Island funfair, and as the annual winter and spring migration of Northern college students to sun-worshipping Florida or surf-worshipping California testifies, the sea, or at least the beach, still counts for something.[45] A sun-tan in February is the modern mark of affluence, a phenomenon which the genteel secluded in Oyster Bay or Nar-ragansett Bay in the 1890s could scarcely have comprehended.

Robert Lewis
Department of American History, University of Birmingham

Notes

1 H. Colman, *European Life and Manners, in Familiar Letters to Friends*, 2 vols. (Boston, 1850), I, 281.
2 See R. W. Malcolmson, *Popular Recreations in English Society 1700–1850* (1973); P. Bailey, *Leisure and Class in Victorian England: Rational recreation and the contest for control, 1830–1885* (1978).
3 H. J. Perkin, 'The "social tone" of Victorian seaside resorts in the North-West', *Northern History*, xi (1976 for 1975), 180–94.
4 G. Curtis, *Lotus-Eating: A summer-book* (New York, 1852), *passim*, 113; J. Z. Grover, 'Luxury and leisure in early nineteenth-century America: Saratoga Springs and the rise of the resort' (Ph.D. thesis, University of California, 1973); F. R. Dulles, *America Learns to Play: A history of popular recreation 1607–1940* (New York, 1940), 149–52.
5 C. Amory, *The Last Resorts* (New York, 1952); R. Barrett, *Good Old Summer Days: Newport, Narragansett Pier, Saratoga, Long Branch, Bar Harbor* (Boston, 1952).
6 On the general development of Atlantic City, see W. McMahon, *So Young . . . So Gay!* (Atlantic City, N.J., 1970), and of Coney Island, O. Pilat and J. Ransom, *Sodom by the Sea: An affectionate history of Coney Island* (Garden City, N.Y., 1941); E. McCullough, *Good Old Coney Island* (New York, 1957); L. P. Gillman, 'Coney Island', *New York History*, xxxvi (July 1955), 255–90.
7 B. J. Danforth, 'Hoboken and the affluent New Yorker's search for recreation, 1820–1860', *New Jersey History*, xcv (Autumn 1977), 133–44.
8 'Scene at Coney Island, sea bathing illustrated', *Frank Leslie's Illustrated Newspaper*, 20 Sept. 1856, 226. See also J. H. Browne, *The Great Metropolis; A mirror of New York* (Hartford, Conn., 1869), 361.
9 G. G. Foster, *New York in Slices: By an experienced carver* (New York, 1850), 89.
10 'A Sunday Excursion to Long Branch', *Harper's Weekly*, (30 Sept. 1882), 614.
11 'A Sunday at Coney Island,' *Temple Bar*, lxv (June 1882), 263.
12 J. Whyman, 'A Hanoverian Watering-Place: Margate before the Railway', in A. Everitt (ed.), *Perspectives in English Urban History* (1973), 138–60.
13 See also J. K. Walton, 'Residential amenity, respectable morality and the rise of the entertainment industry: the case of Blackpool, 1860–1914', *Literature and History*, 1 (1975), 62–78; J. Myerscough, 'The Victorian development of the popular seaside holiday resort', *Victorian Seaport*. (Fifth Conference Report of the Victorian Society, 1967) (1969), 28–31; J. Lowerson and J. Myerscough, *Time to Spare in Victorian England* (1977), 23–64.
14 Speech of T. M. Dale, 1896, quoted in Funnell, *op. cit.*, 23; M. M. Howard, 'Our American Brighton', *Potter's American Monthly*, xv (Nov. 1880), 321–33.
15 Cony [sic] Island', *Chambers Journal*, lvi (4 Jan. 1879), 15; *Temple Bar*, 1882, *op. cit.*, 266.
16 'Coney Island'. *Scribner's Magazine*, xx (July 1896), 19.
17 W. E. Meehan, *Rand, McNally and Company's Handy Guide to Philadelphia, and Environs, Including Atlantic City and Cape May* (Chicago, 1895), 163, 168–9, quoted in Funnell, *op. cit.*, 54.
18 F. W. O'Malley, 'The Board-Walkers: ten days with Bertha at Atlantic City', *Everybody's Magazine*, xix (Aug. 1908), 233–43.
19 'New York in Summer', *Harper's Monthly*, lvii (Oct. 1878), 694–5; A. B. Paine, 'The New Coney Island', *Century Magazine*, xlvi (Aug. 1904), 528–38.
20 W. M. Tuttle, Jr., *Race Riot: Chicago and the Red Summer of 1919* (New York, 1970), 3–8.
21 F. W. O'Malley, *op. cit.*, 243. On segregated recreations in Philadelphia's ghetto, see W. E. B. DuBois. *The Philadelphia Negro: A social study* (1899; New York, 1967), 309–21.
22 *Coney Island and the Jews: A history of the development and success of this famous seaside resort, together with a full account of the recent Jewish controversy* (New York, c. 1879).
23 D. Wecter, *The Saga of American Society: A record of social aspiration 1607–1937* (1937; reprinted New York, 1970), 437–8.
24 On anti-semitism and upper-class summer resorts see J. Higham, *Send These To Me. Jews and other immigrants in urban America* (Princeton, 1975), 148–59; E. D. Baltzell, *Philadelphia Gentlemen: The making of a national upper class* (1948; reprinted Chicago, 1971), 220–2, 285; A. H. Rhine, 'Race prejudice at summer resorts', *Forum, iii (1887)*, 523–31.
25 I. Howe, *The World of Our Fathers: The journey of East European Jews to America and the life they found and made* (New York, 1976), 208–18; J. Adams and H. Tobias, *The Borscht Belt* (New York, 1959).
26 N. Glazer and D. P. Moynihan, *Beyond The Melting Pot: The Negroes, Puerto Ricans,*

Jews, Italians, and Irish of New York City (Cambridge, Mass., 1963), 161. There were an estimated 2000 food stands in 1910, and some must have catered for Jews.: 'The mechanical side of Coney Island – where the imaginative inventor holds sway', *Scientific American*, ciii (6 Aug. 1910), 104.

27 F. Thompson, 'Amusing the million', *Everybody's Magazine*, xix (Sept. 1908), 386.

28 *Scribner's Magazine*, 1896, *op. cit.*, 17.

29 *Steel Pier, Atlantic City* (n.d. [1907]), quoted in Funnell, *op. cit.*, 129.

30 D. Braithwaite, *Fairground Architecture: The world of amusement parks, carnivals and fairs* (New York, 1968); U. Pastier, 'The architecture of escapism – Disney World and Las Vegas', *AIA Journal*, lxvii (Dec. 1978), 26–37; R. Banham, *Los Angeles: City of four ecologies* (1971).

31 F. S. Mines, 'A Pilgrimage to Coney Island', *Harper's Weekly*, xxxv (12 Sept. 1891), 694. See also *Valentine's Manual of Old New York*, x (1926), 131–6.

32 F. Thompson, 'The summer show', *Independent*, lxii (20 June 1907), 1460–1, quoted in Kasson, *op. cit.*, 66, 69; R. Hughes, *The Real New York* (New York, 1904), 310.

33 B. M. Hall, *The Best Remaining Seats: The story of the golden age of the movie palace* (New York, 1961); D. Sharp, *The Picture Palace and Other Buildings for the Movies* (1969); N. Harris, 'Museums, merchandising, and popular taste: the struggle for influence', in I. M. G. Quimby (ed.), *Material Culture and the Study of American Life* (New York, 1978), 140–74.

34 'The mechanical joys of Coney Island', *Scientific American*, ic (15 Aug. 1908), 108–10; W. F. Mangels, *The Outdoor Amusement Industry from the Earliest Times to the Present* (New York, 1957); R. E. Snow and D. E. Wright, 'Coney Island: a case study in popular culture and technical change', *Journal of Popular Culture*, ix (Spring 1976), 960–75.

35 *Temple Bar*, 1882, *op. cit.*, 266. See also E. E. Slosson, 'The amusement business', *Independent*, lvii (21 July, 1904), 135.

36 R. L. Hartt, 'The Amusement Park', *Atlantic Monthly*, xcix (May 1907), 677.

37 See, for example, the brilliant essay in N. Z. Davis, *Society and Culture in Early Modern France* (1975), 97–123.

38 B. Bliven, 'Coney Island for battered souls,' *New Republic*, xviii (23 Nov. 1921), 372–4.

39 J. K. Walton, 'Holidays and the discipline of industrial labour: a historian's view', in M. A. Smith (ed.), *Leisure and Urban Society* (1977), no. 18, 1–11.

40 *Everybody's Magazine* (Aug. 1908), *op. cit.*, 233.

41 J. R. McGovern, 'The American woman's pre-world War I freedom in manners and morals', *Journal of American History*, lv (Sept. 1968), 315–33.

42 E. B. Harris, 'The day of rest at Coney Island', *Everybody's Magazine*, xix (July 1908), 24–34; Slosson, *op. cit.*, 139.

43 There is a representative collection of postcards more scenic than saucy in H. Bridgeman and E. Drury (eds), *Beside the Seaside: A picture postcard album* (1977), and R. E. Snow, 'Greetings from Coney Island: old postcards,' *American Heritage*, xxvi (Feb. 1975), 49–55.

44 It continued, however, to fascinate artists: R. Cox, 'Coney Island, urban symbol in American art', *New York Historical Society Quarterly*, lx (Jan.–April 1976), 35–52.

45 Even at Coney Island – see the photographs of H. Lapow, *Coney Island Beach People* (New York, 1978).

Death and survival in the city: approaches to the history of disease

Now that the debate about the standard of living during the first half of the nineteenth century appears to have entered a relatively quiescent phase, historians have begun to turn their attention towards the more elusive concept of the quality of life.[2] The incidence of fatal and non-fatal disease is clearly central to research of this type and so, too, is a delineation of the physical context in which infections have flourished and in which those who have been afflicted by them have lived. Although there has been a tendency to underestimate the ferocity of epidemics in rural areas in the period after about 1750, historians working on disease in the modern period are inevitably most usually concerned with processes which are specifically urban in character. And urban historians, especially those interested in such topics as the development of utilities, the growth of administrative bureaucracies or the spatial segregation and different life experiences of the classes, can undoubtedly benefit from a knowledge of patterns of infection in the past.

There are, in fact, a number of wholly unforced and fruitful connections to be made between urban history and the history of disease. It would also seem reasonable to assume that the historian of disease and the urban historian who makes use of selected epidemiological material would gain from a close acquaintanceship with the venerable discipline of the history of medicine. But, paradoxical though it may seem, historians of medicine have in fact written remarkably little about the actual incidence and mass experience of disease in history. Why this should be so (why, that is, the history of medicine should have remained largely indifferent to what would seem to be a crucial field of inquiry) is an intriguing and complicated question: and an explanation of this historiographical peculiarity, even the abbreviated account offered in the introduction to this paper, should reveal something of the intellectual pedigree and current state of the history of disease.

1

The failure to confront the 'hard facts' of disease in the past is partly explicable in terms of the history of the history of medicine itself – a discipline which has traditionally been the province of those whose main interests have been in the evolution of medical theories and practice rather than in relationships between medicine, disease and society at large. It is a style of history which has been more concerned with the development of diagnosis and therapy, of sub-disciplines and specialisms – anatomy, physiology, surgery, anaesthesia, paediatrics, psychiatry and so on – than with the great mass of people in whom ill-health has, as it were, been physically and psychically located.

Medical history, like all history, has also been strongly influenced by current preoccupations. Therapies which cannot be shown to have contributed to an ever more effective body of medical expertise have been largely ignored. And with a few exceptions – the very different work, for example, of Foucault and Abel-Smith[3] – the institutional history of hospitals and of hospitalization has been dominated by assumptions that are rooted in the here-and-now. Improvements in medical practice and education have, according to this view, been made to flow in a linear and predetermined manner from what has gone before, and to lead on to what is known to have followed. It is not simply that discontinuities have remained unclear as a result of this approach: but, more seriously, that the most fundamental of all historical processes, that of change, has been tacitly excluded.

Nevertheless, a small number of scholars have over the years fashioned a rather different type of medical history. Erwin Ackerknecht has propounded challenging hypotheses about connections between a prevailing political climate and dominant theories as to the transmission of disease:[4] the late George Rosen has charted the long-term behaviour of the major European infections and the ways in which medical and political bureaucracies have reacted to the threat of epidemics:[5] and Joseph Needham, in his magisterial researches into the history of East Asian science and medicine, has challenged numerous Whiggish and Eurocentric orthodoxies.[6]

More recently, a growing though still small number of social, political and urban historians have been engaged upon work on the historical incidence of disease and the ways in which it has been perceived and treated. In his studies of the plague in the city states of Italy, Carlo Cipolla has indicated how individual communities organized themselves against epidemics and the extent to which economic self-interest determined which from among a range of competing theories of disease was the most likely to be adopted by particular social groups.[7]

In *Religion and the Decline of Magic* Keith Thomas has demonstrated how historians may make use of anthropological concepts to shed light on differences between specialist and popular images of therapy and disease.[8] In a number of provocative articles, in which he has applied contemporary findings in epidemiology and the food sciences to reconstituted demographic data of the type assembled by the Cambridge Group for the History of Population and Social Structure, Andrew Appleby has sought to disentangle the relative contributions of malnutrition and infection to high levels of mortality in preindustrial society.[9]

Phillipe Ariès and Ivan Illich, the latter in his polemical *Medical Nemesis* which sparked off a small-scale debate within the medical profession, have traced changing attitudes towards suffering and death.[10] In the field of nineteenth-century studies, with which this paper is primarily concerned, three pioneering historians, Sidney Finer and R. A. Lewis in their complementary studies of Edwin Chadwick, and R. S. Lambert in his seminal work on John Simon, have described the political and environmental assumptions of the vanguard of the first national campaign for the improvement of public health in an industrial society.[11]

There has as yet, however, been little detailed research into the explicitly quantitative incidence of disease, or of specific infections, in the late eighteenth and nineteenth centuries.[12] It may be the case, of course, that social and economic historians have tended to be intimidated by the technical demands posed by medical history and, in this respect, it can hardly be a matter of chance that the standard articles by Thomas McKeown and his colleagues at the University of Birmingham on changes in aggregate mortality between the later eighteenth and mid-twentieth centuries should have been written by specialists in social medicine.[13] But this is an argument which cuts both ways. It is hardly surprising that social and urban historians venturing into medical territory should feel that their hypotheses are likely to be demolished by the medical expert. But it may also be the case that researchers whose primary training has been medical will oversimplify findings in social and economic history.

The remainder of this paper will examine ways in which urban and social historians may set about tackling topics which were, until quite recently, assumed to lie exclusively within the domain of the research worker blessed with a specialist medical background. A brief comment on the quality of the statistical data relating to infectious disease in the nineteenth century is followed by an account of how such evidence may be made to throw light on otherwise elusive aspects of environmental change. The ensuing discussion of the variables which must enter into any attempt to clarify the changing behaviour of infections with the passage of time leads into a critique of what is here loosely defined as 'microorganic determinism' – the hypothesis that shifts in mortality due to a number of demographically important diseases have been less powerfully influenced by medical intervention or by programmes of urban reform than by purportedly 'random' biological and/or ecological modifications. The article concludes with some remarks on recent work in the social and political interpretation of epidemics during the nineteenth century.

2

The fundamental source material for the historian of disease in the nineteenth century, the annual and decennial *Reports* of the Registrar-General, must be approached with a high degree of caution and scepticism. The ever-changing categorization of disease during the first 20 years or so of registration, and the failure to achieve a convincing differentiation between several of the most important infections until after mid-century, involves the research worker in a constant battle to ensure that like is being compared with like. To take a single and representative example: the symptomologically similar but etiologically quite distinct infections of typhus and typhoid only came to be reliably differentiated from one another in the Registrar's *Reports* in the late 1860s. In this, as in several comparable instances, the historian is forced to seek out other categories of evidence which may clarify the epidemiological nuances obscured by the medically misleading aggregates contained in the official returns. Thus in London in the mid-nineteenth century, and many of the examples in this paper will be based on the epidemiological experience of the capital; progressive medical men at the Fever Hospital in Islington as well as a number of well-informed medical officers of health made calculations of what they believed to have been the approximate incidence of the two diseases from the late 1840s onwards.[14]

Another weakness of the registration material is that it fails throughout the nineteenth century to make allowance for patients whose 'normal place of residence' was deemed to be in district A but who actually died in a hospital or public institution in district B. It is extremely difficult to make adjustments for distortions of this type in the early post-registration period. But from about 1870 onwards it becomes increasingly feasible to cross-check the Registrar's *Reports* against the admissions registers of those public hospitals which were beginning to accept larger numbers of working-class patients, and thus to 'redistribute' deaths from one district to another.[15] It should be noted, however, that this juggling with data at district level – and most urban historians will inevitably be more interested in differentials within large urban areas than in crude aggregates for the community as a whole – can be exceptionally time-consuming. The results, that is, do not always seem to justify the very large numbers of calculations which have to be undertaken to construct a corrected, cause-specific district mortality schedule.

Yet probably the most debilitating shortcoming of all is that the registration material fails to provide an indication of the incidence of non-fatal illness. It hardly needs emphasizing that, in the almost total absence of unemployment benefit and minimal health care, a serious bout of illness affected wage-earners and their dependants in a number of debilitating ways. Lengthy periods of unemployment led to a reduction of income available for rent and food, with the result that families were forced to move to cheaper and less healthy accommodation and to purchase smaller quantities of less nutritious food.[16] Lower intakes of food weakened both the sufferer's resistance to secondary infection and the general level of health of the family as a whole. Illness bred poverty: increased poverty yet further eroded resistance to fatal infection.

It is considerably easier to outline the impact of morbidity than to give it an accurate quantitative expression. In the period before about 1870 case fatality rates derived from the records of the small number of hospitals which accepted substantial numbers of working-class patients may be applied to data in the Registrar's *Reports*, but care must, of course, be taken to assess both the typicality of the hospital catchment area and the size of the intake in relation to the non-hospitalized population. For the period after 1870, case fatality rates for specific infections in large towns are more fully documented in the reports of medical officers of health and an increasingly authoritative epidemiological literature.

Providing, then, that sufficient attention is given to the weaknesses and ambiguities of the official registration material, and especially to the vagaries of cause-specific mortality at district level, it should be possible to arrive at moderately reliable estimates of mortality and morbidity for individual infections from about mid-century onwards.

In addition to revealing the epidemiological profile of a given urban community, and of its component sub-communities, mortality and morbidity figures may also be used to assess the scale of pollution in the period before environmental deterioration came to be monitored through independent indicators. The value of retrospective environmental assessment of this type may be more fully appreciated in the context of the impressive range of qualitative evidence, dating from the 1820s onwards, which shows that town-dwellers from very nearly every social class were fully alive to the newly emergent dangers of pollution. Dominant medical orthodoxies did not, of course, acknowledge that disease such as cholera and typhoid were principally spread via the mass distribution of unsafe water, but this did not inhibit contemporaries from being aware of and protesting against the widespread despoliation of the natural world, and it is, in fact, during the period between about 1820 and 1840 that the word 'environment' first takes on its distinctively modern meaning. It was during this period, also, that public controversy about what are now known as 'environmental problems' – the impact, for example of river pollution on income derived from fishing in the Thames in the late 1820s, or of massive chemical fall-out over the residential districts of St Helens in the 1850s – became unprecedentedly intense.[17] This awareness of the undesirable side-effects of industrialization and urbanization spread rapidly, yet the effectiveness of the protests of those who condemned the baleful effects of uncontrolled pollution on drinking water or on the saleability of vegetables grown on allotments backing on to factories was necessarily dependent upon impressions which were highly subjective. Industrialists, local authorities and the owners of urban utilities were therefore well placed to argue that a particular instance of pollution had not in fact taken place: to admit that it had taken place but to disclaim responsibility for it: or to accept responsibility but deny that there was a proven medical connection between an alleged incident and increased mortality from a specific cause. Individual crusaders might declaim against the dangers of pollution but the miasmatic theory of disease dictated that those who contended that there was a link between, for example, a polluted river and a wide-ranging outbreak of typhoid or cholera, were usually outgunned.

In our own time, of course, scientists and administrative bureaucracies have access to indicators which enable them to monitor levels of pollution and of diseases which are known to be heavily influenced by particular types of environmental change. The historian of disease, though, is in a less fortunate position and is seriously restricted by the weaknesses of the available evidence – especially the absence, until about the final quarter of the nineteenth century, of any kind of reliable and meaningful environmental series.[18] Since, however, it is now indisputably established that particular infections are invariably associated with particular types of pollution, cause-specific mortality data may be used to yield information about the gravity of such pollution during the nineteenth century. In this sense, rising mortality from cholera, dysentery, 'diarrhoea' and typhoid from the 1840s onwards confirms the validity of the claims of those who campaigned against the unconstrained pollution of the water environment at that time. An analogous but, because of the continuing haziness of Victorian medical categorization, probably a less decisive association may also be posited between what contemporary medical men termed 'diseases of the lungs and chest' and rising levels of atmospheric pollution.

3

An explanation of the changing behaviour of a given infection over time involves consideration of a number of social, economic and environmental factors. The availability and reliability of evidence on the most important of these variables for the historian of the nineteenth-century city – population densities, rates of migration, changing levels of *per capita* income and associated levels of nutrition – will now be briefly examined.

Since the mode of transmission of the (in quantitative terms) most important diseases in the period under review was predominantly air-borne, mortality and morbidity were decisively influenced by levels of over-crowding. There is now a growing body of literature on this topic as well as on the strengths and weaknesses of the various indices, whether of persons per acre, per house or per room, by which contemporaries attempted to measure population densities.[19] As for migration, the reactivation of epidemic diseases which were transmitted through person-to-person contact or via an insect vector, rather than through an intermediate environment, were frequently sparked off by the arrival of infected individuals into a susceptible population. The precise dynamics of epidemics of this type are more likely to be elucidated by charting sudden and relatively small-scale inter-urban movements, especially those undertaken by the very poor during periods of acute economic distress, than by computing the more conventional net inter-county rates from *Census* material. The scale and impact of these often socially disruptive migrations may sometimes be partially recovered by exploiting the archives of those large urban hospitals which accepted the poorest of the poor and recorded either their place of birth or their 'normal place of residence'.[20]

The actual death-toll exacted by the individual epidemic was in many instances affected by standards of living and levels of nutrition. Changing *per capita* income, the proportion of income spent on food, its quantity and quality, and when such information finally becomes available, probable *per capita* intakes of calories – all these are essential, though all too often elusive, determinants of nutritional change.[21] Once assembled, material of this type must be interpreted in the light of what is definitively established as to the impact of nutrition on the individual infection – and this is a complex and highly contentious field. (There is, for example, still no absolute agreement as to the precise effect of marginally improved diet on the incidence of typhus in the nineteenth or the twentieth centuries.[22])

A further determinant of the incidence of infectious disease is how people live, their customs and their patterns of behaviour. From this perspective, a crucial question currently facing historians of disease is whether, beginning in the late eighteenth century, it is possible to identify a slow but irreversible sea-change in attitudes towards personal cleanliness: and, a related issue, how much this as yet underdocumented transformation may have contributed to the long-term decline of such infections as cholera, typhus, typhoid and infant diarrhoea.

Statistics relating to the consumption of water for domestic purposes, vital to any systematic examination of changing patterns of communal hygiene, were studiously collected throughout the nineteenth century. But material on regional increases in the consumption of soap, which may have hastened the eradication of the 'dirt diseases' is sparse. So, too, is quantitative and qualitative evidence which might confirm the hypothesis that the mass introduction of cotton clothing was inimical to the louse population which had for so long sustained the ferocity of epidemic typhus. Nor, to complete this catalogue of material for a rigorous account of hygiene in history, is much yet known about the numbers, and the spatial and social distribution of baths, washbasins and water-closets in the new urban areas.[23]

Economic, social and behavioural variables should not, of course, be artificially abstracted from their larger environmental context. There are, broadly speaking, two aspects of the environment which have an important bearing upon infectious disease among humans: the external environment, comprising the natural world, man-made artifacts and the technologies, for the supply of water and the disposal of sewage and waste, with which urban man has sought to minimize filth and infection: and the internal or domestic 'microenvironment', comprising the contents and arrangement of the individual dwelling, the method of conserving food and drink, and the distance between areas used, on the one hand for living and eating and, on the other, for the short-term storage of waste. Although it has not yet been fully tested against the experience of any single nineteenth century urban community, the hypothesis that it was primarily the modification of the external environment between about the mid-1840s and 1870 which precipitated the decline in diseases of the faecal-oral route, notably typhoid and cholera, will probably be found to be substantially correct.[24]

The improvement of the domestic 'microenvironment', on the other hand, only got under way during the first decade of the twentieth century when infant mortality, which the late George Rosen has called 'one of the most sensitive indicators' of the quality of community health, finally began to decline to levels which may be meaningfully compared with those in the developed world today.[25] This amelioration, which made an important impact on the infections of infancy and childhood (and particularly on infant diarrhoea) has not yet been at all adequately explained, although it is reasonable to suggest that it could not have occurred without continuing increases in *per capita* income, a slowly improving supply of public housing and greater public awareness of the germ theory of disease. And yet the behaviour of a number of infections remains elusive and apparently unrelated to socio-economic or environmental change. There has therefore been a growing tendency in recent years, supported by such historians as Braudel, Henry and Chambers, to explain epidemiological history – and by extension, the history of population – in terms of 'random' biological and ecological transformations.[26] This emergent 'microorganic determinism', a complement to the geographical and climatic determinism which have proven so attractive to French historians, and particularly to the *Annales* school, presents man as merely one among a multitude of different types of life on this planet, potentially at the mercy of autonomous change in the ecologies of the bacteria, viruses and insect vectors which cause disease among humans. Insofar as it implies the termination of the absolute supremacy of *homo sapiens* both in nature and in history, and thus devotes more attention, in the style of the pioneering virologist MacFarlane Burnet, to the natural history of micro-organic life *per se*, this is a potentially exciting enterprise.[27] But, in its currently over-generalized form it may, as Paul Slack has noted, merely serve as a convenient though unilluminating escape-route for historians whose other explanatory schema have proven inadequate.[28]

The conception of an 'autonomous' change in the nature of a disease is itself exceedingly complex for, depending upon the characteristics of the infection, a very large number of factors and/or interactions between factors may be involved. These may include a shift in the toxicity or invasiveness of the micro-organism, a sudden environmental or climatic modification exerting a dramatic effect on the bioecology of bacteria outside the human body, or a disturbance in the insect populations which transmit infections to humans. One technique of deciding whether the virulence of an infective micro-organism may have changed – in the manner in which, according to McKeown and Record, the haemolytic streptococcus responsible for scarlet fever changed during the nineteenth century[29] – is to compare case fatality rates when mortality from the disease is high with comparable rates when mortality has undergone a large and rapid reduction. If such comparisons reveal substantial differentials there will be good grounds for exploring the possibility that biological and ecological factors may have played a dominant role. But, if the difference between the two rates is either small or non-existent, behavioural change is likely to be more satisfactorily explained in environmental or socioeconomic terms. Certainly, as ecologically complex a disease as typhus which several writers, over a long period of time, have believed to have been at least partly affected by sudden 'autonomous' changes in virulence, does not in fact display significant intertemporal differentials in case fatality when the large-scale British epidemics of the 1830s and 1860s are compared with small-scale outbreaks during the later nineteenth century.[30] In this case, it is the highly unpredictable long-term periodicity of the disease, its 'long swings', and the nature of the inter-epidemic reservoirs of infections – how the disease manages to preserve itself, as it were, between its recrudescences among human populations – which will probably eventually provide a degree of insight into short-term behavioural change.

These comments should not be interpreted as a dismissal of what has here been described as 'microorganic determinism' but rather as an indication that the 'natural history' of a disease is invariably highly complex, and that the major infections which have afflicted European society in modern times will only be fully understood through the application of models which accommodate specific biological and ecological variables. These models will not be easy to construct since they will demand that the historian be acquainted not only with the fundamentals of medicine and bacteriology, but also with aspects of bioecology, parasitology, immunology and the food sciences.

4

There is, however, no reason why work of this type should precede research into the political and social implications of epidemics during the nineteenth century. Indeed, the two enterprises – the epidemiological and the socio-political – can, and in my view should, be carried on together.

Following Asa Briggs' seminal article, there has been a steady growth in the number of books, articles and theses devoted to the interpretation of disease, and more particularly, of cholera in the nineteenth century.[31] This body of work has, *inter alia*, documented contradictions between medical and lay ideas on the nature of infection and has shown that sections of the working class believed that cholera epidemics were deliberately spread by Malthusians, seeking to thin out the ranks of the poor, and by medical men eager to obtain supplies of bodies for *post-mortem* dissection.[32] In Britain, in contrast to several European countries, rioting associated with cholera seems only rarely to have interacted and fused with deeper political discontent. Indeed, despite the futility and counter-productiveness of the preventive and therapeutic measures to which they lent their support, both central government and the ruling elites in the hardest hit of the localities appear to have weathered successive visitations with remarkable resilience. We now have monographs on aspects of the epidemiological and social history of cholera in nineteenth-century Britain, Russia, France and the United States.[33] The next priority is a genuinely comparative study which would attempt to explain differential reactions to the pandemic in terms of diverse political, institutional and religious structures.

Yet it would be disappointing if future work were to be concentrated on cholera to the exclusion of other, less dramatic but, in terms of their contribution to aggregate mortality, more important diseases such as tuberculosis, smallpox and the infections of childhood. A distinction may perhaps be drawn between diseases such as cholera, typhus and smallpox, which were traumatic in terms of their observable symptoms and therefore highly visible to large sections of the population, and others, such as tuberculosis and typhoid, the symptoms of which were considerably less conspicuous. The range of provocative questions which might be asked of a highly visible disease such as typhus is very wide – to take just one example, it would be intriguing to know whether and to what extent the large-scale epidemics of the later 1830s and the later 1840s reinforced existing prejudice against newly arrived Irish immigrants in the larger urban areas.

The less sensational diseases will probably generate a different set of questions – whether, for example, it is possible to make a hard-and-fast distinction between the social impact of epidemic and endemic infections in history, how and approximately when endemic disease ceased to be accepted and suffered as part of the natural order of things, the range of treatments (or pseudo-treatments), 'folk' as well as medical, which were available to different social classes, and how non-fatal illness among infants and children was nursed in the individual home.

The theoretical and empirical implications of some of these questions are beginning to be confronted by social historians of medicine.[34] The aim of the present paper has been to argue that the enduring themes of disease, survival and death should now also be taken up and creatively investigated by urban historians.

Bill Luckin
Bolton Institute of Technology

Notes

1   A more 'popular' and much abbreviated version of this paper appeared in the *Times Higher Education Supplement*, 18 June 1976. It was also delivered in a variety of forms to historical and medical seminars in Cambridge, London, Manchester and Bolton. I am grateful to all those who offered comment and criticism. My greatest debt, however, is to the late Professor H. J. Dyos, both for his advice on an earlier draft, and for many other kindnesses over the years.

2   A recent contributor to the debate qualifies what seem to be guardedly 'optimistic' conclusions by stating that: 'The data on mortality rates in early nineteenth century cities seems damning enough, and I find myself in sympathy with the recent shift in emphasis to environmental factors'. G. N. Von Tunzelmann. 'Trends in real wages, 1750–1850, revisited', *Economic History Review*, 2nd ser., xxxii, 1 (1979), 49.

3   M. Foucault, *The Birth of the Clinic*, translated by A. M. Sheridan (1973) and Brian Abel-Smith, *The Hospitals, 1800–1948: A study in social administration in England and Wales* (1964).

4   The classic article is Erwin H. Ackerknecht, 'Anticontagionism between 1821 and 1867', *Bulletin of the History of Medicine*, xxii (1948), 562–93.

5   See, for example, G. Rosen, *A History of Public Health* (New York, 1958) and 'Disease, debility and death' in H. J. Dyos and Michael Wolff (eds), *The Victorian City: Images and reality*, vol. II (1973), 625–67.

6   For a typically dazzling and deeply considered synopsis see Joseph Needham (with Lu Gwei-Djen), 'Medicine and Chinese culture' in Joseph Needham, *Clerks and Craftsmen in China and the West* (1970), 263–93.

7   Carlo M. Cipolla, *Cristofano and the Plague: A study in the history of public health in the age of Galileo* (1973) and *Public Health and the Medical Profession in the Renaissance* (1976).

8   Keith Thomas, *Religion and the Decline of Magic* (1973), 209–52. However, the social and sociological frameworks within which historians might more fruitfully examine interactions between 'specialist' and 'non-specialist' world-views have only recently begun to be discussed. For a brave venture in this field see Janet Blackman, 'Popular theories of generation: the evolution of *Aristotle's Works*. The study of an anachronism', in John Woodward and David Richards (eds), *Health Care and Popular Medicine in Nineteenth Century England* (1977), 56–89.

9   Andrew B. Appleby, 'Disease or famine? Mortality in Cumberland and Westmorland 1580–1640', *Economic History Review*, 2nd ser, xxvi, 3 (1973), 403–33 and *idem*, 'Nutrition and disease: the case of London, 1550–1750', *Journal of Interdisciplinary History*, vi, 1 (Summer, 1975), 1–22.

10   Ivan Illich, *Limits to Medicine: Medical nemesis* (1977); Phillipe Ariès, *Western Attitudes Towards Death: From the Middle Ages to the present* (Baltimore, 1974). Illich's study contains a superlative bibliography on the history and sociology of medicine and disease.

11   S. E. Finer, *The Life and Times of Sir Edwin Chadwick* (1952); R. A. Lewis, *Edwin Chadwick and the Public Health Movement 1832–1854* (1952); R. S. Lambert, *Sir John Simon 1816–1904 and English Social Administration* (1963). These seminal studies have now been complemented by Margaret Pelling's scholarly account of medical and epidemiological thought, *Cholera, Fever and English Medicine 1825–1865* (1978).

12   Exceptions include Peter Razzell, *The Conquest of Smallpox: The impact of inoculation on smallpox mortality in eighteenth century Britain* (1977) and Alan Armstrong, *Stability and Change in an English County Town: A social study of York 1801–1851* (1974), 108–54.

13   The arguments contained in these articles have now been restated and expanded in Thomas McKeown, *The Modern Rise of Population* (1976).

14   Charles Murchison, *The Continued Fevers of Great Britain* (3rd edn., 1884), 52–3; *Report*

of the Medical Officer of Health: Shoreditch (1862), 19; *Report of the Medical Officer of Health: Strand* (1859), 11; and *Report of the Medical Officer of Health: Holborn* (1866), 53–4.

15 Admissions material for London for the period 1848–70 is to be found in Murchison, *op.cit.*, 74–5. Data for the final 30 years of the century may be abstracted from the *Minutes* of the Metropolitan Asylums Board and, from 1887 onwards, from the annual *Reports* of the Board's Statistical Committee. Both the *Minutes* and the *Reports* of the Statistical Committee may be consulted at County Hall, Westminster. The University Library, Cambridge, also keeps a complete run of the *Reports* of the Statistical Committee. These detailed and beautifully presented records, and particularly the meticulously shaded scatter maps which show the annual incidence of infectious disease at district level from 1887 onwards, are among the richest, and least exploited, source materials for the urban historian of disease.

16 Local differentials in levels of rent have not yet been studied in depth but there is much relevant and penetrating material in E. H. Hunt, *Regional Wage Variations in Britain 1850–1914* (1973). On dietary history see D. Oddy and D. Miller (eds), *The Making of the Modern British Diet* (1976) and the trenchant remarks in F. B. Smith, *The People's Health 1830–1910* (1979). The interpretative historical literature in English on this topic is still underdeveloped. For recent work in French, much of it influenced by the *Annales* school, see Illich, *op.cit.*

17 On the Thames question at this time see *Royal Commission on the Supply of Water in the Metropolis*, PP, 1828, IX. 122–23 and 200. On St Helens, see S. G. Checkland, *The Rise of Industrial Society in England 1815–1885* (1971), 170–1.

18 The most important pioneer in the field of applied water analysis was the chemist, Edward Frankland. For a brief biographical note see J. R. Partington, *A History of Chemistry*, vol. IV (1964), 500–1. The crucial figure in the development of the monitoring of atmospheric pollution was the influential Angus Smith. See Roy M. MacLeod, 'The Alkali Acts Administration 1863–84: the emergence of the civil scientist', *Victorian Studies*, ix (1965), 85–112.

19 This topic has been discussed by, among others, Gareth Stedman Jones, *Outcast London* (1971) and A. S. Wohl, *The Eternal Slum: Housing and social policy in Victorian London* (1977). See also S. D. Chapman (ed.), *The History of Working Class Housing: A symposium* (1971).

20 Information of this kind is available for the London Fever Hospital and for institutions which came under the jurisdiction of the Metropolitan Asylums Board.

21 See note 16 above.

22 John C. Snyder. 'The typhus fevers', in Thomas M. Rivers (ed.), *Viral and Rickettsial Infections of Man* (2nd edn, Philadelphia, 1952), 578–610, and Thomas McKeown, R. G. Brown and R. G. Record, 'An interpretation of the modern rise of population in Europe', *Population Studies*, xxvi (1972), 345–82 and, particularly, 356.

23 The general 'hygiene' argument has been put forward by P. E. Razzell, 'An interpretation of the modern rise of population in Europe – a critique', *Population Studies*, xxviii (1974), 5–17. On typhus see J. D. Chambers, *Population, Economy and Society in Pre-Industrial England* (1972), 103–4.

24 This is the general explanation proposed by McKeown, *op.cit.* But note the suggestive qualifications proposed by Robert Woods, 'Mortality and sanitary conditions in the "Best governed city in the world" – Birmingham, 1870–1910', *Journal of Historical Geography*, iv, 1 (1978), 35–56.

25 George Rosen in Dyos and Wolff, *op.cit.*, 650.

26 Fernand Braudel, *Capitalism and Material Life*, translated by Miriam Kochan (1974); Louis Henry, 'The population of France in the eighteenth century', in D. V. Glass and D. Eversley (eds), *Population in History* (1965), 448; Chambers, *op.cit.*, chapter 4. The subject is also clearly examined in John D. Post, 'Famine, mortality and epidemic disease in the process of modernization', *Economic History Review*, 2nd ser., xxix, 1 (1976), 14–38. There is much that is germane to this topic in William H. McNeill, *Plagues and Peoples* (1977), an ambitious interpretation of 'ecological history', based on wide-ranging medico-historical documentation.

27 MacFarlane Burnet and David O. White, *The Natural History of Infectious Disease* (1972).

28 Paul Slack, 'Disease and the Social Historian', *Times Literary Supplement*, 8 March 1974.

29 Thomas McKeown and R. G. Record, 'Reasons for the decline of mortality in England and Wales during the nineteenth century', *Population Studies*, xvi (1963), 94–122, reprinted in M. W. Flinn and T. C. Smout (eds). *Essays in Social History* (1974), 218–55. Scarlet fever is discussed at several points in this influential article but see, in particular, 243.

30 In the period between about 1830 and 1900 case fatality rates ranged fairly consistently

between 25 and 40 per cent. *Fifth Annual Report of the Poor Law Commission*, PP, 1839, XX, appendix C2, 113; annual *Reports* of the Statistical Committee of the Metropolitan Asylums Board 1887–1900; E. W. Goodall, *A Short History of the Infectious Epidemic Diseases* (1934), 88.

31   Asa Briggs, 'Cholera and society in the nineteenth century', *Past and Present*, xix (1960–1), 79–96.
32   Popular hostility towards the medical profession is well described by M. Durey, *The First Spasmodic Cholera Epidemic in York, 1832*, Borthwick Papers, no. 46 (York, 1974).
33   The literature is now becoming voluminous. A basic bibliography, excluding unpublished Ph.D. and M. A. theses, would include R. E. McGraw, *Russia and the Cholera 1823–32* (Madison, 1965); Louis Chevalier (ed.), *Le Choléra: la première épidémie du XIXe siècle* (La Roche sur Yon, 1958); Charles Rosenberg, *The Cholera Years: The United States in 1832, 1849 and 1866* (Chicago, 1962); R. J. Morris, *Cholera 1832* (1976). A more exhaustive bibliography is contained in Pelling, *op.cit.*, in the footnote to page 4.
34   The Society for the Social History of Medicine provides a stimulating point of contact for those engaged upon research in this field. Its journal, the *Bulletin of the Society for the Social History of Medicine*, contains regular summaries of work in progress.

Planning history in Japan

1 Introduction

The planning system which dominates most of the comtemporary world is of European and American origin. It has come out of the particular socio-historical background of these Western countries and has naturally had some implicit assumptions regarding the concepts, purposes and ideology of planning. This system has been exported to, and often imposed upon, countries with different social conditions where those assumptions are not necessarily valid. As a result, in many developing countries, planning is considered ineffective, and planners become frustrated.

Thus, it seems to be important, practically speaking, for each country to develop a planning system which is best suited to its own socio-historical conditions. Equally, it would be important academically to develop a research field in which the planning systems of various countries at various times are compared with each other and are related to their own socio-historical backgrounds. This implies that there is no 'universal planning system', and emphasizes the uniqueness of individual planning systems as well as the differences between them. The Western planning system, which has been widely accepted as *the* planning system, must, in a sense, be 'relativized'. In other words, it is necessary to identify the particularity, not the universality, of the planning systems in the U.S. and Europe.

For this purpose, the planning history of Japan might provide useful suggestions because of the country's different background, enormous challenges, unique achievements, and contemporary problems. First, Japan is the only non-Western country which has, in a little over a century, evolved from a feudal agrarian society to become one of the highly industrialized nations. Japan is a typical, if not average, case of a late developer, who has diligently studied the concepts and techniques of planning in Western countries, and gradually improved, and partly invented, a planning system which is more suitable in her own situation.

Second, the challenges which Japanese planning had to face were varied and enormous. The percentage of urban population rose from 18 per cent in 1920 to 76 per cent in 1975. Most of that population has been concentrated in a narrow strip of land between Tokyo and Osaka metropolises, now forming the Tokaido Megalopolis. Furthermore, Japanese cities have been vulnerable to frequent earthquakes, fires and floods; many of them suffered air raids during the Second World War. Most parts of modern Tokyo had to be rebuilt anew twice, once after the Kanto Earthquake of 1923 and again after the war. The nation needed to fight all these challenges under very severe limitations such as little habitable land, poor endowment of resources and energy, a strong agrarian tradition, and scarce financial resources.

Third, Japan's planning achievements have been unique if not grand. In brief moments of history, she has replaced feudal castle-towns of wood and clay with contemporary cities of steel and concrete. Although often criticized as being designed to suit modern business and industry rather than modern living, Japanese metropolises, after all, are exceptional when compared internationally, for their low rate of crime and still high rate of population growth. In a sense, the nation has succeeded in building distinctive Japanese cities without destroying the traditional sense of urbanism and social order. High-density living, efficient mass transportation, human-scale and mixed-use developments, and a unique land-consolidation technique are just some of these Japanese attainments. They are quite different from the ones suited to the affluent West, but may be very relevant to the presently developing countries.

Fourth, despite these attainments, Japanese planning still has serious unsolved problems, such as soaring land prices and a threatened residential environment in metropolitan areas. The conventional planning system, which was effective for securing urban land for public works, is not so helpful in protecting the residential environment. Local governments complain that the planning system, which is strongly controlled by the central government, lacks flexibility and does not meet local needs. In fact, the Japanese planning system is now at a turning point. This is one reason why the Japanese experience is of interest to the comparative study of national planning strategies.

Unfortunately, the history of the Japanese planning system is not yet available in Western languages. Furthermore, it is only recently that a handful of Japanese planners and historians have started historical researches and, naturally, their achievements are still rather limited. There are only a few universities where planning history is now taught as an independent subject.[1] Even in these cases, planning history is mostly limited to that of Japan and the West, and does not consider either the socialist countries or the Third World. Nevertheless, Japanese planning history is a potentially interesting and useful field of study and there is ample room for foreigners to contribute. The following brief survey is made in the hope of stimulating this interest.

2   Brief history of Japanese planning

A brief outline of planning history in modern Japan seems to be not only a convenient, but also a necessary, guide for foreign readers. Although an authoritative subdivision of historical epochs has not been established for Japanese planning, four major periods can be roughly identified: namely, the Meiji (1868–1912), Taisho-Early Showa (1912–30), Wartime (1930–45) and Post-War (1945–present) periods.[2] The period *preceding* the Meiji is also important, since most contemporary Japanese cities have evolved from castle-towns and other feudal towns built and developed then.[3] Thus, a researcher on modern Japan's planning ought to pay a good deal of attention to these feudal towns, even though his main concern may be their evolution, rather than their origins.

Modern Japan started with the Meiji Restoration in 1868. The same year, the Meiji Emperor moved from Kyoto to Edo, which was renamed Tokyo and became the national capital and seat of the new government. The period following this event, for slightly less than half a century, is known as the Meiji period. With the official slogan of a 'wealthy nation and strong army' (*fukoku kyōhei*), the Meiji government tried hard to create governmental and social institutions after Western models. Industrialization was pushed forward under the strong leadership of the central government and ambitious enterpreneurs. The main attention in public policies, however, was directed to the rural society and its economy, as Japan then was basically an agricultural society.

The urban concern of the Meiji governments was discernible only in the nation's new capital. The governments' leaders, eager to revise unequal treaties with the West, were worried that their Imperial capital could not visually compare with those in the West, say for example, Haussmann's Paris. More basically, they found the urban structure of Castle-Town Edo completely inadequate for modern functions. Thus, their strategy for the capital, but not for cities in general, was a radical surgery of urban structure, not for the entire area but for certain areas or functions of crucial importance.

One of the earliest examples was a redevelopment project for the shopping area in Ginza (*Ginza renga-gai keikaku*), 1872–7. Another was a project to concentrate government office buildings (*kanchō shūchū keikaku*), 1885–8, for which several plans were prepared by British and German architects, although none of them was ever implemented. In 1888, Tokyo City Improvement (*shiku kaisei*) Ordinance was enacted after some 12 years of preparation. This programme aimed at building a network of major streets in the already built-up area and at facilitating water-works for the prevention of epidemics. It covered almost the entire urban area of Tokyo and took three decades until its curtailed completion in 1918. Japanese planners tend to consider this programme as Japan's first modern planning, but it was only a large-scale, fairly systematic public works programme in the nation's capital, although it had an immense impact upon the later planning system. The nation had to wait until the Taisho period in order to have a planning system dealing with land use and public works in a more comprehensive manner.

The Taisho-Early Showa period corresponds to the entire Taisho era (1912–26) and the first five years of Showa (1926–30). This is, according to the writer's under-standing, the formative period of the Japanese planning system, but with import-ant roots in the Meiji period.

The Japanese economy started to grow after the Russo-Japanese War (1904–5), dramatically so during the First World War (1914–18). Rapid industrialization and urbanization brought new kinds of social classes into being. The urban labour-ing class provided the expanding industries with a cheap labour force and mostly lived in slums and industrial areas. Together with other classes at the bottom of society, they often caused urban unrest such as mass riots, labour troubles and socialist movements. All these presented to the 'enlightened' bureaucrats of the Home Ministry (naimusho) a crucial urban problem, and in consequence a new urban policy was called for as an important national concern (as distinct from rural measures). The other emerging class was the white-collar group, who were engaged in such expanding fields as business, government, education and other service industries. They tended to move away from the crowded central area into the urban periphery. Thus, suburbanization began.

Hence, the demand for planning legislation also came from other large cities and from the architectural profession around 1917. The government decided to institu-tionalize a planning system of general applicability and, the next year, established the City Planning (toshi keikaku) Section in the Home Ministry. Thus, the new word toshi keikaku got official recognition. The first Section chief was Ikeda Hiroshi, who drafted the City Planning Bill, which was enacted in 1919, together with the Urban Building Act (shigaichi kenchikubutsu hō). The City Planning Act (toshi keikaku ho, later nicknamed the 'Old Act') provided, at least theoreti-cally, a fairly comprehensive planning system by combining the traditional city improvement programme with such new techniques as zoning, building-line con-trol, and land consolidation. The number of cities where the Act was in effect rose from six to 31 in 1913, and went to over 100 in 1931. The Old Act, by its continua-tion for the following half a century, became the cornerstone for Japanese plan-ning.

Only four years had passed since the Old Act was enacted, when the Tokyo area was hit by the Kanto Earthquake (magnitude 7.9). The capital was almost com-pletely destroyed. The Reconstruction Agency was then established, which carried out the reconstruction programme for Tokyo and Yokohama during the next seven years, ending in 1930. This disaster gave planners a rare opportunity for large-scale planning and implementation, especially through land consolidation under the Special City Planning Act of 1923.

The Wartime period lasted for about 15 years until the end of the war in 1945. All the national policies were gradually directed toward military expansion to neighbouring countries and the execution of the war. Peacetime planning practice was replaced by such wartime measures as national resource mobilization plan-ning, the anti-air raid programme, and the building of war-industry towns. Although there was little room for ordinary types of planning, Japan's colonies and occupying areas abroad provided a good opportunity for planning experiments and training for many Japanese planners who later played an active part in the post-war planning in Japan.

The Post-War period could be subdivided into three periods of reconstruction

(1945-late 1950s), rapid growth (late 1950s-early 1970s), and the present 'uncertainty'.

Post-war Japan started with a completely destroyed economy, food shortage, a massive repatriation problem and 215 air-raided cities. An urgent problem was how to provide the homeless with 300,000 houses before the first winter. The occupation force, denouncing the Home Ministry as the source of militarism during the War, proceeded to dismantle it. Now planning came under the charge of the new Ministry of Construction established in 1948. The Urban Building Act was replaced by the Building Standards Act (*kenchiku kijun hō*); the City Planning Act remained effective, though supplemented by the Special City Planning Act (1946–54), which made possible the reconstruction of war-damaged cities through intensive land consolidation programmes.

During some 15 years, beginning in the late 1950s, Japan enjoyed a miracle of rapid economic growth. Industry and population were concentrated in the major metropolitan areas. Central business districts were filled with high-rise office buildings and fringe areas with the sprawl of suburban development. The entire country was intensively developed with heavy industrial plants, highway systems, Bullet Train lines, new towns and golf courses. All these have brought the Japanese people material prosperity and physical convenience, but at the same time, soaring land prices, a deteriorated environment and a loss of non-material values.

During this period, three important Acts were enacted, all closely related to Japan's planning system. The half-a-century-old 'Old Act' was replaced by the City Planning Act of 1968 (nicknamed the 'New Act'), which introduced the designation of areas to discourage developments, the restrictive permission of developments, the partial delegation of planning powers to prefectural and municipal governments, and procedures for citizen participation. The new Urban Redevelopment Act (*toshi saikaihatsu hō*) of 1969 consolidated former and new redevelopment programmes into the New Act planning system. The Building Standards Act was twice amended: to remove the restriction upon building heights (then 31 metres) in 1963, and to allow more detailed zoning control in the New Act framework in 1970. It is important to note that the New Act was a major legislative change from the Old Act, but the basic framework of the Old Act planning system (e.g. the concepts, purposes, bureaucracy, and ideology of planning) was hardly changed.

Finally, the Japanese post-war boom was shut down by the oil shock in 1973, leading to the present period of 'uncertainty'. Private investment and public expenditure declined; the concentration of urban population slowed down. The age of massive construction is over, and concern for a better living environment is increasing. This is surely a turning point in Japan's planning history when a new philosophy and perspective is needed. Planners are eager to know where they are heading. The increasing interest in planning history in recent years seems to reflect this.

3   Existing research activities

Urban history is not an unfamiliar field of study in Japan. Historians and geographers have long studied Japanese medieval and feudal towns at large, and often the planning of these towns. Yet so little interest developed in the history of post-Meiji cities, except for the local history of individual cities, that 'urban history' is often associated with the study of pre-modern towns. A systematic study of modern urban history hardly exists.

Partly due to a strong Marxist influence, many Japanese social scientists have been preoccupied with the nature of Japanese capitalism. Popular topics include the silk and cotton industries in rural areas and the manual industries in provincial towns during the Meiji era. They have repeatedly discussed how Japanese capitalism developed out of those industries and how different it is from the

British form of 'pure' capitalism. In other words, the social scientists have tended to seek modern Japan's origin in rural areas and provincial towns, not in emerging metropolises. Thus, many works are available on agricultural landlordism, but historical analyses of urban areas are practically nonexistent.

Recent trends, however, are rather encouraging. Some social scientists have started pioneering works in urban industry, urban mass movement, urban policy and even urban planning. Mention must also be made of the recent formation of research groups for urban history and for planning history. In 1971, a group of historians who are mostly interested in comparisons between European and Japanese medieval towns organized themselves into the 'Comparative Urban History Group.' Their monthly *Urban History Newsletter*,[4] however, shows little interest in modern Japan's urban problems, and even less in the history of urban planning abroad or in Japan. One problem is that Japanese academism categorizes urban planning into the engineering sector, rather than arts or public administration. So planning's nearest kinfolk are architecture, landscape architecture and civil engineering, including transportation and sanitary engineering. Besides architecture, which has a long tradition of historical studies, these fields are slowly developing interest in their own histories, though achievements are still very few. However, in November, 1978, the City Planning Institute of Japan held a workshop session entitled 'Toward the Start of Research on Japanese Modern Urban Planning History'.[5] The panel discussion was 2½ hours long and was attended by over 70 scholars and students who shared interests in Japanese planning history. The meeting was the first of its kind in Japan and was considered successful. The core members who had prepared the workshop decided to organize themselves into a group called 'Planning History Group' and to hold regular meetings quarterly. This is a loosely connected group of young scholars and students, and its present purpose is to stimulate research interests in planning history through meetings and information exchange. Foreign scholars were also welcomed. The Group plans to hold a second workshop session on 'Home Ministry and Urban Planning' during the City Planning Institute's 1979 annual meeting. The following survey on the existing research works and potential topics in modern Japan's planning history and related fields is based upon the bibliography which the Group prepared for the 1978 workshop.[6]

4   Research works: general

The academic maturity of any field of historical studies may be measured by the presence or absence of readable works in its general history. This holds true for planning history in Japan. There are only a few general histories available, and they are by no means comparable with English or American studies.

The best work so far is found in a long section in a book on the history of architectural studies in modern Japan.[7] This section as a whole is devoted to the general history of Japanese planning from the Meiji Restoration up to 1950. It includes a chronological list, and 11 chapters of individual papers written by 15 architectural historians and former planning-building bureaucrats. The topics each chapter covers are: major cities at the beginning of the Meiji era, The Tokyo City Improvement Programme, industrialization and local cities, architects and planners in the Taisho era, the Kanto earthquake and reconstruction programme, housing policy, the development of planning and building administration, planning in colonial and occupied areas, architects and planners in the Early-Showa and Wartime periods, wartime planning, and post-war reconstruction.

The writers of each chapter were either architectural historians who were specializing in their respective topics, or former planning-building bureaucrats who were in charge of the named programmes. Most of the important themes of Japan's planning history were covered, and some chapters are significant contributions as individual achievements.

The entire section, however, has two basic shortcomings. First, its general history centres around statutory planning: relatively neglected areas include urban planning and development outside the statutory framework, the urban policies and thoughts related to planning, and the socio-historical background against which urban planning evolved. Second, the whole work tends to be chronology rather than history; the writers are interested more in *what* happened (or what they did), *how* and *when*, than in *why* it happened then. These weak points are not inherent in this particular work, but are more or less common in most of the existing works in Japan's planning history.

Two other works are worthy of a brief mention. Professors U. Nishiyama (Kyoto University) and S. Yoshino (Kyoto Furitsu University) have written articles interpreting, rather subjectively, the history of Japan's planning 'theories' against their social background from Meiji to the end of the War.[8] In addition, Professor Y. Ishida (Tokyo Toritsu University) intends to publish an article on the general history of Japanese planning, the first of its kind to be written by a single person.[9] This brief paper, like the first mentioned work, covers neatly the major topics centring on statutory planning, but adds some new facts of the author's finding. Ishida has compiled a concise chronological list, and included it in his article.

A reference should be made also to Professor H. Kawakami's (Tokyo University) chronological list of Japanese modern planning.[10] It was originally prepared as the appendix to the first mentioned work, and Kawakami has revised and updated it for his students. Now it is the richest listing of planning-related events at international, national, and local levels from 1868 to 1976. A careful reader of this detailed list would be able to find a number of possible research topics in modern planning history. However, comprehensive bibliographies in Japanese planning history can hardly be said to exist. Probably the nearest work would be the present writer's unpublished data sheets containing some 200 Japanese 'classic' titles since the Meiji period with their detailed information.[11] The Tokyo Institute of Municipal Research (*Tokyo Shisei Chosa-kai*), which possesses a library that is indispensable for historical research on Japan's modern planning, has compiled a catalogue of its collection about Tokyo.[12] Tokyo Toritsu University has published several bibliographical lists of books and articles in planning history, urban history and urban studies.[13]

5   Research works: chronological

The Meiji period, with its historical significance as the starting point of modern Japan, greatly influenced by the West, reflecting the ambitions and agonies of a rising nation, has attracted the interest of historians and planners. Among them Professor H. Ishizuka (Tokyo Toritsu University), stands out, having made several contributions to the study of urban history and planning history of this period. He is a socio-economic historian who seriously considers the crucial role of the city in the developmental process of Japanese capitalism. Ishizuka's main concern is Meiji Tokyo, upon which he has published several stimulating papers.[14] His interests range from urban social structure to urban problems, urban policy, and even urban planning. He has written a brief general history of Meiji planning,[15] and two papers on the Tokyo City Improvement Programme, one analysing the planning process of the Programme,[16] and the other examining the Council-bourgeoisie relationship over the water-works programme.[17] It may be fair to say that Ishizuka is a pioneer in modern urban history, an expert in the local history of Tokyo, and a great stimulus to other students of planning history.

In connection with the Tokyo City Improvement Programme, two more papers are worthy of mention. K. Ogura has published a series of articles on the Tokyo City Improvement Programme, based upon his analysis of a wealth of materials including parliamentary records.[18] In a paper published in English, Professor Kawakami elucidated the scheme's basic character by comparing four plans which were prepared during the entire programme.[19]

A. Fujimori (Tokyo University) has recently discovered German records concerning architects Ende and Boeckmann, who participated in the government blocks project in 1886. He has successfully reconstructed the whole story of this rather forgotten project.[20] Fujimori concludes that the idea of this project was originally conceived by the Ministry of Foreign Affairs, which wanted to have a grand seat for the central government, but was turned down by the Home Ministry, which had the hegemony in planning administration and did not want such a costly project. He further argues that this aborted project has great historical significance because any planning efforts in the Meiji period should be evaluated by their intention to change the physical structure of Castle-Town Edo into that of the modern city.

Fujimori seems to reflect some aspects of the architectural historians' approach. He attaches importance to the role of 'heroes', be they architects, politicans, or critics, in determining the physical structure of the city, but he shows little interest in the role of legislative controls or that of the common people. In a sense, Meiji Japan was controlled by a small number of the political and business elite, often very attractive figures, and their personal ideas, interests, and influences were crucial in urban policy and development. This is quite different from the following Taisho era, when bureaucracy was firmly established and many fragmented interests and powers were liable to influence the formation of urban structure.

The Taisho-Early Showa period (1912–30) is the formative period for Japan's planning system. The present writer considers this period to be crucial in any attempt to examine the characteristics of Japanese planning.[21] His hypothesis is that the social character of a planning system of a country is strongly influenced and even biased by the socio-historical context in which that system is institutionalized for the first time. This seemed evident from historical studies of America's modern urban planning and how it developed out of the various reform movements of the late nineteenth and early twentieth centuries, with the ideologies and interests of the downtown merchants and the emerging middle-class suburbanites being brought into it. Physical determinism, middle-class bias, the idea of 'community' as a mutual defence institution of 'haves' versus 'have-nots':[22] all these are familiar themes of recent studies. The planners' so-called *apolitical* stance was in fact a very *political* stance. Most of these themes were heavily challenged in the 1960s, a period which is considered a turning point in America's modern planning.

It is an interesting fact that these themes have been held valid for over half a century. It may be that planning legislation and bureaucracy, once established, will form a framework which will basically control later planning systems. In countries with a strong tradition of professionalism like the U.S. and Britain, the ideology which the first generation of a profession brings into the planning system will be transmitted to the succeeding generations through professional activities and training. All this implies the importance of the formative period of the planning system.

Thus, one of the most important research areas of Japanese planning history seems to be the Old Act planning system. Crucial questions would centre around the concept of 'city planning' (*toshi keikaku*), such as: how did pioneer planners develop and formulate the concept? In what sense was it different from the concept of 'city improvement' (*shiku kaisei*)? Which Western country had the strongest influence upon the formulation of the Japanese concept? How and why was the Japanese concept different from the Western one?

There is no research directly answering these questions but three works are worth mentioning. Professor S. Takagi (Kokugakuin University) has published an article sketching the background of the enactment of the Old Act, and the characteristics of the legislation and its operation.[23] S. Fukuoka has written a stimulating article on the origin, development and collapse of the 'housing-planning vision', which was put forward by Goto Shimpei, Ikeda Hiroshi, and their group, (*Toshi Kenkyu-kai*) in the early Taisho era.[24] Professor S. Akagi's (Tokyo Toritsu University) contribution is a detailed analysis of the enactment process of the Old Act and an interpretation of why the Act lost its comprehensive character.[25]

Furthermore, the Old Act planning system could be analysed from several other approaches, such as: the Home Ministry's role in planning; the role of men like Ikeda Hiroshi, Goto Shimpei, and other pioneers; and the impact of the British Garden City theory. (All these topics will be discussed in the following 'thematic' section.) Other topics would include: the suburbanization which the Act aimed to control; public health, welfare, and housing issues and the Act; and the land problem and the Act.

The last topic concerns more specifically the treatment of land value increments (British 'betterment') due to urban planning and development. What did the Old Act intend to do with, and how did it actually deal with, the increments? Who gained and who lost under that planning system? The answers to these questions would clarify the economic and political backgrounds and the social characteristics of the Old Act planning system. It seems the Japanese rule has been a *private* recovery of land value increments as in the U.S., which is quite contrary to the British idea of *public* recoupment of betterment.

The Kanto Earthquake Reconstruction Programme (1923–30) is an unavoidable topic in this period. Although there are a few writings on this topic, its significance relative to planning history has hardly been recognized. Did the programme reinforce or damage the Old Act planning system? Or did it have nothing to do with it? In addition to these questions, the reconstruction programme has another interesting aspect. Charles A. Beard (1874–1948)[26], a noted American scholar of public administration, visited Japan before and after the earthquake of 1923. He was invited by Baron Goto, then Mayor of Tokyo, who as the Home Minister had pushed through the enactment of the Old Act. Beard's recommendations for the reconstruction programme, with a strong flavour of America's progressive ideology, were not accepted by the people and the Government. This case provides an interesting example of how it is extremely difficult to transplant a planning system to completely different soil.

The Wartime period (1930–45) has produced few considerable achievements in planning practice, and therefore little attention and few works in planning history. This marks a sharp contrast with the British wartime period, during which it is possible to discover the origins of the epoch-making 1947 Act system. For Japanese wartime planning, only a very brief general history has been written by Professor K. Kawana (Nihon Joshi University).[27] Regional and national planning was a fashionable topic then, and S. Sugai, who participated in national planning, has published its history and compiled related documents.[28] Professor A. Sato's (Seikei University) book on regional development in Japan also contains an historical review starting with the Hokkaido Colonialization Plan in the Meiji era, the Tohoku Region Development Plan in the early Showa era, and wartime regional and nation planning.[29] Another topic for this period is Japanese planning in colonies and occupied areas abroad, and A. Koshizawa (Tokyo University) has done preliminary research on planning in Manchuria.[30]

The Post-War period (1945–present) has now lasted for well over three decades, a period longer than the two preceding periods combined. It is naturally a very important standpoint from which historians can look back at history. Yet it has attracted little historical interest so far, probably because it is too recent to be an object of any historical study. Professors Kawakami and Ishida have made a useful review of the reconstruction period, relating ideas about planning to the reconstruction programme until 1960.[31] Ishida also published an interesting article on Tokyo War-Damage Reconstruction Planning.[32]

Planning history after the late 1950s is not yet written. Efforts must be made to analyse the role of urban planning in that boom age. After all, it has been over a decade since the New Act was enacted. The time is ripe to follow the process of its enactment because those who participated in it still remember it and many of them are now in positions in which they are free to tell what they did, and why.

6   Research works: thematic

The following is a list of research works on various topics which the foregoing chronological section could not cover adequately.

The historical account of urban land and population, the very basic information for urban and planning history, is crucially lacking. One of the few works is Professor S. Kobayashi's (Yokohama National University) doctorate dissertation analysing Tokyo's land ownership in the early Meiji, late Meiji and Taisho eras.[33]

Zoning, which was institutionalized by the Old Act, is the most important tool for land-use control, but has been rather neglected until recently. Kobayashi made an intensive survey of zoning literature,[34] from which he has been writing some papers.[35] R. Horiuchi (Tokyo Metropolitan Government) has recently published a book on the past and future of zoning in Tokyo, viewed from the perspective of a planning bureaucrat.[36] Professor Ishida, whose interest in planning history is rooted in his research concerning the control of urban sprawl, made an analysis of the historical development of zoning techniques.[37]

Land consolidation is probably a unique Japanese invention. It is a planning tool so widely used for so many years that it is often called 'the mother of urban planning' especially by its advocates. Yet no history, except for R. Iwami's preliminary work,[38] has been written on the changing concept of land consolidation and its significance in Japanese planning history. However, building-line control was recently picked up as an object of historical study by Professor Ishida and T. Ikeda.[39]

Housing is obviously a field strongly related to planning, and yet both have tended to develop as distinctly different fields in Japan as in many other countries. Professor Kawana has produced a general history of housing problems, issues and policies mainly for Tokyo from the late Tokugawa to the post-war boom period.[40] Considering the increasing public interest in housing and residential environment, more historical studies seem to be needed in this field.

Japan may be the only country in the world where anti-disaster planning is considered as a legitimate field in urban planning. Yet, other than H. Sugiyama's preliminary survey of the literature,[41] hardly any historical studies have been undertaken. This is another frontier for planning historians.

The impact of the British Garden City theory upon Japanese planning is another interesting topic, but again few works are available except for those of the present writer who researched into it, beginning with a case study of Japan's Garden City Co., Ltd (1918–28), which developed into one of the best suburbs in Tokyo. He has analysed how Ebenezer Howard's original concept was used, misused and not used in the actual Japanese situation. This paper is available in English.[42] Another paper was devoted to the historical analysis of the first introduction of the Garden City idea to Japan by the Home Ministry in 1907.[43] It was found that the Ministry bureaucrats had encountered the idea via A. R. Sennett, not Howard, and that they had made use of the idea, not as a planning matter but as propaganda for the Local Improvement Movement, which they were then promoting.

The Home Ministry, as was suggested earlier, may be a key to understanding the unique characteristics of Japanese planning. Until the end of the war, the Ministry was responsible not only for planning but also building, housing, engineering, local government, police and other domestic administration. So a wide range of historians and social scientists should have been concerned with the Ministry, but there is a notable absence of such studies. The reason is obvious. At the end of the war, the Ministry's documents were either destroyed by the officials or confiscated by the occupation force. And, to make matters worse, Japanese scholars have simply accepted the condemnation that the Ministry was the stronghold of militarism. Some recent trends, however, are encouraging. A four-volume history of the Home Ministry was compiled by its 'alumni'.[44] Professor K. B. Pyle (University of Washington) has presented his unique interpretations of the important role played by the Ministry bureaucrats in the nation's modernization process.[45] M. Miyachi (Tokyo University), in his book on political history after the Russo-Japanese War, analyses the local improvement programme and its historical background.[46]

The promoters of the Old Act planning system, as was stressed in Fukuoka's work, were those people centring around the *Toshi Kenkyu-Kai*. Stationed at the Home Ministry, the group campaigned for urban planning with Goto's political leadership and Ikeda's theoretical contributions. Ikeda Hiroshi (1881–1939) was not only the draftsman of the Old Act, but also the top bureaucrat, theorist, and critic in the mid-Taisho and early Showa periods. In a sense, he was the embodiment of the Old Act planning system. A huge collection of his publications is available and his biography has now been co-written by Y. Sadayuki and the present author.[47] A summary of his life as related to his writings is also available.[48] Other planning pioneers in the Meiji and Taisho eras are waiting for their life and thoughts to be recorded and their role in planning history evaluated.[49]

Urban thought, as expressed by people outside the planning field, constitutes another interesting subject. Dr T. Shibata (Tokyo Metropolitan Government) has been studying the thoughts of such opinion leaders in the Meiji and Taisho eras as Mori Ogai, Katayama Sen, Abe Isoo, Taguchi Ukichi, Goto Shimpei and Charles A. Beard.[50] H. Toki has recently published an article analysing Katayama's 'urban socialism' (*toshi shakai-shugi*).[51]

Local cities are another neglected topic in planning history. Cities in Hokkaido, for instance, are mostly 'new towns' built after the Meiji period in an American-style gridiron pattern as in the notable case of Sapporo. The planning and building of these cities preceded national planning legislation. So far, most planners have been preoccupied by the problems of, and the planning for, Tokyo. Here again there is a need for 'relativizing' Tokyo's planning in the national context, and for researching the planning history of other cities. Professor T. Tamaki (Osaka Kogyo University), for example, a one-time Ministry planner and now an urban historian of castle-towns and Osaka, is publishing a series of articles on the construction history of Osaka from the ancient to the present times. Here, the planning in post-Meiji Osaka is well documented.[52]

Tokyo, again, has a wealth of research works devoted to it. Professor Ishizuka's paper on the socio-economic history of Tokyo is a unique contribution to the general urban history of Tokyo.[53] Covering the crucial period between the restoration and the earthquake. Ishizuka portrays this huge urban system and its capitalistic development from the viewpoint of the urban masses. The book is a readable local history of Tokyo and provides informative socio-historical background against which Tokyo's urban planning has emerged. Another unique contribution about Tokyo was made by Professor H. D. Smith (University of California, Santa Barbara), whose strong weapons are linguistic structurism and fully mastered Japanese. In his 'Tokyo as an ideal: an exploration of Japanese urban thought until 1945',[54] Smith successfully restructures the Japanese concept of the 'city' out of the unconsciously conceived one. Following his analysis of the structure of Japanese traditional urban thought, Smith subdivides modern Tokyo's history as: Restoration Tokyo – the city as a showcase, 1868–1900: Streetcar Tokyo – the city as a problem, 1895–1923; Post-earthquake Tokyo – the city as a modern life, 1923–37; Wartime Tokyo, 1931–45. Professor Smith has recently extended his analysis of the conception of the city to a comparative study of Tokyo and London.[55] Written in English and full of unique interpretations, this paper should have a special interest for British readers.

Although most academic writing is in Japanese, a number of British and American Ph.D. candidates have written their dissertations on various aspects of urban history, not necessarily planning history, of modern Japan. They include Hoare's Japanese treaty ports,[56] Staubitz's local government in Meiji,[57] Hayase's career of Goto,[58] and Downard's Tokyo in the depression years.[59] In addition, other useful writings are also available in English, such as Professor D. Kornhauser's (University of Hawaii) *Urban Japan: Its foundations and growth*,[60] and Professor G. D. Allison's (University of Pittsburgh) *Japanese Urbanism: Industry and politics in Kariya, 1872–1972*[61] and 'Japanese cities in the industrial era'.[62]

In conclusion, this survey shows that planning history in Japan is still in a formative stage. More efforts are made for finding historical facts than interpreting them, and it is in this matter of interpretation that foreign scholars would be able to contribute greatly to Japanese planning history by means of a comparative approach.

Shun-ichi Watanabe
Building Research Institute, Ministry of Construction, Japan

Notes

This paper is an expansion of: Shun-ichi Watanabe, 'Planning History in Japan', unpublished paper presented at the American Historical Association, San Francisco, December, 1978.

1   To the writer's knowledge, professors teaching planning history are as follows: Prof. H. Kawakami (Dept of Urban Engineering, Tokyo University), Prof. S. Ishihara (Dept of Social Engineering, Tokyo Institute of Technology), Prof. Y. Ishida (Dept of Architecture, Tokyo Toritsu University), Prof. M. Tajima (Dept of Social Engineering, Tsukuba University).

2   Meiji, Taisho, Showa represent three successive emperors of modern Japan, the present Showa era starting in 1926.

3   John W. Hall, 'The Castle Town and Japan's modern urbanization', in John W. Hall and Marius B. Jansen (eds), *Studies in the Institutional History of Early Japan* (Princeton, N.J., 1968), 169–88.

4   *Urban History Newsletter* (Group in Comparative Urban History, July 1975). The group is represented by Professor K. Ugawa (Faculty of Economics, St Paul's (Rikkyō) University).

5   Toshi Keikaku-shi Kenkyū-kai, 'Nihon Kindai Toshi Keikaku-shi Kenkyū no Shuppatsu ni Mukete', *Tochi Jūtaku Mondai*, liv (February 1979), 37–46.

6   *Ibid.*, 'Nihon Kindai Toshi Keikaku-shi Kenkyū Bunken List', *Tochi Jūtaku Mondai*, lv (March 1979), 64–76.

7   Nihon Kenchiku Gakkai (ed.), *Kindai Nihon Kenchiku-gaku Hattatsu-shi* (Maruzen Shoten, 1972), Part 6 'Toshi Keikaku,' 975–1114.

8   Uzō Nishiyama and Shōji Yoshino, 'Toshi Keikaku Gakusetsu-shi Gaisetsu', in Yoshikatsu Kawano (ed.), *Toshi Jichi Gakusetsu-shi Gaisetsu: Tokyo Shisei Shōsa-kai 50 Shūnen Kinen Ronbun-shū* (Tokyo Shisei Chosa-kai, 1973), 100–29.

9   Yorifusa Ishida, 'Chiiki Keikaku-Toshi Keikaku no Rekishi', in *Kenchiku-gaku Binran* (Maruzen Shoten, 1979 as scheduled), I. 'Planning', part 5 'City planning', chapter 1.

10   Hidemitsu Kawakami, 'Kindai Nihon Toshi Keikaku-shi Nenpyō' (lecture material, 1978).

11   Shun-ichi Watanabe, 'Meiji-Taisho-ki Toshi Keikaku Bunken Shiryō Card', unpublished paper.

12   Tokyo Shisei Chosa-kai Shuto Kenkyū-jo (ed.), *Tokyo ni Kansuru Bunken Mokuroku* (Shuto Kenkyu-jo, 1964).

13   Fumihiko Isshiki *et al* (eds), *Toshi-shi Toshi Keikaku-shi Kenkyū Bunken Mokuroku: Nihon-hen* (Tokyo Toritsu Daigaku Toshi Kenkyū Iinkai, 1971).

14   Hiromichi Ishizuka, 'Meiji Shoki no Tokyo ni okeru Cholera-byō Taisaku to Minshū (1): Toshi Seisaku-shi Kenkyū Oboegaki', *Jinbun Gakuhō* (Tokyo Toritsu University), cxiv (March 1976), 87–106; and 'Meiji-ki no Toshi Kenkyū: Tokyo ni Tsuite', *Iwanami Kōza Nihon Rekishi Geppō*, xiv (June 1976), 1–3; and 'Dokusen Dankai no Toshi Mondai: 1900 Nendai Hajime no Tokyo o Taishō to shite', *Jinbun Gakuhō*, cxviii (March 1977), 97–116; and '"Fukoku Kyōhei-gata" Toshi Tokyo no Seiritsu: "Tokyo-shi" Kenkyū no Hōhō Kasetsu to shite', *Sōgō Toshi Kenkyū*, vi (1977), 3–10.

15   *Ibid.*, 'Meiji-ki ni okeru Toshi Keikaku: Tokyo ni Tsuite,' in Tokyo Toritsu Daigaku Toshi Kenkyū-kai (ed.), *Toshi Kōzō to Toshi Keikaku* (Tokyo, 1968), 481–97.

16   *Ibid.*, '19 Seiki ni okeru Tokyo Kaizō-ron to Chikkō Mondai', *Toshi Kenkyū Hōkoku*, xxii (1971), 33–59.

17   *Ibid.*, 'Tokyo Shiku Kaisei Jigyo-shi Kenkyū Josetsu: Jōsuido Kairyō Jigyō to Shikai-Bourgeoisie no Ugoki o Megutte', *Toshi Kenkyū Hōkoku*, lv (1975), 23–35.

18   Kuraji Ogura, 'Tokyo Shiku Kaisei Jōrei Zengo (I), (II), (II), (Supplement)', *Toshi Mondai*, lv, 6–9 (June-September 1964).

19 Hidemitsu Kawakami, 'Tokyo City Improvement Program, 1884–1918', unpublished paper presented at the First International Conference on the History of Urban and Regional Planning, London, September 1977.

20 Terunobu Fujimori, 'Ende-Boeckmann ni yoru Kanchō Shūchū Keikaku no Kenkyū (1)', Nihon Kenchiku Gakkai Ronbun Hōkoku-shū, cclxxi (September 1978).

21 Shun-ichi Watanabe, 'Toshi Keikaku-shi Kenkyu e no Izanai (An Invitation to the Research on Planning History)', Tochi Jūtaku Mondai, liii (January 1979), 35–43.

22 Shun-ichi Watanabe, America Toshi Keikaku to Komyniti Rinen (American Urban Planning and the Community Ideal) (Tokyo: Gihōdō, 1977).

23 Shōsaku Takagi, 'Toshi Keikaku-hō', in Nihon Kindai-hō Hattatsu-shi, vol. X (Keisō Shobō, 1960).

24 Shunji Fukuoka, 'Taishō-kiino Toshi Seisaku: Jūtaku Toshi Keikaku Kōso no Tenkai (1)–(3)', Tokyo Toritsu Daigaku Hōgakkai Zasshi, xi, 2 (March 1971), 243–97; xii, 1 (October 1971), 219–72; xiii, 1 (October 1972), 1–81.

25 Suruki Akagi, 'Toshi Keikaku no Keikaku-sei', in Toshi Kōzō to Toshi Keikaku, 499–566.

26 Charles A. Beard, The Administration and Politics of Tokyo: A survey and opinions (New York, 1923).

27 Kichiemon Kawana, 'Shōwa Shoki no Toshi Keikaku', in Toshi Kōzō to Toshi Keikaku, 567–76.

28 Shirō Sugai, Kokudo Keikaku no Keika to Kadai (Taimeido, 1975). idem, (ed.), Shiryō Kokudo Keikaku (Taimeido, 1975).

29 Atsushi Satō, Nihon no Chiiki Kaihatsu (Miraisha, 1965).

30 Akira Koshizawa, Shokuminchi Manshū no Toshi Keikaku (Asia Kenkyu-jo, 1978).

31 Hidemitsu Kawakami and Yoshifusa Ishida, 'Henbō suru Toshi: Tenki o Mukaeta Sengo Nihon no Toshi Keikaku', in Kenchiku Nenkan, 1960 (Bijutsu Shuppansha, 1960).

32 Yorifusa Ishida, 'Daitoshi-Ken no Hattatsu to Keikaku: Sengo no Tokyo Daitoshi Keikaku no Hensen', in Toshi Kōzō to Toshi Keikaku, 621–64.

33 Shigetaka Kobayashi, Toshi Keisei to Tochi Shoyū: Toshi-chi Tochi Shoyū Jōkyō to Toshi Keisei ni kansuru JisshōtekivKenkyū (Ph.D. dissertation, Tokyo University, 1970).

34 Ibid., 'Yōto Kisei no Hensen ni kansuru Bunken Chōsa oyobi Jakkan no Kōsatsu', in Kenchiku-butsu Yōto Jittai Chōsa Hōkoku-sho (Housing Bureau, Ministry of Construction, 1977), part 3, 119–66.

35 Ibid., 'Waga-kuni ni okeru Yōto Kisei no Rekishi-teki Hensen ni kansuru Kenkyu: Yoto Kisei Keimō-ki o Chūshin ni', Nihon Tochi Keikaku Gukkai Gakujutsu Kenkyū Happyō-Kai Ronbun-shū, xiii (1978), 289–94.

36 Ryōichi Horiuchi, Toshi Keikaku to Yōto Chiikisei: Tokyo-to ni okeru Sono Enkaku to Tenbō (Nishida Shoten, 1978).

37 Yorifusa Ishida, 'Nihon ni okeru Shigaika Yokusei no Tame no Chiikisei no Hatten: 1945 Nen made', in Toshi Keikaku to Kyojū Kankyō: Kawana Kichiemon Sensei Taikan Kinen Ronbun-shū (Tokyo Toritsu Daigaku Toshi Keikaku Kenkyū-shitsu, 1978), 181–202.

38 Ryōtaro Iwami, Tochi Kukaku Seiri no Kenkyū: Kukakū Seiri no Mondaiten to Sono Kōzō (Jichitai Kenkyūsha, 1978).

39 Yorifusa Ishida and Takayuki Ikeda, 'Kenchiku-sen Seido ni kansuru Kenkyū (1)', Sōgō Toshi Kenkyū, vi (1979), 33–72.

40 Kichiemon Kawana, 'Jutaku Mondai no Tenkai', in Toshi Kōzō to Toshi Keikaku, 283–384.

41 Hiromu Sugiyama, 'Toshi Bōsai-ron no Keifu: Toshi Saigai Taisaku ni kansuru Ronsetsu no Shiteki Kōsatsu', Toshi Keikaku, lxxxix (1976), 7–17.

42 Shun-ichi Watanabe, 'Nihon-teki Den-en Toshi-Ron no Kenkyū (1): Den-en Toshi Kabushiki Kaisha (1918–28) no Baai', Nihon Toshi Keikaku Gakkai Gakujutsu Kenkyū Happyō-Kai Ronbun-shū, xii (1977), 151–6. An English version is: idem, 'Garden City Japanese style: the case of Garden City Co., 1918–1928', unpublished paper presented at the First International Conference on the History of Urban and Regional Planning, London, September, 1977. A further revised version will appear in Gordon E. Cherry (ed.), Planning and the Environment in the Modern World. Vol. 2, Shaping an Urban World: Planning in the Twentieth Century (forthcoming).

43 Shun-ichi Watanabe, 'Nihon-teki Den-en Toshi Ron no Kenkyu II, Naimushō chihō Kyoku Yūshi (ed.), Den-en Toshi (1907) o Meggute', Nihon Toshi Keikaku Gakkai Gakujutsu Kenkyū Happyō-kai Ronbun-shū, xiii (1978), 283–8.

44 Taikakai Naimushō-shi Henshū Iinkai (ed.), Naimushō-shi (4 vols, Taikakai, 1971).

45 Kenneth B. Pyle, 'The technology of Japanese nationalism: the local improvement movement, 1900–1918', Journal of Asian Studies, xxxiii, 1 (November 1973), 51–65; and idem, 'Advantage of followership: German economics and Japanese bureaucarats, 1890–1925', Journal of Japanese Studies, vi, 1 (Autumn 1974), 127–64.

46 Masato Miyaji, *Nichi-Ro Sengo Seiji-shi no Kenkyū: Teikokushugi Keisei-ki no Toshi to Nōson* (Tokyo, 1973).

47 Shun-ichi Watanabe and Yasuhiro Sadayuki, 'Ikeda Hiroshi Den Shiron,' *Tochi Jūtaku Mondai*, lvi (April 1979).

48 To appear as: *idem*, 'Chosaku Jidai Kubun kara Mita Ikeda Hiroshi no Shōgai', *Nihon Toshi Keikaku Gakkai Gakujutsu Kenkyū Happyō-kai Ronbun-shū*, xiv (1979).

49 These pioneers other than Ikeda and Gotō would include: Seki Hajime, Kataoka Yasushi, Sano Riki, Uchida Shōzō, Kasahara Toshirō, Iinuma Kazumi (Issei), Takei Kōshirō, Ishikawa Hideaki (Eiyō).

50 Tokuei Shibata, 'Nihon no Toshi Shisō', in *Nihon no Toshi Seisaku* (Yuhikaku, 1978), part 1, chapter 2.

51 Hiroshi Toki, 'Meiji Toshi Shakai-shugi no Shatei: Katayama Sen o Chūshin ni', *Toshi Mondai*, lxx, 4 (April 1979), 90–110.

52 One of the recent articles is: Toyojirō Tamaki, 'Osaka Kensetsu-shi Yawa, 22: Meiji Jidai no Osaka no Taika Kiroku to Kenchiku Torishimari Kisoku', *Osaka-jin*, xxxii, 4 (April 1978), 42–50. Also see: *idem*, 'Osaka no Toshi Keisei to Toshi Keikaku no Tokusei', *Toshi Keikaku*, lxxxiv (1975), 6–17.

53 Hiromichi Ishizuka, *Tokyo no Shakai Keizai-shi: Shinon-shugi to Toshi Mondai* (Kinokuniya Shoten, 1977).

54 Henry D. Smith II, 'Tokyo as an idea: an exploration of Japanese urban thought until 1945', *Journal of Japanese Studies*, iv, 1 (Winter 1978), 45–80.

55 *Ibid.*, 'Tokyo and London: comparative conceptions of the city', in Albert Craig (ed.), *Japan: A comparative view* (Princeton, N. J., (1979), 49–99.

56 James Edward Hoare, 'The Japanese treaty ports, 1968–1899: a study of the foreign settlements (Ph. D. Dissertation, University of London, 1971).

57 Richard Louis Staubitz, 'The establishment of the system of local self-government (1880–1890) in Meiji Japan: Yamagata Aritomo and the meaning of "Jichi"' (Ph. D. dissertation, Yale University, 1973).

58 Yukiko Hayase, 'The career of Gotō Shimpei: Japan's statesman of research, 1857–1929' (Ph. D. dissertation, Florida State University, 1974).

59 Douglas J. Downard, 'Tokyo: the depression years' (Ph. D. dissertation, Indiana University, 1976).

60 David Kornhauser, *Urban Japan: Its foundations and growth* (London and New York, 1976).

61 Gary D. Allinson, *Japanese Urbanism: Industry and politics in Kariya, 1872–1972* (Los Angeles and London, 1975).

62 *Ibid.*, 'Japanese cities in the industrial era', *Journal of Urban History*, iv, 4 (August 1978), 443–76.

Decline and decay in late medieval towns: a look at some of the concepts and arguments[1]

The fortunes of late medieval towns seem to have become rather a contentious topic.[2] That is probably a good thing. It is a poor historical proposition that cannot be illustrated by *some* evidence, but proof of an historical phenomenon like general decline or decay requires something more than illustration and something that argument may help to secure. So far, however, as S. H. Rigby points out,[3] the debate has suffered from an uncertainty over terms that may frustrate the advance of knowledge and understanding. Two words which he did not mention but which seem to me particularly unclear are 'decline' and 'decay' themselves. Until they are examined more closely we may not be sure enough of what anyone is trying to prove to know whether he has succeeded or not.

The arguments about urban decline or decay are closely connected with the generally accepted view that a fall in population during the later Middle Ages caused a fall in economic activity. The word 'decline' for this fall in population has the authority of Postan,[4] but it may be misleading, for, although it suggests a steady downward trend, it continues to be used by some who think that, however much population dropped in the fourteenth century, it was no longer falling in the fifteenth.[5] It is not always clear whether those who refer to 'declining population' really mean what Saltmarsh, with admirable clarity, called 'not simply a population that had fallen, but one which was falling progressively'.[6] This is particularly important when one comes to consider the economic effects of population changes. If population was static (or 'stagnant', though that makes it sound more sinister), or even if it fluctuated, should we expect that the economy as a whole, or urban economies in general, continued to contract? Though J. H. Hatcher argues forcefully that population continued to decline throughout the fifteenth century, the scale of the decrease which he himself postulates is still not such as to make its economic impact very easy to assess[7] and some of the evidence he adduces might serve as well to explain failure to rise as to explain an actual decline. Even if one takes the steepest possible curve within his 'plausible estimates' of decline, is it clear that fifteenth-century England was subject to 'prolonged and remorseless demographic attrition ... capable of explaining the ubiquity of the urban malaise'?[8] If it is not, is there any other *general* cause which can do so? Are we after all sure that the 'malaise' was general, or are we just looking for evidence which will illustrate a malaise that we expect to be general because the concept of 'declining population' invites us to do so?

Everyone agrees that some towns had periods of prosperity. York and Coventry, the respective starting-points for Dobson's and Phythian-Adams's impressive surveys of the evidence of decline and decay both seem to have done well until about the middle of the fifteenth century.[9] The problem is to decide which times, and which towns, were typical and which exceptional. Distance telescopes time for us, but the 'later Middle Ages' cover a long stretch, even before they are extended to include most of the sixteenth century. Given the scarcity of demographic evidence between the Black Death and the 1520s it is not surprising that we keep harking back to the earlier fourteenth century for comparisons,[10] but we should not assume that people in the fifteenth century did the same. Even if (as seems probable) most towns were smaller and less rich than they had been in 1300 that does not necessarily mean that they were all 'in decline' in the fifteenth century or that the long-term demographic trends were the chief determinants of the fortunes of individual places. Historians love origins and long-term trends and perhaps nowadays we are particularly drawn to them when they are gloomy. Nevertheless, to discount periods of urban prosperity in the late Middle Ages as fleeting, almost illusory 'Indian summers' may be like discounting the nineteenth-century growth of the British empire because of the loss of the American colonies in the eighteenth and the dissolution of the whole thing in the twentieth.

The previous paragraph, moreover, illustrates a further difficulty in that one is tempted to slide (rather than to reason) not only from population to the economy but from economic activity to prosperity. The questions Rigby asked about economic growth in a late medieval context apply equally, or more, to prosperity. What does it mean and how does one prove it – or its opposite? Is one talking about a change in the total wealth of a town, in the number or wealth of its richest citizens, or in the mean or modal income or standard of living of everyone? It is this sort of uncertainty, and emphatically not the desire for a soggy compromise or 'neutralist text-book orthodoxy' that makes me want the evidence looked at more closely. Dobson and Phythian-Adams have presented a strong case.[11] It is not only based on much evidence but has the vital scholarly merit of being firm enough (once a few fuzzy edges to some of the terms are clarified) to be testable. The next stage in advancing knowledge is to test it – that is, not merely to accumulate convergent illustrations but to see how much evidence can be found to modify or contradict it and how much is equally, or more, compatible with alternative explanations. To doubt the proposition, or parts of it, meanwhile is not to impugn the scholarship of its proponents. It is a scholarly duty and a compliment to the stimulating quality of their work.

There are many points which need further examination. The evidence of fine private houses and the chronology of their building in, for instance, Lynn and Southampton, suggest that falling overseas trade (or its monopoly by aliens) did not impoverish the burgesses as much as has been thought.[12] As more evidence of buildings emerges, it is important not to close our minds to its significance – either way. Some evidence is hard to interpret chronologically: churches are unlikely to be closed, for example, until some time after their congregations have shrunk, so that closure need not imply (though it may) that things are still getting worse. Phythian-Adams sees no need to doubt the reluctance of substantial citizens to fill posts of fiscal responsibility and Dobson says that examples 'derived from published town records alone could be multiplied *ad nauseam*',[13] but we have no right to take even their words, based on even their knowledge of the sources, on trust. We need to weigh the evidence – to know how often fines were actually imposed and whether the records will show the problem to have been more serious in some places or some decades than in others.[14] Similarly, we now have a number of cases in which the reduction of tax quotas or fee-farms is prima facie likely to reflect genuine poverty, but alternative explanations cannot be eliminated merely because we have evidence – even a lot of evidence – to support an explanation already propounded by good scholars. A. P. M. Wright's study, the most detailed that I have consulted, suggests that Exchequer procedures themselves accounted for some of the apparent difficulties in payment. That may be partly because he was interested in governmental procedures and relations between Crown and boroughs rather than in economic trends, but if the fiscal system (along perhaps with other political trends of the time) encouraged a tax-evasion culture, then the use of the fiscal evidence must take that into account.[15] Another detailed study which I for one have ignored until too recently is that on Battle by Eleanor Searle. Here several types of evidence which might on their own suggest decline (loss of privileges, abandonment of the market place and hall, investment in rural rather than urban property) go along with seemingly 'solid prosperity' until the Dissolution.[16] If Battle suffered thereafter, as seems highly probable, it was not apparently as the last stage in a long decay.

The debate is on. With the Dobson/Phythian-Adams thesis to guide and stimulate research we should learn much more about late medieval towns – particularly if we concentrate on refining and testing hypotheses and do not treat them as labels which, however we interpret them, enable us to accept or reject the whole package without further enquiry about what it really contains.

Susan Reynolds
Lady Margaret Hall, University of Oxford

Notes

1   Professor R. B. Dobson and Mr C. V. Phythian-Adams have kindly both read this paper in typescript, though no doubt they disagree with much of it. Mr Phythian-Adams also allowed me to read *Desolation of a City* in proof and to refer to it.
2   S. H. Rigby, 'Urban decline in the later Middle Ages', A. Dyer, 'Growth and decay in English towns 1500–1700', and C. V. Phythian-Adams, 'Dr Dyer's urban undulations', all in *Urban History Yearbook* (1979); also D. M. Palliser, 'A crisis in English towns? The case of York, 1460–1640', *Northern History*, xiv (1978), 108–25.
3   S. H. Rigby, *Urban History Yearbook* (1979), 56–7.
4   M. M. Postan, 'Some economic evidence of declining population in the later middle ages', *Economic History Review*, 2nd ser., ii (1950), 221–65 (or as 'Some agrarian evidence . . .' in *Essays on Medieval Agriculture*, 1973).
5   e.g. J. R. Lander, *Conflict and Stability in Fifteenth-Century England* (1969), 22, 28, 35; F. R. H. du Boulay, *An Age of Ambition* (1970), 32–6.
6   J. Saltmarsh, 'Plague and economic decline in England in the later Middle Ages', *Cambridge Historical Journal*, vii (1941), 30. Postan does not distinguish very clearly a population static in the fifteenth century from one still falling: Postan, *op. cit.*, 245.
7   J. H. Hatcher, *Plague, Population and the English Economy, 1348–1530* (1977), *passim*, especially 11, 12, 68–9, 73.
8   R. B. Dobson, 'Urban decline in late medieval England', *Transactions of the Royal Historical Society*, 5th ser., xxvii (1977), 20–1.
9   On York, *ibid.*, and Palliser, *op. cit.* On Coventry, C. V. Phythian-Adams, 'Urban decay in late medieval England', in P. Abrams and E. A. Wrigley (eds), *Towns in Societies* (1978), 159–85 and *idem, Desolation of a City: Coventry and the urban crisis of the late Middle Ages* (1979). It is not my intention to quarrel with the evidence of Coventry's (or York's) sixteenth-century troubles, let alone with Phythian-Adams's fascinating study of Coventry society, which seems to me to stand entirely independent of any argument about earlier decline there or general decline elsewhere.
10   I omit here the issue of declining or static population before 1348, but it should be noted that the 'Malthusian' thesis has not gone unchallenged. If there was a 'Malthusian' situation the Black Death in any case seems to have eliminated it, so that the situation was sufficiently changed to justify treating it as a separate problem.
11   Their arguments seem to me sufficiently similar to make it not improper, I hope, to consider them together in this way as making a single case.
12   V. Parker, *The Making of King's Lynn* (1971), 4–5, 11–12, 30, 166; C. Platt, *Medieval Southampton* (1973), 145–7, 152–71, 182–5, 203–4, 215–24; see also e.g. J. Campbell, 'Norwich' in M. D. Lobel and W. H. Johns (eds), *The Atlas of Historic Towns*, ii (1975), 16–17.
13   Phythian-Adams, 'Urban decay', *op. cit.* 164; Dobson, *op. cit.*, 14.
14   The evidence of reluctance in late fifteenth-century Worcester comes from the *fixing* of fines: A. D. Dyer, *The City of Worcester in the Sixteenth Century* (1973), 191; there is no evidence before the mid-sixteenth century to show whether they were imposed there. After that they were 'almost unknown': *ibid.*, 196. At Coventry no fines were apparently imposed before 1495: Phythian-Adams, *Desolation of a City*, op. cit., 47, 250–2, 287–8. Cf. Platt, *op. cit.*, 56–7, 176–7.
15   A. P. M. Wright, 'The relations between the king's government and the English cities and boroughs in the fifteenth century' (Ph. D. thesis, University of Oxford, 1965), 160–250. Dobson's comment (*op. cit.*, is fair but note e.g. pp. 172, 184, 192, 212, 222–4, 230–50. See also Platt, *op. cit.*, 169–75.
16   E. Searle, *Lordship and Community: Battle Abbey and its banlieu. 1066–1538* (1974), 351–66.

The topography of seventeenth-century London: a review of maps*

Since the mid-sixteenth century London has received attention from many map-makers and publishers. Before the arrival of the Ordnançe Survey, however, only a handful of London maps are both topographically reliable (in terms of contemporary technical ability) and based on original surveys. These are: the lost mid-Tudor copper-engraved map, original of the so-called 'Agas' woodcut map, Hollar's uncompleted map of 1661–6, Rocque's maps of London and its environs of the 1740s, and the two post-Fire maps considered here. Of this group only 'Agas' and Rocque's maps are familiar and fairly widely used by historians, although, one has to say, more often as book-illustrations for their ornamental and quaint character than for the information they give.

London historians are fortunate in having these two massive maps of the city, the earlier published by Ogilby and his partner Morgan (hereafter Ogilby) and the later by Morgan alone, taken shortly after the Fire of 1666 but preserving the essential structure of the medieval town. Both of these maps have been previously published in facsimile, in 1894 and 1904 respectively, but have been relatively little used, partly because of lack of confidence in their accuracy and topographical value and perhaps because of their sheer size and scale. Ogilby's 1677 City map measures about 8 by 5 feet when put together and Morgan's of Greater London (1681/2) about 8 by 6 feet. Also the facsimile of William Morgan's map (*London Etc.*) published by the London Topographical Society was taken from a later copy in the British Museum with heavy colouring over the ward and parish boundaries which obscured the engraved detail beneath. The title commonly used for this map in the past, of 'Morden and Lea', refers to this later B.M. edition. The unexpected appearance of a first edition of Morgan's map in 1967 (now in the Museum of London) made the present facsimile possible. This joint publishing venture by the Guildhall Library and Harry Margary has brought the two complementary maps of Ogilby and Morgan out again in a series of physically convenient formats (both as single sheets and bound sets), and at an accessible price. The intention of this article is to draw attention to their value for topographical studies.

In the crisis after the Fire of 1666 with its wholesale destruction of those properties on which virtually every city institution depended for income, it was immediately recognized that a survey of the burned area should be produced as quickly as possible. In *London Reviv'd* (1666), John Evelyn demanded both a relief map and 'some more particular iconographical plan of the whole city *membratim*' for planning purposes. In October 1666 the City, to speed up rebuilding and reduce disputes over property boundaries, employed surveyors to record every plot in the burnt area. Fair copies of their surveys, covering roughly two-thirds of this area and perhaps half of the City, have been published by the London Topographical Society (*Mills and Oliver's Survey*, vols. 1–5, between 1962 and 1966). These surveys can be pieced together to produce a detailed plan of much of the City before the Fire. Meanwhile, a general survey of the streets was made and engraved by Wenceslas Hollar, of which only a reduced version survives. However, there was as

* *A Large and Accurate Map of the City of London – John Ogilby and William Morgan: 1676 in 21 Sheets, with An Explanation of the Map   John Ogilby: 1677* (Harry Margary, 1976); and *London Etc. Actually Surveyed – including, A Prospect of London and Westminster – Taken at several Stations to the Southward thereof – William Morgan: 1681/2 in 16 sheets.* (Harry Margary, 1977).

Both maps are published in several formats, the cheapest, in sets of loose sheets, being £7.50 (Ogilby and Morgan) plus £3.50 for a bound copy of Ogilby's *Explanation*, and £10.00 for Morgan's *London Etc.*, to be ordered direct from Harry Margary, Lympne Castle, Kent.

yet no printed map of the City showing the post-Fire alterations.

The Scotsman John Ogilby had no formal background in cartography. His successive careers included being a dancing instructor, Master of the Revels in Ireland, theatre manager in Dublin, poet and successful publisher of lavishly-illustrated books. He was author of the 'Speeches, Songs and Inscriptions' for Charles II's coronation procession in 1661, following this up with a superbly-illustrated account of the coronation. By 1670 he was well-established as a publisher, despite severe losses in the Fire, and in that year received from the City of London the privileged grant of a shop in the newly-rebuilt Royal Exchange to promote his publications. His project of preparing a survey of the City to a uniquely large scale was only one of a series of such proposals in the post-Restoration flush of enthusiasm for semi-scientific publications. Customers and patrons interested in topography and geography had earlier bought his travel books about Cathay and other exotic spots, and volumes of his *English Atlas* on Africa, America and Asia appeared between 1670 and 1673. The British volumes, to be called the *Britannia*, were to include large-scale town surveys as well as road maps in strip-form. Although routes have been prepared in strip-form at least since the time of Matthew Paris, Ogilby was the first to present the information consistently and coherently with a full picture of the hazards and pleasures of a particular route, ancestor to the AA's route-guide.

By 1672 Ogilby was an experienced cartographic publisher, closely in touch with potential customers and, under the patronage of the City authorities, ideally placed to commission surveys of the capital. When Ogilby's surveyors (William Leybourne, John Holwell and Gregory King) started work, the process of domestic rebuilding was virtually complete. In April 1672, the busiest building month of the year, there were only 58 building 'starts' (as indicated by the foundation certificates) compared with 297 in April 1669. Ogilby was thus able to distinguish between house sites and their gardens or courtyard areas. He showed the sites of 35 forgotten churches which had been destroyed in the Fire and were not to be rebuilt, and the post-Fire street improvements such as the widening of Fleet Street, Cornhill and Cheapside.

His information as to two major improvements of the post-Fire City is fairly well borne out by other sources. The Thames Quay, a massive clearance of the medieval confusion of private wharves and warehouses along the river, was proposed by the City in emulation of the splendid open waterfront of Genoa, but was never fully realized although some owners did lay open their frontages. As the late Professor Redaway wryly commented 'no amount of poring over unreliable maps is likely to establish their exact dimensions' (*Rebuilding of London*, 238), but Ogilby does show the partial clearance achieved by 1676 and for one section, west of the Fleet River to the Temple Wall, his line corresponds exactly with a manuscript survey showing an alteration made in 1672–4. The Fleet Canal, another attempt to regularize and purify London's river frontages, is shown as though it were completed. Contemporary comments suggest that the embanking was never as wholesale as Ogilby's map shows.

Ogilby's survey received direct encouragement from the City authorities and he worked closely with some at least of the official surveyors. Robert Hooke's diary contains repeated references to discussions over half-engraved sheets of the map with Ogilby at Garraway's coffee house and elsewhere and it is said that Hooke proposed the scale adopted by Ogilby ('a Hundred Foot in an Inch' or approximately 52in. to the mile, the largest scale used for any city map until the Ordnance Survey skeleton plan of London in the mid-nineteenth century).

Whatever the exchange of information between Ogilby's employees and the city surveyors, the description of the methods employed, which Ralph Hyde discusses in section 8 of his introduction, demonstrates that most of the basic information must have been gathered by solid 'on the ground' point-to-point surveying, taking sightings and measurements with the chain according to the most up-to-date Stuart techniques and not transferred from the existing official surveys. In any case, the greater proportion of the map's area was not covered by the post-Fire surveyors.

A demonstration exercise described by Ralph Hyde compares sections of Ogilby's map with three near-contemporary plans of city properties. In each case the number of properties delineated is correct, the ground plans are also correct, but there is a tendency to be diagrammatic behind the street lines. As far as tested, therefore, Ogilby's map coincides with other contemporary sources, limited by the ability of his surveyors to penetrate into private property.

A further element in this process of testing Ogilby's accuracy arises from the current programme of archaeological research in the City of London. Detailed examination of particular sites enables us to draw tentative conclusions as to the value of Ogilby's map. Several of the sites investigated by the Department of Urban Archaeology cross groups of city waterfront tenements, whose boundaries normally appear to remain fossilized and unaltered from the Middle Ages. These properties, with their measurements and abuttals, are naturally fully recorded in the many medieval and Tudor land transfer documents preserved by the Corporation of London. The burst of surveying of private and institutional properties undertaken in the seventeenth century, both before and after the Fire, by surveyors using the same methods and covering the same ground as Ogilby's surveyors (albeit in greater detail) gives a further, contemporary, check-point. However, Tony Dyson, historian of the Department of Urban Archaeology (Museum of London) who in an earlier review welcomed Ogilby's map as a valuable tool for archaeologists and historians (*London Archaeologist*, 1977) now tells me that he finds it necessary to modify his enthusiasm for its authority. He kindly discussed for me some cases where he had matched up the map with other contemporary sources.

At Trig Lane, a waterfront site belonging to the Armourers' and Brasiers' Company, surveys of 1669 and 1679 conveniently bracket the period of surveying for Ogilby's map. Here the boundaries on the manuscript surveys and on the printed map agree, although in this case confirmation from excavation was lacking; the rear of the site close to the river seems not to have been clearly divided by walls into separate warehouses or wharves for each property. Another medieval waterfront site east of St Magnus Church towards Botolph's Wharf contained seven precisely described and identifiable tenements. At the street end seven properties are correctly marked on Ogilby and Morgan and excavations behind the frontage demonstrated that the pre-Fire, i.e. medieval, boundary walls and the post-Fire lines more or less agreed with one another. Apparently there had been no substantial sub-division or pairing of properties in the interval. However, Ogilby's property lines near the river could not be reconciled with those recovered by the archaeologists, suggesting that his surveyors plotted what they could see from the street and if denied access by the tenants, invented what seemed to them a reasonable pattern of ownership behind the frontage. With perhaps some 20,000 properties to record, who can blame them?

In one instance, Ogilby's information is confirmed by a mid-Tudor record of property boundaries. In 1545 the Canons of St Paul's granted a lease of one of 20 tenements running from the Church of St Mary Aldermanbury to Adbryght (Addle) Lane, the parish boundary with St Alban Wood Street. Ogilby and Morgan give 21. The agreement is sufficiently close to be reassuring; there are several acceptable explanations of the appearance of an extra tenement in the intervening 130 years. Not until more of this detailed matching of the map with building contracts and property surveys has been completed, a task which is to be undertaken by the team under Derek Keene now surveying medieval London, can a final assessment be made as to Ogilby and Morgan's accuracy. There is undoubtedly an enormous amount of information about property boundaries in the pre-Fire and indeed medieval City to be gained from detailed study of the map, in conjunction with appropriate contemporary sources.

Stuart Londoners lacked a firm, clear and generally acceptable term to describe the built-up area of London, divided as it was between distinct and often warring jurisdictions. The City and its Liberties clung to their separate existence, as they still do. In the title to his City map, Ogilby specified that it was 'distinct from Westminster and Southwark'. Westminster had its Court of Burgesses; Southwark was partly a Ward of the City and partly independent and those communities in Middlesex which were already effectively integrated into the urban sprawl such as Clerkenwell, were governed by Justices of the Peace. This great area, containing as it did some 700,000 people, could only be described by various clumsy additions or such circumlocutions as William Morgan's 'London Etc.'. In 1662 John Graunt estimated that the walled city formed only a quarter or a fifth of the total area of London. This Greater London area was described by various formulae devised for administrative purposes; thus the 'Incorporation of the Suburbs', Charles I's short-lived attempt to set up a predecessor of the London County Council in 1636, was followed by references in the civil war to the area 'within the Lines of Communication', referring to the 18-mile run of trenches and forts constructed in 1642 and 1643 around the suburbs to keep out the royalist army. An alternative and more common reference was to the parishes 'within the Bills of Mortality', that is, those making weekly returns of their dead to the Parish Clerks' Company. This uncertainty as to how to define and name London remained a problem to cartographers until the nineteenth century. Several unwieldy titles occur such as *A New Map of the Cityes of London, Westminster and the Burrough of Southwark together with the Suburbs as they are now standing* (1707), and at least one mapmaker, John Rocque, marked the boundary of the Bills of Mortality with crossed bones on his 1754 Middlesex map.

William Morgan, Ogilby's colleague and partner and relation by marriage, was left on Ogilby's death in 1676 with surveys of Westminster and Southwark to the same large scale as the City. They were not an economic publishing proposition; probably by Ogilby's death the relative lack of interest (as expressed in advance orders from subscribers) had convinced Morgan that it was unrealistic to continue at that scale. His 1681/2 map of London, Westminster and Southwark, which shows the built-up area from Piccadilly to Limehouse, and from the New River Head in Islington to Lambeth, was prepared at a scale of almost 18 inches to the mile. It is the first map to demonstrate the massive growth in the suburbs, particularly to the west and south of London, and was to be frequently reprinted and copied at a reduced size until the 1730s. This was a common practice among map publishers and it is curious that Ogilby's City map only seems to have been published once. This may be due to its rather purely topographical character; it lacked the views of buildings and other decorative elements common to contemporary mapping.

An important element in the value of both of these maps lies in the lists of streets, alleys, rents and courts, many here documented for the first time. Ogilby's 1677 references are confined of course to the City and listed rather confusingly by localities according to a letter and number key, rather than alphabetically. However, this street gazetteer or *Explanation*, published as a separate small volume, has been reprinted with an introduction and alphabetical index by John Fisher of the Guildhall Library. Lists of streets were already a familiar element in London maps; compare for example the rather crude reissue of Norden's 1593 London map with a street guide for visitors. The large scale of Ogilby's map allowed many more obscure corners and by-ways to be identified.

Morgan's references in the map *London Etc.* are particularly useful in the extramural districts. Of his almost 1800 place-names, many make their first appearance on a London map, enabling the location of alleys and courts previously known only from documentary sources to be determined. However, Morgan's tendency to discriminate in favour of the more prosperous parts of London means that, for example, very few indeed of the alleys and courts east of the Tower are named. He is also biased in the naming of inns and taverns, so giving a somewhat misleading distribution. Of the 176 named most appear in Westminster and the City, although it is common knowledge to social historians that Southwark had more than its fair share, supplying not only visitors to the pleasure quarter of London but also all those weary travellers who needed refreshment before crossing the Bridge.

Since John Ogilby did not, in the contemporary fashion, ornament and confuse his City map with elevations of prominent public buildings, confining himself to bands of decorative foliage to be cut out and pasted up when the map was framed, he was not obliged to discover, for example, how St Paul's Cathedral might appear once rebuilt. William Morgan in his map of London published five years later not only included bird's-eye views of major buildings, as customary, but even advertised his willingness to depict subscribers' houses. As Ralph Hyde says, this offer 'seems to have met with almost no response'. Of the 18 private houses in the tables of reference, 12 are town houses of aldermen, three of whom were dead before its appearance in 1682. Morgan's St Paul's 'as much as is built is taken from the work itself'! The rest, he somewhat vainly hoped, 'may not be very unlike when finished', which of course it was not to be for another 30 years. One invaluable element common to both the City map and Morgan's *London Etc.* is the indication of ward and, outside the City, parish boundaries. These appear for the first time on any London map; since many London parishes were substantially altered by the creation of new parishes to serve the growing areas outside the City in the late seventeenth and early eighteenth centuries, they are an invaluable record.

The information on Morgan's map was as up-to-date as he could make it. He shows St James's Church, Piccadilly, completed only in 1684. Morgan preserves the evidence for building developers in action; the vacant site of Arundel House, demolished in 1678, and the site of Exeter House, purchased by Dr Nicholas Barbon and divided into building lots, can be seen by comparing Morgan's map of 1682 with Ogilby's earlier coverage of the same area. This enthusiasm for new information is shown even in the ornamental elements which crowd the map. In St James's Park William Morgan shows an ostrich, a reminder of the 30 ostriches presented by the Moroccan Ambassador to Charles II in January 1682, just as the map sheets were going to press. Morgan's potential customers would expect and be entertained by such awareness of contemporary news. His obsession with ornament induced Morgan to provide a *Prospect of London and Westminster* 'taken at several stations to the southward thereof', a long view of the Thames and the buildings rising behind the waterfront, which is a far more accurate representation than the rather better-known views of the pre-Fire City by Visscher and Norden.

Morgan's map was intended to be pasted up in entrance halls, stairways and other large spaces and copies were presented by Morgan to many institutions with this hope in mind. Inevitably the effect of such exposure to damp led rapidly to decay and I know of only one copy of Morgan's map, at the Vyne in Hampshire, which looks as though it might still be in the position for which it was originally intended. There are indeed only two copies of the first edition, one in the Royal Library in Copenhagen and another (with one sheet missing) in the Museum of London which was used for this facsimile. The quality of the reproduction is all that we have come to expect from Harry Margary's facsimiles. One small quibble is the inconvenience of consulting Ralph Hyde's excellent introductions; they can only be read (being printed on sheets at least 2 feet wide, the same size as the map sheets) when standing up!

The Guildhall Library has done a great service to historians, archaeologists and topographers through its current programme of republishing important large-scale early maps of the capital with their excellent introductions by Ralph Hyde; we look forward to the forthcoming joint publication of the Library with the London Topographical Society which is to be the earliest London map, the so-called 'Agas', with copies of its cartographic progenitors, overprints and index.

Philippa Glanville
Tudor and Stuart Department, The Museum of London

Title deeds:
a key to local housing markets*

Title deeds are an invaluable source of information on the evolution of local housing markets. They are also a key to three other data sources. First, they complement plans registered with a local authority before a house was built. Second, by recording the deaths of most rentier landlords they give an entry point into the Probate Registry. Third, they check property ownership as listed in rate books. Finally, they are complementary in a more general sense. They are reliable (because solicitors take special care to see that the facts are correct) and each event in the history of a house is made intelligible by being recorded as part of a time sequence. But information is limited to one house or at most a block. Only by painstaking accumulation of a large number of deeds is it possible to discern economic patterns. Even then a sample of deeds drawn from a whole city might be insensitive to the finely balanced economic equations of, for example, landlords' rental income and their offsetting payments to mortgagees, agents, and ground landlords. Confined to a more manageable suburb, a sample of deeds may be atypical of the city. On the other hand, complementary data from the other registers is comprehensive, covering big geographic areas and large numbers of houses or people. But it comes as snapshots, aggregated appearances which are difficult to make socially or economically intelligible: the atomised names of otherwise anonymous builders on a building plan, landlords in a rate book, and property owners in the Probate Registry.

1   Title deeds

Title deeds can be difficult to obtain because owners consider their property dealings as essentially private transactions, and worry about releasing and losing documents which are the primary proof of their ownership. For example, deeds are released from mortgage with the Halifax Building Society in a wallet which 'should be kept in a safe place such as fireproof safe. Banks or solicitors can usually provide such facilities. Loss or destruction of these deeds could cause you great difficulty and expense in selling or otherwise dealing with your property.'

The technical barriers to research coincide with traditional assumptions about the important characteristics of a housing market. Investigators have generally been content to describe appearances – the housing condition of the working classes – leaving anonymous (unless long dead) those who own or control the markets. For example, writing in the shadow of the 1957 Rent Act, Cullingworth[1] considers it strange that no serious enquiry has been made into the private ownership of rented houses. On the other hand, a long list of Government Reports from the 1908 *Inquiry into Working Class Rents*[2] to the technical volumes of the recent government Green Paper[3] recount endless details of rent and mortgage repayment levels, of occupancy rates, and the numbers of pensioners living alone in more than five rooms rented unfurnished from a private landlord in England and Wales on census night in 1971. Random sample surveys, aggregating the questionnaire responses of anonymous residents, are now the principal research tool for collecting data about these symptoms.

To uncover the market forces behind these appearances there must be a different approach; one which applies some of the searching methods of urban historians to the contemporary, more sensitive and secret arrangements for accumulating

* Based on evidence from the research programme sponsored by the S.S.R.C. at the Centre for Urban & Regional Studies, Birmingham University.

wealth. When most houses were rented, landlords and their solicitors controlled access to this information. With the spread of owner-occupation into even the poorest working-class suburbs ordinary people now own through their deeds a partial record of their local housing market. They are less concerned than their middle-class counterparts to keep it private and willing in return for services, or out of friendship, to release it. In my case it is given in return for helping lease-holders to buy the freehold of their house. It complements similar, less extensive information from traditional local authority sources.

A bundle of title deeds should describe the history of a house, and if it were built for rent, the early history of neighbouring houses built together in a street block. Each time the property is sold, a transfer document, either a conveyance of free-hold or assignment of lease, records the name and address of buyer and vendor, their occupations (before this practice lapsed in the mid-1950s), the selling price, and for leasehold property, the annual ground rent and various restrictive cove-nants. Mortgage documents, usually associated with a transfer, show the name and address of lender, borrower and any guarantor, the amount to be lent, the ini-tial interest rate, and conditions under which it can be varied, how this translates into monthly repayments, and when the mortgage was paid off. Banks, which have displaced building societies in many inner city areas, generally lend money for house purchase on equitable mortgage. The documents record similar details about the lenders and borrowers but do not refer specifically to the amount of money lent or the interest charged.

Searches made with the Land Registry and local authority supplement this in-formation. The enquiry form sent by solicitors to the Registry records the names and addresses and (prior to 1955, though occasionally later) the occupations of the vendor, buyer and any past owner. When returned the same form now shows mort-gages or other legal charges secured on this or other property by any of its owners. Searches against owner-occupiers usually reveal no more than mortgage docu-ments in the bundle of deeds, but against landlords they might show other pro-perty holdings (disguised usually as a Land Registry number). Local searches show whether the house is subject to any statutory notices administered by the local authority – for example, requiring the owner to repair it, or sell it as part of a compulsory purchase order. Both kinds of search are generally made by solicitors whose names are recorded on the enquiry forms. It is possible then to piece together which firms acted for vendor and buyer, whether particular firms domi-nated a local market and whether they acted for both parties before (and some-times after) the Law Society generally banned the practice in 1972.

Owners keep deeds to show they have a title to the property. They will not be able to produce early original deeds where a block of rented property has been split up and each house sold separately into owner-occupation. Where this happens, usually in inner city areas of old byelaw housing, the owner can produce an abstract of title which summarizes the history of the terrace block when it was owned by successive landlords. Information has been taken from original deeds examined by the buyer's solicitor when the house was first sold separately. More recent abstracts of title furnished by vendors to prospective buyers often include this information together with a recent history of conveyances or assignments taken from the original documents in their possession. Because abstracts are shortened versions they sometimes omit legally redundant information which is important to a researcher – for example, the occupation and address of a landlord. Then there is a second reason why data is discarded. To prove title to a property an owner need only produce a record of the conveyance or assignments within the last 15 years (subject to a record of the lease where the house is leasehold). There is no legal necessity to retain early documents. In practice most owners and solicitors keep them as a precaution. If they are thrown away then there is a good chance that the relevant research data will be in the title deeds of the house next door.

Many bundles of deeds are becoming legally redundant as compulsory state regi-stration of title applies to more and more areas of England and Wales. 'One of the principal objects of registered conveyancing is to abolish the repeated investigation of title each time a property is sold . . . it does not assist (the purchaser) in deciding whether the title is good or defective'; and Barnsley,[4] a leading authority on conveyancing, continues: 'A purchaser is not concerned to know about the past history of a property.' We are. Registration is slowly destroying information on past ownership and control of housing markets. There was no conspiracy between owners and exchange professionals to do this (though the secrecy of Land Registry information protects owners from public scrutiny and reinforces the virtual monopoly of solicitors over the information we need). Avner Offer[5] shows how solicitors opposed registration 'despite pressure from property owners and law reformers'. Their acquiescence was finally bought by the State in return for higher conveyancing fees and a concession that mandatory registration would be brought in only very slowly. This has generally helped us, though the completeness of information differs from area to area, depending on when registration was introduced.

2 Building plan registers

Peter Aspinall[6] has comprehensively described the scope for statistical analysis of Building Plan Registers. The Saltley deeds support his division of private residential developers into three groups. Most of our deeds (covering 724 houses) record first a builder leasing land and within a year selling the lease together with completed houses to a landlord. Some builders lease land and retain the houses they build for investment (198 houses); yet others retain houses for a year or two before selling to a landlord or owner-occupier (presumably when the market allows). Peter Aspinall describes all these entrepreneurs as speculative builders. In Birmingham they are nearly always recorded in the building plan registers as the 'building owner' (the land or lease owner more precisely), and sometimes also as the 'plan depositor'. For the Saltley area between 1892 and 1900 there are 112 entries of identifiable builders as 'owners' of 1746 houses. Only on 34 occasions (69 houses) are they recorded as plan depositor and on 16 occasions (116 houses) as both. Nearly always the plan depositor is the architect or surveyor who draws it. Their names and business addresses are usually written on the plans but, since they never own the property, they are not referred to in the deeds. All this evidence conflicts with two assumptions made by Jim Dyos[7]: first, that the plan depositor is more likely to be the builder than the 'building owner'; second, that speculative builders are to be identified primarily if the names of plan depositor and building owner coincide.

In Saltley, speculative developers – Peter Aspinall's second group of 'specialists in the entrepreneurial side of housing creation and not necessarily a house builder'[8] – are a much smaller group than the builders themselves, and involved with only 125 houses. Title deeds record them as leasing large plots of land from a landowner and subletting them at higher ground rents to a builder. Sometimes they are recorded in the Register as building owner and they must have sold or passed on the plans they commissioned with the underlease. More often the builder who underleased their land had his own plans prepared and his name is recorded as the building owner. Either way the Register under-records the operations of one entrepreneur since it is rare for both to submit plans for the same plot. This is less of a problem in the equally large numbers of cases where a builder simply transfers the lease on a plot of land, or part of it, to another. Presumably this is done to rationalize the supply of land for building when one builder discovers he cannot build the number of houses within a time specified in the covenants of the lease, and another builder has productive capacity in excess of his landbank.

Lord Norton, Saltley's biggest landowner, granted a number of leases (23 out of 137 covering 73 of the 994 houses for which we have all the relevant information) to people who were clearly not builders or developers like those already described. They fit precisely into Peter Aspinall's third cryptic category 'of the owners of plans of one or a few houses . . . likely to have been intending owner-occupiers or small scale investors whose contribution to the building process was an isolated or short lived event'. Deeds build up a picture of these people as a local *petite bourgeoisie*, investing and sometimes living in better houses, but they record nothing of the builder. They may, like the others, record mortgages taken out to pay for the construction, and they may even detail a sequence of payments made by the mortgagee as the building proceeds. But it is difficult to determine whether the owner employed one builder or subcontracted parts of the work. The Building Plan Register gives the only clue. Original application forms are attached to the plans recorded in the Birmingham Register (where they have not been lost) and they ask for the occupations of depositor as well as owner. Where the depositor is an architect or surveyor this suggests the owner might parcel the work out under his supervision; where the depositor is a builder then there seems a good chance that he will be employed by the owner to carry out the building.

Many indices of building cycles are based on building plan registers. Since house completion dates are not usually recorded, John Parry Lewis[9] estimates them by lagging six months the plan approval dates which are generally recorded and reducing the numbers by a percentage which accounts for abortive plans. John Parry Lewis admits 'There are obvious criticisms to be levelled at this device', and one of them surely is that the time lag between approval and completion will itself probably vary with the building cycle as builders slow down construction in response to market depression. This indeed appears to be a problem when the Saltley deeds are used to supplement the Birmingham Register, though we have not yet accumulated enough evidence to be sure. Beyond doubt however, is the very wide variation in the time lag between application dates and sales of completed houses to landlords even within the same year. Some builders sell their houses within three months of submitting their plans, others take a year.

3 The probate registry

'Since the First World War the private landlord has declined both relatively and absolutely as a supplier or intermediary in the housing market', writes John Greve, summarizing the evidence in *Private Landlords in England*.[10] Consistently the Saltley deeds record sales into owner-occupation of formerly rented houses from 1920 onwards. Many substantial terraced houses with interwar rateable values between £13 and £16 were sold to artisans and clerks before 1928, but it has taken another 50 years to eliminate all but a handful of rentier landlords of the poorer property. During that time ownership changed, though often by inheritance. The deeds usually record this in detail; who each owner was, where they lived, their occupation, when they made their wills, who they appointed as executors, trustees and benificiaries; when they died, where and when each will was proved. So it is possible to trace the history of a rentier family and discover how they responded to the market. Despite the 1925 Law of Property Act which allowed trustees much more easily to dispose of real estate, families retained houses until in the 1950s mounting repair costs and premium vacant possession values made the economic case for selling overwhelming.

An abstract of title which records the early ownership of a block of houses sometimes squeezes out legally redundant information on a landlord's occupation or address, which is vital to locate their economic and social status. At other times an owner is recorded simply as a gentleman, married woman, wife or spinster. Again, these courtesy titles, a product of Victorian social values, mask the occupation by which an owner or her husband accumulated capital to buy the property. Title deeds of a neighbouring house might fill some gaps. The Probate registries certainly should; copies of wills are kept for public inspection at the relevant District Registry and the original in the Principal Probate Registry at Somerset House in London. Grants of Probate or letters of Administration (for those who die without wills) are kept in the same places. According to the standard order form (PR 102) they tell you 'who are the administrators or executors entitled to collect and distribute the estate and the name of any solicitor acting for them. It also tells you the total value of the estate . . . The Registry has no other details of the estate; and the capital taxes office, Minford House, Rockly Road, West Kensington, London W14 0DF, which has the details cannot disclose them without the written consent of the administrators or executors.' In other words, it is normally difficult to uncover the extent of someone's property, and how it is distributed. Wills are suitably discreet about real property holdings referring vaguely to 'Freehold and Leasehold property'. Title deeds show the distribution of property relevant to the house in question and sometimes by chance the testator's other property holdings. More often other property is described as just that, 'inter alia', or 'not the subject of this assignment'.

Wills give a better idea of family structure, of the owner's wife, children and other dependents and friends who agree to be executors. They often record his occupation more accurately than title deeds, but if he persists in calling himself a gentleman, a better guide might be his death certificate which costs £2.50 from Somerset House (expensive research) or marriage certificate from the same place. If this fails, then the marriage or birth certificates of his children will record his occupation. Deeds usually supply an owner's date of death and his will, and a Grant of Probate takes only a minute to locate. But neither title deeds nor wills usually record births and marriages: in practice this means competing with tourists and genealogists to flick through the registers (in St Catherine's House in the Aldwych in London) for a range of probable years to discover the certificate index number.

Since legal title to property is proved by evidence of 15 years ownership, an abstract may not only squeeze out information on occupation or address, but also leave out some early transactions altogether, simply lumping them together as 'divers assignments'. In some cases wills or Grants of Probate fill the gap by linking the names in one recorded transaction and the next. For example, an abstract of title for a house in College Road, Saltley, shows that it was once part of a terrace of six bought by David Smith from a builder, Thomas Turley, on 15 March 1899. It records nothing more about David Smith other than his sometime mortgage with Birmingham Incorporated Building Society, which was paid off in 1911. The next recorded transaction is the sale of the six houses on 12 May 1924. Joseph Spruce Smith and Rowland Alfred Blantern assign them to Eleanor Charlotte George. Only the names of the vendors are recorded, but since one is called Smith, and there are two of them it seems likely that they are executors of David Smith, the first landlord. A search of the probate register confirms that David Smith died on the 13 December 1923, and Joseph Spruce Smith, a railway clerk, his son, and Rowland Blantern, a commercial traveller, were appointed as executors. David Smith himself is described as a gentleman of 9 Link Road, Edgbaston, Birmingham, and he so describes himself in his will. His son's occupation and his own estate of £1,876 (modest for a landlord even in the 1920s) suggests that his designation 'gentleman' merely reflects his living off the capital accumulated in a job or trade. An earlier document might record his occupation more precisely. His will made in 1914 describes Rowland Blantern as his son-in-law, married to his daughter who is to receive a half share of his estate 'providing always that if my daughter Jennie Elizabeth Blantern shall die in my lifetime leaving a child . . . etc.' This implies, though it is not clear, that his daughter was of childbearing age in 1914, and must have married some time after 1890. An hour's search at St Catherine's House pinpoints it to the 3 July 1900 and her marriage certificate describes David Smith as an engine driver. It was common for drivers – 'aristocrats of labour' – to own a few houses in Saltley. It was a railway suburb and their average weekly income of 42s. (£2.10) before the First World War was twice that of a labourer, affording them some surplus for investment.

4 Rate books

Rate books allow 'a detailed analysis of the structure of house ownership, both as an investment and for self occupation', argues M. J. Daunton in an article 'House ownership from rate books' (*Urban History Yearbook 1976*) and in his later book *Coal Metropolis*.[11] Evidence from the Saltley deeds generally confirms this claim up to the First World War but shows the Birmingham rate books, at least, to be less accurate after 1920 in identifying either landlords or owner-occupiers. Birmingham Council has retained ratebooks for five-yearly intervals until 1911, and thereafter consecutively. The 1906 Saltley rate book compiled in the early part of that year squares nearly completely with deed evidence of landlords on 31 December 1905. In these early years any inaccuracy is reduced by comparing one rate book with the next which sometimes records the agent as acting on behalf of a named owner. In the 1930s this is more difficult as the practice of listing agents in the owners column of the rate book becomes more widespread. After the Second World War the Birmingham rate books are unreliable as a guide to the names of owners. In 1950, for example, agents are listed instead of owners for over half the houses where we have deed information. The position is further confused because many landlords' agents became dealers after the war, buying and selling houses in their own right. Then, even if a landlord's name is correctly identified, there remains the problem of identifying his or her social and economic status. It is easier, M. J. Daunton admits, to place those who occupy a house in a block they own. A street directory – Kelly's for Birmingham – will often identify their occupation. But resident landlords are exceptional; in Saltley they are commonly artisans owning less that half a dozen of the better houses. Birmingham's rate books record neither the occupation nor the address of that overwhelming majority of landlords who do not live near the houses they let. M. J. Daunton's 'success rate in locating the bulk of smaller (non-resident) owners was low, making an accurate analysis of their social composition impossible'.[12]

None of Lancaster's 853 landlords identified by Barry Cullingworth in 1960[13] were property companies; although a third of the 269 who yielded interviews for John Greve[14] were, half of these owned five or fewer houses. Surveys of this kind underestimate their impact. Like rate books they are snapshots picturing the durable rentier landlord but not sharp enough to catch the dealer who buys and sells as quickly as possible. The post-war market in many old areas of our cities has been dominated by the dealers' logic of buying blocks of rented houses and splitting them up for resale to owner-occupiers. At one time or another two-thirds of the houses covered by the Saltley deeds have passed through their hands, owned ephemerally by their property companies. Yet a random sample survey at any time in the last 35 years would have recorded only the failure of dealers to rid themselves of some property as quickly as they disposed of the bulk of it. For example, 95–105 Bowyer Road were rented for 55 years from Samuel Hutton and his heirs and have

Table 1: Number of owner-occupiers in Saltley (from rate books)

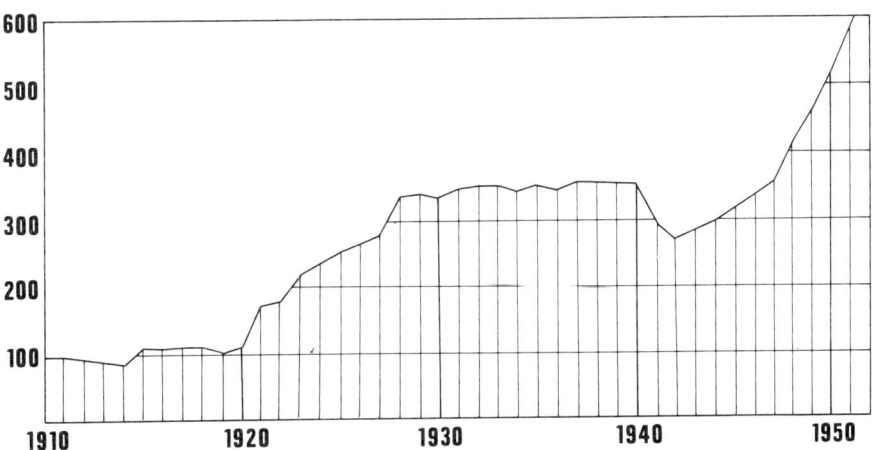

been owner-occupied (with one exception) ever since. Only in a few months of 1949 might a survey have uncovered a dealer managing the tenure transition. Denmar Investments, who bought the block of six houses for £2,000 and sold five for an average of over £600 apiece to tenants and others within six months, were unlikely to have been recorded in the rent books: so even if a survey took place in these crucial months, the chances of uncovering the dealer are much less than of locating the average rentier landlord.

Rate books, too, tend to gloss over the dealer intermediary, though their intervention is clear enough when a long-standing landlord of a block of houses is suddenly replaced in the rate book by new owner-occupiers interleaved with the dealer or his agent recorded as owner of yet unsold houses. In such cases rate books take forward the history of a group of houses when the deeds available record only the first few sales into owner-occupation. Our two deeds from the block of six houses referred to above record two houses sold into occupation in 1949. The rate books show three of the others sold similarly in the same few months, and the remaining one of the six in 1953. Pepper, Tangye and Winterton, executors of Samuel Hutton in the 1948 rate book, are replaced by owner-occupiers' names in the 1949 rate book, with the one exception recorded until 1952 as owned by Bright Willis, a firm of estate agents, presumably agents for Denmar.

Current rate books (if they are available; generally they are not) and registers of fair rents (kept by local Rent Officers for public inspection) both pinpoint houses in a block which are still rented. Tenants' rent books are required by the 1962 Landlord and Tenant Act to name the owner, and there are provisions in the 1974 Housing Act to force disclosure, so it is possible to gain an impression of dealer intervention in the market without access to the deeds. This was how Benwell Community Development Project first uncovered ownership patterns described originally in their booklet *Benwell's Hidden Property Companies*[15] and incorporated later into *Private Housing and the Working Class*.[16] Deeds additionally provide the (often illegible) signatures of a director and secretary of the property company dealing in a house, but these names are only a starting point; like the isolated names of earlier landlords they reveal little of their control of a local housing market. The records at Companies House (in Cardiff and London) fill out the picture within limits. Christopher Hird in *Your Employer's Profits*[17] correctly argues that 'As a result of (their) desire to minimise the amount of money paid to the taxman the information supplied in the accounts of private companies is often meagre and misleading.' Other legally required information is more helpful – lists of directors together with their other directorships, of share holders and of mortgages taken out by the company – all help build a picture of the connections between property companies and the extent of their property holdings.

The Saltley rate books record fairly accurately, as far as we can tell by cross checking with title deeds, the first surge into owner-occupation during the 1920s and the second, much bigger surge after the Second World War. Title deeds accurately record owners, and in 1920 confirm as owners almost all of 100 'rate book' owner-occupiers for which we have deed information. On the other hand rate books identify occupiers more clearly than deeds which usually record only a buyer's previous address. Sitting tenants buying a house are clearly recorded in the deeds as owner-occupiers, but not those buying with vacant possession. Only when these latter resell the house does their recorded address indicate that they may have been its sometime owner-occupier. After 1957 there is a change in the recording procedure in Birmingham rate books which diminishes their research value. Occupiers of houses of less than £21 rateable value are no longer recorded; neither are the owners of houses above this limit unless they are occupiers also. Since the bulk of old working-class houses fall below the rateable divide, their owners can be checked against occupiers recorded in the relevant electoral register to establish the level of owner-occupation, but there are problems. Rate books record ownership each April whereas electoral registers for each year are made up the previous October. Aliens are not included on electoral registers: non-resident shop-keepers may be. Commonwealth citizens are included in principle, but in practice it takes time for them to be recorded.

Owner-occupation has extended into even the poorest areas of our cities; yet the nominal ownership of slum property by its occupiers can only in a tenuous sense constitute control, either by an individual of a house or owners collectively of the local housing market. Once owner-occupation becomes the dominant tenure form a precise empirical measure of its size is less important in explaining a housing market than its internal price mechanism. The key contradiction in many city suburbs built to rent at the end of the nineteenth century is rising prices for houses which are physically deteriorating visibly. Title deeds can help explore the dilemma by providing reliable information on exchange values, but' it must be related to the material conditions of those who live there. Only residents themselves can point to the concrete ways in which the market oppresses them or provides ephemeral gain. Our task is to build out of their experience, suspend the abstract categories of random sample surveys and explore the secret world beyond appearances.

Geoffrey Green
Centre for Urban and Regional Studies, University of Birmingham

Acknowledgments

I am grateful to Martin Durham who helped collate the statistics, and commented on the draft, to Mr Smallwood in Birmingham Rates Department who gave us access to the rate books, and to the staff in the local studies section of Birmingham Reference Library for their help with the Building Plan Registers.

Notes

1　J. B. Cullingworth, *Housing in Transition: A case study in the City of Lancaster 1958–1962* (1963), 105.
2 ⸳ *Report of an Enquiry into Working Class Rents, Housing and Retail Prices together with the Standard Rates of Wages in the Principal Industrial Towns of the United Kingdom* (Cd 3864), Board of Trade (1908).
3　*Housing Policy*, Technical Volumes I, II and III (*HMSO* 1977)
4　D. G. Barnsley, *Conveyancing Law and Practice* (1975), 302.
5　Avner Offer, 'The origins of the law of Property Acts. 1910–1925, *Modern Law Review*, xl, 5 (1977), 505.
6　Peter Aspinall, '*Building applications and the building industry in 19th century towns: the scope for statistical analysis*' (Centre for Urban and Regional Studies, Research Memorandum, 1978).
7　H. J. Dyos, *Victorian Suburb: A study of the growth of Camberwell* (1966), 126, 218.
8　Aspinall, *op.cit.*, 34.
9　John Parry Lewis, *Birmingham Cycles and Britain's Growth* (1965), 302–3.
10　John Greve, *Private Landlords in England* (1965), 9–10.
11　M. J. Daunton, 'House ownership from ratebooks' *Urban History Yearbook 1976*, 21–7; and *idem*, *Coal Metropolis: Cardiff 1870–1914* (1977).
12　*Ibid.*, 118.
13　Cullingworth, *op. cit.*, 105–6.
14　Greve, *op.cit.*, 28.
15　*Benwell's Hidden Property Companies* (Benwell C.D.P., 1976).
16　*Private Housing and the Working Class* (Benwell C.D.P. 1978).
17　Christopher Hird, *Your Employer's Profits* (1975), 69.

Conference reports

Urban history group, annual conference, University of Sheffield, 5–6 April 1979

A meeting of the Urban History Group without its guiding spirit was both a time of sadness for past occasions when Jim Dyos's bustling good humour had pervaded our meetings, and also a time of reflection about the future organization of the Group. Such was the tone established for the two days at the opening business meeting. Before this, the excursion led by Dr HEY and Dr SUTCLIFFE had inspected medieval sites, model mining communities, and the Cottage Exhibition of 1907; they had not, however, planned to experience the more modern urban phenomenon of a two-hour traffic jam in Doncaster.

The opening lecture was given by Professor Stephan THERNSTROM (Harvard) on 'Urbanization and ethnicity: patterns of assimilation of white and non-white ethnic groups in urban communities'. Did the melting pot melt? In the past, it had been assumed that it did, at least for the whites, but more recently persistence of ethnic identity has been both stressed and applauded. The extent of assimilation may be measured, argued Thernstrom, by using five indices: language, occupational change, educational mobility, residential concentration, and intermarriage. First he applied these indices to white immigrants, and found in each case a trend away from initial disparity towards the native norm. But if the melting pot has melted for the whites, what of the blacks? Professor Thernstrom admitted a more optimistic assessment than in *The Other Bostonians*. Until the Second World War the experience of the blacks had been different from the white immigrants: they stayed in menial jobs as a caste rather than a class; residential segregation was higher; marital assimilation was not possible; and black education was inferior. But, he argued, this has been changed by a revolution in race relations since the Second World War, so that remaining disparities are not the result of *current* racism, but rather of cultural characteristics created by *past* racism. These cultural characteristics may now be expected, as for white immigrants, to wither away and so allow assimilation.

The discussion was opened by Professor E. P. HENNOCK (Liverpool) who wondered if the same questions and techniques of measurement could be applied to similar experiences in other parts of the world. Thernstrom accepted the need to see how the American experience fitted with other cases, but felt that other measures might be needed: political assimilation might be one criterion, whilst a measure of inter-marriage might not mean much in a society where the mother's ethnicity determined socialization. Dr G. J. CROSSICK (Essex) asked, 'assimilation to what?' The existing structure should not be assumed to be static, for the immigrants were themselves changing the culture as they assimilated to it. Thernstrom agreed that it was not a case of everybody assimilating to the culture of a charter group. Rather it was a matter of blending, as initial differences disappeared, which makes it unnecessary to define 'American culture'.

Iain C. TAYLOR (Athabasca University) and J. D. WILLIAMS (Stirling) raised the issue of which variable was most important: ethnicity or class; colour or culture. Thernstrom argued that ethnicity had been substituted for class, and that colour had become relatively unimportant. It could have been said just as much of the Jews, Japanese or Chinese that they were 'visible', yet they had been assimilated, and there was no reason why the same was not possible for blacks. But P. RENSHAW (Sheffield) wondered if the number of blacks in comparison with pre-

vious groups might not be significant. Thernstrom was sceptical, for the presence
of the blacks was no greater than that of the Irish in the 1850s.

The Irish reappeared the next morning, when a double session chaired by Charlotte ERICKSON (L.S.E.) was given over to a discussion of migration and urban
development. Five papers were presented. Dr R. A. P. FINLAY (Lancaster) spoke
on 'The magnet of the metropolis: migration and the early modern city', stressing
that the metropolitan cities in the early modern period could not grow without
migration, and that this affected the demographic history of their regions. He illustrated this by the examples of Holland and London, bringing out the imponder-
ables rather than any definite conclusions. In his discussion of 'Population,
migration and urban development in the north-west, 1851–1901', Dr C. POOLEY
(Lancaster) outlined the theories of migration and the weakness of his sources
before reaching three conclusions from his study of the north-west of England: that
migration switched from sources close at hand to long-distance movement between
towns; that there was a high degree of occupational selection in migration; and
that most long-distance migration occurred as steps up the urban hierarchy as
part of a social process of adjustment.

After two papers which were theoretical in motivation and impersonal in
approach, it was welcome to turn to two papers in which it was easier to perceive
the migrant in his historical reality. Or rather, according to Nick TIRATSOO
(L.S.E.) in his paper on 'The Coventry ribbon-trade in decline, 1860–70: the place
of out-migration in the popular repertoire of strategies for survival', the non-
migrant. Migration, he argued, was only one response to depression; the question
is why other groups selected different strategies for survival. In Coventry, the
problem of depression was redefined so that blame was not placed upon employers
within the town but upon groups outside the town. This allowed a consensus ideology to develop, so that depression led not to class conflict but to moderation. Migration as a response can only be understood within this context of class relations. He
concluded with a plea, which was most pertinent after the first two papers, that
migration should not be allowed to languish in an isolation ward of flows, but
should be integrated into a wider approach. The study by Brenda COLLINS
(Coleraine) of 'The social experience of Irish migrants in Dundee and Paisley
during the mid-nineteenth century' was an excellent example of how this can be
done. Rather than assume that rural-urban migration caused major changes in
life-styles as the migrant adjusted to the host community, she asked how far cultural traditions could be carried from the point of origin to the point of destination.
By a subtle analysis of the development of the domestic linen textile industry in
the distinct areas of northern Ireland which supplied migrants for Dundee and
Paisley, she was able to show how the attributes of the industry in the Scottish
towns fitted the attributes which the migrants brought with them. It was not
simply an adjustment of migrants to the places in which they settled, but a more
complicated interaction between the local industry and the family economy
brought by the migrants from their place of origin. This formed a useful link with
Professor Thernstrom's paper, for recent American studies have been based precisely upon this realization, rather than upon a somewhat mechanistic measurement of assimilation.

In the final paper, Bronwen WALTER (Cambridgeshire College of Arts and
Technology) considered 'Time-space patterns of second-generation Irish immigration into British towns'. Recent Irish migrants have settled not in Scotland and the
north-west but in the south-east and the West Midlands. Did the Irish migrants
move direct to the new areas, or did they settle in the old communities as 'reception
centres' before moving to the optimum location? She concluded that most took the
second option.

Dr D. E. BAINES (L.S.E.) acted as commentator. He raised a number of issues on
the nature of Irish migration. Were there two labour markets or one? In the nineteenth century, there was a choice between Britain and America, and it might be
that Britain was seen as a place from which it was possible to return. On movement

to Dundee, he was sceptical whether its requirements drew out one group rather than another. He was uncertain whether the argument was that the nature of this workforce shaped the industry, or that the nature of the industry allowed them to come. The interesting question would be to compare textiles with other industries, and ask why the demands of Dundee were met by the Irish rather than by the Scots. After raising some methodological points with Pooley and Tiratsoo, he turned to Finlay's paper to suggest that the Wrigley hypothesis that London required half the population increase of the country was incorrect. He argued that the Wrigley estimate assumes the migrants were impotent, that their rate of natural increase was nil; if the migrant birth-rate were added, then the demand of London for population would be reduced to a quarter of the country's natural increase. He concluded by making a number of general points. The first was how we are to link ideas that migrants followed well-defined paths (for example, to relatives), with ideas that they moved in their best interests. The second was how to get at total movement, for the data shows only highly stable moves rather than migration itself as a phenomenon. And third, the relationship between migration and emigration might be complementary rather than supplementary.

The discussion opened with a technical argument between E. A. WRIGLEY (Cambridge), W. A. ARMSTRONG (Kent), P. LAXTON (Liverpool) and Dr Finlay on the question of how to measure the contribution of migration to urban growth. Wrigley maintained that he had allowed for births amongst migrants, since these were recorded in the birth registers. Dr Armstrong proposed a counter-factual population history; by taking a given population, it should be possible to estimate its demographic growth potential; the contribution of migration should then be apparent by comparing the estimate and reality. Laxton thought that this was unreal, and with a plea by G. J. CROSSICK (Essex) to consider what migration meant rather than to analyse flows, attention turned to the papers of Tiratsoo and Collins. The question Crossick raised was what the out-migrants from Coventry thought they were dealing with: decline or a fluctuation. Professor Thernstrom was of the opinion that out-migration was less sensitive to economic conditions than in-migration, for the level of out-migration was similar for all towns whilst the level of in-migration varied significantly. A number of speakers then turned the discussion towards the relation between migration and economic opportunities in the receiving area. J. D. WILLIAMS remarked that women's jobs might not be available in mining or heavy industry, which might have increased the attractiveness of Dundee. P. LAXTON felt that the textile industry in Dundee might be responding to the existence of Irish labour which reduced the incentive for technical advance, rather than that migrants were responding to opportunities. R. J. MORRIS (Edinburgh) took the example of Middlesbrough to illustrate these points. The town had a large number of Irish but few women's jobs. This suggested that the question was not that a particular occupational structure attracted the Irish, but that it might aid assimilation once they had arrived.

The session was closed by Charlotte Erickson who pointed to the gaps in our knowledge and the dearth of information.

The closing paper was by Professor Lynn LEES (Pennsylvania) on 'Strikes and the urban hierarchy in English industrial towns', in which she sought to elucidate the relationship between city size and political and social conflict. It has often been argued that large towns generate more conflict, and to test this in the case of England she took strike activity in Yorkshire, Lancashire, Leicestershire and Nottinghamshire as a useful surrogate for conflict. She found that strikes were both more frequent and larger in small and middle-sized than in large towns. The low propensity of large towns to strike was explained for the 1840s in terms of their incorporation which entailed a more active political life and local agencies of authority. This difference was perpetuated in the later nineteenth century by other institutional structures, namely Trades Councils and Boards of Conciliation or Arbitration which were found in the larger but not the smaller towns. The employers for their part usually had formal associations. The complex political interests of employers and unions meant that they found it better to conciliate; disputes were rarely intensified for there were complex industrial and political interests to balance. The propensity to strike was dampened; labour consciousness was present but not militancy. In the smaller towns, there were fewer political outlets and a lower level of organization. Strikes were more likely to develop, and relations were a mixture of deference and defiance. The general conclusion was thus that size, through its institutional expressions, channelled conflict into less aggressive forms.

The chairman, Dr D. FRASER (Bradford) suggested that there were four issues: the use of strikes as an index of tension and consciousness; whether city size was the key variable or if that was hiding something else; if city size was the key variable, was it because of the differences in institutions; and did these institutions suggest class conciliation rather than conflict? R. J. MORRIS followed up these points. A particular type of conflict was being considered, which ignored radical politics, non-attendance at church, or whatever. Conciliation did not necessarily mean that there was no consciousness; it could indicate that people were better at conflict rather than that there was less of it. He also wondered whether the size of the unit of production might be relevant. Retailing, merchanting and services created small units, and had few fluctuations in the return to labour. The consequence was fewer strikes, and these occupations were concentrated in the larger towns. Dr J. WALTON (Lancaster) queried the use of a strike index which lumped together industries of different types, for strikes in cotton were short and frequent, whereas in mining they were less frequent and longer. He wondered if it was possible to allow for the duration of strikes. J. D. WILLIAMS felt there was some confusion in the use of the terms class consciousness and conflict, and sought clarification.

Professor Lees promised to consider strike duration and the nature of the industry. She denied using the term class consciousness; she was only prepared to use the term labour consciousness. This inspired Dr MORRIS to remark that class consciousness should not be defined by the impossible criteria of everyone being out on the streets demanding a total change in society. All that is required is an awareness of fundamental differences in the access to power. Class consciousness should not be reserved for the extreme situation.

Dr CROSSICK queried the statistical basis of the argument. He was concerned at the use of periods of high strike activity, for at such times unions were spreading into previously unorganized areas so that what is being considered is weakness manifesting itself at peculiar times. Professor Lees did not accept that strike waves distorted matters, for the pattern was the same at periods of low strike activity, and between areas of high and low unionization.

A number of speakers suggested possible alternative measures of conflict, be they civil disturbances and criminality (I. C. TAYLOR), levels of suicide and illegitimacy (E. A. WRIGLEY), or membership of co-operative societies (J. WALTON). As R. J. MORRIS remarked, the problem is what is measurable, for otherwise the analysis must fall back upon two or three towns. There was also some concern about the areas covered by the statistics. Professor M. DRAKE (Open University) pointed out that administrative boundaries might not reflect the size of population concentrations, whilst E. A. WRIGLEY wondered if the same units were being used for the recording of strikes as for population figures in the census. Professor Lees promised to consider some of the suggested measures.

Professor F. P. HENNOCK felt that if the concern was with strikes, priorities should be reversed. The starting point should be the industry and not the town. He argued that the strikes of 1889–91 were outside the existing framework of institutions, and that the two periods of 1842 and 1889–91 should not be treated as the same phenomenon explicable by the same set of factors. Professor Lees agreed that it would be useful to control for industry, but she did not accept that the activity of 1889–91 was outside the existing framework. Until comparisons were made over time it was not possible to know if 1842 and 1889–91 were indeed different.

P. S. JONES (Leicester) took up the examples of Leicestershire and Nottingham-shire. There industry was moving into the country in order to pay low wages, and strikes might be a first attempt to oppose the trend rather than a measure of strength. Dr FRASER remarked that whilst Professor Lees argued that institu-tions defused conflict, to John Foster the institutions were used to work out con-flict. Dr J. LOVELL (Kent) indicated that if big cities were defusing conflict in the nineteenth century, in the years before and after the First World War strikes were concentrated upon the big cities.

Professor Lees summed up the session by accepting that phenomena were dif-ferent at different times, and that data was lacking. But what was required was to be systematic. The structural argument used in her analysis was not amenable to rapid change over time, but she was not willing to drop the hypothesis, for the institutions operated in the social arena and ought therefore to be taken into account.

The members of the Urban History Group now had the choice of dispersing, or of transforming themselves into economic historians. The Economic History Society's conference did have some interest for urban historians, with papers by Frank MANDERS (Newcastle) on the new poor law in Gateshead, by C. BROWN (S.S.R.C.) on churches and the labour movement in Glasgow, by Malcolm FALKUS (L.S.E.) on the British gas industry, and by M. D. REILLY (Liverpool) on urban electric railways.

Gregynog Seminars in Local History 1977–8

Philip Riden reports that during the 1977–8 session the Department of Extramu-ral Studies of University College, Cardiff, organized two residential seminars at the University of Wales conference centre at Gregynog, near Newtown, Powys. The aim was to bring together amateur and professional historians, and scholars in related disciplines such as archaeology or historical geography, to discuss a chosen topic that can be approached through local case-studies. The events were arranged particularly to give an opportunity for the experienced amateur resear-cher involved in extramural studies to take part in a conference run on profession-al lines, rather than with a divide between teachers and taught. The subject selected for the two seminars last year was one of wide interest applicable to all parts of Great Britain and indeed attracted contributions from both Wales and Scotland as well as England. The general theme of the pre-industrial town in Britain was divided, so that a meeting in December was devoted to the medieval town and another in April to the post-medieval town. There were about 30 partici-pants at each gathering, drawn, as intended, from among the teaching staff and postgraduate students of universities, extramural students and elsewhere, espe-cially archaeology units. The surroundings at Gregynog are exceptionally pleas-ant for a residential conference of this kind and both occasions proved a success socially as well as academically, with a lively and informed discussion following each paper.

It was the intention of the host department from the start that the proceedings of each seminar should be published, if only on a fairly modest scale, to provide a per-manent record of the occasion. As so often happens, publication has not followed as quickly as at first hoped, but by the time this report is published the papers from the December 1977 conference, and possibly those of the second one also, should be available from the Extramural Department at Cardiff. There will be two separate volumes, each containing revised versions of the papers delivered at the two seminars, with most of the contributions illustrated with maps and tables. The Department welcomes enquiries about the publications, which will be produced as cheaply as possible. It may be helpful here simply to list the authors and titles and to conclude with the hope that in the next *Yearbook* it will be possible to include the proceedings among the year's published work in urban history.

December 1977: **The Medieval Town in Britain**
John Blair (Oxford): Gilds and chantries of medieval Chesterfield
Barbara Champion (L.S.E.): Gilds and chantries of medieval Beverley
Peter Clack (Durham): The origins and growth of Darlington
Geoffrey Martin (Leicester): The medieval town in Britain: a survey
Huw Owen (Cardiff): The Welsh town in the later Middle Ages
Alan Rogers (Nottingham): The value and use of deeds for medieval urban history
Eric Talbot (Glasgow): The Scottish medieval town
Tim Tatton Brown (Canterbury): Canterbury's urban topography: some recent
work

April 1978: **The Post-Medieval Town in Britain**
Joan Dils (Reading): Traders and craftsmen in Tudor Reading
Alan Dyer (Bangor): The early modern town: problems and themes
Joyce Ellis (Loughborough): The river dragon: Newcastle upon Tyne in the early
eighteenth century
John and Sue Farrent (Brighton): Brighton 1650–1820: the antecedents of a
seaside resort
Richard Rodger (Liverpool): Town planning in Scottish burghs since 1500
Sandra Wheatley (Aberystwyth): Urban change in the small town: Aberystwyth
in the eighteenth and nineteenth centuries

**Stockholm: growth and transformation of a city: University of Stockholm,
11–15 September 1978**

Dr A. R. Sutcliffe reports that this ambitious symposium, held to celebrate the centenary of the University of Stockholm, was the brainchild of Professor INGRID
HAMMARSTRÖM, and was organized by Dr THOMAS HALL and other staff of
her research project, 'Swedish urban environment: building and housing during
the past hundred years'. Professor Hammarström sought to relate key themes in
the physical development of Stockholm to urban evolution in the Nordic countries
and elsewhere in the world. Three main topics emerged: changes in the arrangement of urban areas in the nineteenth and early twentieth centuries under the
impact of industrialization; twentieth-century planning, with special reference to
central-area redevelopment; and the future of planning and urban studies.
    Half the communications dealt with the first theme. From the presentations of
MARIANNE RÅBERG (Stockholms Stadsmuseum), OLE HYLDTOFT (University of Copenhagen), and THOMAS LUNDÉN (University of Stockholm), together with an *in absentia* paper by SVEN-ERIK ÅSTRÖM (Helsinki), there
emerged a picture of Nordic capital-city development very much on the Berlin
model. Stockholm, Copenhagen, and to some extent Helsinki, were all large
enough by the mid-nineteenth century to have built up a solid pre-industrial structure which the sudden onset of industrialization could not sweep away overnight.
Mechanized industry established itself from the very first in the suburbs, while a
tradition of authoritarian planning was adapted to new needs, permitting the
creation of logical street networks at the expense of a reinforcement of high-
density, tenement housing. However, the centrifugal dynamic of industry eventually generated hopes of a suburban solution to the cities' housing problems, and
deconcentration was gradually incorporated into municipal policies before and
after the First World War.
    Råberg outlined the growth of Stockholm from its origins until the late nine-
teenth century. Settlement spread from the rocky islet of Stadsholmen onto
Södermalm and Norrmalm. When Sweden's success in the Thirty Years' War
brought a spurt of development, building was regulated by sweeping royal street
plans. With stagnation setting in from the early eighteenth century, this network
continued to serve until the middle of the nineteenth. However, rapid growth
thereafter required the planning of new districts, and a general renewal of the

city's equipment, which were carried out under the leadership of Albert Lindha-gen. In 'Industrialisation and urbanisation: Copenhagen 1840–1914', Hyldtoft took up the story in respect of the Danish capital. He showed how the new factories, most of which were set up outside the cramped, fortified city of the 1840s, became major forces in the shaping of new districts. Gradually, the new suburbs came to outweigh the old town both in economic importance and population density, but tertiary activities clung to the virtually unaltered central areas. Hyldtoft went on to discuss the effect of this structure on housing provision and journey-to-work, showing that an acceleration of the centrifugal process from the 1890s coincided with an improvement in housing standards. Lundén, in 'Stockholm – a hundred years of suburban growth: aspects, factors and functions', pursued the suburbani-zation process from the 1870s to the present, doing much to explain the marked suburban emphasis in the recent planning of the Stockholm region.

The geographical emphasis of these papers was complemented by two studies of the building cycle by Ingrid Hammarström (University of Stockholm) and RICHARD RODGER (University of Liverpool). In 'Building fluctuations 1860–1930: some Swedish evidence', Hammarström analysed the rich Swedish evidence on the lines pioneered in recent years in Britain and the United States. Having identified the operation of a building cycle in the main Swedish towns, she found that it had much the same relationship to the industrial investment cycle as we have come to expect. The type of housing erected by speculative builders varied according to the stage of the cycle. She also discovered an inverse relationship between the Swedish and English building cycles, and sowed the seeds of a Baltic/ North Sea economy debate to succeed the flagging controversy on the Atlantic building economy. Many of her points were echoed by Rodger in his brief discus-sion of the Scottish nineteenth-century building cycle.

With the contributions of BARBARA MILLER LANE (Bryn Mawr), SAM BASS WARNER (Boston University), and ANTHONY SUTCLIFFE (University of Sheffield), attention switched to some of the qualitative aspects of nineteenth-century urban development. In 'Monumental and modern: a reinterpretation of architecture and city planning around 1900', Lane questioned the orthodox inter-pretation of design developments between 1890 and the First World War. Reject-ing the view that these years witnessed the inevitable rise of modernity, she suggested that the dominating preoccupation of architects was with monumenta-lity. The spread of the city and the multiplication of similar buildings, usually linked in continuous façades, had cramped the architects, who sought to escape by isolating their structures and incorporating features which stressed their three-dimensionality. Support for this interpretation came from Sutcliffe's 'Architecture and civic design in nineteenth-century Paris', a critique of the façade-architecture generated by high building densities and the mechanistic improve-ment policies of Haussmann and his successors. Sutcliffe went on, in 'Town planning in European capitals, 1860–1914', a comparison of London, Paris and Berlin, to suggest how, and why, the quality of government in nineteenth-century primate cities generally failed to match the gravity of the exceptionally serious problems which they generated, thus allowing provincial centres (Birmingham, Lyon, Frankfurt) to earn the title of 'best-governed city' in each country. Warner, in 'The transformation of private and public space in the American metropolis, 1870–1970', moved beyond the façades to discuss the links between public space (the street) and the private space of houses, shops and hotels. He argued that in the compact, 'walking city' of mid-nineteenth century America many important ac-tivities took place in the street, and that individuals behaved and dressed in ways designed to maximize their security and well-being in the face of constant encoun-ters with people different from, and possibly threatening to, themselves. As the city began to expand, providing more space and facilities for specific purposes, public space increasingly became a neutral area, with more and more taking place in private accommodation which could be controlled by its owners and users. The massive American hotel lobby, maintained Warner, was a product of this movement, as was the garden of the suburban house. Secure in spaces from which disturbing elements could be excluded, people were able to dress and behave more casually and naturally, but individuals, and especially the poor, were increasingly restricted and surveyed by the guardians of various public spaces. Thus the street, having once been the centre of urban life, was reduced to a marginal zone in which, by the 1970s, the casual stroller risked arrest on suspicion of evil intent.

Warner's wry reflections added a piquancy to the discussion of modern urban redevelopment which centred around papers by THOMAS HALL (University of Stockholm), JOHN ALLPASS (Copenhagen), and PETER HALL (University of Reading). In 'The central business district: planning in Stockholm 1929–1977', Thomas Hall provided an analysis and critique of the reconstruction of central Stockholm in the 1950s and 1960s. He maintained that the rebuilding was decided, in the interests of government, big business and the motor car, by a small circle of officials and councillors. The public was hardly consulted at all until a popular conservation movement helped to halt the demolitions in the later 1960s. Allpass, in 'The urban core – for whom?', agreed in favour of conservation and rehabilitation, citing Copenhagen's example. These criticisms were firmly refuted by a representative of the Stockholm municipality, but the planners' credibility was further undermined by Peter Hall's 'Great planning disasters of our time', a romp through Concorde, BART, the third London airport, and various other flops and white elephants. So lengthy has the planning process become, argued Hall, that big projects inevitably face obsolescence, escalating costs, and complete reversals of circumstances which are liable to make them appear completely misguided.

Where, then, did salvation lie? Hall and Warner now reappeared in positivist guise, announcing the early results of big investigations into the urban phenomenon in the second half of the twentieth century. In 'A research strategy for metropolitan history', Warner made a strong case for taking metropolitan areas rather than cities as the basic unit of urban analysis. Hall's 'The city in the year 2000' supported him, predicting a continuation of the decentralization processes already detectable in the most heavily urbanized areas of Europe. Coming from a historian, Warner's display of versatility was especially impressive, suggesting that the urban historian can help directly in the shaping of the future. After these two papers, moreover, Stockholm began to appear in a more favourable light, with the extraordinarily decentralized structure imposed by its planners seemingly foreshadowing a world-wide, end-of-century urban reality.

The only disappointment in this exciting programme was the lack of lively debate. Scandinavian academic etiquette seemed to demand that praise be lavished on every contribution, and doubts and disagreements repressed. National differences between Nordic countries were kept carefully in the background, except when the Stockholm planner, goaded by Allpass's eulogy of Copenhagen's quaint courtyards, permitted himself some tight-lipped reflections on Danish urban decay. The Swedish social consensus appeared to make efficiency the only respectable goal of urban planning, and the discussion on the redevelopment of Stockholm was amazingly placid, once Allpass had been damned with faint praise by his Swedish hosts.

Towns in Pre-modern England, Institute of Historical Research, London, 1 December 1978

Peter Clark reports that nearly 40 participants heard three papers on various aspects of urban development in the early modern period. BILL CHAMPION (Leicester) talked on 'A late medieval urban crisis? The case of Shrewsbury, 1450 – 1570'. He presented evidence from tolls, rentals and other sources to suggest that Shrewsbury experienced severe demographic and economic difficulty in the late fifteenth and early sixteenth centuries. JOHN SCHOLFIELD (Museum of London) gave an illustrated paper on 'Sixteenth and early seventeenth century housing in London', in which he argued that the limited rebuilding of the capital during the period reflected the conservative building policies of those principal city landlords, the livery companies. In 'The taming of the landscape: street and square in the early modern town c. 1660–1760', PETER BORSAY (Lampeter) emphasized the development of more uniform, classical housing and improved streets after the Restoration. In the lively debate which followed medievalists pointed to the existence of planned groups of buildings in an earlier period, while questions were also raised about land and building costs, and the degree to which classical innovations affected smaller towns.

Those present agreed to hold a similar conference in London in December 1979 and to form a Pre-Modern Town Section of the Urban History Group. Enquiries should be made to the committee, which includes Caroline Barron (Bedford College, London), Peter Clark (Leicester), and David Hey (Sheffield).

History of Planning Group: Planning for Housing in Britain, 1850–1940, Department of Civic Design, University of Liverpool, 17 March 1979

About 30 people – including all the speakers but not the organizer – fought their way to Liverpool through the blizzards. Professor E. P. Hennock stepped in as chairman, and four papers were delivered. M. J. DAUNTON (Durham) in 'Housing peculiarities: the north-east of England, 1850–1914' attempted to explain both the architectural features of working-class housing in his area, and the low quality of the housing stock by contemporary English standards. DAVID WITHAM (Oxford Polytechnic) provided, in 'Like honey from the carcase of the lion: state housing and the Great War', a detailed account of government action in supplying housing for munitions workers in Scotland. In his paper 'An insurance against revolution: British housing policy and housing standards, 1918–1921', MARK SWENARTON (University College London) attempted to argue that the large-scale public housing programme of 1919–21 was a conscious government attempt to abort a putative revolution. Once the threat disappeared, a more narrowly conceived programme was possible. In discussion, he manfully attempted to maintain his conspiracy view of housing policy against other possible explanations such as financial constraints, the impact of rent and mortgage controls, and the realities of local responses to national legislation. The final paper by SIMON PEPPER (Liverpool) on 'Ossulston Street: early L.C.C. experiments in high rise housing' took one housing scheme and traced the changing attitudes to high-rise building, and to mixed working- and middle-class development, which could be found between its inception in 1925 and its completion.

At no time was housing in Liverpool itself – an early pioneer in local authority housing – mentioned, but the participants could return to the blizzards with a greater knowledge of Tyneside, Clydeside and London.

Fourteenth Irish Conference of Historians. 'The Town in Ireland', Queen's University, Belfast, 30 May–2 June 1979

Brenda Collins reports that the theme of this year's conference provided a wide-ranging forum for both historians and political scientists with the timespan of the papers ranging from the eleventh to the twentieth centuries. Of the medievalists, Professor G. MacNIOCAILL (U.C.G.) in 'Socio-economic problems of the medieval Irish towns' argued that the fluid nature of the oligarchy in fourteenth- and fifteenth-century towns such as Dublin, Kilkenny and Waterford could not be understood without reference to the adjacent rural areas both in the provision of migrants to the urban power base and in furnishing adequate grain supplies to allow the towns to expand. The inter-relationship between the functions of Irish 'plantation' towns and their hinterlands was also discussed by Professor G. MARTIN (Leicester).

Subsequent papers, however, emphasized the separation of town and country in the development of Irish urban society. Dr L. CLARKSON's (Q.U.B.) paper

'Armagh 1770: portrait of an urban community' stressed the ways in which the three elements of late eighteenth-century Armagh, adherents of the Established Church, Dissenters and Roman Catholics, formed an interlocking cohesive community with a sense of urban function and specialization. Miss M. MURPHY (Leicester) in 'The economic and social structure of nineteenth century Cork' described the transformation of Cork city from a mid-nineteenth century artisan manufacturing town to a late Victorian mercantile and commercial centre.

The contributions of Dr P. JUPP (Q.U.B.) on 'Urban politics in Ireland, 1801–1831' and Dr C. O'LEARY (Q.U.B.) on 'Belfast 1840–1910: its political and social structure' served to illustrate nicely two juxtaposed but complementary themes of similarity and difference in the wider British context. Dr Jupp outlined some of the differences in the structure of Irish urban politics compared with England, while Dr O'Leary drew attention to the similarity in the effects of 'municipalisation' in nineteenth-century Belfast and in the northern English textile towns. The latter theme also formed part of the opening paper of the conference 'Industrialisation and health in Belfast in the early nineteenth century' by Professor P. FROGATT (Vice-Chancellor, Q.U.B.), although he stressed the gap between contemporary knowledge of the origins of environmental diseases and the will to effect social change to improve the urban quality of living.

The last session of the conference moved forward to the early twentieth century with papers on Belfast and Dublin. Mrs S. GRIBBON (Bangor) in 'An Irish city: Belfast 1911' continued the theme of similarity yet difference by comparing aspects of Belfast life in the early twentieth century with those of other Irish and British towns. Her conclusion was that, in the last analysis, the distinctive and enduring characteristics of the economic and social life of Belfast were an outcome of the urban industrial development of a 'plantation' society. In 'Late nineteenth century and early twentieth century Dublin', Mrs M. DALY (U.C.D.) contrasted the differing industrial/commercial trends in both cities around the turn of the century, and demonstrated how one of the consequences of the Dublin employment structure was a widening gap between 'respectability' and poverty.

The conference papers are to be published early in 1980.

Review of periodical articles

Once more, the cascade of articles published during 1978 and 1979 means that this can only be a limited and selective review. The increased flow of work on the medieval and early modern period reported last year seems to continue in full force, while the torrent of post-1800 articles shows no sign of drying up.

Pre-1500

Recent work on distant and ancient societies is a salutory reminder that nineteenth-century England was far from being the world's first urban civilization. In 'Town and country planning in Ancient India according to Kautilya's *Arthasastra*', *Scottish Geographical Magazine*, xciv (1978), W. Kirk investigates a treatise on the science of government composed between 300BC and 300AD, and explores its vision – not entirely utopian – of the ideal Indian city state. Politics, power and government were, he notes, an urban game: the countryside was seen as a resource base from which wealth was acquired, and as a territory to be taxed and governed. In the same way, A. F. Burghardt argues in 'The origins of the road and city network of Roman Pannonia', *Journal of Historical Geography*, v (1979), that the Romans saw the city as the best way of occupying and controlling space. Hence, in Pannonia at least, the first decision was to set up a garrison, and settlements, roads and trade followed later. Major centres, Burghardt concludes, were site specific: devotees of central place theory be warned!

Decision-making and its role in the creation and establishment of towns is also the concern of B. Graham, 'The evolution of urbanisation in medieval Ireland', *Journal of Historical Geography*, v (1979). He, too, stresses the importance of strategic considerations in the founding of settlements. But this time, he takes the argument one stage further, by trying to relate it to the social structure of Ireland after the Norman Conquest. For, he suggests, the settlement was more likely to succeed the more important and powerful was the feudal lord who took the initial decision. The hierachy of town size is a constant inducement to evolve such elegant correlations and, in 'Patterns of migration in the late middle ages: the evidence of English place-name surnames', *Economic History Review*, 2nd series, xxxii (1979), P. McClure gives another example. His analysis of place-name surnames lends statistical support to the hypothesis that the bigger the town, the greater the catchment area from which it drew its migrant population. But, of course, the danger here is in reaching a circular explanation of the dynamics of urban growth: towns grew biggest which exerted the strongest attraction for migrants; but migrants only travelled long distances to towns which were already large.

One way out of this circular impasse is, perhaps, to stress the economic functions of medieval towns as centres of trade and commerce. D. Nicholas, investigating 'The English trade at Bruges in the last years of Edward III', *Journal of Medieval History*, v (1979), notes how, even after the removal of the wool staple to Calais in 1363, Bruges remained an important centre for English trade, an entrepôt through which luxury items from Italy and Castile were imported. Some, no doubt, made their way to London which, as G. Milne explains in 'The making of the London waterfront', *Current Archaeology*, lxvi (1979), was already zoned, prosperous and thriving by the fourteenth century, with extensive port facilities at Billingsgate. More generally, in what is one of the all-too-few wide-ranging articles this year, he tries to relate the development of London docks over a millennium to the changing level of the river, shifts in economic needs, and to developments in shipping.

Trade, indeed, gets star billing among medieval urban historians this year. In his study of 'Italian merchant organisation and business relationships in early Tudor London', *Journal of European Economic History*, vii (1978), M. E. Bratchel examines the large but diminishing Italian mercantile community, and tries to explain both how it worked, and why it declined. During the first half of the sixteenth century, he argues, the family unit remained of fundamental economic significance. But thereafter, the employment of commission agents removed the need for direct representation abroad, and also enabled operating costs to be reduced substantially. A different approach to the Italian merchant family is to be found in S. Blanshei, 'Population, wealth and patronage in medieval and renaissance Perugia', *Journal of Interdisciplinary History*, ix (1979), where an ambitous attempt is made to relate economic change, social structure and cultural developments. Between the late thirteenth and early sixteenth century, she suggests, the decline in the wool industry weakened the power of the popular party, while at the same time the growth in the mercenary business served to increase the wealth and power of the great family clans. And this change in the distribution of power was reflected in a shift from the old patterns of communal art patronage to more restricted patronage by the nobility. As the ruling oligarchy became narrower, its cultural dominance became more complete.

Clearly, there is much we still do not know about the politics of the Italian city states and, if the findings of two recent articles are any guide, some of what we know may itself be in need of re-thinking. In his account of 'Guild republicanism in trecento Florence: the success and ultimate failure of corporate politics', *American Historical Review*, lxxxiv (1979), J. M. Najemy tries to modify the popular image of republican Florence derived from fifteenth-century civic humanists such as Bruni, by exploring an earlier – and now forgotten – concept of republicanism based on the corporate politics of the guild system, which flourished between the early thirteenth and late fourteenth centuries. In a similarly iconoclastic vein, J. E. Law, 'Verona and the Venetian state in the fifteenth century', *Bulletin of the Institute of Historical Research*, cxxv (1979), suggests that the Burckhardtian picture of the Italian city-state as a 'work of art' is, at least in this particular case, inapplicable, for his investigation of the way in which the Venetians conquered and then controlled Verona suggests that their concept of the state was far more ambiguous, flexible and hesitant than it was abstract, unified and coherent.

Yet, as E. Muir demonstrates in 'Images of power: art and pageantry in renaissance Venice', *American Historical Review*, lxxxiv (1979), such equivocation on the part of the governors was not allowed to spill over into the public image which the state manufactured for itself. Through the use of symbolism and allegory, the plastic and performing arts were successfully employed to elevate political ideas – however tawdry, however vague – to a persuasively transcendent level. And, in unconscious corroboration of Blanshei's study of Perugia, he subtly demonstrates how the tightening of the ruling oligarchy in the sixteenth century resulted in corresponding changes in the art and pageantry itself. Although it takes us across the great divide of 1500, Muir's account of renaissance Venice invites comparison with P. Burke's more general survey, 'Investment in culture in three seventeenth-century cities: Rome, Amsterdam, Paris', *Journal of European Economic History*, vii (1978), where he argues that investment in art and pageantry was undertaken by different towns for different reasons and with different results. In Rome, for example, an administrative and religious centre, there was extensive papal investment in grandeur and ceremonial. But in Amsterdam – more a trading city than a political centre – expenditure was concentrated on buildings for commerce and welfare. And Paris, where the rulers were glorified at the same time as the streets were improved, came half way between.

1500–1800

If trade dominates the medieval period, religion overwhelms the early modern, as urban historians exchange the excitement of the counting house for the agony of the inquisition. The most ambitious work here is E. W. Monter, 'Historical demography and religious history in seventeenth-century Geneva', *Journal of Interdisciplinary History*, ix (1979), which ingeniously utilizes the rich data of baptisms, marriages and burials to plot the ebb and flow of refugees from France, to investigate the working of Calvinist morality (the illegitimacy rates in Geneva were quite incredibly low), and to relate the age of marriage in Geneva to broader European trends. In approach and subject matter, this article twins up well with J. Davies, 'Persecution and protestantism: Toulouse, 1562–1575', *Historical Journal*, xxii (1979), another piece of quantitative analysis, in which the numbers, social background and ultimate decline of the Huguenot community are examined. The dramatic fall in numbers between 1562 and 1575 is well demonstrated: it would be interesting to know how many refugees from Toulouse ended up in Calvin's Geneva.

A century later, as R. M. Golden explains in 'Religious extremism in the mid seventeenth century: the Parisian *Illuminés*', *European Studies Review*, ix (1979), ideas reminiscent of the ranters, diggers and fifth monarchy men were to be found across the Channel. But this extreme branch of *Frondeur* activity was never more than a tiny minority, which makes Golden's attempts to fit it into a more general framework of mid-seventeenth-century European extremism not entirely convincing. In London, by contrast, the Presbyterians fared much better, as M. Mahoney shows in 'Presbyterianism in the city of London, 1645–1647', *Historical Journal*, xxii (1979), in which he painstakingly reconstructs the lists of personnel and rudiments of organization of the High Presbyterian group at parochial level. Another study of urban dissent is J. J. Hurwich, '"A fanatick town": the political influence of Dissenters in Coventry, 1660–1720', *Midland History*, iv (1977). As the author ably demonstrates, despite the penal laws in effect between 1660 and 1688, to say nothing of the restrictions on political activity which continued after the Act of Toleration in 1689, the Dissenting community in the town remained extraordinarily influential, as Crown attempts to suppress them were effectively thwarted by local indifference and obstruction.

Second only to religion comes the attraction of London. The most important article here is V. Pearl's inaugural lecture 'Change and stability in seventeenth-century London', *The London Journal*, v (1979), in which – although ostensibly surveying and synthesizing recent work in the field – she launches a formidable attack on those early modern urban historians who have, she claims, given an incomplete account of town life by stressing crisis, conflict and polarization, and by invoking misleading analogies which liken seventeenth-century English towns to contemporary third-world cities. In a provocative attempt to overturn such views, she suggests that the central question to be asked about Stuart London is not, as some insist, 'Why was it so disorderly?', but rather, 'Why was it so stable?' Her answer – the high, unique degree of neighbourliness and of participation in local government – may not please those whose interpretations she attacks: but her invitation to consider more deeply the question of how, exactly, mid-seventeenth-century London actually held together is surely one which should be accepted. Anyone wishing to contribute would do well to ponder the findings of L. D. Schwartz, 'Income distribution and social structure in London in the late eighteenth century', *Economic History Review*, 2nd series, xxxii (1979), which shows that, despite its reputation as the 'Athens of the artisans', London in fact contained a far higher proportion of employed members of the working class than is generally supposed. Perhaps the economic interdependence between classes which this implies should be pursued backwards into the seventeenth century.

Apart from the oblique references to popular protest in these two metropolitan articles, studies of crowd activity, riots and demonstrations have been rather thin on the ground. W. Albert investigates 'Popular opposition to turnpike trusts in early eighteenth-century England', *Journal of Transport History*, v (1979), and suggests some revision of the prevailing view which sees turnpikes as a value-free force for good, and their opponents as either foolish or wicked. Basing his argument on E. P. Thompson's 'moral economy' work, he claims that turnpikes, like enclosures, were promoted in the interests of a particular social group (the gentry), and that they were opposed, in a disciplined, purposeful manner, by those who saw such changes as a threat to their established rights of free passage along the king's highway. The argument is well developed, but suffers from the fact that there is a large gap between the plausibility of the explanation and the very limited frequency of the riots thus analysed. Part of the problem, as D. Wells makes clear in 'Counting riots in eighteenth-century England', *Bulletin for the Study of Labour History*, xxxvii (1978), lies in the difficulties of evidence and definition for, as he points out, any evidence which might be used for counting the incidence of riots is by its nature flawed, biased and selective. And in any case, even if accurate statistics could be compiled, the problems of definition remain. When is a riot not a riot? What is the difference between a non-violent crowd and a demonstration?

Other areas of inquiry are, it seems, mercifully free from such problems. I. D. Whyte, for instance, seems to have had little difficulty in measuring 'The growth of periodic market centres in Scotland, 1600–1707', *Scottish Geographical Magazine*, xcv (1979), and shows a spectacular increase for the years after 1660. The explanations, he suggests, lie in the general expansion of the economy, the increasing commercialization of agriculture, and the rise of processing and exports. But, as he himself admits, the central problem which remains is to discover exactly how established and upstart market centres interacted as part of an integrated hierarchy of markets. Less broad ranging, but conveying some useful information, is another study of Scottish urban history, D. G. Lockhart, 'The planned villages of Aberdeenshire: the evidence from newspaper advertisements', *ibid.*, xciv (1978), which looks at previous research on planned villages for the period 1750–1850, and argues persuasively that newspapers have been a much neglected source, since many settlements were extensively advertised before building began, and some were advertised which were never built at all.

A last fling north of the border is T. M. Devine's study of 'An eighteenth-century business elite: Glasgow-West India merchants, c1750–1815', *Scottish Historical Review*, lvii (1978), which examines the size, financial interests, social origins and local political influence of the 40-odd merchants who rose to prominence at the end of the eighteenth century as a result of the cotton, sugar and rum trade with the Caribbean. But, he argues, while they were an important influence in local society, they were never the dominant oligarchy as the tobacco lords had been earlier in the century. By the late eighteenth century, the ever-broadening industrial base of the town made it impossible for the elite of one trade to dominate. The rise of the West India trade, he concludes, postponed, but could not halt, the relative political decline of Glasgow's old mercantile elite. In Liverpool, on the other hand, as F. E. Sanderson explains in 'The structure of politics in Liverpool, 1780–1807', *Historic Society of Lancashire and Cheshire*, cxxvii (1978), the old mercantile, dock-building elite retained its grip on the town's affairs for much longer. Indeed, political life in this period was remarkable for its extraordinary parochialness: 'national' issues rarely intruded; party labels meant little; power and place was the name of the game. Shades of Sir Lewis Namier!

Post 1800

The most impressive contribution here is the special issue of the *Institute of British Geographers*, new series, iv (1979), which was given over completely to the Victorian city. Some of the articles are preoccupied with exploring the physical form of the city, and try to locate specific towns somewhere on that haunting, elusive continuum which is supposed to run unbroken from the pre-industrial city of Sjoberg to the post-industrial metropolis of the Chicago school. C. R. Lewis, 'A stage in the development of the industrial town: a case study of Cardiff, 1845–75', does this for the 'coal metropolis', and concludes that by 1870 its internal structure was already relatively highly differentiated. R. C. Fox, using different kinds of data, looks at 'The morphological, social and functional districts of Stirling, 1798–1881', and reports similar changes in a town whose nineteenth-century expansion owed more to its prominence as a market centre than to any spectacular industrial expansion. A similar transition is described by G. Gordon, 'The status areas of early to mid-Victorian Edinburgh', where particular stress is laid on the importance of land-ownership in influencing the timing of development and the particular types of building which might be constructed.

More ambitious – in scope if, perhaps, less so in results – is M. Shaw's attempt at 'Reconciling social and physical space: Wolverhampton, 1871', where he tries to link dimensions of social differentiation with the physical and spatial differentiation of the residential environment. There is a need, he argues, to explain social patterns with reference to those physical and human factors which influenced the development process. But the problem remains of deciding exactly what the social patterns were: a mere statistical aggregation of (say) middle- or working-class areas, or something more intangible (but historically more significant) such as class consciousness? The question is more easily posed than answered, and so it is not surprising that H. Carter and S. Wheatley, in their contribution, 'Fixation lines and fringe belts, land uses and social areas: nineteenth-century change in the small town', explicitly disclaim any attempt at looking at the links between the shapes on the ground and the shapes in society. But what they do succeed in integrating, in their study of Aberystwyth, is the evolution of the physical structure of the town, the consequent disposition of its land uses, and the organization of its social space.

By contrast, K. A. Cowland, 'The identification of social (class) areas and their place in nineteenth-century urban development', suggests that these lines of causality might be reversed, or at least looped back for, as he argues persuasively in the case of Wakefield, using concepts which Walter Firey would have appreciated, once the distinctive social character of an area was established, it tended to be self-perpetuating. It was not just that the city fashioned society; society also moulded the city. How much further such snapshots of the Victorian city at specific moments in time can take us is not entirely clear. What we really need to know more about are the thousands of decisions taken by city-dwellers as to where they should live, when they should move, and what type of housing they should look for, which in aggregate create those trends in city evolution so far preponderantly investigated from outside. The most promising article in this volume, which focuses its attention on this central problem, is C. G. Pooley, 'Residential mobility in the Victorian city', which examines intra-urban mobility in mid-Victorian Liverpool. He concludes that short-distance movement predominated; that the wealthy bourgeoisie moved infrequently but over relatively long distances; and that the workers moved often but only a few houses or streets away. For all the difficulties of research and analysis, this attempt to re-discover what the people in the town actually did seems a more fruitful line of inquiry than further efforts to locate Victorian cities along that curiously appealing Sjoberg-Burgess continuum.

Two other articles in the same journal suggest that the history of urban retailing is about to become a boom subject. G. J. Holyoake, looking at 'Consumers' co-operatives in Victorian Edinburgh: the evolution of a locational pattern', notices that, because the labour aristocracy and *petite bourgeoisie* constituted the co-op's main customers, its stores tended to be distributed in working- and lower-middle-class areas rather than in the central business district. Indeed, if the argument of M. T. Wild and G. Shaw is convincing, it may well be that British urban retailing has always been more widely distributed than, for instance, in America. In 'Trends in urban retailing: the British experience during the nineteenth century', they note how far retailing had become decentralized *before* the advent of the tram or the development of those great changes in the nature of retailing itself at the end of the nineteenth century. But how far this English experience was actually unique remains unclear. For, as M. P. and K. N. Conzen argue, in 'Geographical structure in nineteenth-century urban retailing: Milwaukee, 1836–1890', *Journal of Historical Geography*, v (1979), there was also a well-developed hierarchy of dispersed shopping centres in this American city well before the advent of the streetcar. Clearly, there is important and stimulating scope for some more rigorous attempt at Transatlantic comparison here.

As these studies of urban retailing imply, the impact of mass transport on cities on both sides of the Atlantic remains an enormously important area of study. In an attempt to evaluate more rigorously some of Sam Bass Warner Jr's generalizations, J. Modell, 'Suburbanisation and change in the American family', *Journal of Interdisciplinary History*, ix (1979), tries to discover precisely when it was that the changing form of the city itself came to influence the type of family life which town-dwellers wanted. His conclusion – that in this regard the impact of the car was greater than that of the streetcar – implicitly supports the arguments of M. W. Dupree and D. O. Wise, 'The choice of the automobile for urban passenger transportation: Baltimore in the 1920s', *South Atlantic Urban Studies*, ii (1978). Showing a healthy scepticism for romantic attempts to explain the appeal of the automobile for inter-war Americans with reference to the limitless vistas of travel, excitement and adventure which it opened up, the authors argue persuasively that the demise of the tram and the triumph of the car may most plausibly be explained in terms of rational choices made by commuters, who traded off costs against time and land prices. In England, of course, the love-hate affair with the car came much later, which makes it important for twentieth-century urban historians to heed the request of A. G. Newman, 'Bus services and local history', *Local Historian*, xiii (1979), and make more use of the voluminous documentary sources which bus companies and local authorities have left behind.

In Russia, as M. Crouch shows in 'Problems of Soviet urban transport', *Soviet Studies*, xxxi (1979), the picture was different again. Assuredly, by 1914, in Moscow as in Boston, the streetcar was the predominant form of mass urban transport. But since then, the combined effects of the revolution, the civil war, the Second World War and the restrictions imposed on private transport mean that Soviet city transport has evolved in a way fundamentally different from Western countries. Since 1945, buses and trolley buses have so proliferated that, even without a large private motoring sector, urban congestion has become a major problem. Rapid city growth, inadequate investment, and problems of management and innovation are seen as the main reasons for this. Indeed, the more articles which appear on twentieth-century urban Russia, the more it becomes clear that the U.S.S.R. is *sui generis*. For instance, the problems explored by R. Szporluk, 'West Ukraine and West Belorussia: historical tradition, social communication and linguistic assimilation', *Soviet Studies*, xxxi (1979), and by T. Shabad, 'Some aspects of central Asian manpower and urbanisation', *Soviet Geography*, xx (1979), strike few familiar chords in Western experience. One looks at the role of the Press in an attempt to explain why some recently-assimilated parts of the Soviet Union have become Russian-speaking and others have not; the other explores the problems for Soviet planners which are raised by the distinct preference on the part of Central Asians for a non-urban, non-industrial mode of life.

As this article reminds us, urbanization – and therefore urban history – is not just about large, growing, industrial cities. Although decay and decline are intrinsically less glamorous subjects than expansion and prosperity, they do make up a considerable – if neglected – part of the nineteenth-century urban experience. So it is a pleasure to record two forays into this field for this year. In 'The demographic impact of economic growth and decline: Portpatrick, 1820–1891', *Scottish Historical Review*, lvii (1978), N. L. Tranter explains how a thriving port declined during the second half of the nineteenth century, when the advent of the steamship robbed the town of its unique locational advantages for the Scottish-Irish route in the days of sail. Predictably, he finds this decline reflected in a diminished total population, lower crude birth rates, higher ages of first marriage, and a growing preponderance of women over men. Very similar conclusions are reached by D. Foster, 'Poulton-le-Fylde: a nineteenth-century market town', *Historic Society of Lancashire and Cheshire*, cxxvii (1978), another port and market town which, in the second half of the nineteenth century, stagnated. What it was like to be poor in such relatively undeveloped communities is described, rather anecdotally, in J. Donaldson, 'Mid nineteenth-century poverty in Dumfries', *Dumfries and Galloway Natural History Society*, liii (1977–8), although its conclusion, that Dumfries was 'representative in many ways of the country as a whole', is more easily asserted than proven.

Perhaps these towns would have thrived more if they had boasted energetic and indigenous entrepreneurs. That is certainly the conclusion to be drawn from S. A. Royle, 'The development of Coalville, Leicestershire, in the nineteenth century', *East Midland Geographer*, vii (1978), where the growth of one of the most important mining towns in the east Midlands is persuasively explained in terms of the entrepreneurial flair and energy of William Stenson. A different example of the same phenomenon, but on a much more spectacular scale, is explored by R. W. Lotchin, 'The city and the sword: San Francisco and the metropolitan-military complex, 1919–41', *Journal of American History*, lxv (1979), who shows the extent to which the bay city's economic recovery in the inter-war years was due to the success with which local government and big business were able to persuade the U.S. government to make San Francisco the hub of the west coast defence system. The degree to which that extraordinarily beautiful city was succoured by the presence of the Pacific Fleet certainly lends support to Lotchin's argument that, in the twentieth century at least, militarism and urbanization should be seen as part of an interacting process.

A more conventional study of a nineteenth-century American town is R. Flowerdew, 'Spatial patterns of residential segregation in a southern city', *Journal of American Studies*, xiii (1979), which argues with some force that the effect of earlier black immigration into Southern towns was to produce a different spatial structure from the ghettos characteristic of immigrant communities in northern cities. Other aspects of minority and immigrant experience in the city are dealt with in a variety of articles. S. M. Neild examines 'Colonial urbanism: the development of Madras city in the eighteenth and nineteeth centuries', *Modern Asian Studies*, xiii (1979), and shows the town to have been an amalgam of three separate but overlapping societies: suburban villages of the pre-colonial period; predominantly Indian town centres which expanded largely in response to British trade; and the British urban and suburban community which developed from the late eighteenth century onwards. Changing continents again, D. Coplan, 'The African musician and the development of the Johannesburg entertainment industry, 1900–60', *Journal of Southern African Studies*, v (1979), surveys the decline of indigenous black urban culture, and argues that it was, ironically, the very desire of talented African musicians to equal the black Americans in their own artistic idiom, and join with them in the international entertainment arena, which enabled white commercial interests to gain such complete control over the economics and development of the performing arts in South Africa.

Nearer home, W. Williams, 'The Jewish immigrant in Manchester: the contribution of oral history', *Oral History*, vii (1979), skilfully shows how oral history can restore the full context of Jewish life in a way which ordinary written history – more interested in perpetuating than investigating communal myths – cannot. The assumptions that Jewish immigrants at the turn of the century formed cohesive communities, and that many of them went into the rag trade because observance of the Sabbath was easier, are both impressively debunked. Divisions within the immigrant community are also investigated by G. R. Andrews, 'Race versus class association: the Afro-Argentines of Buenos Aires, 1850–1900', *Journal of Latin American Studies*, xi (1979), who argues that the divisions between middle- and working-class blacks, combined with a lack of opportunities for unskilled workers, meant that the immigrant community was as isolated as it was divided. Far from making racial integration easier, Andrews concludes that the buoyant expansiveness of late nineteeenth-century Buenos Aires only served to exacerbate racial tensions.

The lessons which informed contemporaries drew from this are sketched in by R. M. Morse, 'Latin American intellectuals and the city', *Journal of Latin American Studies*, x (1978). But how typical or representative were the responses of the three 'positivists' and three 'eclectics' whom he investigates is not at all clear. More systematically impressive is A. Lees, 'Critics of urban society in Germany, 1854–1914', *Journal of the History of Ideas*, xl (1979), which guides the reader securely through the mass of literature produced by the city haters, who wanted to put the clock back to an idealized rural world, and by the city reformers, who took the more realistic view that since the city was here to stay, the only sensible policy was to try to make the best of it. A similar attitude is to be found in P. Richards' study 'R. A. Slaney, the industrial town and early Victorian social policy', *Social History*, iv (1979), who urges that more attention should be paid to M.P.s than to 'statesmen in disguise' in attempts to explain the movements for sanitary reform in the 1830s and 1840s.

The responses to urbanization and industrial growth of those less fortunate have received full coverage this year. J. F. Barnes, 'The trade union and radical activities of the Carlisle handloom weavers', *Cumberland and Westmorland Archaeological Society*, lxxviii (1978), is merely a narrative of events, with little attempt at analysis or interpretation. Much more impressive is J. Dinwiddy, 'Luddism and politics in the northern counties', *Social History*, iv (1979), which shows acute awareness of the problem of distinguishing between industrial and political action, and handles the evidence of spies and informers with great discernment. His conclusion – that there was real political content in the Luddites' programme, but little revolutionary leadership or organization – seems judicious and convincing. The need to handle evidence carefully is also illustrated in J. V. Corrigan, 'Strikes and the press in the north east, 1815–44', *International Review of Social History*, xxiii (1978), who points out that if newspapers are to be used as source material for studies of industrial unrest, it is vital to look at the broadest possible range of publications. But some sources, however ingeniously treated, stubbornly refuse to yield unequivocal results. And of none is this more true than the real wage figures which have been endlessly debated in the standard-of-living controversy; as G. N. von Tunzelmann shows, 'Trends in real wages, 1750–1850, revisited', *Economic History Review*, 2nd series, xxxii (1979), if the figures are manipulated with sufficient statistical ingenuity, they can be made to show that real wages doubled, or that they stayed constant.

Faced with such a tiresome conclusion, von Tunzelmann suggests that the figures should be abandoned, and that historians should direct their attention more energetically to exploring the nature of the environment in which people actually lived. And the signs are that this is exactly what is beginning to happen. M. Lewis, for example, looks at 'Sanitation, intestinal infection and infant mortality in late-Victorian Sydney', *Medical History*, xxiii (1979), and relates the decline in the high death rate resulting from diarrheal diseases to changes in the spatial pattern of the city, improvements in transport, and extensive provision of sewerage and water supply. Much less aware of context is S. T. Anning, 'The history of medicine in Leeds', *Leeds Philosophical and Literary Society*, xvi (1978), which merely provides an antiquarian's account of hospitals, doctors, nurses and diseases, with no attempt to relate such information to general issues of urban growth. By contrast, N. Evans, '"The first charity of Wales": Cardiff Infirmary and South Wales society, 1837–1914', *Welsh History Review*, ix (1979), does precisely that, by setting the history of Cardiff's premier hospital firmly and perceptively within the context of Cardiff's growth and changing attitudes to philanthropy.

It would be an unusual year which did not see more writing on the Welsh capital by M. J. Daunton. In 'Jack ashore: seamen in Cardiff before 1914', *Welsh History Review*, ix (1978), he explores the reasons why it was so long before the National Amalgamated Union of Sailors and Firemen, set up in 1887, was recognized in Cardiff. The life-style of the seamen, the problems of competition from foreign labour, and the fluid nature of wage negotiating are all explored with characteristic thoroughness. Another article, on a closely related subject, which is equally sensitive to place and circumstance is E. L. Taplin, 'Dock labour at Liverpool: occupational structure and working conditions in the late nineteenth century', *Historic Society of Lancashire and Cheshire*, cxxvii (1978), which draws out the important distinction between porters and stevedores and explains why it was that, despite its critics, the system of casual dockside labour lasted for so long.

Both writers draw attention to the spendthrift habits engendered by casual labour and irregular, uncertain income. But, as R. I. McKibbin shows in 'Working-class gambling in Britain, 1880–1939', *Past and Present*, lxxxii (1979), it is dangerous to view this quintessentially working-class activity through the eyes of biased and ill-informed middle-class observers. For, as he convincingly demonstrates, most working-class people gambled because it was rational, rather than profligate, so to do. In a related article, 'Social class and social observation in Edwardian England', *Royal Historical Society Transactions*, xxviii (1978), the same author explores attempts to investigate the domestic lives and social attitudes of the working classes made by Mrs Bosanquet, Miss Load and Lady Bell, and shows how, simultaneously, they accepted the concept of class, yet failed fully to understand it. Even more revealing of middle-class attitudes to the lower orders is P.A. Dunae, 'Penny dreadfuls: late nineteenth-century boys' literature and crime', *Victorian Studies*, xxii (1979), which argues that the shift from disapproval of such literature in the 1870s to admiration two decades later, is more to be explained by changing middle-class attitudes than by changes in the nature of the product. What was denounced as 'blood and thunder' in an age of peace and internationalism was acclaimed as 'wholesome and patriotic' in a period of international tension and crisis.

The urban middle classes themselves are carefully scrutinized this year. P. Searby, 'Progress and the parish pump: local government in Coventry, 1820–1860', *Birmingham Archaeological Society Proceedings and Transactions*, lxxxviii (1976), shows that the relationship between the reform of local government in London and what actually went on in the localities is far from simple. In Coventry, at least, the impact of that supposedly epoch-making piece of legislation, the Municipal Corporations Act, was distinctly limited. Even before 1835, the council had already become relatively honest and efficient, and the changes resulting from the legislation of 1835 'created no additional measure of these qualities'. A similar problem is explored by G. T. Rimmington, 'Leicestershire school boards, 1871–1903', *Leicestershire Archaeological and Historical Society Transactions*, lii (1976–7), who tries to explain why some towns and villages adopted school boards, and others did not. Another local elite finds itself under the microscope in E. D. Steele, 'The Leeds patriciate and the cultivation of learning, 1819–1905: a study of the Leeds Philosophical and Literary Society', *Leeds Philosophical and Literary Society*, xvi (1978), which explains how this bastion of middle-class corporate identity and self-assurance came into being, how it flourished in the mid-Victorian era, and why it was that it suffered a crisis of finance and of support in the years 189'–1905.

Across the Pennines in Lancashire, the Manchester middle-class has also been the subject of a variety of studies. S. D. Chapman, 'Financial restraints on the growth of firms in the cotton industry, 1790–1850', *Economic History Review*, 2nd series, xxxii (1979), questions Gatrell's recent suggestion that it was the attitudes of the entrepreneurs which kept firms small, and suggests that a more plausible explanation lies in the difficulty of obtaining capital without which it was impossible to break into the important (but precarious) overseas market. The role of foreign trade is further examined by B.M. Ratcliffe, 'Commerce and empire: Manchester merchants and West Africa, 1873–1895', *Journal of Imperial and Commonwealth History*, vii (1979), which explores the relationship between the merchants on the spot in Africa, the mercantile lobby in Manchester, and government attitudes in Whitehall. Yet a third facet of the middle-class elite of Cottonopolis is investigated in D. A. Farnie, 'An index of commercial activity: the membership of the Manchester Royal Exchange, 1809–1948', *Business History*, xxi (1979), who plots the rise and fall of the greatest meeting place for merchants and manufacturers in the cotton industry.

Even higher up the social scale, F. Harcourt, 'The Queen, the Sultan and the Viceroy: a Victorian state occasion', *The London Journal*, v (1979), shows how, as a result of the unprecedented pageantry of July 1867, it was first realized that London possessed potential as the ceremonial centre of a great empire. But cities were not, of course, merely the setting for establishment ritual. In '"Red Wednesday" in Hamburg: social democrats, police and lumpenproletariat in the suffrage disturbances of 17 July 1906', *Social History*, iv (1979), R. J. Evans mounts a sustained and impressive assault on the Tillys' attempts to measure violence, by arguing that such an approach divorces protest completely from its historical context, without an understanding of which its meaning cannot be plausibly or convincingly interpreted. Much more sinister activities in the twentieth-century German town are reported in E. G. Reiche, 'From "spontaneous" to legal terror: S.A., police and the judiciary in Nürnberg, 1933–4', *European Studies Review*, ix (1979), in which the process whereby the Nazis obtained control over the police and the judiciary is painstakingly reconstructed. Very different is the picture of police activity revealed by R. Harrison, 'New light on the police and the hunger marchers', *Bulletin for the Study of Labour History*, xxxvii (1979), where, despite some evidence of police spying, he concludes that the British force deputed to control the London Hunger March of 1934 was more muddleheaded and amateur than it was violent or sinister.

Some of the hunger marchers – if they were lucky – might have been the beneficiaries of the government's inter-war housebuilding programme, an important subject which has recently begun to attract scholarly attention. An early foray by the central government into building homes fit for heroes is described by S. Marriner, 'Sir Alfred Mond's octopus: a nationalised housebuilding business', *Business History*, xxi (1979). More generally, E. Roberts compares 'Working-class housing in Barrow and Lancaster, 1880–1930', *Historic Society of Lancashire and Cheshire*, cxxvii (1978). She concludes that in Barrow, the gross overcrowding of the pre-1914 period was largely eradicated in the inter-war years, not by council house building, but by the complete economic collapse of the town which resulted in a massive decline in population. In Lancaster, by contrast, it was the energetic programme of housebuilding instituted by the council which was responsible for improvement. Another study of inter-war government intervention is R.H. Campbell, 'The Scottish Office and the special areas in the 1930s', *Historical Journal*, xxii (1979), where he shows convincingly that attempts by Scottish Office officials to encourage new industrial development in depressed areas were largely frustrated by the Whitehall mandarins.

Nor, as another clutch of articles demonstrates, are we any closer to making planning and industrial rejuvenation work. In 'New towns in the Paris region: an appraisal', *Town Planning Review*, l (1979), J. Tuppen describes the ambitious French proposals which were evolved in the late 1960s, and contrasts them with the less-than-successful communities which have actually taken shape, with lower target populations, a weaker economic sub-structure, and less satisfactory buildings and layout, than had once been anticipated. In England, too, there has been a shift in government thinking in the 1970s away from new towns, and towards a policy of reviving the central areas of ailing big cities. But, as A.W.Cox explains, 'Administrative inertia and inner city politics', *Public Administration Bulletin*, xxix (1979), it has not been accompanied by the evolution of an administrative structure of sufficient flexibility for there to be any real chance of its effective implementation. And this pessimistic view is largely corroborated by W. A. K. Struthers and C. B. Williamson, who examine 'Local economic development: integrated policy planning and implementation in Merseyside', *Town Planning Review*, 1 (1979); their investigation of the ways in which the new metropolitan county of Merseyside has tried to tackle the serious economic problems of the area is more a description of administrative structure than an account of projects successfully implemented.

Indeed, the problems of contemporary urban life get a very full airing this year. B. Kruijt, 'The changing spatial pattern of firms in Amsterdam: empirical evidence', *Tidjschrift voor Economische en Sociale Geografie*, lxx (1979), describes the decline of the manufacturing and service industries which has in turn resulted in a reduction in population in both inner city and urban renewal areas. M. Boddy and F. Gray examine 'Filtering theory, housing policy and the legitimation of inequality', *Public Planning*, vii (1979), and argue that public policy which is based on the old faithful of the Chicago school merely perpetuates its underlying ideology of *laissez-faire*, and therefore fails to solve the problem of housing for the urban poor. The survival of the fittest in the contemporary urban environment is also the subject of D. Mclennan, 'Information networks in a local housing market', *Scottish Journal of Political Economy*, xxvi (1979), which looks at the way in which individuals obtain and use information when searching for furnished, rented accommodation. He concludes that those who have access to informal sources of information have the highest success rate in finding the type of accommodation they want; but ·that such sources only tend to become available after those in search have spent a long time looking.

Finally, to end where we began, some articles on town planning. In a wide-ranging general survey, G. Cherry, 'The town planning movement and the late Victorian city', *Institute of British Geographers*, new series, iv (1979), tries to refine the prevailing evolutionary model of town planning development by explaining the growth of interest in the subject at the end of the nineteenth century with reference to the precise issues and problems of late Victorian urban society. More specifically, M. Wynn examines 'Barcelona: planning and change, 1854–1977', *Town Planning Review*, 1 (1979), and shows how attempts to lay out the city systematically have constantly been thwarted by developers, speculators and landowners. Hopping continents again, R. F. Haswell, 'South African towns on European plans', *Geographical Magazine*, li (1979) deftly illustrates the way in which the planned Boer and British communities of the nineteenth century reflected the different priorities – economic, cultural, social and religious – of their respective societies. But the most interesting piece on this subject is J. W. R. Whitehand, 'Long-term changes in the form of the city centre: the case of redevelopment', *Geogfiska Annaler*, lx (1978), which is a pioneering attempt to quantify and explain the re-development of the centre of Glasgow since 1840. Another aspect of Whitehand's work – this time the expansion of the urban fringe – finds support in R. G. Rodger, 'The building cycle and the urban fringe in the Victorian cities: another comment', *Journal of Historical Geography*, v (1979), which also reports 'the recent defection of Cannadine from a supporter of the idiosyncratic landowner approach to that of price determination in the land market' as being 'most interesting'. It is always a pleasure to read other people's articles to discover what one is thinking!

David Cannadine
Christ's College, Cambridge

Reviews of books

An index to authors and titles has been provided at the end (pp. 178–9).

1 GENERAL AND THEMATIC

Josef W. Konvitz, *Cities and the Sea: Port City Planning in Early Modern Europe.*
   Baltimore and London: The Johns Hopkins University Press, 1978. xv + 235 pp.
   No price stated.

In this ambitious study of how and why Europeans since the Renaissance have built new port cities and rebuilt existing ones, Josef Konvitz heralds 'the beginning of a new age of maritime exploitation' by a wide-ranging comparison of urban cultures across time and space. It is his contention that the work of city planners, with which the book is literally illustrated, not only demonstrates the process of early modern urban growth but also represents a conscious effort on the part of contemporary rulers and intellectuals to place an understanding of maritime affairs at the centre of urban civilization. Changes in the traditional maritime world in the early seventeenth century meant that maritime affairs took on more profound political and social implications than ever before and that the old monolithic view of the sea as a hostile place became outmoded. Thus the Dutch combined successful exploitation of sea-power with cultural change and with the acceptance of urban planning as a means to prevent growth choking the development of their ports. Konvitz contrasts their pragmatic approach with the increasingly grandiose schemes adopted by Baltic rulers who drew the wrong conclusions from the Dutch example and hoped that port city planning would serve as a matrix for sea-power, in defiance of evidence that planning styles were no substitute for demographic and material resources. This proliferation of monumental, impractical plans is seen as one reason for the declining importance of city planning in the eighteenth century and for its replacement by engineering as a means of tackling the problems of urban growth. However, Konvitz is also concerned to link this decline with broader cultural developments, claiming that the planners' role as mediators between society and sea-faring had been usurped by the writers, artists and theorists who were now offering more stimulating approaches to the crucial issues.

   This dual explanation of the declining importance of planning in the modern world illustrates Konvitz's own uneasy combination of the practical and the ideal. The detailed analysis of Louis XIV's new port cities which forms the core of the book seems marooned amid the lofty cultural speculations that brush against the experiences of so many countries in passing. He admits that relatively few people contributed to the arguments that port city planning stimulated; and in a sense the most interesting – and unanswered – question is why the English remained stubbornly convinced that planning had nothing to do with sea-power.

Joyce Ellis
University of Loughborough

R. Forster and O. Ranum (eds), *Family and Society. Selections from the Annales Economies, Sociétés, Civilisations.* [Translated by E. Forster and P. M. Ranum.] Baltimore and London: The Johns Hopkins University Press, 1976 x + 261 pp. $3.45. £2.75.

The history of the family can be both a delight and an embarrassment. Its practitioners have produced some of the most original and invigorating, but also some of the most pretentious and muddled, historical writing of recent years. This welcome collection of essays can be placed firmly in the former category. The second in a series of volumes of translations from *Annales E.S.C.*, for which the Johns Hopkins Press deserves the gratitude of all teachers of social history in the English-speaking world, it provides 11 essays linked by their concern with the sociology of the family in the past. All save one, in fact, originally appeared in the well-known special issue of *Annales E.S.C.* for July-October 1972, the exception being N. Belmont's 1973 article. It might be objected that the editors could have cast their net wider in order to achieve a greater degree of chronological or geographical unity than this volume possesses. Such criticism would, however, lack justice. The principal virtue of the collection is not its potential usefulness as a course reader, but rather the way in which it renders more accessible a wide range of approaches to diverse aspects of family history.

A simple rehearsal of the contents serves to make the point clear. Belmont examines ancient rituals of child-recognition and assesses their significance. Duby explores the evolution of the feudal seigneury of the Mâcon region through genealogical analysis. Le Roy Ladurie carefully summarizes the inheritance patterns revealed by sixteenth-century French customary laws. Klapisch and Demonet reconstruct rural Tuscan household structure from the 1427 *catasto* listing. The problems of widowhood and parental loss in the early-modern Paris region are sensitively handled by Bauland, while Bourdieu's essay provides a fascinating analysis of marital strategies among Pyrenean peasants. Moving further afield, Kula investigates the influence of the manorial regime in eighteenth-century Poland on peasant family life and Cuisenier analyses, with striking sophistication, the role of kinship in the social organization of medieval Turcoman tribes. Finally, Burguière discusses attitudes to contraception and the origins of the pattern of late marriage in early-modern France, while Lautman examines the problems of conceptualizing change in family organization in the face of the coexistence of distinct family types in particular societies.

Of the 11 essays, only one, Depauw's study of illegitimacy from the *déclarations de grossesse* of eighteenth-century Nantes (the only example available in English of the extensive French literature on illegitimacy and abandonment), is of direct relevance to urban historians. Nevertheless, the volume is to be recommended for its broader relevance. British urban history for periods earlier than the nineteenth century has not yet carried the analysis of the structure and dynamics of urban society far beyond studies of the distribution of wealth, migration, poor relief and the composition of governing elites. Those who wish to extend the field of enquiry will find both the questions raised and the techniques adopted in this volume an excellent point of departure.

Keith Wrightson
Department of Modern History, University of St Andrews

Peter Burke, *Popular Culture in Early Modern Europe*. London: Temple Smith, 1978. 365 pp. £9.75.

It is over 15 years since Mandrou's book on the content of the 'bibliothèque bleue de Troyes' first appeared in France, and proved the seminal work which led to the growth of the 'mentalité' school, which attempts not only to examine popular attitudes and changes in them, but also to provide quantified evidence for these extremely slippery subjects. Now we have Peter Burke's book as a first general survey in English of the whole field of popular culture in Europe. His Europe extends from the Hebrides in the west to Russia in the east, from Norway in the north to Sicily in the south, geographically speaking, and from 1500 to 1800, temporally speaking. His subject matter includes dancing, mumming, plays, chapbooks, ballads, and their dominant themes and heroes, as well as popular festivals and rituals, iconography and the decorative arts. The book is likely to act, as Mandrou's did, as a catalyst to refocus the thinking of social historians.

Peter Burke sets his massive survey within the historiographical framework of the 'rediscovery' of popular culture by intellectuals from the mid-eighteenth century onwards. One of his main theses is that the elite of Europe, lettered and Latin-speaking, shared in the festivals, listened to the sermons, read the chapbooks, and sang the ballads of the common people for amusement until some time in the seventeenth or eighteenth centuries, when the upper classes withdrew from participation. The nobility and bourgeoisie were affected by the refinements of the Renaissance, the clergy and the gentry by both Puritan and Catholic Reformations. The time-lag involved in the spread of these movements meant that by 1800, when the Russian nobility was gradually stopping revering icons, watching buffoons and reading chapbooks, the academic revival of interest in the taste of the common people as a proper object of study was elsewhere in full swing.

Within this frame, Peter Burke looks not only at change in the context of popular culture within his period, but also at regional and occupational differences within it. He surveys, for instance, the 'sub-culture' of farmers and herdsmen, shepherds, craftsmen, and miners, in the countryside, and weavers, shoemakers, journeymen and apprentices in the towns, as well as itinerants belonging to neither. He never falls into the trap of rigid classification, and is good not only on borrowings of popular culture from the elite, as on the sinking of the medieval chivalric story into the seventeenth-century chapbook, but also on the reverse process. He drives home his points with fascinating detail; how many of us knew Handel used the music he heard the shepherds of the Abruzzi play in 1707, in the *Messiah*?

He surveys professional and amateur performers, the craftsmen, singers, showmen, preachers, whose wanderings carried popular works across Europe, and then looks at the various type of performances they put on, and analyses their form and content. He devotes a chapter to the heroes and villains of popular mythology, since they reveal much about the tastes of the audiences to whom they appealed.

One of Peter Burke's virtues is his commendable caution, shown perhaps best in his consideration of the 'mediators', the Villons and Mrs Browns, who transmitted the *argot* of fifteenth-century Paris, or the late seventeenth-century ballads of rural Scotland, and yet were themselves M.A.s of Paris or daughters of professors of Greek. Oral traditions, faithfully recorded by ballad-collector or folklorist, often turn out to be less faithful reproductions of earlier cheap print. Peter Burke is very aware of the pitfalls involved, and his suggestions of 'oblique approaches' to the problems, using, for instance, surviving customs, plays or ballads recorded in the nineteenth century, as palimpsests, and working backwards through time to discover their early modern equivalents, as Bloch used eighteenth-century field-maps, are extremely interesting.

The limitations of the book on the whole are those of space, or of the regional materials which were available for synthesis. One of the themes Burke suggests, the iconographic, he does not follow far, perhaps for reasons of space, or perhaps because the concrete appeals to him less than the abstract. He is much more detailed on the articulate expressions enjoyed by the common people than the tangible residue of their living. Songs, story-telling, festivals and dancing engage him much more than surviving peasant artifacts, from houses, to marriage-chests, to pottery.

England was one of the regions where materials were short for him. There were no studies of the English chapbook and the English chapmen before the eighteenth century for him to draw on, for instance. It was a pity, though, that he missed R. S. Thomson's thesis on the development of the English broadside ballad trade, since it has so much valuable evidence on the way print fed into the oral tradition. It was also a pity he missed Cressy's work on literacy and its social distribution which would have supported some of his themes well. As a result his few pages on literacy in England have a slightly old-fashioned air. I myself doubt whether the English upper-classes ever became completely unaware of popular culture. There is evidence that schoolboys acted as the new cultural intermediaries, and, in the intervals of their elite education, avidly read the old chapbook stories.

It is ridiculous, however, presented with such a masterly synthesis, which will spark off a range of questions which are new to many historians, to cavil at items missing from the footnotes. What is amazing is the breadth and inclusiveness of the study. Why, though, could the publishers not make these same end notes more accessible to the serious reader by heading each page of them with the page numbers to which they refer, and so cutting down the constant chore of hunting for them?

Margaret Spufford
Department of History, University of Keele

Christopher Duffy, *Siege Warfare: The Fortress in the Early Modern World, 1494–1660*, London and Henley: Routledge and Kegan Paul, 1979. xii + 289pp. 82 illustrations. 20 maps. Annotated bibliography. General index. £9.95.

The bastioned enceintes thrown up against siege artillery dominate urban history between 1600 and 1860. All over Europe cities and towns were cut off from the country, their expansion contained by the ever-increasing depth of costly and complex defences. Vauban's magnificent Neuf-Brisach is protected by works 700 ft deep. The outermost glacis of the defences of Valletta in Malta ends 1800 yds from the main gate. Military architects or engineers were often also intimately concerned with important aspects of urban life; with sanitation and the water supply, granaries and stores, certain industries and trades, and with the alignment and layout of streets.

The best general survey of the evolution of fortification is Quentin Hughes, *Military Architecture* (London, Hugh Evelyn, 1974). Christopher Duffy is concerned mainly with war and the tactics of offence and defence. This study is the first part of what promises to be an important work on the role of fortification and siege in various theatres of war. The next volume will be *Siege Warfare II. The Fortress in the Age of Vauban and Frederick the Great*.

The value of this study to those working on urban history is that Mr Duffy relates the human and physical defences of a particular city or fortress and its experience under siege to its role in a specific war. Mr Duffy firmly makes the point that for the historian fortifications and sieges are only part of a general picture, other foreground features of which are battles in the field, the movement of armies, diplomacy and so on. The architect on the other hand tends to be more interested in design, proportion and symbolism. Thus while Mr Duffy discusses the methods and tactics developed by the attacker and the counter-measures taken by the defender he is careful to give the human factor its due weight. During siege the civil population is invariably taxed and generally imposed on; robbed and at times starved, bombarded, expelled, often decimated by pestilence and occasionally massacred.

The main body of the book deals with wars in Italy, France, the Low Countries, the Baltic and Germany. The lucid and well-illustrated account of the horribly complicated campaigns and siege upon siege in the Low Countries, 1566–1648, is, I think, the best chapter in the book. The periphery gets reasonable coverage too. There is a good chapter on Britain and its sieges during the civil and Irish wars. Others are on the Ottoman war zones in the Mediterranean, south-east Europe, southern Russia and Asia, and a very interesting introduction to fortress building and siege outside Europe – North America will be dealt with in the second volume. The sections on India, China, south-east Asia and Japan are fascinating and cry out for more illustrations.

There is an excellent, comprehensive, annotated bibliography of over 400 entries and in general the illustrations and maps are of high quality – though I am disappointed by the plan on p. 194 illustrating the defences of Malta. There are better ones.

Of course, because the book covers two centuries Mr Duffy has had to be selective and the result is unavoidably patchy especially as regards the European periphery where the thread of development in siege and defence running through the principal chapters is inevitably lost. More serious in my view, taken from the central Mediterranean, is the very thin coverage of Italian military engineering in the seventeenth century. There is no reference, for example, to Pietro Paolo Floriani's *Difesa et offesa delle Piazze* (Macerata, 1630), which Quentin Hughes (*op. cit.*, 122) describes as 'one of the most influential treatises of the period'. Perhaps Mr Duffy intends to introduce Vauban by discussing those of his precursors who did consider fortification and siege as scientifically soluble problems.

But it is unfair to highlight weak points when the book is, generally, of such high quality. In the second volume Mr Duffy will be on his own stamping ground and we can expect an even more impressive study. I have kept a few superlatives against its appearance and hope we can have a third volume on siege warfare in the wars of the French Revolution and Napoleon.

Roger Vella Bonavita
Department of History, Old University, Malta

R. A. Griffiths (ed.), *Boroughs of Medieval Wales*. Cardiff: University of Wales Press, 1978. xii + 338pp. £12.50.

Studies of individual medieval English towns have accumulated rapidly in the last few years and two recent syntheses by Colin Platt and Susan Reynolds have been based on this detailed local work. Research on Welsh towns is, however, at a very different stage. There has been no general survey of Welsh medieval urban history since E. A. Lewis' *The Medieval Boroughs of Snowdonia* (1912) and no future survey can be attempted without 'a preliminary series of local studies which will demonstrate the variety of burghal development as well as its common features'. The collection under review is the first step towards providing such a body of local research. Griffiths' volume consists of his own introduction to the study of Welsh medieval urban history and his studies of Aberystwyth and Carmarthen, together with chapters on Brecon, Caernarvon, Cardiff, Denbigh, Newport, Oswestry, Ruthin, Swansea, and Tenby by nine other scholars.

Although dealing only with a limited number of towns, which were themselves small even by English standards, these individual studies bring out the diversity of Welsh urban life, from Carmarthen, a Roman fort in the late 70s A.D., to Aberystwyth founded in 1277, from Brecon with its overwhelmingly local economic orbit to Tenby with its international trade. Further diversity is provided by the sources available for each town. For Newport ecclesiastical records are important in the absence of records of the borough administration. In Oswestry charters help to fill this gap. At Tenby architectural remains offer useful evidence, whilst W. R. B. Robinson has the unenviable task of writing about Swansea, a town where architectural evidence has been obliterated and documentary sources are slight.

Despite the fact that the book consists of individual studies of diverse towns drawn from a wide range of sources, a number of common themes can be discerned. These themes are made plain by the town maps which accompany each chapter. In Ruthin, for instance, the focal points of the town were the castle, the market-place and the collegiate church of St Peter. Such administrative, military, mercantile and religious functions give a unity to the studies, whether of towns of Anglo-Norman or Edwardian foundation, inland market or coastal port. In the Norman settlement of Wales 'castle, town and priory . . . were the triple bastions of the new regime'. In Oswestry the castle physically loomed over the town, Caernarvon was always primarily a garrison town, Newport was the headquarters of the regional seignorial administration. The church was not only a geographical focus within the towns but also 'one of the most effective weapons in the armoury of the new conquerors'. In Carmarthen, Benedictine monks helped to wean the Welsh from their traditional religious practices, while Brecon was the focus of religious life in its district. The market place was, of course, crucial to borough development. In

Aberystwyth, the town enjoyed a virtual market monopoly within a radius of 15 miles. Denbigh's burgesses enjoyed a similar privileged position.

The map of Ruthin provides another clue to one of the common themes of the collection in its Welsh Street, where in 1324 of 27 known burgesses 22 were Welsh. In Ruthin itself the Welsh became burgesses from the early days of the borough. Although varying in pace, the general trend was towards integration of the Welsh into urban life. Indeed, by the sixteenth century, Oswestry (technically in England) was 'more Welsh than the English boroughs of Wales'. Caernarvon and Camarthen were also in Welsh hands by the sixteenth century, though in Denbigh English families still managed to maintain their grip on borough offices.

These 11 case histories, united by common themes and well furnished with maps and references, are a welcome addition to our knowledge not only of the Welsh town but of medieval urban history in general. Covering no more than a small proportion of the 90 Welsh medieval boroughs, the volume permits only tentative and provisional general conclusions. Nonetheless, R. A. Griffiths and his contributors have provided a solid foundation for much future research.

S. H. Rigby
Department of History, Bedford College, London

John Patten, *English Towns 1500–1700*. Folkestone: Dawson, and Hamden, Connecticut: Archon, 1978. 348 pp. £12.00.

John Patten is already well known to students of the early modern town from a number of articles on migration, occupational ranking and the use of the hearth tax records. Together with other historical geographers he has played an active part in rolling back the blanket of ignorance which once shrouded towns in Tudor and Stuart England. Not surprisingly his new book on the demographic and economic development of those towns has much to offer. Though his detailed field-work is confined to Norfolk and Suffolk he reveals a wide knowledge of recent published work and unpublished doctoral dissertations.

The first part of the book is introductory providing an over-view of urban society in the period. One chapter scans recent urban studies, notes (without attempting to resolve) the difficulty of defining a town, and concludes with an impression of life in the pre-industrial community. A second chapter describes the urban hierarchy (without adding much to the accepted picture) and then considers some of the factors affecting urban change. Among the 'forces inhibiting change', Patten ranges the slow pace of agricultural development, the small scale and rural bias of most industry, the vicissitudes of foreign trade, and more specific urban disasters such as fire, plague and civil war damage. He has some very useful data on the turmoil of the 1640s and on the impact of fires (although he neglects the way that fires, such as those at Northampton and Warwick in the late seventeenth century, could also open up a bright future for some places with fashionable new buildings attracting large numbers of gentry and professional men to town). In the case of plague Patten puts forward a pessimistic view of the urban consequences, though recent work has tended to argue that the long term effects were fairly limited. Among the 'forces promoting change' were population growth, 'the openness and free institutions' of certain towns, migration and the influence of London.

The second part of the book is thematic, looking in turn at urban population, the economy, and the relations of towns and their hinterlands. Population estimates of various towns are provided for various periods and there is also an account of the regional ranking of town populations. All this is valuable, fleshing out our limited knowledge of demographic trends. Less successful is the analysis of the processes of demographic change with mortality and fertility receiving fairly superficial treatment. The chapter on the urban economy makes good use of freemen and other records to shed light on occupational structures and argues persuasively that 'whole areas of England had few specialized towns of any sort, no large ones of any kind, and only the most generalized urban economies'. By the late seventeenth century, however, there was growing occupational diversification in towns, while more specialist centres – dockyard towns, spas, industrial towns – were also putting in an appearance; London and its differentiated suburbs set the pace for both developments.

Patten rightly emphasizes the vital relationship of the town and its rural hinter-land. He illuminates this through a survey of urban markets and marketing (based on Everitt's work), the growth of urban-style shops in the countryside, and immigration – attempting to plot migrational fields mainly from apprenticeship data. Particularly good is the discussion of the changing fortunes of the small ports whose prosperity was increasingly derived from the buoyant coastal trade. The last part of the book, a case study of East Anglia, brings together in shortened form several pieces which have been published already.

The book has numerous strengths: the presentation of a mass of demographic and other data from a kaleidoscope of sources; the constant awareness of and will-ingness to tackle methodological problems; the appreciation of the importance of seeing towns interacting one with another in regional networks; and the light shed on the structural weaknesses and problems of towns during the period. But at the same time there are disappointments. While we learn of the long-term trends affecting urban populations and economies there is little serious consideration of the medium and short term fluctuations which may have afflicted towns: one thinks here of the early Tudor crisis described by Phythian-Adams, or the major dislocation in many older towns during the 1620s and 1630s. The focus on demo-graphic and economic variables tends to mean that social, political and other influences on urban growth are under-estimated – the impact, say, of large-scale pauperization or the patronage by an aristocrat of a small market town. Again the book is rather disorganized: the same theme tends to jump up like a startled rabbit in a variety of unexpected places while the direction of the general argument is never very clear (exemplified by the introductory remark 'that change, not growth, was the diagnostic characteristic within individual towns and within the growing urban system'). Most serious, though considerable data is presented on a large number of towns, the cream is spread somewhat thinly; we never get to know any one town, with its own complex demographic and economic structures, at all well. This is not entirely Patten's fault, of course. We badly need more detailed studies of individual towns. Monographs must be at the top of the agenda for historians of the early modern town during the next decade. No doubt this study, so wide-ranging and interesting, will do much to stimulate the new work.

Peter Clark
Department of Economic and Social History, University of Leicester

Bernard Capp, *Astrology and the Popular Press: English Almanacs, 1500–1800.* London: Faber and Faber, 1979. 452 pp. £15.00.

Almanacs were probably the most popular form of reading in the seventeenth and eighteenth centuries, and certainly the best-selling, next to the Bible, yet so far they have been discussed only in articles in learned periodicals. Bernard Capp's pioneering book inevitably takes the form of a series of essays – 'Almanacs and pol-itics', 'Almanacs and religion', 'Society', 'History and literature', 'Astrology, science and medicine' – but it is a welcome first survey of the subject as a whole, and gives us a mass of illuminating detail by the way.

The great Puritan theologian William Perkins denounced almanacs for producing 'contempt of the providence of God' (p. 32). But almanacs suffered impartially from the Laudian and post-Restoration censorship. They flourished most freely in the 1640s and 1650s (pp. 47–50). Even after 1660 'they preserved a public awareness of political events and issues. Their partisan violence helped to sustain party loyalties and divisions. In publicizing threats to liberty or religion they helped also to establish the idea that political issues were of vital importance to all; to that extent they reduced the likelihood of royal absolutism' (p. 101). The radical Whig attitude of Old Moore 'must have been an important formative influence in the growth of English radicalism in the early 1790s; even Paine's *The Rights of Man* reached only a fraction of the homes which possessed an annual copy of the almanac' (p. 266).

The main usefulness of this book for most historians will derive from the incidental light thrown on social history. 'While contemporary French almanacs seem not to have advanced beyond platitudinous advice on when to sow and reap', English almanacs gave information on new crops and new techniques, and on remedies for diseases of livestock (pp. 113–14). In general English almanacs were much more political than French, more aware of change and progress (p. 271). Bernard Capp attributes the emergence of English almanacs as 'a forum for the discussion of major contemporary issues' to the mid-century Revolution. They also helped to popularize scientific changes (pp. 271–4). Many almanac-writers were mathematicians, astronomers or serious astrologers: almanacs did much to popularize the Copernican theory at a time when 'within the universities, paradoxically, the ancient Ptolemaic universe lived on in the undergraduate syllabus' (p. 199).

Almanacs forwarded the cause of the Moderns against the Ancients, and so gave currency to 'an implicit concept of progress' (pp. 180–204), a concept which was reinforced by the chronological lists of British achievements which featured in many almanacs (pp. 221–2). 'The medical notes contained in almanacs amounted also to a sustained attack on the monopoly of the élitist College of Physicians and on the secrecy and exclusiveness of the medical profession'. The almanac-writer Nicholas Culpeper was 'the standard-bearer of the campaign to throw open all medical secrets' (pp. 205–12).

Useful bits of information can be found here on contraception (p. 122), wife-sale (pp. 125–6), millenarianism (164–74), insurance (p. 184), nostalgia for Cromwell's foreign policy after 1660 (pp. 218, 223), and on many other subjects. For all their crudity and superstition, Bernard Capp suggests, almanacs must have been a significant force for popular education (pp. 280–7). The value of his book is enhanced by an Index of Dedications, a 40-page bibliography of English almanacs before 1700, and an even longer list of almanac-writers, including a hitherto unnoticed radical lady, Sarah Jinner (fl. 1658–64).

Christopher Hill
Department of History, The Open University

Ian H. Adams, *The Making of Urban Scotland*. London: Croom Helm; Montreal: McGill-Queen's University Press, 1978. 303 pp. £14.95.

This book is the first to examine the origins of Scottish urban settlements over an extensive period. The 14 chapters span the 'Urban beginnings' of prehistoric and Roman Scotland to the 'Urban future', one of four chapters concerned with planning and government policy in the 1960s and 1970s. The main emphasis is, however, devoted to the foundation and expansion of eighteenth- and nineteenth-century towns and the impact of industrialization. The approach is that of an historical geographer employing cartographic, pictorial and diagrammatic evidence to support the textual material. This is principally concerned with spatial developments in an urban context, and tends to eschew consideration of social and political structures and the religious, cultural and ethnic aspects of Scottish urban life.

In a work entitled *The Making of Urban Scotland* one might reasonably expect an assessment and analysis of the forces shaping urban communities. Unfortunately, such hopes are unfulfilled. The dynamic aspects of the process of urbanization are not subject to detailed examination and a conceptual framework is nonexistent. Typical of the treatment is chapter five, entitled 'Industrial towns'. Here industrial expansion is assumed to be synonymous with urban expansion. The links, the functional relationships between industrialization and urbanization remain unexamined. Thus, sequentially, we are offered descriptive passages, easily available elsewhere, on cotton, linen, woollen and jute textile industries, iron, steel and shipbuilding sectors, and coal and shale mining. The performance of each industry is recounted in relation to appropriate burghs. Precisely why urban expansion occurred in any particular location is rarely investigated. General issues, such as the relative costs of production in alternative locations, supply elasticities for factors of production, the availability, price and functional specialization of land use, and the structure of demand are not covered in any co-ordinated manner. The role of migration is unconsidered (there are no index entries for this subject)! Was political and administrative control in a burgh a relevant factor in attracting industry? Is the pattern of landholding and estate development a consistent feature influencing urban development? Such issues, prevalent in the current literature, are not investigated. Furthermore, the reader cannot distinguish between special cases and the more general pattern of urban development without reference to an analytical framework. In short, attention is devoted to the particular circumstances of a town; systematic treatment of the fundamental mechanics of the process of urbanization is lacking.

This approach recurs in other chapters. The dates of new transport routes are related to the circumstances of a particular town; but discussion of the varying stimuli resulting from the differential impact of alternative transport systems is avoided. Similarly, a chronicle of public utility provisions also lacks a synthesizing overview.

While Adams has successfully employed much new archival material from the Scottish Record Office's holdings of twentieth-century Scottish Development Department files, he has overlooked significant published contributions relating to urban development in Scotland. In the otherwise sound sections on the early origins of Scottish communities the absence of references to Laing's work is a significant omission, and, astonishingly, Smout's *History of the Scottish People* is not mentioned. This is all the more remarkable because of the incisive observations made by Smout regarding the political and social structure of urban areas. Indeed, this raises a methodological reservation concerning Adams' work, namely whether the making of urban Scotland can really be reduced to a consideration of the physical fabric alone. Other bibliographical omissions are curious. Can the impact of Scottish railways on urban development be considered without reference to Vamplew's several contributions, or, more recently, Ochojna's work on Glasgow and Edinburgh tramways? Furthermore, Cramond's study of subsidized housebuilding in Scotland and the sociological perspective of Elliott, McCrone and Damer are clearly unknown to the author, or at least, the wider implications make little perceptible impact. Because Adams fails to incorporate much of the recent historical research in the field he consequently does not tackle some of the central issues currently under discussion amongst urban historians.

Errors of bibliographical omission are matched by errors of commission. Sources of data and evidence presented are frequently not acknowledged. This is most noticeable in the numerous graphs and figures which, with a number of blank pages between chapters, account for 42 per cent of the book. While the author skilfully uses maps and diagrams to good effect there is considerable room for economy in this area. Another irritating aspect is the conversion of historical data into metric distances and weights.

The author is on firmer ground when recounting specific developments relating to modern planning, providing a cartographic representation of historical material and, more specifically, in the treatment afforded to the growth of village settlements in eighteenth-century Scotland. While there is, therefore, an acknowledged need for published work on urban Scotland, this volume is just the start. After all, when the central feature of urban Scotland, the tenement, is an unexplained, indeed an unattempted phenomenon, as it is in this book, the door is open to a more co-ordinated, thematic and ambitious approach.

Richard Rodger
Department of Economic History, University of Liverpool

R. G. Fox, *Urban Anthropology: Cities in their Cultural Settings*. Englewood Cliffs: Prentice-Hall, 1977. xii + 169 pp. Bibliography. £4.80. $7.65.

Like urban history, urban anthropology is a relatively new field without consensus about the questions to be asked, let alone the answers. In a lucid introductory chapter, Richard Fox explains how anthropologists have become interested in cities and discusses the problems arising because the holistic approach and the method of participant observation do not combine as easily in urban research as in the study of tribesmen or even villagers. In his final chapter, he offers an acute critique of colleagues who describe the ethnography of contemporary urban ghettos without explaining why ghettos exist, continuing to practice participant observation but abandoning holism. Fox's own solution is to emphasize holism, cross-cultural comparison and change over time but to place less emphasis on participant observation. In the main body of his book he describes five types of city, illustrates each with examples from different cultures and draws attention to the links between cities and the societies of which they form a part. Fox distinguishes three types of pre-industrial city, criticizing Sjoberg as he does so; regal-ritual cities, small-scale settlements but potent symbols, exemplified by Charlemagne's castles and Rajput forts; administrative cities, like Paris and Edo in the seventeenth century; and mercantile cities like Renaissance Florence and Javanese bazaar towns. The juxtapositions are illuminating, but the ethnography of medieval and early modern Europe leaves much to be desired. The rather flat and occasionally distorted summaries of Ranum on Paris and Brucker on Florence provided by Fox do little to answer his own questions. If he was not prepared to dig deeper into European history himself, he might have been better advised to have sent his questionnaire to the authors concerned and to have printed their replies. The author is more at home with his fourth and fifth types, colonial and industrial cities, and at his best in summarizing his own work on a small North Indian town over the last century or so. He is perhaps a little hasty in rejecting the concept of 'modernisation', since some of his own data fits into the explanatory framework of 'structural differentiation'; and he is perhaps a little too anxious to distinguish anthropologists from sociologists. In the world city of today, such occupational ethnicity is surely out of place. Although it is primarily intended for students of anthropology, many urban historians might benefit from reading this book.

Peter Burke
Emmanuel College, Cambridge

Brian J. L. Berry (ed.), *Urbanization and Counter Urbanization*. London: Sage Publications, 1977. [Urban Affairs Annual Reviews, Vol. II.] No price stated.

This is a collection of stories about where people and activities are moving to in different places. There is little in the way of conceptual theorizing, although a number of contributors imply that 'technology' makes this or that happen. Part I, 'Emerging contrasts, East and West' includes a chapter by Robert Jenson comparing the urban environment in the U.S.A. and the U.S.S.R. We learn that the U.S.S.R. has been keen on planning since the 1920s but the U.S.A. is not so keen; as a result 'the urban system of the United States, in sharp contrast to that of the Soviet Union, has taken form with relatively little government intervention.' More usefully Drewett, Goddard and Spence provide a summary of the attempt to update the PEP study of the containment of urban England to 1971. The story of urban change and decentralization in the 1960s is interesting. I learn that Canterbury, where I live, was previously classified as outside 'urban Britain' but is no more. It is becoming 'increasingly urbanized': by more people living in the country, I suppose. Elisabeth Lichtenberger deals with the rest of Europe. In market societies commuting continues to grow as people move out to lower density housing in the suburbs. They do not allow that kind of thing in eastern Europe which 'has been most successful to date in maintaining the traditional European concept of the city core as the centre of urban life and economic activity.'

The second part of the book is about what are called 'the western margins': that means Australia, Canada, South Africa and Brazil. A lot of urban dispersal goes on there too. The final part of the book is entitled 'The Third and Fourth Worlds': that seems to mean everywhere else. Here we learn that cities are important and we had better watch out or all sorts of problems are going to be with them for a long time unless they are sensible and stop breeding so quickly and plan those which are already here. Things may well be different in China as a result of the distinctive approach of Mao, but even there 'the old Adam has proved to be very resistant.' Naughty Chinese come to live in cities when they are not meant to and some try to get favours by dealing through their kin.

Really it would seem to be pretty sensible for the world to get used to the idea that sooner or later the American experience of urban development will become a world-wide phenomenon. I feel much comforted that whichever way the people flow, I am sure that Brian Berry and his colleagues will be there to record it diligently. Since the need for such documentation never ends it should perhaps be organized by the United Nations. It is very reassuring to look out of the window of my university office, to see the sheep grazing in the fields and to know that it's all part of the urban scene.

R. E. Pahl
Department of Sociology, University of Kent at Canterbury.

V. F. Costello, *Urbanization in the Middle East*. Cambridge: Cambridge University Press, 1977. viii + 121 pp. £4.95 hard cover, £1.95 paperback.

This is a perceptive study of the process of urbanization in the Middle East, largely neglected until now. Although quite readable this study provides neither the detail nor the depth of discussion necessary to give the enquiring reader – even at undergraduate students' level – a clear insight into the problems of the Middle East's rapidly expanding cities. However, readers will be quickly convinced that urbanization in the Middle East – like elsewhere – is a complex and a multidimensional subject. But whether they will get 'a clear and concise account of one of the most significant aspects of the Social revolution taking place in this region' is much more doubtful. The insight provided in this volume is too superficial, too oversimplified and uninformative. Both in content and methodology the book has not much to offer in so promising a field and it is valid to question whether it makes a good text-book for students.

The range of topics covered is not comprehensive. Very little information and comparative study is presented especially in chapter 4 (on rural-urban migration) and in chapter 6 (on occupations and social stratification). Ironically these are the vital subjects to comprehend urbanization in general terms. The author blends excerpts borrowed from some 163 references. Oddly enough – with only two exceptions – all of them are published in English and are works of scholars of Western orientation. His book therefore appropriately demonstrates why Western notions of what constitutes urbanization in general do not help in understanding urbanization in the Middle Eastern cities.

One of the author's biggest mistakes (as almost every scholar of Western orientation) is to misinterpret the common feature of the urban past of the Middle Eastern cities, the religion of Islam. Costello's study is also an excellent example of dimensionless study, since 'the territories grouped here under the title Middle East include: Libya, Egypt, the countries of the Arabian peninsula, Israel, Lebanon, Iraq, Iran and Turkey'. That's quite a region, even for a geographer's unlimited sense of limitation.

The lack of a time dimension is also painfully felt in the sketchy treatment of the common urban past. Distinctions must be made in the Islamic city of different time periods and places. Ideal and prototype models should be cast aside. Neither the simplistic and rigid framework of the conventional Islamic city model nor the ideal pre-industrial city model should be applied to Middle Eastern cities. What is needed is a developmental model of the Islamic city.

Costello's macroanalysis of the urbanization in the region is far from being comprehensive, avoiding a rigid division into qualitative and quantitative aspects. The author admits that 'statistical material on the region is far from comprehensive even now; it is often unreliable and may lack comparability over time and between countries'. Therefore he simply avoids the quantitative approach. This leads to an overall misrepresentation of the facts.

Moreover the literature cited in the book combines an extraordinary mixture of research, reports and a range of opinions and prejudices on anything from the marriage of women to coffee-houses; from the development of economies down to urban microdynamics. Sketchy and anectodal treatment of the past and the present situation leaves almost no space for the predictions about future. The logical systematic link between the retrospective and the prospective is therefore non-existent. The author would appear to have been unable (or unwilling) to carry out such an important task. This probably is impossible. But someday some braver academic soul may write a book to cover it all.

Engin Yenal
Department of Urban Planning, National Academy of Fine Arts, Istanbul

Susan Migden Socolow, *The Merchants of Buenos Aires 1778–1810. Family and Commerce.* Cambridge: Cambridge University Press, 1978. xv + 253 pp. Appendices. Tables and figures. Bibliography. £12.50.

Bryan Roberts, *Cities of Peasants. The Political Economy of Urbanization in the Third World.* London: Edward Arnold, 1978. vii + 207 pp. Bibliography. £4.50.

Both these books deal with aspects of the history of urban growth in Latin America, although their aims and approaches are quite distinct: Susan Socolow is essentially a social historian, concerned with the role of less than 200 individuals, the wholesale merchants, and their families in late colonial Buenos Aires, while the concern of Bryan Roberts is nothing less than to introduce the student to the problem of the impact of capitalism in underdeveloped countries by focusing upon Latin American urbanization in its historical context.

Throughout its history Latin America, and in particular Spanish America, has been *par excellence* a continent dominated by cities, despite the fact that until the twentieth century agriculture and mining provided the wealth to sustain its urban elites. The Spanish *conquistadores* took with them to a New World already characterized by the existence of major cities in the centres of high Indian civilization a profound tradition of urban life inherited from medieval Spain: literally the first acts of Cortés and his fellow-*conquistadores* as they entered new territories were to lay out towns on the traditional grid-iron pattern, promulgate municipal ordinances, and appoint their principal followers as magistrates and councillors in newly-created corporations; the great *encomenderos* of sixteenth-century Mexico and Peru, although drawing their wealth from their thousands of rural vassals, lived in cities, whether former Indian capitals like Cuzco and Mexico, or new foundations like Lima, partly for reasons of defence and convenience but above all for reasons of tradition. The elaborate bureaucratic imperial structure developed by the Habsburgs compounded this tendency by concentrating political, judicial, and commercial authority in the viceregal capitals and a dozen or so subordinate cities scattered throughout their vast American possessions. Until the second half of the eighteenth century Buenos Aires, capital of modern Argentina and one of the great cities of modern Latin America, was little more than an isolated outpost of empire, notorious more for its illicit commercial relations with Portuguese and British merchants than as an important centre of Spanish authority. The River

Plate territories looked primarily to Upper Peru (modern Bolivia) and Peru proper, with their great mining centres, for both commercial stimulus and political control. The Peruvian market provided a healthy demand for the agrarian and pastoral products of the interior Plate provinces and, in return, supplied both specie and European manufactures imported through Lima, but commercial control rested essentially in the hands of the great merchant houses of Lima.

This relationship of economic interdependency – one of the key general themes pursued by Bryan Roberts – was already changing in the first half of the eighteenth century, as Lima's commercial monopoly grew increasingly unrealistic. It was dramatically reversed in the 1770s by two dramatic changes in royal policy inaugurated by the reforming Bourbon king of Spain, Charles III: the creation in 1776, largely for strategic regions, of a new South American viceroyalty, to include not only modern Argentina, Uruguay and Paraguay but also Bolivia, with Buenos Aires as its capital, and in 1778 the opening of Buenos Aires and other ports to direct trade with the major ports of Spain. These reforms brought rapid growth for both the city and the region, as the export of hitherto unprofitable products, notably cattle hides, expanded rapidly; the installation in the capital of a new bureaucratic and military elite helped create, moreover, a demand for the expensive foreign manufactures which the mercantile community could now import directly. It is in this context that one has to assess Susan Socolow's exhaustive group biography of some 178 merchants, the majority of whom were listed in a census of 1778. They are pursued vigorously through notarial records, parish registers, estate papers, bills of sale, and the minutes of the city council and lay religious brotherhoods. A convincing analysis is presented of their origins – the great majority were Spanish-born – marriage patterns, life-styles, commercial activities, political and social awareness, and so on. One interesting feature to emerge is that, although they had extensive investments in urban property, the merchants of Buenos Aires did not invest in the rural sector until the second decade of the nineteenth century when, following the repudiation of Spanish control in 1810, they were eclipsed in their traditional commercial role by an influx of British merchants. It was thus that the sons of the eighteenth-century merchants became the great *estancieros* of the nineteenth century. This monograph is not primarily a work of either economic or urban history but essentially of social history. Although an impressive piece of work, it does not entirely escape from the danger of becoming self-justifying and introspective, with little attempt being made to relate its conclusions to wider issues.

Bryan Roberts, on the other hand, displays the admirable breadth of vision that one would expect in a scholar of his experience and standing. After a general theoretical discussion, which considers the linkages between urban growth and economic development, he examines the general pattern of urbanization in Latin America in both the colonial and pre-contemporary period, with an emphasis upon the effects of industrialization on agrarian structures and the increasing concentration of economic control in urban centres in Argentina, Brazil, Mexico, and Peru. He explains lucidly why migrants flood to the cities, the nature of 'urban economic dualism', the ways in which the poor cope with urban life. He concludes, somewhat pessimistically, that authoritarian government tends to emerge as a solution to the class and social problems created by industrial and urban development and the inability or unwillingness of governments to promote the social policies demanded by economic growth.

J. R. Fisher
Department of Modern History, University of Liverpool

David Popenoe, *The Suburban Environment. Sweden and the United States.* Chicago and London: University of Chicago Press, 1977. xii + 275 pp. 14 plates. 7 figures. £12.95.
This book centres on an intriguing contrast. After the Second World War both the

United States and Sweden experienced a housing shortage which made some form of suburban expansion inevitable. In both countries the strong consumer preference was for single-family detached houses, and in the United States this preference was soon acted upon. Aided by federal highway programmes and mortgage guarantees, private developers turned the farmland around American cities into endless expanses of tract houses.

In Sweden, however, planners controlled urban growth; and, as David Popenoe rightly observes, planners have always disliked the waste and formlessness of the low-density suburbs. The Swedes may have wanted single-family houses, but what they got was 'low-rise, high density' development. The basic living unit was the three-storey apartment building within walking distance of a 'centrum' with shops, offices, and a subway connection to downtown Stockholm. Where the American suburb divided the land into private enclosed 'yards' around the houses, the Swedish plan provided public open spaces and playgrounds. And where the American design exalted the automobile into an absolute necessity of life, the Swedes reduced it to a marginal luxury.

In *The Suburban Environment*, Popenoe poses the basic question: which plan has better served its residents and the larger society? To answer this question he examined in detail a representative American suburb – Levittown near Philadelphia, named for its builder, the archetypal developer Alfred Levitt – and a Swedish counterpart: Vällingby outside Stockholm, the best example of the work of planner Sven Markelius. Both suburbs were begun in the early 1950s, and, in the abbreviated life-span of these settlements, both now qualify as 'mature'.

At a time when planners and planning arouse almost universal suspicion, David Popenoe arrives at the unorthodox conclusion that the Swedish planners made the right decision in disregarding citizen preference, and that the environment they designed at Vällingby is clearly superior to Levittown. This is not merely an American academic's long-distance romance with the Welfare State, nor 20-20 hindsight based on the current petrol crisis, nor a snobbish disdain for the populist preferences of 'middle America'.

Popenoe readily concedes that the characteristic Levittown family – an affluent middle-aged couple with two teenaged children – is very well served by their community. Nevertheless, the American low-density suburb can be very hard on many 'uncharacteristic' residents: the family living beyond its means; the widowed or divorced female head of household who must struggle to keep up house and family while driving long distances to work; the trapped housewife or lonely older woman; and teenagers who feel confined and bored by the unvarying acres of neat little houses.

In contrast, the strength of Vällingby is precisely its ability to serve the needs of many different households. The varied opportunities for work and leisure, all within easy bicycling or walking distance, are well adapted to the life-styles of teenagers, single people, and childless couples. And the compact environment makes possible a wider range of social services for larger families than Levittown could economically provide.

David Popenoe is a sociologist but, fortunately, he does not write like one. His book is a model of unpretentious clarity. He has discovered nothing very surprising about either Levittown or Vällingby, but his comparative approach leads one to see even the more familiar American material in a new light. He is a sympathetic interviewer and a perceptive observer, and his observations on the complex 'fit' between people and their environment ring true. Above all, he believes that a well-structured environment does make a significant difference in people's lives – a proposition which is obvious to anyone except the now-dominant school of American sociologists. Popenoe's book is, among other things, an argument for an American housing policy along Swedish lines.

It is ironic, therefore, that the Swedes themselves have in the 1970s abandoned the purity of Markelius's doctrines and opted for more single-family houses. And, while Swedish suburbs spread out, American suburbs have been increasing in density as higher land values mean fewer detached houses and more apartments. Both Levittown and Vällingby are becoming less and less representative of the total suburban environment of their respective nations.

If American and Swedish postwar suburbs started from very different design principles, their recent development has shown a remarkable convergence. Both have gone beyond the pre-war model of the 'dormitory suburb' to a disparate mixture of housing, industry, and services, with so many opportunities for work and leisure that the traditional urban centres have become almost irrelevant for most suburbanites. Both are becoming formless regions too crowded for Levittown's pattern of detached houses but too amorphous for Vällingby's compact convenience.

In this context, Professor Popenoe's advocacy of 'low-rise, high density' suburbs is eminently sane but as difficult to implement as squeezing toothpaste back into the tube.

Robert Fishman
Department of History, University College, Rutgers University

Shulamit Volkov, *The Rise of Popular Antimodernism in Germany. The Urban Master Artisans, 1873–1896*. Princeton: Princeton University Press, 1978. ix + 399 pp. Tables. Bibliography. £15.50.

Taking as her point of departure the general view of social and political movements in late nineteenth-century Germany developed by her mentor, Hans Rosenberg, in his *Grosse Depression und Bismarckzeit*, Shulamit Volkov gives us a richly detailed account of one well-defined social group's experience of and increasingly hostile response to modernization. Volkov refers to conservative intellectuals such as Adolf Wagner and Julius Langbehn but only to emphasize that popular antimodernism had a life of its own, quite independent of the efforts of 'half-baked philosophers'. This is a study in the social history of *mentalité* rather than the history of ideas, and it is very well done indeed.

The growing despair of the urban master artisans – numbering between 600,000 and 800,000 independent practitioners of the traditional handicrafts – stemmed in the first place from the process of industrial growth and the obvious threats it posed to their economic and social status. They also suffered from the cyclical economic fluctuations of the last quarter of the nineteenth century, which resulted in much sharper declines in the prices they received for their goods than in the wages they paid their employees. Widening splits between the masters and their men, already in evidence during the revolutions of 1848–9, and increased social isolation both from the upper middle class and from other groups within the *Mittelstand* similarly exacerbated the masters' sense of insecurity.

What Volkov emphasizes most strongly is the way in which the artisan elite came to feel isolated from all of the major political forces within the Empire. She tells us a great deal – sometimes perhaps more than we need to know – about the intricacies of the shifting relationships between the craftsmen and the political parties, and sometimes (as in her discussion of disputes within the artisan estate) the reader may wish that she would come more quickly to the main point. But her argument does finally come through with great force. Not only were the artisans increasingly separated from the liberal parties and the Social Democrats; they were also frustrated in their dealings with the Catholic Centre and the Conservatives. These parties were ostensibly friendly to the handicrafts, but they hesitated to support many of the artisans' demands for protective legislation out of unwillingness to jeopardize their ties to big business. As a result, even though industrial freedom was undermined by numerous pieces of legislation during the imperial era, the master artisans came to feel a sense of 'political homelessness' that left them susceptible to the extremist ideology of the incipient radical right. Antiliberalism, anti-capitalism, anti-socialism, and anti-Semitism all became components of their attitude toward the modern world. Thus, Volkov argues, there emerged a basic orientation that provided a foundation for Nazism, to which these men turned *en masse* after the renewed hardships of the 1920s and early 1930s.

Two observations may be made about topics on which the book is relatively uninformative. While quite thorough with regard to the economic and political environment in which the artisans functioned, it says much less about non-occupational aspects of their life-style in areas such as education, leisure, and family life. In addition, although the concluding pages apply an interesting bipolar model based on a contrast between Germany and England to several German cities in an effort to explain regional variations in the intensity of anti-modernism, there is not much attention in the rest of the book to the significance of the urban milieu. We are told briefly that urban artisans experienced greater insecurity than rural ones, but on the whole the city remains very much in the background. Nonetheless, the book still has a great deal to say about a vital segment of urban society that remained a force to be reckoned with well into the twentieth century precisely because of its deep roots in the German past.

A. Lees
Department of History, Rutgers University

Nora Levin, *Jewish Socialist Movements, 1871–1917. While Messiah Tarried.* London: Routledge & Kegan Paul [The Littman Library of Jewish Civilisation], 1978. xii + 554 pp. 10 illustrations, 3 maps. £9.00.

Much is now being written on the migrations of the Russian-Jewish population, both within Western Russia and out of it, during the years between 1870 and 1914. Earlier issues of the *Urban History Yearbook* have paid some attention to various books on this subject, commenting on the ways in which this population movement created new minority groups in many of the cities of a wider-spread Diaspora, and above all deposited in them a different sort of urban proletariat. There have in fact been many studies of these immigrants' occupations, but there has been less attention paid to their intellectual activities, or the impact which these might have made upon their contemporaries and fellow-workers.

One of their fundamental religious beliefs had originally been a Messianism, the belief that at the end of the day all would be for the best, and there were many who held that in the meantime it was difficult, if not indeed impossible or even sacrilegious, to attempt anything more than the merest amelioration of distress. But there were many others who recognized that for many reasons the advent of the Messiah had been delayed and that in the interim it was necessary to do something substantial towards a more immediate Utopia. This clash was not in itself a result of the events of the late nineteenth century, but they became of significance to the rest of the world with these population movements.

Nora Levin has now undertaken a study of these quasi-Messianic ideas and has discerned three major trends. The creation of a Jewish urban proletariat in New York spawned a great deal of thought that was specifically socialist and Jewish. The way in which a Jewish labour movement developed in New York, and the differentiation between Jewish and non-Jewish unions, is one of the themes on which she expounds, pointing out that whether or not they had originally desired to maintain a connection between their religious or social origins and their socio-political organizations they had in practice no real alternative but to accept it.

A second aspect discussed is the development of socialist thought amongst the Jewish masses left in Russia. The author spells out the ways in which Jewish socialist thought initially differed from the other movements inside Russia, but eventually disappeared before the all-powerful embrace of Bolshevism. Her third theme is the way in which Jewish socialist thought in Russia turned as an alternative towards the ideas of Socialist Zionism and in consequence developed the Kibbutz ideal in Palestine before the First World War.

It is indeed interesting to reflect upon these three very divergent patterns of thought emerging from the one area, but the author does leave some questions to be answered. Dr Fishman has for example discussed in great detail the ways in which the East End of London spawned Radical (or Anarchist) thought in these years, and the ways in which there was considerable flow of ideas through England to the new world; it would certainly be unfair to say that Nora Levin has ignored his work, but the few pages which she devotes to Jewish thought and organizations in London do not, I think, give enough weight to these influences. She could also have spent a little time reflecting upon the interrelations between the thought of western Europe and Jewish migrants in this period. Her analysis of New York ignores any parallel thoughts elsewhere in the United States (were there no thinkers in Chicago?) while in practice she spends more time on the history of the American Jewish Labour movement than on its thought. Her allocation of attention between the first two themes on the one hand and the third on the other seems also a little out of balance. Much of the third section is a narrative of the struggles to establish some form of socialism, rather than an analysis of the way in which the socialist theories within Zionism developed and adapted to the environment – both in Russia and in Palestine – in which they found themselves.

Nonetheless this is an important study of one of the ways in which Eastern European urbanization affected the intellectual climate of the late nineteenth and early twentieth centuries. It cannot be ignored by those studying either urbanization or intellectual developments in these years, but it does need to be studied by those who already have a considerable understanding both of the three backgrounds involved and of the habits of thought on which this Messianism was super-imposed.

Aubrey Newman
Department of History, University of Leicester

Jack Simmons, *The Railway in England and Wales 1830–1914*, Leicester: Leicester University Press, 1978. 295 pp. £12.00.
John P. McKay, *Tramways and Trolleys: The Rise of Urban Mass Transport in Europe*. Guildford: Princeton University Press, 1976. 266 pp. £10.00.
Carl W. Condit, *The Railroad and the City: A Technological and Urbanistic History of Cincinnati*. Columbus: Ohio State University Press, 1977. xii + 335 pp. $15.00.

These three works are all of interest to transport historians, but of varying value to students of urban history. Perhaps the most peripheral to urban history is Professor Simmons' *The Railway in England and Wales*, volume I, which is subtitled *The system and its working*. We are promised three more volumes, the next of which will consider the railways' impact on London and the provinces; and in later volumes the part played by railways in social, economic and political life. If this first instalment is a foretaste of the readable and clear treatment to be expected the series will take its place amongst the indispensable reference works on the history of rail transport. A detailed end-map summarizes the development of the system in four main chronological phases, and sets an example (which urban historians cannot afford to neglect) of the unobtrusive use of cartography to relieve a narrative of the tedious repetition of place names. His tables, in the body of the book, though somewhat meagre, are fully discussed and absorbed into the text; and there are two fuller appendices. The line-drawings of sections of track and signals will no doubt gladden the hearts of railway enthusiasts, of which Professor Simmons is perhaps the doyen. There is an engaging glimpse of him reacting to the London and North Western Company's persistent use of the 'inadequate Clark and Webb chain brake' – 'one smiles wryly as one reads, perhaps bitterly' [p. 257]. Needless to say the four chapters on the permanent way, equipment and control systems are a mine of technical information, frequently illuminated by discussion of matters usually passed over: the special market considerations which dictated the much-criticized use of small waggons, the special role in Britain of privately owned rolling stock, and our reasons for not adopting compound engines – 'not obtuse conservatism'.

His chapters on the sequence by which the system came into operation and the part played by chairmen, directors, politicians and the great contractors makes full use of work by Gourvish, Irving, Mitchell and Parris, with perceptive observations of Professor Simmons' own, and a reprimand to those whose 'mistaken partisanship' has confused the history of individual companies. The only chapter directly concerned with urban matters is chapter 5, 'Greater London', which contains a useful narrative of the 'Quadrilateral' ruling of 1846 excluding railways from the central area, of the 'cut-and-cover' phase of Metropolitan underground railways, and a short account of the forceful entrepreneurship of the Americans, C. T. Yerkes and J. P. Morgan. On suburbs, tantalizingly, 'there will be more to say in the succeeding volume of this work'.

C. T. Yerkes and J. P. Morgan also figure in John P. McKay's *Tramways and Trolleys* which, although at first sight a slight work, presents a remarkable amount of original research material and of stimulating analysis in the still neglected field of intra-urban transport. Of course there have been excellent monographs, and classic individual studies, but no-one has yet ventured to give an international comparison of urban tramway systems through an economic historian's eyes. This is the daunting task undertaken by John McKay with admirable address. His study necessarily is selective and concerns itself only (if only is the word) with the street-car systems of France, Germany and Great Britain; with a few backward glances to the United States' pioneering role in technical developments and management techniques. A further study on Russian and Belgian tramways is promised: 'I have no intention of waiting for others to grind my grain', McKay declares.

Naturally, in a short work, however condensed, further selection is essential if the study is not to consist of unsupported generalizations, but to gain from sharply focused case histories. McKay is particularly successful in the choices which he has made for illustration and analysis. There is a minimum of repetition, and each example is chosen for a special reason. The systems at Rouen and Bordeaux are examined because the records of the *Credit Lyonnais* (brilliantly used by McKay) provide a key to explain exactly how a run-down and overcapitalized system could be rejuvenated and re-financed, and the financial methods of the Thomson Houston and General Electric companies illustrated. Berlin is brought into the analysis to throw light on Germany's clear lead in European tramway electrification, Hamburg to show the importance of local taxes and aesthetic and environmental lobbies, Glasgow as a model to discuss the pros and cons of municipal enterprise.

McKay holds energetic and controversial views upon the merits of the different municipal approaches. The relatively slow diffusion of tram tracks and the lag in electrification in this country is seen as 'a sign of the hardening of British entrepreneurial arteries'; and his case is sufficiently well argued to command attention. Conversely the hectic spread of U.S. street-car operation reflected the ethos of American business and civic life: grant 999-year franchises; allow overhead wires to be strung across prominent streets and squares; and provide fiscal encouragement for the promoters, rather than safeguarding the public interest through low fares and uneconomic extensions of the track. The whole is epitomized in the contrast between the $70 wooden poles in American cities, and the splendid cast-iron double-bracket standards at $2500 each in some European cities. The result of America's lead in both the initial phase of construction, and of later electrification, McKay argues, was the invasion of Europe by American entrepreneurs, who played a role not dissimilar to that of the great railway contractors Peto and Brassey in Victorian urban railways. The inflated profits made by G.E.C. and Thomson Houston in their widespread European ventures in construction and equipment sales 'introduced at the producer's level the substantial entrepreneur's profits which public authority denied at the operating level'. This is only one of the many thoughtful and challenging opinions in McKay's book. At a more detailed level it also provides summaries of the arguments and experiments concerning the operation of steam, cable, battery, double-decker and trailer trams, together with several chapters which provide excellent short surveys for student use. Altogether a remarkable amount of general interest in small compass.

Unfortunately the same cannot be said of *The Railroad and the City*, by Carl W. Condit, which only lives up to half of its subtitle 'a technological and urbanistic history of Cincinnati'. There are several passages which attempt to relate a very detailed narrative of railway construction in Ohio to the growth of the city of Cincinnati; but unfortunately the links made are of too general and perfunctory a nature to give any new insights. Perhaps the most interesting parts for readers of the *Yearbook* would be chapters 3 and 4, which discuss the considerations influencing the actual construction and location of the urban termini in Cincinnati. These are chapters of great expertise, and form a most valuable contribution to the corpus of factual knowledge indispensable for inter-city comparisons.

John R. Kellett
Department of Economic History, University of Glasgow

James Walvin, *Leisure and Society 1830–1950*. London: Longmans, 1978. ix + 181 pp. Bibliography. £2.95.
Peter Bailey, *Leisure and Class in Victorian England, Rational Recreation and the Contest for Control 1830–1885*. London: Routledge & Kegan Paul, 1978. x + 260 pp. Bibliography. £5.75.
Paul Boyer, *Urban Masses and Moral Order in America 1820–1920*. Cambridge: Harvard University Press, 1978. xi + 387 pp. 26 plates. $18.50.

These books are all informative and entertaining but vaguely unsatisfactory in the task of explanation and adding to historical understanding. Walvin's wide-ranging survey identifies many variations of leisure activity with social classes. Bailey and Boyer chart various efforts to guide working-class morality especially in the use of their leisure time, and relate these attempts to something called 'social control', but they never break the mild air of unreality in their accounts.

For Walvin urbanization played an important part in the changes which took place in the use of leisure time in early nineteenth-century Britain. Like Bailey he traces the decline of traditional events like communal street football, bull running, ox roasts and the like, and the repression of cruel sports, at least the lower-class ones. This produced the poverty of working-class entertainment commented on by the Hammonds. The lack of space in urban areas was one explanation, but given that urbanization was not new, we have as yet been offered little evidence by the historians of leisure as to why this particular phase of urban growth should be the crucial one. If, as the 1834 S.C. on Public Walks believed, enclosure was the culprit, we need more detail of the manner in which this became intolerable. Like many historians Walvin relates the decline of traditional and violent sports to the need for work discipline. This is explanation by analogy. If history had created a range of violent and disorganized sports in the nineteenth century, we should be talking wisely about the need to 'let off steam'. Bailey looks to the needs of factory production and the activities of factory owners as an explanation but in 1830, by which time most of these changes were under way, such production only affected a portion of the textile industry (cotton spinning) and even in 1851, the factory labour force was a minority of most urban populations. The factory will not do as a direct explanation of changes in leisure use. The repression of such working-class traditions seemed to be done all too easily. Bailey suggests why. Working-class leisure was occupied quite nicely with the public house free and easy, friendly society meetings, street entertainments, and, we might add after reading T. W. Laquer, in Sunday School.

Although Bailey begins by proposing the importance of middle-class efforts to make working-class leisure 'respectable', much of his book shows in fact that such activity was unimportant at least in the sense that it resulted in the direct control of the activities of one class by another. Change in working-class leisure habits did take place (well documented in both books) but to call this the 'house training' of the working classes (Bailey, p. 174) is a denial of the evidence for working-class autonomy, present in much recent historical writing and in Bailey's own book. Faced with the cultural products of the middle and upper classes, the nineteenth-century working class showed an outstanding ability to select and transform those items which suited their own needs and purposes. The creation of organized sport after 1870 challenges all class-based 'social control' explanations. Football was transformed in the public schools, and brought to town by Old Boys and by young persons organizing their boys' clubs. It was promptly taken over by the working classes they attempted to patronize. By 1885, Blackburn Olympic had beaten the Old Etonians in the F.A. Cup and professionalization had been forced upon the F.A. by Lancashire. The fate of the Clubs and Institutes Union created by Solly was another working-class take-over. The Music Hall sprang without assistance from the public house and although Bailey assumes that an 1880s campaign in London to oppose the licences of the music halls was a major class threat and notes that changes did take place in the halls during that period, his evidence also suggests that such changes might equally well have been a sound commercial response to a growing market for family entertainment and a wise move which drew more of a growing middle-class audience. Not all clerks were satisfied with the Y.M.C.A. Recent studies of artisans in Edinburgh and London and of the Volunteer movement have shown similar relationships. Class bargaining it might have been but 'social control' it was not. A more limited meaning of this last term is applicable to a broadly based middle-class concern with the law and order aspects of recreation which showed in the suppression by the police of sports like pedestrianism but the implications of police action are not explored in these books.

Bailey and to a lesser extent Walvin both use a two-class model of society, which is inadequate for their purpose. The relationships and activities of leisure time need to recognize several status groups within classes, artisans, the lower middle class and a middle-class elite. They both use these terms and then fall back on the two class model for overall analysis. Such an analysis also needs to explore the division between the respectable and non-respectable in each social class. We need know why an evangelically inclined fraction of the middle classes has come to represent the total of middle-class cultural aggression in many historians' accounts of the nineteenth century, as well as to trace the relationship between respectable and non-respectable working-class cultures.

Walvin is at his best in his descriptions of the impact of technology on leisure, above all the railways which transformed possibilities for all social classes. This leads him naturally to the seaside on which he has already written with such vigour, and Blackpool Tower, penny in the slot machines and the seaside leisure industry. Both Bailey and Walvin finish their books with comments on the commercialization of leisure. It is clear that the profit motive and the market won the battle for control, not middle or working classes, and the implications of this have scarcely been explored, least of all in class terms.

Boyer sets out to demonstrate the continuity of the nineteenth-century American elite's response to urban growth. Moral reformers attacked gambling, prostitution and drink and successively used tracts, missions, Sunday Schools, the Y.M.C.A., charitable visitors, legislation, housing reform and playgrounds. Each phase followed a cycle of enthusiasm, effort and disillusionment, and tried to recreate the uniform moral discipline of an idealized rural society. Boyer plays down the importance of the break between those who sought to manipulate the environment in the late nineteenth century and those who earlier laid the blame on individual moral responsibility. The real break in approaches to urban moral reform came in the 1920s when the vitality and heterogeneity of the city was accepted by Wirth, Park, Mumford and others. The continuity is well demonstrated with a mixture of analysis and anecdote, but the importance of this strand of continuity for the lives of the bulk of the urban population is not examined; hence the unreality which surrounds the account.

There was a class dimension to the use of leisure and attempts to influence the development of its use, but the full complexity of this relationship has not yet been outlined. Urbanization had a major place in the changes which took place, especially in providing the massed populations which were the market for the commercialization and increasing variety of leisure activity. These three books all reflect the great increase in our knowledge of leisure in the past but they also show an ability to analyse change only in broad and general terms.

R. J. Morris
Department of Economic History, University of Edinburgh

Duncan Bythell, *The Sweated Trades, Outwork in Nineteenth Century Britain.* London: Batsford Academic, 1978. vii + 278 pp. £12.50.

The author has written an illuminating book on a somewhat neglected but very important aspect of industrial change. In a work of synthesis bringing together the information which in general has been available previously only in scattered sources, he directs our attention to the 'putting-out' system not merely as the residue of the past – which has to be replaced – but as an integral part of the economic organization of Britain in the nineteenth century. He suggests that further work on local sources may correct errors which have become part of the accepted story and deepen our understanding, and this may well be true. The Bradford woolcombers' strike of 1825 was not caused, as is usually supposed, by the fear of mechanization, for there was no serious threat for nearly another 30 years. It was a much more complicated struggle to establish the dignity of the wage-earning operative in a period when the small master comber was almost extinct. The elimination of the hand combers eventually took place in two phases of investment between 1847 and 1853 and between 1859 and 1866, and a close study of the events might throw up some interesting ideas. But the main outline is clearly established and firmly expounded by Duncan Bythell.

Outwork persisted because of the large and cheap supply of labour available to do the work. It was this which gave the system its greatest strength and flexibility. It did not depend simply on the pace of technical invention. Entrepreneurs could chose an appropriate time for investment. Large or small – firms continued to use outworkers for years after their replacement became possible. A proportion of fixed costs was thus borne by employees and the entrepreneur could maintain a level of liquidity which facilitated expansion. It meant also that the cost of starting a business was not high, so that, although few poor men profited, a reasonable competence might well suffice. It would be ridiculous to under-estimate the risks of business in Victorian England; mortality rates were very high, but the 'putting-out' system helped to make life a good deal easier for the businessman.

Bythell identifies the workers in the 'putting-out' system as the elderly, the young, housewives, and, in the large centres of population, immigrants – the defenceless and the trapped. For them the principal consequence was massive degradation. Although occasionally, groups of workers in a crucial position in the productive process could benefit in the short run from mechanization in another branch of an industry, labour was generally so abundant that piece rates were constantly forced down and conditions worsened. This could happen whether the introduction of machinery was an imminent threat or not. The Bradford woolcombers, to cite them again, were pleading with employers to provide combing sheds at the factory site by 1845, at least 18 months before a decisive technical breakthrough was accomplished, for conditions in their homes had become intolerable already. Employers using the system were not mere brutal capitalists, indifferent to public and private opinion; and some men, particularly handloom weavers, refused factory work out of pride. Nevertheless, Duncan Bythell's last sentence sums up the experience. 'Outwork' he writes, 'is rightly relegated to one of the darkest chapters of economic history; and now that it is virtually dead, none should regret its passing.'

J. Reynolds
School of Social Sciences, University of Bradford

J. H. Treble, *Urban Poverty in Britain, 1830–1914*. London: B. T. Batsford, 1979.
   216 pp. £12.50
James Dawson Burn, *The Autobiography of a Beggar Boy*. [Edited with an Introduction by David Vincent.] London: Europa Publications, 1978. vi + 205 pp.
   £8.50.

Nineteenth century poverty began, in J. H. Treble's view, 'at the point at which aggregate family income failed to yield, or barely yielded, a subsistence standard of living for the family unit as a whole'. In the first two chapters of his book, he exa-mines the main reasons for this shortfall in family income – low pay, unemploy-ment and underemployment. He then goes on to discuss other causes of poverty, many of which stemmed from individual misfortune or failure, sickness, widow-hood, old age or the maladministration of limited resources. After a brief investi-gation of the alleviation of poverty in which more attention is given to devices like credit or child labour than to the more familiar institutional agencies of relief, the author moves on to the second main aim of his study, an examination of the socio-economic characteristics of poverty as reflected in the feeding and housing of the urban working classes.

His book provides a valuable guide to the large and complex subject of nineteenth-century poverty. As he shows, there were few distinctive marks of poverty. To draw a 'poverty line' and then to attempt by aid, exhortation or threat to raise those below it up to comparative comfort was to ignore the dynamic, shift-ing nature of the problem. Few members of the manual working classes were not threatened by severe material deprivation at some time in their lives, with the early and late stages of the life cycle constituting the periods of greatest risk. Drink, sickness, sudden death could mean poverty for a family even in a period of general affluence, whilst the inexorable forces of trade depression or seasonal slump could sink even the thrifty and hard-working.

In charting the course of poverty over his chosen span of 80 years, J. H. Treble demonstrates that the social revolution which created an urban society in Britain in that period brought with it 'a series of modest, but cumulatively significant, improvements' in the quality of urban life for the majority of the working classes. Nevertheless he is quick to warn that 'national averages often obscure rather than illuminate the socio-economic position of the poor'. None of the causes of urban poverty had been removed by 1914. Indeed the expansion of some areas of casual work and low pay, the increasing number of evictions for rent arrears, and the more stringent policies of relief pursued by some poor law authorities and philan-thropists may have added to the miseries of the urban poor after 1870.

For many Victorians, the means of escaping from poverty lay within the indivi-dual. 'Whatever men may feel upon this subject, there is one thing certain, that well directed energy backed by habits of industry and common prudence, will always make way for itself', wrote James Dawson Burn in one of his letters to his son. These letters were published as *The Autobiography of a Beggar Boy* in 1855, and the book had gone through four editions by the time Samuel Smiles published *Self-Help* in 1859. Burn chronicled his rise from the depths of pauperism, as the illegitimate son of an itinerant hawker, to artisan status in the hatting trade, and then, by way of positions of responsibility in the trades union and friendly society movements, to a series of white-collar positions. In the course of this struggle with circumstance, Burn acquired a high degree of self education yet, as David Vincent points out in his perceptive but unobtrusive introduction to this new edition of the *Autobiography*, he still lacked a confident sense of his own identity. Bamford-like he regretted the folly of his involvement in the working-class movement of the

1830s. He took pride in his sturdy individualism, yet felt himself still deficient in the virtues of prudence and foresight which marked the successful man of business.

The *Autobiography* provides an interesting study of the individual's perception of social status: a book to be read perhaps in conjunction with Foster on Oldham or Crossick on Kentish London. Burn's life also illustrates dramatically some of the matters raised by Treble's analysis of poverty. Wife desertion, drink and the exploitation of children as causes and characteristics of poverty are fully revealed in Burn's account of his early years. His experiences in hatting show that skilled status was no protection against poverty, particularly in a trade exposed to the whims of fashion. His constant wanderings in search of work illustrate the considerable mobility of both skilled and casual labour. His failure to attain security even after the publication of his book show how high up the social scale the tentacles of poverty could reach. Self help provided no solution, yet the feeling that it could was by no means confined to a self-satisfied group of middle-class philanthropists.

The most entertaining parts of the *Autobiography* are the early chapters describing Burn's picaresque boyhood in the company of his mother and his erratic stepfather, Mcnamee. A surprising feature of this account is the hospitality extended to wayfarers like the young Burn and his stepfather, especially in the Border country which Burn regarded as his homeland. 'Every house on the Border at that time was a welcome home for the wayfarer – the beggar was treated kindly and bountifully supplied with food.' Such treatment contrasts strongly with the extreme harshness of the poor law system towards the vagrant, especially after 1834. Was it that this tradition of mutual help and hospitality for the unfortunate was lacking in the urban context of poverty? J. H. Treble dismisses mutual assistance as being on too small a scale to raise its recipients above the poverty line, yet he admits that it was an integral part of working-class social life. The often sentimentalized 'friendliness' of the street was an important if ineffective defence mechanism against the many-headed monster, poverty.

Michael E. Rose
Department of History, University of Manchester

F. S. Schwarzbach, *Dickens and the City*. London: The Athlone Press, 1979. xii + 258pp. 9 plates. £10.50.

Walter Bagehot said of Dickens that he described London 'like a special correspondent for posterity'. The observation is famous and often-quoted: it appears, understandably, on the first page of F. S. Schwarzbach's *Dickens and the City*. But its epigrammatic neatness is deceptive. A special correspondent who mystified the readers of his newspaper as much as Dickens has mystified posterity by his portrayal of London and London life would not keep his job for very long. For the non-specialist, non-academic reader there is, of course, no real problem – there rarely is with Dickens. It is the professional critic with a thesis to justify who cannot bear to think that Dickens' London resists easy classification. Bagehot was clearly right that we would turn to Dickens more readily than to any other writer in order to find out what life was really like in Victorian London, but dreadfully wrong if he meant by the 'special correspondent' tag that we would have little difficulty in understanding what we found.

Modern literary critics who have dealt extensively with this topic tend to find whatever they want to find, and this writer is no exception. 'I have tried to keep before me', he writes in his preface, 'the main concern, Dickens and the City, and rigorously to exclude everything that did not illuminate it.' But the truly difficult question is precisely, what *is* relevant to the subject of Dickens and the city? The author answers firmly, the events of Dickens' own life and, as he promises, nearly everything else is rigorously excluded, with the result that *Dickens and the City* is more a contribution to psycho-biography than to urban history.

The central argument is not unfamiliar. As a child Dickens was moved from Chatham to London where he was abandoned by his parents to humiliating work in Warren's Blacking Warehouse. He survived this experience and became the most famous living writer in the English-speaking world, but at the very moment when his fame seemed assured his adored sister-in-law, Mary Hogarth, died, and because she died in London this reinforced Dickens' conviction that the great city was a place of 'danger and distress'. If we pursue the significance of these events we can see that the London of Dickens' novels is not so much a real city as a mental projection compounded of Warren's Blacking Warehouse and Mary Hogarth's place of death, while set against this city of death and horror is the pastoral ideal of Chatham he carried with him from childhood: 'Dickens' deepest creative and imaginative forces had been invested in a complex psychological and fictional struggle between a mythic vision of pastoral innocence and a hellish nightmare of urban experience.'

Of course this interpretation may be right, but there is no way of knowing whether it is or not. F. S. Schwarzbach offers a few basic statistics about life in London and the occasional reference to historical reality – most interestingly in connection with the architectural significance of *Martin Chuzzlewit* and the possible influence of Angela Burdett Coutts' home for fallen women on *Bleak House* – but these issues can never be given the detailed attention they deserve because the psychobiographical interpretation turns each novel into a stage in Dickens' struggle with deeply personal, possibly subconscious, problems. It is all very well to say, for example, that, 'The terrifying message of *Little Dorrit* is that the crutch which props up the decrepit social structure is our own continuing, self-deluding belief in the system', but, in this context, what does such a statement mean? Can it, in effect, strongly political as it is, have any significance beyond a profound personal meaning for Dickens himself?

To this last question F. S. Schwarzbach appears to want to say yes, but close-reading and a thesis topic combine to force him to say no. For *Dickens and the City* has a happy ending: in *Great Expectations* Dickens at last succeeds in confronting, through Pip, the guilt he had suffered since childhood, and *Our Mutual Friend*, which has so often been seen as a final, and frighteningly prophetic, instance of Dickens pessimism about the future of city life, becomes a 'celebration' of change and 'first and foremost a celebration of the real, of the future transformation and imminent resurrection of London'. In the same novel the riverside pub, The Six Jolly Fellowship Porters, is seen as a 'positive symbol of the possibility of creating an environment of life, love and human fellow-feeling within the city'. It is not too loud a celebration as F. S. Schwarzbach admits, but at least Warren's Blacking Warehouse is finally buried and that seems to be the main thing.

Peter Keating
Department of English Literature, University of Edinburgh

M. Jeanne Peterson, *The Medical Profession in Mid-Victorian London*. London: University of California Press, 1978. x + 406 pp. Tables. Bibliography. £12.25.

A. J. Youngson, *The Scientific Revolution in Victorian Medicine*. London: Croom Helm, 1979. 237 pp. £9.95.

F. B. Smith, *The People's Health, 1830–1910*. London: Croom Helm, 1979. 436 pp. Bibliography. £14.95.

Three new books about the Victorian medical profession, and all good ones – a reviewer's delight! And they are timely, since at the moment the position of the British medical profession in the nineteenth century is rather ambiguous. On the one hand due recognition continues to be given to its major scientific achievements and to its key role in the evolution of urban public health services and in the enormous expansion of hospital provision both by the State (through the Poor Law) and by private enterprise. On the other hand, however, is Professor McKeown's iconoclasm. With various colleagues, McKeown has exposed the extreme feebleness of the medical armoury against ill-health. By whatever means the reductions in morbidity and mortality at any time before the 1930s (when the antibiotics and sulphonamides were introduced) are to be explained, it is not in terms of any advances in the capacity of medical science to cure. Until well into the twentieth century, in other words, doctors could comfort, use their common sense, and possibly make sensible suggestions for prevention; but they could do very little actually to cure. McKeown, a professor of Social Medicine, dealt a blow at the image of former generations of doctors from which rehabilitation will clearly be a difficult task.

These three new books are all directly relevant to this debate. Jeanne Peterson sets out to study the ways by which the metropolitan elite sought to raise the uncertain social status of their profession while at the same time retaining their controlling position through the Royal Colleges and hospital consultancies. Her book starts conventionally but usefully with a careful description of the various forms of medical qualifications available in the first half of the nineteenth century, the formal trainings associated with each of these qualifications, and the routes to careers in the profession open to qualified entrants. When she moves on to her main subject-matter of the struggles within the profession both for general professional status and for the maintenance of the existing internal pecking-order, she becomes much more original and interesting. It is clear that, given the financial resources available for medical services in the mid-nineteenth century either from local authority rates (virtually no central government money found its way into doctors' pockets at this time) or from private individuals in the form of fees, the medical profession was over-supplied, so that while a small elite enjoyed substantial, sometimes enormous, incomes, most doctors had the greatest difficulty in earning incomes commensurate with the 'respectability' (size of house, number of servants, etc.) that was a prime criterion for status in mid-Victorian society. The spectacle of people scrambling for money and status is seldom edifying, and with much both to lose and to gain, the doctors were no better, possibly worse, than other social groups on the make. So, while Jeanne Peterson's fascinating and carefully-documented study does much to illuminate the problems of education, qualification, career and rewards in the nineteenth-century profession, it clearly contributes little to the rehabilitation of its reputation.

A. J. Youngson also concerns himself with internecine struggles within the profession, though the context here is scientific advance. He calls his book *The Scientific Revolution in Victorian Medicine* but restricts his investigation solely to two developments – Simpson's anaesthesia and Lister's antisepsis. What Youngson explores with inumerable well-chosen quotations from letters, pamphlets and the medical press is, in his own words, 'the resistance to new ideas'. He is able to show that the two new ideas he studies were resisted not merely because 'those who resist new ideas are dull or obscurantist or . . . have a vested interest in the *status quo*' (he offers enough evidence of these motives to leave no doubt of their potency), but also because of the inability of those expounding the new ideas to convince the doubters and even some of those willing to believe of their merits. It was almost as easy to pick holes in the statistics designed to illustrate the high success rates of the new methods as it was in the frankly disingenuous 'proofs' of the virtues of methods we now know to have had a high chance of being lethal. So long as the inventors were unable to *prove* lower mortality with their new techniques in the face of doubters who preferred the guidance offered by biblical texts ('in sorrow thou shalt bring forth children'), even when these were shown to be mistranslations of the Hebrew, general acceptance was bound to be slow. Youngson therefore offers us an acute analysis not so much of the 'resistance' to new ideas, as of the reasons why ideas that seem to us in the late twentieth century to be self-evidently sensible and humane did not immediately command universal support. What emerges from his original and entertaining study are some slightly tarnished heroes, and much ignorance and stupidity. He is, nevertheless, dealing with very important advances in life-saving medical techniques which ultimately became general practice. In showing how wisdom and humanity ultimately prevailed, he may be said to have contributed valuably, if cautiously, to the process of rehabilitation.

F. B. Smith's book is the most weighty of the three in terms both of scope and detail. He examines the treatment offered, and the institutions through which that treatment was offered, in the event of the ill-health of successive age-groups, starting with childbirth and proceeding through infancy, childhood, youth and maturity, to old age. It is a largely unmitigated horror-story. Confirming implicitly throughout most of this long book, and explicitly in a brief final chapter, McKeown's thesis of medical inability to cure throughout the nineteenth century, Smith illustrates in infinite detail the ineffective treatment offered by nineteenth-century doctors – much of it harmless, fortunately, but enough of it sufficiently lethal to invoke throughout the century a succession of prosecutions for manslaughter. Most of these failed as magistrates and judges demonstrated solidarity with brother professionals.

F. B. Smith has read widely in all sorts of curious but relevant places, but the fascination and importance of what he writes derive most of all from his humanity: he is no Whig historian aiming to trace the march of science or applaud the heroes of medicine (there are precious few of the latter in his account), but a social historian endeavouring to find out what Victorian medical treatment actually meant at the receiving end. 'Patients loom small in medical history', he protests: 'most medical history in the past has been compiled by medically trained men and published by medical publishers only for medical men'. Seen through the eyes of the people – mostly poor people – in this way, the nineteenth-century medical profession emerges as occasionally painstaking and sympathetic, mostly ineffectual (necessarily), but not infrequently callous, brutal and mercenary. Diagnosis rarely transcended guesswork and treatment was random when not cynical.

F. B. Smith devotes much of his space to an examination of the hospitals, the quacks and the Poor Law that represented medical provision for large sections of the population. Though he explicitly disclaims either the intention or the ability to resolve the dispute about the role of hospitals in reducing mortality in the eighteenth and nineteenth centuries, he makes a considerable contribution to it by showing how previous students of the hospital records have been seriously misled by their failure to interpret their terminology correctly. Like the doctors, the hospitals, particularly the Poor Law infirmaries, emerge rather scathed from Smith's scrutiny.

All three authors are surely right to emphasize the element of charlatanry in the nineteenth-century profession, but might perhaps have softened the severity of their exposures by some recognition that while all these terrible things were going on some valuable scientific work was also proceeding. The foundations of the understanding of physiology, anatomy, bacteriology and biochemistry which underlie modern medical success were being laid at this time. It was a time of learning, even if much of it was by trial and error: the learning, and even the trial and error, which some patients failed to survive, were necessary stages in the mastering of the art of curing and the creation of a viable profession which could command the respect of society by virtue of its genuine skills and not of its posturings and protestations. In these books the seamier side of Victorian medical practice and behaviour predominate; but we should not lose sight of the favourable omens, however few they may have been. As after McKeown's seminal articles, after these books Victorian medicine can never be quite the same again. That makes them all important.

M. W. Flinn
Brownshill, Glos.

G. W. Jones and Alan Norton (eds), *Political Leadership in Local Authorities*. Birmingham: Institute of Local Government Studies, University of Birmingham, 1978. 233 pp. Tables. £4.50.

Urban history, child of stern, numerate, economic history and soft, passionate, social history has had, like its parents, a serious problem in relating to people. To 'urban history', people appear either as card-carrying representatives of tides of opinion, classes, interests, or as clowns for light relief between the serious business of jargon-packed analysis and columnar statistics.

Political studies has had a similar maladjustment to real people, but, with skilled American guidance in social psychology, a few have noticed that events are often the consequence of individual initiatives and skills.

The volume under review considers post-war local political leaders in a variety of urban and rural settings in Great Britain and signals a substantial shift away from analysing local politics in terms of local elections and the domestic arrangements of political parties. One editor, George Jones, provides an introductory essay setting a general framework for analysing political leadership, while the other editor, Alan Norton, contributes a concluding essay trying to draw the varied contributors' essays together into George Jones' framework. Since the contributors had a free hand to report whatever they found in whatever analytic framework they found convenient, the theoretical essays of the editors are, like the other essays, written clearly, with only the necessary minimum of specialized technology.

All the contributors find some heroic quality about the leaders they have studied. Some combinations of social and political structure make leadership difficult, and some leaders do not succeed at their heroic task, whether it be keeping an increasingly complex system afloat, developing it, giving it new objectives, or simply representing it to outsiders. However, it is impossible, having read the volume, not to look with fresh eyes at the working of local affairs.

This is where the volume may be of particular importance for urban historians – to stimulate them into rethinking the boundaries of their subject. Instead of discarding the information about individuals that they collect, they might consider this to be the real story that needs to be told. Urban history will be cured of its maladjustments when it takes real people as its heroes.

Owen A. Hartley
Department of Politics, University of Leeds

Charles H. Levine (ed.), *Managing Human Resources. A Challenge to Urban Governments*. Beverly Hills and London: Sage Publications, 1977. 319 pp. No price stated.

This book is volume 13 of the *Urban Affairs Annual Reviews*, a (now semi-annual) series of reference volumes treating policies, programmes, and current developments of interest to urban specialists. The current volume consists of a dozen essays loosely linked under the heading of municipal public personnel management in the United States.

In his introduction editor Charles Levine has carefully established the *raison d'être* for the collection by noting that a new era of politics has recently emerged in U.S. cities. The major political antagonists of this new era are no longer the machine politicians and 'good government reformers' of the past. Instead, the cities today are witnessing the increasingly bitter struggles of taxpayers and elected officials with public employee unions, battles between governmental bodies over scarce resources, and disputes involving local and federal governmental officials over compliance with federal law and court decisions.

As a result of these new challenges and the new management techniques which have arisen to meet them, the old *unitary* conception of public personnel administration has collapsed. In its stead there now exists a conceptual fragmentation of the subject of public personnel administration – a fragmentation which Levine argues 'reflects the operational fragmentation of the human resource system itself'.

The 12 readings which have been selected for the volume are intended to represent the principal developments impinging upon public personnel management in the 'post reform era'. They may be loosely grouped into five major areas: the changing roles of the municipal employee, the hiring of minority groups (affirmative action), collective bargaining, human resource development techniques, and federally-designed public employment programmes. It is possible, of course, to discuss only a few of the varied contributions here, and my preferences as an economist will almost certainly differ from those of individuals in other disciplines. David Stanley's essay, 'The ambiguous role of the urban public employee,' raises the question of whether today's municipal worker is primarily a public servant, a beneficiary (who may owe his job to someone or some programme), a political tactician, or a participant in the managerial process. For those who might wonder what difference it makes as to which pair of shoes the urban employee wears, Stanley presents a convincing argument.

In his 'Institutional barriers to equity in local government employment,' Frank J. Thompson reports on a survey of attitudes of local public personnel officials regarding affirmative action programmes and the hiring of women and disadvantaged minorities. As is well known, such programmes have generated much controversy in the U.S. (during the 1970s especially) to the extent that they have clashed head-on with the more traditional merit-based selection process. Thompson's attitudinal data suggest that there is only a very limited supportive environment for reducing the institutional barriers to hiring the disadvantaged in local government jobs.

The fiscal crises faced by many local governments in the past few years have brought forth cries for greater productivity and efficiency of public employees. But as Roy Bahl and Jesse Burkhead point out in their 'Productivity and the measurement of public output', there is very little in the public sector that is amenable to output measurement. Even if this were not the case, such measurements might be wholly misleading in terms of how citizens or administrators view public output. (For example, do more police arrests mean safer streets?) Instead, Bahl and Burkhead suggest that we analyse local government service delivery in terms of a system of vectors: environment, input, activities, output, and consequences. They also review and criticize the attempts made by other researchers to use governmental expenditures as a proxy for governmental output.

Because of the variety of subjects treated in the other essays, it is safe to say that most students of U.S. urban affairs will find something of interest in the collection. However, it should be pointed out that the variety of offerings is also mirrored by the widely different disciplinary perspectives of the various authors (e.g., economics, behavioural science, statistics and quantitative methods). This may serve to limit somewhat the book's appeal.

R. J. Thornton
Department of Economics, Lehigh University

2 INDIVIDUAL TOWNS AND REGIONS

D. E. H. de Boer, *Graaf en Grafiek. Sociale en economische ontwikkelingen in het middeleeuwse "Noordholland" tussen + 1345 en + 1415.* [Count and Counting. Social and economic changes in medieval 'Noordholland' between c. 1345 and c. 1415.] Leiden: New Rhine Publishers, 1978. xiv + 395 pp. With English summary. No price stated.

Though this book is not devoted to urban history as a main theme, dealing primarily with the countryside, it surely deserves notice in this Yearbook, not least because of the methods of research and presentation which are new for the study of the later Middle Ages in Holland. This work examines the considerable social and economic changes which took place in the fourteenth and fifteenth centuries in the region of 'Noordholland' (at that time a part of the county of Holland between

Haarlemmermeer and Maas, in the north and middle of the present-day province of South Holland). The main sources for this investigation are the unedited accounts of the comital officials (hence 'count' in the title of the book) and other serial records suitable for illustrating long-term development through statistical analysis ('counting'). The study consists of three parts: 1, population; 2, money, wages and prices; and 3, productivity and trade at the local and regional level. Some conclusions of the investigation can be summarized as follows. The country-side of the region suffered a decline of population because of epidemics; cultivation, especially corn-growing, underwent a decrease owing to physical-geographical conditions; unemployment in the countryside encouraged migration into towns, also affected by epidemics. As to towns in this context, a distinction has been made between smaller and the larger centres. In the former the relatively prosperous industrial production declined in favour of the latter, major towns like Delft, Gouda, Haarlem, and Leiden, which specialized in export industries (cloth, beer). The smaller towns would henceforth play a role in the trade and distribution of the products of the larger ones and would only produce for the local market. In the second half of the fourteenth century the urban economy, especially of the larger towns, became the basis for the regional and international trade which would flourish in the sixteenth and seventeenth centuries.

P. H. J. van der Laan
Municipal Archives, Amsterdam

J. H. Moran, *Education and Learning in the City of York 1300–1560*. [Borthwick Papers 55.] York: St Anthony's Press, 1979. 49pp. Annual subscription £1.50 post free, non-subscribers 80p + 10p postage.

In this paper, which is based on his doctoral thesis, J. H. Moran examines education and learning in the city of York in the later medieval period – a period that has often been neglected by historians of education. He comes to the conclusion that the state of learning was more highly developed before the Reformation than many previous scholars had thought (with the exception of Nicholas Orme, whose theories, based upon work in the West Country, are confirmed by J. H. Moran). The main sources that are used are the records in York Minster Library and the wills in the Borthwick Institute of Historical Research, both of which unfortunately yield only patchy evidence. Nevertheless they do provide the material for a good analysis of St Peter's Grammar School which flourished in the fifteenth century with perhaps 100 to 150 pupils, and also the Minster song school. The author's arguments are strongest when he deals with the grammar, song and reading schools in the city, but they are weaker when he tries to look at the general state of learning by examining libraries and sermons. He also admits that no attempt can be made to assess the level of literacy in the city. Another weakness is that some of his footnotes are misleading, but despite these criticisms he has produced a very readable and informative study which adds to the gradually emerging picture of urban life in later medieval England.

Barbara Champion
Department of Political Economy, University College London.

Thomas A. Brady, Jr, *Ruling Class, Regime and Reformation at Strasbourg, 1520–1555*. Leiden: E. J. Brill, 1978. xxi + 458 pp. No price stated.

Thomas Brady's study of the politics of the Reformation in Strasbourg has been widely discussed as a controversial contribution to Reformation studies. It is also an important piece of urban history.

The author believes that 'One can no more choose between structural and narrative history than one can between theory and practice.' Accordingly, his book is divided into two parts which deal respectively with structure and with change.

The structural analysis in part one aims at answering what might be called the Dahl-Pahl questions; whose city? where did the ruling elite come from? and by what means did they rule? Thomas Brady's conceptual apparatus is neo-Marxist (the Marxism of Ossowski, Bourdieu, Poulantzas). His method is prosopographical: the backbone of the book is Appendix A, the biographies of the 105 members of the two key 'privy councils', the XV and the XIII, from 1520 to 1555. His main conclusion is that the ruling class, despite its divisions into patrician and guildsman, rentier and merchant (divisions which overlapped but did not coincide), were a united group who intermarried and had important economic interests in common, in the city and also in the countryside around it. Only these men had the leisure to devote to committees, so in practice it was they who ran the city.

So far, the book may be judged a distinguished contribution to the recent work on the quantitative social history of German cities by such scholars as Erich Maschke, Hans-Christoph Rublack, and Ingrid Bátori. Even historians who do not speak the language of 'social fractions' and 'symbolic capital' may agree that Thomas Brady has put forward a plausible explanation of Strasbourg's celebrated – almost Venetian – political stability.

The author is well aware of the dangers of a static picture of a changing situation and he accepts what he candidly calls 'the unproven assumption that regimes are most likely to reveal their true social character at times of greatest stress'. Hence he goes on in part two to study the Reformation as a threat to the political stability of Strasbourg and to the dominance of its ruling class. He concentrates on two crises. That of 1523–5 was a storm successfully weathered. Despite their divisions of opinion, the ruling class presented a united front, made sacrifices in the interests of survival and satisfied the main popular demands. In 1547–8, however, caught between the contradictory demands of the emperor and the people (or at least the lesser guildsmen), the ruling class 'collapsed'.

The author emphasizes that he is not offering a history of the Reformation in Strasbourg, and so the criticisms of 'sociologism' which have been levelled at him are less than fair. Yet, for all its brilliance, part two is less convincing than part one. The 1523–5 story of the victory of the 'politiques' in the elite over their colleagues (Protestant 'zealots' no less than Catholic 'old guard'), is plausible, but the evidence for it is thin, and the assumption that the moderates must all have put politics before principle is, to put it mildly, not proven. The 1547–8 story is less coherent. After their collapse, we find the ruling elite come bouncing back, but how the crisis came to be resolved remains unclear. Like his oligarchs, Thomas Brady does not meet the challenge of 1547–8 as well as that of 1523–5. Despite that he has written a lucid, vigorous, penetrating and provoking book.

Peter Burke
Emmanuel College, Cambridge

W. J. Sheils, *The Puritans in the Diocese of Peterborough 1558–1610* [Northamptonshire Record Society, vol xxx]. Northampton. 1979. xi + 166 pp. 2 plates. 3 maps. 4 tables. Bibliography. £7.50.

It is good to have a solid, well-documented account of puritanism in the diocese of Peterborough to add to the few case studies already in print on this important movement. All credit to the Northamptonshire Record Society for publishing this study. While this book will please the specialist, general readers should perhaps be warned that the author has attempted to capture more of the diversity of the puritan tradition than is often the case. The resulting detail of this work may confuse the unwary. After a rather brief introduction to Peterborough diocese, which might have been made clearer by reference to a map, the work falls into two sections. Four chapters provide a narrative account of puritanism in the diocese covering a period usefully extended to 1610, thus placing Bancroft's work in an Elizabethan perspective. There are one or two adjustments to the record, notably with a call to heed the activities of puritans *not* involved in the *classis* movement of the 1580s, but otherwise this section upholds the general framework established by Professor Collinson, whose inspiration W. J. Sheils acknowledges. The four remaining chapters follow a more analytical format. The education, family connections and eventual role of the puritan ministers are examined and due attention is paid to the differing degrees of support afforded by the laity – gentry and lower orders alike. Of most interest to readers of this journal is the short chapter on 'the godly town' of Northampton. The author paints a convincing picture of the Geneva which ministers like Percival Wiburn and Robert Catelin strove to create. Their battle with the clerical authorities is well caught, but unfortunately, in a section only 12 pages long, there is little room for elaboration on how these ministers related to factions within the corporation or to particular social groups in the town. This is a short book crammed with information and it would be too much to expect full treatment of all aspects of a complicated subject. We can only regret that the author did not find space to comment more systematically on the 11 of the 15 market towns of the diocese cited as puritan centres during this period. It is also sad that more could not be said about the diminutive cathedral town of Peterborough. Perhaps W. J. Sheils will be kind enough to satisfy these specialist interests at a later date.

Andrew W. Foster
Department of History, West Sussex Institute of Higher Education

Ed Taverne, *In 't land van belofte: in de nieue stadt.* Maarssen: 1978. No price stated.
While economic activity in the period covered by this book (1580–1680) was either stagnant or in decline in large parts of Europe, the young Republic of the United Provinces boomed. In spite of a long war against Spain, coastal provinces in particular succeeded in establishing a highly efficient urban economy, accompanied by demographic growth of 145 per cent between 1514 and 1622. The towns of Holland profited most from this increase, but at the same time, housing the immigrant masses created huge problems. Taverne's book is primarily concerned with the question: how did urban planners and four leading cities deal with urban expansion in this period? The first part of the book focuses on the emergent humanistic renaissance view of how towns should be built, the 'città ideale'. This was an essentially Italian concept in which the need for modern fortification often dictated the urban physiognomy. Architects concentrated on the walled space and designed the optimal grid, location, centrality, etc. of the town. The 'città ideale' philosophy often went further than merely discussing optimal morphological form; however, the author is clearly more interested in this than in showing us what social and moral ideas influenced the architects.

The major contribution of part I is Taverne's rehabilitation of Simon Stevin (1548–1620) as a town planner. Although widely known as a mathematician, Stevin also happens to have had original and practical ideas about a Dutch 'ideal city'. Perhaps his skill, like that of architect-scientist Salomon de Bray from Haarlem, was forgotten after the attacks which were launched against classical urban design at the beginning of the twentieth century. Camillo Sitte, Eisler and the Dutch architect Berlage highly valued the medieval city, in which they admired organic growth and irregular shape as contrasted to the classical grid with its severe angles and dead straight roads. In doing so, Taverne explains, they did no justice to the creativity of Dutch humanist town planners, who unfortunately hardly ever got a chance to realize their plans in the young Republic. Here, the surveyor and military engineer were prominent. It was in Christian IV's Denmark and in some German principalities that Dutch architects could realize their plans.

How, then, did the Dutch cities cope with overcrowding? This forms the main theme of part II, in which the author turns out to be an excellent urban historian.

Taverne has selected four cities which were facing a rapid rise in numbers: Amsterdam, Leiden, Utrecht and Haarlem. In each case the author examines the main countervailing powers in the local struggle for urban space. Real estate speculators and rack-rent landlords tried to maintain a situation of overcrowding and sky-high rents, and consequently tried to block any extension of the city. On the other hand, the city as a whole was forced to handle the problem of overcrowding, pollution and pre-modern Bidonvilles outside the city walls. High rents usually meant high wages, which in turn threatened the city's competitive position. There was always the very real threat of nearby villages luring away labour and capital by offering workers low-cost accommodation and housing. The urban extensions actually built represented compromises in a protracted warfare between urban pressure groups, each of which laid its own specific claim to urban space, and none of which was able or willing to step back in favour of the common interest. There were some individuals who sought to define what was good for the city as a whole: Burgomaster Cornelis Pietersz. Hooft of Amsterdam and architect de Bray of Haarlem both philosophized about the 'Ideal City'. But practically none of their ideas were ever realized.

One of the reasons why strictly planned developments failed was the high cost of military fortification. In a period of chronic warfare modern city walls were essential for survival. Medieval defence systems were outdated, and a new complex of earthen walls, ditches and redoubts had to be built. Each urban development started with fortifications, which in turn forced the municipality to sell walled empty lots as soon as possible for prices which could finance the military expenditure. Over-strict rules on quality and quantity of buildings, streets and canals would deter buyers. This was the moment when real estate speculators moved in. Lack of building regulations and inefficient enforcement of existing ones made high-density, multi-storey building possible. The result was far from 'classical': a fairly chaotic façade, where each house differed in both form and size.

This phenomenon – high fortification costs forcing the municipality to sell land at the highest possible price – was more or less the same in each of the four cities. At the same time the author makes clear how local circumstances provided different arenas for the urban power struggle. This makes for interesting variations on the main theme: what societal forces created the net morphological result, after years of deliberation and open conflict? If the aim was to clarify the often blurred and intricate motives behind the power politics for urban space, the author has fully succeeded.

Still, there remain questions. How do the two parts of the book – sixteenth-century urban theory and local urban practice – relate to one another? What the author makes clear in part II is that plans were essentially frustrated instead of being put into practice. Why then were these critics of 'classicism', of grid patterns and the like so upset when urban building was highly eclectical in reality? Another question: why was it that real estate speculators, building contractors and landlords succeeded in taking over urban developments? Fortification and consequent money shortage on the part of the municipalities, we are told, is the answer. But was not the Republic one of Europe's richest states, despite a war against Spain? 'Ideal Cities', however, were built in absolutist states, where omnipotent sovereigns imposed their will upon city and citizen. Their will was the common interest. In the Republic there was no strong, supra-urban power structure available to enforce a common interest upon the cities. The Revolt itself was, for a large part, carried out by the cities, anxious to defend their local autonomy. There was simply nothing and nobody to enforce 'ideal city' plans.

Questions and criticisms are, however, largely overshadowed by the great qualities of this book. It is still rare to find a study of urban history in this country in which 'urban' stands for something more than the casual 'locus' for all sorts of history. Taverne succeeds in presenting the vivid interaction between socio-economic development and the concrete morphological environment as both resultant and constraint. Moreover, he introduces Simon Stevin as a highly original and interesting urban planner. Dutch urban history has been enriched by an important contribution.

Michiel Wagenaar
Department of Human Geography, University of Amsterdam

Richard Alan Ryerson, *The Revolution is now Begun: The Radical Committees of Philadelphia, 1765–1776*. Philadelphia: University of Pennsylvania Press, 1978. xv + 305 pp. £18.65.

This book is, as the title suggests, more a case study of the mechanics of revolutionary political mobilization than an analysis of political life within a fully-documented urban milieu (there is little attention paid to Philadelphia's social and economic structure in this book). Its true historiographical context is to be found in the current orthodoxy that the American Revolution can ultimately be explained in ideological terms. For Ryerson, however, if the development of a particular world-view explains why the Revolution took place, such a focus is of limited use where questions of process and timing are concerned. Explaining why the Revolution occurred does not tell us how it occurred. It is to the latter question, set within the context of Philadelphia (and, more generally, Pennsylvania), that this book is addressed.

On the eve of the Revolution, Pennsylvania was governed by a well-entrenched Quaker oligarchy. The Pennsylvania Assembly was an extremely conservative body, consisting primarily of middle-aged, experienced, Quaker legislators of English and Welsh descent. In two years – from 1774 to 1776 – this hegemony was at first undermined and then overthrown. The author's searching and thoroughly exhaustive analysis of the numerous extra-constitutional committees that rose to prominence in these two years is an attempt to explain both the speed and extent of this revolution and to gauge its precise revolutionary character. Less than 200 Philadelphians served on major resistance committees in the years 1774–6. With the aid of 20 well-presented tables and graphs and various appendices, Ryerson explores the wealth, age, occupation, religious affiliation and ethnic origin of these men. Analysis of the membership of successive committees reveals a uniform decline in their average wealth, a dramatic increase in the number of 'mechanics', and an increasing diversity of ethnic groups and religious denominations. For Ryerson, this development was revolutionary not only in paving the way for independence but also for ushering Pennsylvania into an age of mass politics. Indeed, Philadelphia's radical leaders are credited with creating 'the prototype of a modern American urban party'. The author does not, of course, simply rely on prosopography to explain the coming of the revolution to Pennsylvania; the greater part of the book is devoted to an extremely detailed narrative which focuses on shifting tactics and goals (as well as composition) of the radical committees. Without doubt, Ryerson has succeeded in illuminating the process and identifying the key turning points of Pennsylvania's struggle for independence.

Whether he has succeeded so well with some of the broader implications of his study is another matter. For instance, in the preface, the author mentions that he aimed to study 'the process of radical committee politics within one community'. He has certainly succeeded in the first half of that aim; unfortunately, the 'community' receives neither definition nor exploration. If 'the resistance committee system was oriented toward mass politics', if 'its representation was by neighborhood or ward, by ethnic-religious group, by occupation and by relative economic standing', then the relationship between committee men and their constituency deserves more attention than it receives in this book. We need to know how widespread public support was for the radical committees, how that support was maintained or lost, why some men were recruited to the committees and others not – all questions that involve more analysis of this urban 'community'. Furthermore, one suspects that these questions cannot simply be answered from 'the domain of reality and action' but also require moving into 'the realm of theory and rhetoric'.

'How' and 'why', action and ideology, cannot be separated as easily as Ryerson seems to think.

Philip Morgan
Department of History, Johns Hopkins University

David D. Buck, *Urban Change in China. Politics and Development in Tsinan, Shantung, 1890–1949.* Madison: University of Wisconsin Press, 1978. xvi + 296 pp. 5 maps. $15.00.

David Buck makes available to the West a new dimension of Chinese urban history. He has selected a single city, Tsinan, in the northern province of Shantung, and traced its responses through the changes that have overtaken China since 1890. Tsinan has been chosen as being more typical of essentially Chinese experience than the cities that have tended to attract so much attention in the West, namely the treaty ports. It is a city of considerable size and antiquity, lying inland from the direct impact of the westerners, yet organically related in market and transport terms to its region of China. In earlier times it manifested its own logic of traditional development, with its own trading system and administrative and security functions, but from *c.* 1890 it had to respond to new forces operating on a national scale. There is, therefore, a powerful duality, consisting of China as the larger whole and Tsinan as a city-region within it. David Buck offers a city-region biography, but in terms that are novel, both as to the general Chinese setting and the particular experience of a city seen as undergoing a transition to something different from its former self, and yet manifesting important continuities.

The author is able to present a useful generalized introductory paradigm of the urban response to change in Western terms, and to contrast it with that of China. This raises the question of value systems as they relate to the role of cities: for the West the city has been the outcome of forces generated by the market and private property, with a minimum of State control; in the Chinese case there has been and there still is no automatic acceptance of the city. Recent history and traditional realities have both contributed to this Chinese attitude. On the one hand the idea of the city is tainted by recollections of the foreign dominance exercised through the treaty ports. On the other hand Mao was intensely aware of class conflict in the countryside, and adapted Marx accordingly: the village rather than the city was where reality lay. Urban growth has not therefore been left free to assert itself, but has been controlled and limited by official policy both in the past and in the present. Tsinan, then, like other Chinese cities, has not been allowed to respond to the modern age in the uninhibited manner of the West, but has been kept within a containing framework of national values and priorities. All this, of course, poses a challenge: how far is it possible to create and preserve an alternative to Western-type urbanization, following a philosophy as with Gandhi's view of India or Khomeini's of Iran? Can whole nations be deflected from market 'inevitability', maintaining some kind of chosen balance between agriculture and industry and between country and town, containing the pressures thus generated? Is it possible to promote the principles of 'socialist urban construction', within the towns, rejecting 'imperialist urban construction' (p. 203)?

To this kind of problem this study makes a useful contribution. The author traces the experience of a single city as it passed through time. Approached in this dimension the simple choice between market and socialist alternatives is heavily complicated by real experience. The phases are dramatic: the encroaching impact of modernization stemming in part from the treaty ports, the attempted official reforms in the search for a conservative compromise with the new forces, the first revolution and the early republic, the chaos of near-disintegration in the war-lord era, the decade of the Kuomintang, the foreign attack by the Japanese and, finally, the communist revolution and the struggle to consolidate it. In each phase the same groups of actors are present – there are the men of business, the bureaucrats, the military, the landed magnates and the peasantry, each responding to success-ive immediate situations. Each era is given its chapter, with a useful summary.

Returning from the particular (in the form of his chosen city) to the general (in terms of Chinese urban experience), the author concludes that the case of Tsinan 'reveals quite clearly the overall pattern of Chinese urban development to 1949' (p. 210). It is one in which, though significant beginnings were made, Chinese cities 'failed to reach the levels of economic and political modernisation necessary to achieve success along the lines of the Western model'. This would seem to be a fairly self-evident statement. The value of the book lies in the way in which the author has delineated the relationships between the forces of modernization and those of constraint. It does not appear to be possible to cast these relationships into the form of a generalized model of the kind with which the author begins his study.

Are we to deduce that the failure to modernize was inherent in the condition of China, or was it an accident, or perhaps a marginal shortfall? How far was it the consequence of official will, or conversely, of the breakdown of government? What are the implications of such a failure? If Tsinan and the cities which it is taken to represent had moved somewhat further along the road to modernization on the lines of the Western model, would there have been no communist revolution? David Buck provokes such questions by providing a unique study that amplifies our view of urban processes, both as a monograph investigation of a particular city, and as relating cities in general to the nation that formed them.

S. G. Checkland
Department of Economic History, University of Glasgow

J. D. Wirth and R. L. Jones (eds), *Manchester and Sao Paulo: Problems of Rapid Urban Growth*. Stanford: Stanford University Press, 1978. 234 pp. $17.50.

The aim of this book is incautiously ambitious – no less than a comparison of the experiences of two cities in different countries and at periods a full century apart. That it fails to match the demands of so herculean a task is not surprising, particu-larly given that there is no comparative framework to which its nine contributors work. Some do make direct comparisons between Manchester in the heyday of its growth and São Paulo in the postwar years, but most look simply at aspects of one or other city and it is left to one of the editors to draw some unhelpfully cursory parallels in a brief introduction to this set of conference papers. The rapid expan-sion that each city underwent during the early period of industrialization in Britain and Brazil may provide grounds for comparison, but the contexts of their growth were literally worlds apart and none of the authors surmounts the problem of holding constant such contextual differences. Roberts does succeed in setting the two cities against the contemporary background of the broader societal and economic structure in his essay on growth and organization: Morse is rather less successful in doing this for his somewhat strained thesis that Manchester 'chose' economics because it had a clear view of the nature of society whereas São Paulo 'chose' sociology because it had not. Most of the essays, however, are content to discuss only one city – and one contributor throws Liverpool in for good measure – and cover a broad spectrum from the perceptual views of contemporary writers and poets, to the relationship of city and hinterland in the process of growth, the evolu-tion of government, and such social responses to mass society as religion and foot-ball. The individual chapters have a good deal of meat to them and add to our knowledge of two cities which act as litmus in our understanding of the structural changes accompanying urbanization and industrialization; but without a stronger comparative framework and with the perspectives of history, politics, anthropol-ogy and sociology jostling with one another, the whole seems no greater than the sum of its parts.

B. T. Robson
Department of Geography, University of Manchester

Richard Cobb, *Death in Paris: The records of the Basse-Geôle de la Seine, October 1795–September 1801*. Oxford: Oxford University Press, 1978. ix + 134 pp. Appendices. Bibliography. £4.95.

In his recent writing Richard Cobb has moved perceptibly away from the history of politics and institutions, from the police and the *armées révolutionnaires* of his earlier research, towards the study of people as private individuals responding to the demands of Revolutionary society. He shares some of the characteristics of both the novelist and the anarchist, exploring with great compassion the lives and feelings of the poor and vulnerable, and showing little regard for the needs of governments and bureaucracies. His evocative use of language is unparalleled among historians; and in his pittoresque approach he owes more to Restif de la Bretonne than to any living scholar. In recent essays, in works like *Paris and its Provinces* and *A Sense of Place*, this compassion has grown more marked and the stress on the mentalities born of deprivation more persistent. Politics, he insists, was of little interest to ordinary Parisians, and to understand them we must enter their world and follow them in their everyday pursuits. *Death in Paris* happens to be rooted in the documentation of the Revolutionary period, but it is not really a book about the Revolution. Rather it is about habit and custom, the everyday sociability of a large city, the sense of *quartier*, the comradeship and the loneliness of life in a Paris lodging-house. The source materials are totally apolitical: the records of sudden death for that area of Paris which naturally straddles the Seine, between the Pont de Charenton and the Pont d'Asnières. We learn of the brawls and the accidents at work, of swimming tragedies and especially of suicides. We gain, in short, a rather special insight, one based far more on the author's remarkable feel for the city and its varying moods than on the statistical base – some 400 dossiers from the Paris morgue – on which the book is nominally built. For many readers with a liking for the methodology of the sociologist, the demographer or the statistician, this study will seem too slight and impressionistic, too dependent on Richard Cobb's historical imagination. But for the historian of Paris its value lies precisely in that imagination – in seeing how far the private fears and joys, griefs and condolences of a largely unlettered population can be traced from the bleakly bureaucratic entries about the corpses laid out on the mortuary slab. In *Death in Paris* this approach is exploited to its limit, as Richard Cobb uses a rich variety of detail – the network of neighbours and relatives, the timing of suicides, the clothing covering a victim's body, the reassuring daily routine of the *cabaret* – to attempt to penetrate the private and jealously-guarded world of the Paris poor.

Alan Forrest
Department of History, University of Manchester

Daniel J. Walkowitz, *Worker City, Company Town: Iron and Cotton-Worker Protest in Troy and Cohoes, New York, 1855–1884*. Urbana: University of Illinois Press, 1978. xviii + 292 pp. $12.95.

The problem of why workers strike in some towns and industries but not in others is an intriguing one, and it forms the background for Daniel Walkowitz's book, *Worker City, Company Town*. This study of two industrial communities in the Hudson River Valley compares a small city with several major industries with a mill town dominated by one cotton textile firm during the third quarter of the nineteenth century. Walkowitz places primary emphasis on contrasting patterns of workers' protest, and he develops a complex argument to explain large differences in his subjects' abilities to resist changes in working conditions. In Troy, the iron moulders maintained strong and active unions, which retained much control over work processes through the 1880s, but in Cohoes, cotton workers organized relatively late and remained weak in the face of company pressures. The Troy iron workers were male artisans, highly skilled and predominantly Irish. They developed a local community united by ethnicity, work experiences, religion, and associations. Moreover, the city's mix of industries meant that alternative types of employment were available so that family income was cushioned from the effects of strikes or depressions in one industry. Textile workers in Cohoes, however, were largely low-skilled females or adolescents. An influx of French-Canadians into a heavily Irish and English town during the 1870s lessened community solidarity, while the Harmony Mills had enormous power over workers' lives because of their provision of company housing and control of the local labour market.

   Worker City, Company Town is a skilful blend of older and newer styles of social history. Both quantitative data and narrative accounts of local strikes and organ- izing campaigns are combined to produce this carefully controlled example of comparative urban history. The book gains added depth from analyses of wages, the cost of living, women's roles, and family organization. In addition, Walkowitz's familiarity with English social history results in frequent and interesting com- parisons with industrial workers on the other side of the Atlantic. Unfortunately, his sources – largely censuses, city directories, city council reports, newspapers, and a few trade union minutes – are less rich than those available to many histo- rians of English industrial communities. The lack of material written by workers about themselves poses a problem for his discussions of ideologies and mentalities. While he contends that workers generally lacked an active class consciousness, his evidence on this point is limited. Although he sees class struggles in the streets of Troy and Cohoes, the perceptions of those involved in the mounting protests of the 1880s remain obscure. Nevertheless, his argument, that the combination of social mobility, the right to vote, and a liberal, democratic ideology dampened class con- sciousness rings true.

   Questions can also be raised about the homogeneity of the workers he surveys. How important were Irish protestants, non-believers, and non-joiners? Did Troy and Cohoes have their 'respectables' and their 'roughs'? While the sources avail- able limit answers to these questions, the existence of such groups would have limited the solidarity of the labour movement that Walkowitz so vividly portrays.

   The Irish, as a major component of the Troy and Cohoes population, play a large part in the book. Walkowitz probably underestimates the extent of diversity of their pre-famine backgrounds. Those he calls peasants came from a multitude of places and were of differing status. Many early and mid-nineteenth-century Irish migrants were town artisans or the tenants of relatively large farms, and I doubt whether his invocation of an Irish tradition of resistance to authority as an ex- planation of a Celtic propensity to join labour protests can be applied uniformly to the various sorts of Irish migrants. His argument would rest on sounder ground if he could specify the local and social origins of his migrants. His research shows, however, how important migration and ethnicity are as explanations of working- class behaviour in the context of American cities.

Lynn H. Lees
Department of History, University of Pennsylvania

Eugene J. Watts, *The Social Bases of City Politics: Atlanta, 1865–1903.* Westport, Connecticut: Greenwood Press, 1978. x + 188 pp. 26 tables. Bibliographic essay. $17.95.
This book is one of a growing number of recent studies on the history of the urban South. A study in the 'new political history', it attempts to analyse late nine- teenth-century Atlanta politics in order to discover 'persistent social patterns of political behavior' (p. 3). These patterns, the author argues, can best be discover- ed through an examination of the candidates for election to local office. His major research methodology is political prosopography – 'the investigation of the common background characteristics of political actors by means of a collective study of their lives' (p. 4). The group-defining social characteristics of the candi- dates included: property, occupation, age, race, residence, ethnic background and/or region of birth, period of arrival in Atlanta, and length of residence in the city. In addition, three political characteristics of candidates were examined: pol-

itical persistence (or number of campaigns), previous experience in city appointive offices, and prior service in political committees. Information on each of these 11 variables was collected for all candidates for election to the mayoralty, the city council, and the board of aldermen between 1865 and 1903. With this information, the author hoped to test the notion of the 'social filter' – the idea that certain social and political attributes sorted out candidates for office from non-candidates, and then determined political success or failure of those who had become candidates.

In his early chapters, Watts describes the governmental and political structure of Atlanta and discusses the significance of his 11 social and political variables. This portion of the book is based upon extensive research in Atlanta's newspapers and in traditional historical sources. The heart of the book, however, is contained in two long chapters – one examining the social filter in the nomination process, and one analysing the social filter in the actual elections. This section of the book is based upon a statistical analysis of the background characteristics of over 800 candidates. 26 tables present the statistical evidence.

The conclusions Watts draws from the evidence are interesting, although not really surprising. Regarding the first stage of the social filter – the nomination process – he contends that Atlanta's candidates were highly unrepresentative of the population at large. Businessmen and professionals dominated the mayoralty campaigns; they were wealthier and older than candidates for other positions, had been long-term residents of the city, and had previous political experience in appointive offices and/or political committees. Compared to the mayoralty hopefuls, candidates for the at-large alderman positions were younger, less wealthy, and more recent arrivals to Atlanta. Candidates for the city council were more heterogeneous and included larger numbers of newcomers, blue-collar workers, and political novices, as well as younger and poorer men. Watts also detects some changes over time in the character of the candidates. Over the course of the late nineteenth century, early settlers were gradually replaced by newcomers; candidates tended to be older and wealthier, they were more likely to be residents of the outskirts of the city rather than the centre, and a larger number had prior experience in political committees (especially after the development of a citizens' reform movement in the 1880s).

During the actual elections, according to Watts, the second stage of the social filter became operable. Its impact is less clear than in the earlier stage. Before the citizens' reform movement of the 1880s, most successful mayoralty candidates were businessmen, Southerners, previous political campaigners, and men who were not seeking advancement from appointive positions. After the mid-1880s, wealth and age became more important. The social filter made the mayoralty an exclusive and unrepresentative position. However, the social filter did not operate to any significant degree in the aldermanic and council elections. The statistical evidence reveals no strong patterns of political preference among Atlanta's voters, and elections for these posts 'did not hinge to any great extent upon the social or political qualities of the candidates' (p. 154). Thus, Watts concludes, the social filter in Atlanta was more important in the nomination process than in the elections, but 'both stages of the social filter made Atlanta's office-holders highly unrepresentative of the citizenry' (p. 171).

This book has certain obvious uses for those interested in the study of urban political history. It is a careful case study which presents a considerable amount of information in a relatively brief space. It represents an advance over earlier social-filter studies which analysed the background characteristics only of electoral victors rather than all candidates, or examined only mayors but not aldermen and councilmen. It demonstrates that office-holders in Atlanta were different in several ways from those in other cities at the same time. Thus it emphasizes the diversity of urban politics in late nineteenth-century America.

Yet the book contains some basic and underlying weaknesses as well. While it statistically describes voter behaviour, it does not really explain this behaviour. The social filter is an analytical tool which demonstrates certain patterns in the nomination and election of candidates, but it does not tell us precisely why voters preferred candidates who were businessmen, or who were wealthy or older or politically experienced. Moreover, the book suggests that nominations and elections were held in a sort of political vacuum in which issues were meaningless. Surely there were issues in late nineteenth-century Atlanta which influenced the voters at least as much as the qualifications of the candidates; but there is no sense here that a candidate's stand on the issues of the day meant anything. Wrenched from the political context, the nomination and election statistics do not tell the whole story.

Raymond A. Mohl
Department of History, Florida Atlantic University

John W. Briggs, *An Italian Passage. Immigrants to Three American Cities, 1890–1930*. New Haven and London: Yale University Press, 1978. xxii + 348 pp. 12 plates. Tables. Bibliographical Note. £14.40.
Harold X. Connolly, *A Ghetto Grows in Brooklyn*. New York: New York University Press, 1977. xiii + 248 pp. 5 maps. $15.00.

Both these studies are concerned with migration and settlement in North American cities. In narrating the story of the creation and growth of three Italian and one black colony, the authors correctly divert attention away from Manhattan, Philadelphia, Chicago and Detroit which to date have received an overwhelming degree of attention, and concentrate on lesser-known ethnic communities in an attempt to verify hypotheses about the ghetto and lower class culture and, in Mr Connolly's case, to assess what the future holds for the population of the inner city.

Connolly's straightforward, concise account of black settlement in Brooklyn from colonial days to the present is pessimistic in conclusion. From a few slaves at the end of the eighteenth century the black community grew steadily until a century later it was beginning to infiltrate the white middle-class area of Bedford-Stuyvesant. By the forces of migration and natural increase this and adjacent areas have since been transformed into the third or fourth largest black ghetto in the United States, accounting for almost 40 per cent of New York City's black population in 1970. Connolly's case study confirms our understanding that during the last 200 years the relative position of urban blacks has only marginally improved under the multiple afflictions of 'lack of employment, poor education, low income, decayed housing and poor health'. The proliferation of Federal anti-poverty programmes since the middle 1960s has not succeeded in undermining the culture of the ghetto since they have failed to raise black incomes substantially. Connolly asserts that Americans lack the political will to bring blacks into the economic mainstream because of the aversion felt by suburbanites for the central city and through the persistence of racism. He predicts that the relative gap between black and white income and power will persist into the foreseeable future.

While Connolly's study appears to confirm the 'ghetto hypothesis', that is, the causal connection between unwelcome economic, social and psychological characteristics of ghetto inhabitants and entrapment in narrow, closed urban environments, Mr Briggs strikes a more encouraging and optimistic note in his substantial and impressive study. His revisionist interpretation of south Italian emigration to the United States and the settlement of these newcomers in three medium-sized American cities between 1890 and 1930 postulates, on the basis of extensive research in Southern Italian archives and in his chosen urban communities in the United States, that southern Italian immigrants were not a homogeneous class of backward, uneducated and illiterate peasants alienated from, and ill-adjusted to, urban-industrial society and in consequence lacking a positive attitude towards the future. On the contrary, their values, organizational ability, attitudes towards education and stress on individual advancement prepared them to take advantage of the occupational and educational opportunities presented by the American environment, and to create voluntary organizations to meet their various insurance, recreational and fraternal needs. Here Briggs takes issue with Humbert Nelli's conclusion, based on Banfield's concept of 'amoral familism', that Italian immigrants failed to bring with them the seeds of organizational life and were dependent on American models. In the three Italian settlements he has studied, Briggs suggests that the ghetto, in the sense of a totally concentrated, ethnically homogeneous community, did not exist. In Rochester, Italian settlement was based on three or four separate areas and whereas in Utica and Kansas City, there were heavy concentrations of Italians in single wards, they never contributed more than one-third of a ward's total population. Furthermore, and contrary to what appears to have been the case in New York and Chicago, immigrants from particular Italian communes or provinces did not dominate particular blocks since migration patterns militated against this. Consequently particularistic cultural features (promoting *campanilismo*) were harder to maintain and in these cities a more general Italian-American culture was promoted. Briggs' important study offers new and convincing findings to add to those of Barton and Yans-McLaughlin in the construction of a serious revisionist interpretation of Italian-American history.

A. T. Lane
School of Social Sciences, University of Bradford

Louis P. Cain, *Sanitation Strategy for a Lakefront Metropolis: The Case of Chicago.* DeKalb, Illinois: Northern Illinois University Press, 1978. xv + 173 pp. 32 tables. 12 maps. Illustrations. Bibliography. $15.00.
This book, written by an economic historian, is essentially a technological history of sanitation in Chicago. It covers the period from the early nineteenth century, when Chicago was a frontier outpost in a low-lying, swampy area, to the mid-twentieth century, when Chicago possessed the largest sewage and water treatment plants in the world. Unlike most other nineteenth-century American cities, which had ocean or river locations, Chicago was situated on a large fresh-water lake. Seaports and river cities could discharge sewage into adjoining waters and secure fresh drinking water from inland locations. The central sanitation problem for nineteenth-century Chicago, however, stemmed from the use of Lake Michigan for both water supply and sewage disposal. By necessity, therefore, Cain's study requires an examination of the inter-related nature of drainage, sewage disposal, and water supply.

As Cain notes in his introduction, the book 'concentrates on the decisions that were made and examines the motivations of the decision-makers' (p. xiii). Five major sanitation decisions are analysed, and for each of these sequential decisions the author lays out the various engineering alternatives and the economic costs involved. The first significant decision came in 1855, when the city council adopted a sewerage plan recommended by engineer Ellis Sylvester Chesbrough. Before this time Chicago had no sewers and garbage and waste was simply dumped into roadside ditches. Chesbrough's plan required the building of graded, underground sewers which emptied into the Chicago River, which in turn flowed into Lake Michigan. The plan was unique in that it necessitated the raising of street grades substantially; since the city was built on very low land, sewers were laid at street level and the streets then raised ten feet – a plan which also required raising most of the city's buildings. The main problem with Chesbrough's plan was that the sewage entered Lake Michigan quite close to the city's water supply intake.

As the sewer system became operable, the water supply worsened and water-borne diseases increased. These problems brought a recognition of the interdependence of water supply and sewage disposal, and dictated the 1863 water supply decision. Chesbrough, now chief engineer of the city's Board of Public Works, supervised construction of a tunnel under Lake Michigan to a water-intake point in deep water two miles from shore. As the city's water supply needs increased, additional tunnels were constructed, as well as a pumping station and an underground system of mains and pipes for distribution. Preservation of a pure water supply from Lake Michigan became an absolute requirement, and future sanitation decisions focused on improving methods of sewage disposal. In the 1880s engineers reversed the flow of the Chicago River and connected it with the Illinois-Michigan Canal and a newly constructed sanitary canal, both of which flowed into the Illinois River and then the Mississippi. By this means, Chicago preserved the Lake Michigan water supply while dumping its sewage through the Mississippi River drainage area. After the turn of the century, the Calumet-Sag Channel servicing the south Chicago region was built and tied into the existing system, and finally, by the 1930s, an extensive system of sewage treatment plants had been constructed to eliminate the noxious pollution, especially industrial wastes, from Chicago's essentially open sewers.

This book is a useful addition to the literature of American urban history. It logically organizes Chicago's sanitation history around the crucial choices and shows the sequential nature of these decisions, each based upon the preceeding decisions, and it demonstrates the important role of the engineer in determining the physical configuration of Chicago. More studies of this sort which elaborate the decisive place of the engineer in urban history are needed.

However, the book does suffer from some problems in research. Cain's research in primary sources is limited to the reports of the engineers and the annual reports of various official bodies such as the Sanitary District of Chicago and the boards of water commissioners, sewerage commissioners, and public works. He has relied too heavily on secondary sources, especially A. T. Andreas' three-volume *History of Chicago*, published in the 1880s. Excessive reliance on such secondary sources has led to numerous errors. A few examples will suffice. In discussing the early history of the Illinois-Michigan Canal, relying on Andreas, Cain quotes from what he calls the Niles, Michigan *Register*. Most historians knowledgable about the early nineteenth century would immediately recognize this newspaper as the *Niles Weekly Register*, published in Baltimore and edited by Hezekiah Niles. Similarly, in reporting an 1885 storm which swept sewage into Lake Michigan to the water intake point, Cain asserts that the resultant outbreak of disease killed 'approximately 12 per cent of Chicago's population' (p. 64). In 1885 Chicago had a population fast approaching 1,000,000, which was attained by 1890. It seems inconceivable that the 1885 epidemic would kill close to 100,000 people and not even receive mention in the most careful and complete history of the city, Bessie Pierce's *A History of Chicago*. The problem, of course, stems from Cain's source, which apparently is a real estate board report urging better sewage disposal methods. Obviously, the real estate people overstated the public health menace in order to get results, but Cain has accepted this material uncritically. Another basic problem with the book is that the sanitation decisions are discussed in isolation from the political and social context. Research in Chicago's newspapers, in city council records, and in the correspondence of business and political leaders would have eliminated some of the errors and helped to elaborate the larger context of urban Chicago. Nevertheless, Cain has written a helpful book, one which should be of interest to those concerned with urban physical and technological development.

Raymond A. Mohl
Department of History, Florida Atlantic University

Max Foran, *Calgary, An Illustrated History*. [The History of Canadian Cities Series.] Toronto: James Lorimer & Company and the National Museum of Man, 1978. 192pp. *c.* 110 plates, assembled by Edward Cavell. 11 maps. 12 tables. Bibliography. $21.00.

This is the first book-length scholarly history of Calgary and the second volume in a series of Canadian urban biographies sponsored by Canada's National Museum of Man. It is an attractive book, with many excellent illustrations. In keeping with the plan of the series, it seeks a balance between popular and scholarly appeal, and fully half the book consists of photographs. This leaves Foran fewer than 100 pages of text in which to cover a century of Calgary's history. Hence the book is essentially anecdotal and impressionistic, brief accounts of selected leaders and 'typical' individuals having often to serve as a basis for much more general statements regarding important aspects of the city's development. Similarly, where Foran argues for Calgary's distinctive character, he must rely more on assertion than on explicit comparative argument. A number of helpful maps are included. It is, however, confusing that some (e.g. numbers 1 and 7) include anachronistic features, and the reader who is unfamiliar with Calgary will often find himself unable to locate a particular district or street referred to in the text. Some statistics, drawn largely from the printed census, are also provided.

The book is strongest in its account of Calgary's growth before 1914, over 60 per cent of its text being devoted to the first phase of the city's rise. This reflects the emphasis of previous research on the city (some of the best of it by Foran himself), but it means that the whole modern history of the city receives only relatively limited and sketchy treatment. Thus, despite the hopes of the series editor, Alan Artibise, that a 'general and comparative history of Canada's urban development' will ultimately result from the volumes in this series, it is hard to know how solid a foundation for comparison this volume will provide. There is simply not enough sustained and detailed investigation of any local theme, from politics through the economy to land use, local services, social structure, and local culture. Plainly this is not Foran's responsibility, as he has had to work within tight constraints of length and format imposed by the series. His book succeeds admirably as an introduction to the history of what is now Canada's fastest growing city, and it can be recommended very warmly indeed.

Douglas McCalla
Department of History, Trent University

Ruben Bellan, *Winnipeg, First Century: An Economic History*. Winnipeg: Queenston House, 1978. iv + 270pp. Illustrations. $12.95 cloth, $5.95 paper.
Thomas R. Weir, *Atlas of Winnipeg*. Toronto: University of Toronto Press, 1978. xiv + 67pp. $25.00.

In Canadian terms, Winnipeg is a medium-sized city. It is barely 100 years old, having been incorporated in 1874. Yet, despite the age of Quebec (founded in 1608) or Halifax (founded in 1749), or the size and international stature of such cities as Montreal, Toronto, and Vancouver, Winnipeg has for some time been the most written-about city in the country. Unfortunately, neither of these two volumes add much to our knowledge of Winnipeg's development. While similar studies on other Canadian cities would have been welcome, these volumes do not offer urban historians much that is fresh, stimulating, or useful.

Winnipeg, First Century is a slightly revised version of Bellan's Ph.D. thesis completed for Columbia University in 1958 and entitled 'The development of Winnipeg as a metropolitan centre'. During the past two decades, Bellan's thesis has served researchers well since it provided a detailed examination of the city's economic development from the 1860s through to 1939. In addition, the thesis contained an important conclusion which analysed the forces and factors which determined the pace and character of Winnipeg's development, analysed inter-city rivalry under such headings as location versus size, and suggested a theory as to how the development of a new metropolitan centre is likely to proceed: it must battle the claims of older, larger metropolitan centres outside the hinterland, and defend itself against the challenges of younger, smaller cities within the hinterland. Its development will reflect the general progress of the hinterland, and the success of the campaign waged against rivals on two fronts.

Unfortunately and inexplicably, the concluding sections of the thesis were omitted from the book. Indeed, while the book contains two new chapters on the years since 1939, it also omits all of the 27 tables contained in the thesis. The removal of this data turned a very good thesis into a very superficial book. Instead of a solid economic history of Winnipeg, we are presented with a chronicle almost totally devoid of interpretation. Furthermore, even if the book had retained the statistical data found in the thesis, publication in book form should have caused the author to update his material to reflect the considerable amount of research that has been completed since 1958. The author chose, however, to avail himself of neither the new material on Winnipeg nor the interpretative material on Canadian urban development generally. The point is that both economic history and urban studies have progressed far beyond the unsophisticated presentation of *Winnipeg, First Century*. In short, anyone wishing information on the city's economic development would best be served by examining the original thesis and supplementing this work with subsequent publications by other authors.

The *Atlas of Winnipeg*, unlike Bellan's book, is an original piece of work. In fact, it is the first atlas devoted entirely to a single Canadian city. It consists of a short preface and more than 150 maps, many with analytical comments. The maps are grouped into nine sections: physical (plates 1 to 3), historical (4 to 7), political and administrative (8 and 9), land use and transportation (10 to 13), demography (14 to 33), family structure (34 to 39), dwellings and income (40 to 53), occupations (54 to 63), and educational status (64 to 67). There is no question but that Thomas Weir, Professor Emeritus of Geography at the University of Manitoba, has prepared a scholarly volume that will appeal to many urban planners, geographers, economists, and sociologists. For historians, however, the *Atlas of Winnipeg* is most disappointing.

The vast majority of the maps found in this atlas spatially represent data taken from post-1971 federal, provincial, and city data. The result is a volume that is of very limited use to historians since few maps are devoted to the process of change over time. One wishes that the author had chosen to prepare an historical atlas rather than one that presents static impressions of various aspects of Winnipeg during the past decade. Indeed, the *Atlas of Winnipeg* is most successful in the few plates that are devoted to historical processes, such as the sections on political evolution and on spatial growth. Here one gets a glimpse of cartography at its best since these plates are both useful for reference and dynamic, aiding immeasurably in understanding aspects of reality and sets of relationships. The tragedy of this volume is that there are few plates that have these qualities, and the overall impression is one of frustration.

A good historical atlas can serve a variety of purposes. It can stimulate scholarly debate, open up new avenues to old problems, discover major lacunae in the study of a period or a region, and bring together methodically scattered bits of knowledge already extant. An atlas can also summarize the state of research and provide an excellent medium to take stock of what we know and what we do not know. It can also find new patterns and layers of meaning in our geography and history. The *Atlas of Winnipeg* succeeds far too infrequently in these goals to label it a success. It is to be hoped that it will not be used as a model for other cities.

Alan F. J. Artibise
Department of History, University of Victoria

Brian J. Young, *Promoters and Politicians: The North-Shore Railways in the History of Quebec, 1854–85*. Toronto: University of Toronto Press, 1978. xviii + 193 pp. 3 maps. Bibliography. $15.00.

With the coming of the railroad, the St Lawrence River became in important ways not a uniting but a dividing force in Quebec. The south shore succeeded in obtaining railroads connecting its major centres during the 1850s. North-shore cities and towns, notably the city of Quebec, now sought to catch up. At the same time, Montreal groups sought direct rail links to Ottawa and to the projected Canadian Pacific Railway. How these interests combined to produce what eventually became the

C.P.R. lines on the north shore is the subject of Brian Young's study. His is a very complex, essentially political story, in which the central protagonists were the metropolitan interests and rivalries of Quebec and Montreal, the leaders of the colonization movement that was pressing for new rural settlement to the north, the various figures involved in determining Canada's trans-continental railroad politics, and a diverse group of Quebec politicians, entrepreneurs, and schemers. The story is one of waste, public gullibility, and corruption; as Young notes, these were not peculiar to Quebec, however, but were typical of railroad projects in many parts of nineteenth-century North America.

The book rests on very extensive research (though a number of footnotes in chapter 1 to 'Quebec, *Journals of the Assembly*' are incorrect and/or meaningless), but its style and its extreme brevity do not do full justice to the inherent interest and significance of its story. As a result, this is primarily a book for the connoisseur of Quebec politics and of the infighting of Canadian railways and politicians.

Douglas McCalla
Department of History, Trent University

Kenneth Moore, *Those of the Street. The Catholic-Jews of Mallorca.* London: University of Notre Dame Press, 1978. viii + 209 pp. Bibliography. £8.40.

There is no better way to present the subject of this book than to quote the opening sentence of the introduction: 'on the island of Mallorca there lives today a category of people who are designated as Jewish by the local people, but who are at the same time ardent followers of Roman Catholicism'. The author is an anthropologist but his theme is the history, survival and present existence of this unusual community. It is regrettable that the author has apparently been unable to benefit from the works of Baer and Ashtor (Strauss) dealing with the history of the Jews in Christian and Moslem Spain but his general picture carries conviction nonetheless. The history of the *Xuetas*, as the members of the community are known, has its origins in the Jewish community of Mallorca in the early thirteenth century which constituted a typical Jewish community of the Mediterranean Diaspora; that is to say, it formed an acknowledged state within a state by virtue of its autonomous legal and religious system. This happy condition was brought almost to an end by the activities of the Inquisition in the period from the mid-fifteenth century to the end of the seventeenth. This saw the enforced conversion of the Jews, as a result of which some assimilated and some, whilst legally Christian, retained their Jewish communal attachment (as 'converses'), enforced the rules of endogamy and continued to practise Jewish religious ritual, though in an attenuated form. In the last two centuries the position of the *Xuetas* has further declined in that the Inquisition secured a total compliance with Christianity, confiscated the converses' wealth and made the *Xuetas* into a stigmatized and pariah people – which did not however, prevent them from fulfilling specialized economic functions, practising traditions of mutual aid, and retaining the rule of endogamy. This was only possible by reason of their pariah status and, as the author excellently demonstrates, the quasi-isolated and conservative nature of Mallorcan society in general. Now that a measure of industrialization and mass tourism have come to the island, assimilation is on the increase, as shown particularly in an increased rate of exogamy. All that seems likely to persist as specifically *Xueta* is the Street of the Silver Shops in Palma. The remaining *Xuetas* apparently have no desire to change their religious or national affiliation – at least if their negative response to an emissary from Israel is any guide. Kenneth Moore may have composed the swan-song of a dying community but in so doing he has made a valuable contribution to the history of the Jewish Diaspora.

Lionel Kochan
Department of History, University of Warwick

Francis W. Carter (ed.), *An Historical Geography of the Balkans*. London and New
   York: Academic Press, 1977. xxvi + 599 pp. 124 figures. 36 tables. Bibliography.
   £22.00.
Hugh D. Clout (ed.), *Themes in the Historical Geography of France*. London and
   New York: Academic Press, 1977. xxviii + 594 pp. 158 figures. 20 tables. Biblio-
   graphy. £18.00.

These two beefy and not inexpensive books contain much valuable material for the
regional specialist and general reader alike. Despite their titles both are collections of essays; curiously blended *pots-pourri* which even the card-carrying historical geographer may wish to digest in small doses, and which may leave gourmets of
urban history wondering what they are eating. The main ingredient in both these
dishes is the rural cultural landscape; its peopling, its settlements and emerging
economy, its regional contrasts, and human patterning in response to environment and natural resources. In other words, the recipe that the uninitiated used to
read on the brand label 'Historical Geography' before that old jar was dropped and
the contents spilled all over the floor.

   Frank Carter's collection of 15 essays makes available in English for the first
time much hard information on the evolution of the geography of south-east
Europe: 'Balkanology' (even the editor uses quotation marks) remains a mystery
among historical geographers for whom even Mitteleuropa is daringly innovative
research territory. After the editor's introduction which discusses the term Balkan
come two chapters on pre-history by John Nandris and John Bintliff. Both of these
consider settlement evolution, at different scales, in relation to major environmental changes drawing impressively on recent research. These are followed by some
traditional studies of rural settlement and landscapes: Roman roads and settlements in the Balkans; settlements in the Mani peninsula in the seventeenth
century; Brac Island, Dalmatia, from Roman times to the present; Richard
Lawless examines the economy and landscape of Thessaly under Ottoman
rule.

   Other less classifiable contributions cover Ottoman geographical knowledge,
regional names, and early capitalism in Yugoslavia. Some of these also present
primary research but others are stock-taking syntheses which may, nonetheless,
be useful to those led by the title to expect a textbook treatment of the region as a
whole.

   Among these far-flung topics are two summary statements about urban development in Yugoslavia: 'Urban development in the Western Balkans 1200–1800' by
Frank Carter and 'The changing urban pattern in Yugoslavia' by Veljko Rojic.
Carter assembles a substantial Slav literature to summarize the numbers and
distribution of medieval towns. A settlement of 1000 or more inhabitants qualifies
as a 'grad' in this thinly urbanized territory. It is the pattern of these 1400 or so
urban places, and the political, military and economic influences upon it, that
chiefly concerns Carter, rather than the function or evolution of particular towns.
For that the reader would gain greater satisfaction from his *Dubrovnik: A Classical City State* (1972). The canvas is, as the author states, a broad one but on it is a
very useful sketch for the larger picture of urbanization in medieval and early
modern Europe.

   Rojic's shorter essay, after an incongruous and over-condensed discussion of
classical towns moves to the firmer ground of the nineteenth and twentieth centuries. Yet even by 1850 only Trieste exceeded 20,000 inhabitants: the major
urban foci lay beyond the boundaries of present-day Yugoslavia, and remained so
into the present century. Most of the text concerns 'the most recent historico-
geographical period', a very East European phrase meaning in this case the last 30
years or so, and the rise of the first mature urban system in the region. Characteristically enough in the early part of this century the largest towns grew fastest.
More recently the fastest growth rates have been experienced lower in the urban
hierarchy.

   Themes in the Historical Geography of France is a better integrated (and better edited) book, perhaps because Hugh Clout has written nearly half the text. On the other hand the themes and the approach will be more familiar to an English readership. Here is a Whitaker's Almanac of the historical geography of rural France; an impressive and well-presented of a coherent, though very partial, set of concerns. The editor's introduction is a condensed but bibliographically useful summary of the relationship between history and geography in France in which most of the familiar names appear but the *Annales* school receive brief attention, and French demographers even less. It is, however, to Hugh Prince's assertively eloquent essay that we have to look for the persistence of the rural landscape tradition which pervades this book. The lively *civilization agraire* and the distinctiveness of the *pays* survived the changes wrought by modernization in neighbouring parts of Europe and have yielded a rich literature. French demographic experience is a major element in this: not only is it not included in these 'themes' but it might have provided a more convincing starting point than vaguely-formulated generalizations that the answer lies in the soil. We have been told often enough before that the French have a deep attachment to the 'homeland', or that 'French civilization is exceptional both in its firm adherence to its rural origins and in its persistent regional diversity'. Prince may well be close to the heart of the matter but since such observations conveniently defy either verification or refutation they form a weak basis for further analysis. And if analysis is too acerbic a word for the French geographic tradition, then let us by all means stick to reading Vidal de la Blache in the original.

The essays which follow are boldly and often interestingly presented from rich French sources [sic], especially those by the three French contributors. There is admirable detail on the reclamation of the marshlands, the spread and retreat of rural settlement, field systems and enclosure and vernacular architecture. André Fell's essay on the *petite culture* is alone in hinting at other issues lurking in this Cartier-Bresson landscape debrutalized. It is not simply that folk are not counted and their breeding and dying unobserved, but that the issues one has come to expect historians of France, and especially the *paysan*, to confront have been disinfected. Historical geographers, it has been noted, tend to do this and it is insufficient to reply that these are, after all, only themes: to what may we attribute their selection?

Urban history may legitimately occupy a small place in the Balkans: in France this can only result from the partiality just detected. Two essays by Clout tackle urban development before and after 1500, and whilst both have useful summary material they are condensed almost to the level of lecture notes. Themes appear and then suddenly disappear without trace, and the disjointed second essay leaps from an inadequate examination of the processes of urban population growth to the morphology of Paris and back again to selections from provincial France.

Paul Laxton
Department of Geography, University of Liverpool

Richard D. Altick, *The Shows of London: A panorama history of exhibitions, 1600–1862.* Cambridge, Massachusetts and London: The Belknap Press of Harvard University Press, 1978. 552 pp. Illustrated. Textual and reference notes. Index. $35.00.

'Where has pleasure such a field, so rich, so thronged, so drained, so well equipped as London – opulent, enlarged and still increasing London'. These lines from Cowper were used more than once to preface the 'new' London guides, not least by Horace Wellbeloved, M.A., for his publication of 1824: *London Lions for Country Cousins and Friends About Town, being all the new Buildings, Improvements and Amusements in the Metropolis.* Seeing the sights of London had been a ritual since Elizabethan times, and between the 1780s and 1850s especially there were many more sights to see, as well as more people to see them. By then commercial showmen were extolling and catering for the fads and fancies of a pleasure-loving, sight-seeing public, diversifying the range of metropolitan sights with exhibitions and pictorial shows of ever greater ingenuity and novelty. But it has taken a modern American scholar to document fully the rise of these entertainments and to highlight the pre-eminence of London in the development of popular amusements.

Richard Altick is concerned only with non-theatrical entertainments, which he calls exhibitions (for which show was a historically accurate synonym). It is an elastic term which includes pictorial shows and he devotes nearly a quarter of the book to describing the great 'orama' craze which lasted for 40 years or so, beginning with the Eidophusikon, going through panoramas, dioramas, cycloramas, cosmoramas, kineoramas, and their derivatives, ending up with the phantasmagorias which replaced them. Exhibition-type shows had a longer life (and are still with us) – their origins may be found in the private museum collections (the 'cabinets of curiosities' and commercial 'knicknackitoriums') started by seventeenth-century virtuosi and popularized thereafter in that 'filtering-down process which characterised so much of the London museum and exhibition trade' in the eighteenth century. Exhibitions were still going strong in Victorian London: 1851, the year of the Great Exhibition, marked their apogee with numerous other displays of artifacts and objets d'art. From this time, the exhibition-show began to decline somewhat in popularity with competition from theatres and music halls and the proliferation of 'indoor' domestic entertainments, including magic lantern shows. Moreover, the two great streams of appeal for shows – amusement and instruction – which hitherto had 'mingled in a single channel dominated by commercial entrepreneurs', now diverged – 'As the focal point of London shows symbolically moved from Leicester Square to South Kensington the age of exhibitions was succeeded by the age of public museums.'

In this study, examples of all the various types of show are carefully traced and amply described: how they originated, where and when they were shown – in private houses, pleasure gardens, exhibition rooms (with special attention given to such fun palaces as the Colosseum and the more prestigious but exotic Egyptian Hall) down to the travelling circus and the street-corner show – what all these displayed or showed, what they cost to put on, what kind of audiences went to them, and what visitors, journalists and the literati thought about them. There are chapters also on the place of exhibitions in London life, the emergence of a government interest in them, and what might be broadly called the politics of entertainment.

Such a prosaic summary, however, conveys little of the extraordinary way in which the author recovers the atmosphere, the meaning, and the lexicography of these shows. This is, in truth, no ordinary account, and no ordinary book. It is so full of detail, so lavishly illustrated, so elegantly produced as to be in itself a kind of show. One cannot help wonder at the expense and labour that has gone into this massive compilation of information and anecdote, this prodigious feat of research, made possible only with the help of several assistants. What then justifies such an elaborate treatment? The answer must be that this is not just an extravaganza, nor 'raree-show' to use the somewhat old-fashioned derisory term. It is a book with an interesting and serious historical purpose, in effect a companion volume to his earlier work on the role of print in the history of popular culture, but in this case the mass reading public is replaced by a mass sight-seeing public. It is nevertheless an exceedingly long read (over 500 pages) by any normal standards, which takes time and perseverance; and it would be unfortunate if the cost and bulk of this volume, and the apparently esoteric nature of some of the subjects described, were to inhibit its circulation among students and social historians. Yet it is arguable whether an abridged version would have done, and not only by depriving us of much intriguing and enjoyable detail. For the spirit of the work, and the impact it has, depend only in part on the author's commentary – enlivening and instructive though it is on the history of public taste and the nature of the popular mind in the past – but much more on the way he juxtaposes and demonstrates by innumerable examples the inter-connections between so many diverse phenomena.

The subjects of this volume are not randomly selected. There *is* point, he convinces, in a history that puts together such manifestly cultural institutions as museums, art galleries, 'philosophical' lectures, public monuments and national exhibitions, with such an array of popular amusements as the waxworks and *poses plastiques*, automaton shows and other displays of technical ingenuity, hydraulic, pyrotechnic and aerostatic displays, and all the pictorial shows. They are not different genres, but different species, with elements in common. The same is true of shows which traded more crudely on eccentricities, and abnormalities: so he deals with the catchpenny shows, displays of exotic lands and people, the monster-mongers and retailers of human freaks. He is saying that despite all the sophisticated novelties, dependent on lighting effects, perspective, and the machinery of motion, the strange, the magical and the curious in their old forms still persisted, though even here tastes changed. The point being also that in the realm of London shows it is difficult to separate ingenuity and invention from trickery and chicanery, or, indeed, to distinguish between sheer entertainment and the satisfaction of intellectual curiosity and artistic sensibility. Public improvers and instructors concerned with elevating taste had to contend with the 'stubborn insistence of the people on being amused' and try to convert shows into a form of 'rational recreation'; but the development of urban entertainments had important cultural functions in their own right which should not be overlooked. So we are invited to understand the show as a medium for the dissemination of enlightenment thought and the romantic imagination, recognizing the popular interest in the magic of science and the significance of the pictorial show as an art-form; whilst we are shown how developments in science, technology and art were harnessed to the production of commercially viable means of creating illusions.

We know that the diffusion of science and art was important to the making of an urban cultural milieu, but the chief value of this study is to demonstrate how much that depended on the finance and organization of what became a mass entertainment industry. It is the relationship between the media and the message which is so interesting – the interplay between the development of knowledge, catering for popular tastes, and the risk-taking of entrepreneurial showmen. This is what justifies a technical, economic and social history of London's exhibitions and related entertainments as a contribution to the history of a broad stream of urban culture'. It is a disconcerting claim in a way, the interpretation of which, as illustrated here, shows up the limitations of much conventional history of English cultural institutions. How stuffy the latter now seem, how remote from the urban context and the world of popular consciousness to which this volume provides such important clues. By exploring how shows worked to enhance the role of the metropolis as a cultural force, the author reveals unfamiliar and previously neglected dimensions to the concept of cultural diffusion. He not only enlarges our knowledge of the history of metropolitan entertainments, but he challenges our preconceptions, English preconceptions especially perhaps, about what is to be meant by the history of urban culture.

David Reeder
Department of Education, University of Leicester

Lynn Hollen Lees, *Exiles of Erin. Irish Migrants in Victorian London*. Manchester: Manchester University Press, 1979. 276 pp. 6 plates. 4 figures. Tables. Bibliography. £11.50.

Lynn Lees has produced a useful monograph based on extensive and discriminating consultation of a wide range of archival material, together with the indispensable information collected in nineteenth-century parliamentary papers and a good selection of other contemporary printed sources. She naturally owes much to those who have opened up her field; and acknowledges a particular debt to Sheridan Gilley, whose essays on the religion and politics of the London Irish are required, and elegant, reading. Curiously omitted from the text of a work on this scale and from its sizeable bibliography is any mention of the late J. E. Handley's classics on the Irish in Scotland; although there is a footnote reference (p. 44) to one of his books. It was Handley who made the first major scholarly contribution to the specialist study, now expanding fast, of Irish immigrants and their descendants in Great Britain. His achievement measures up well against that of professional historians who have followed where he led. If he was too partisan, his standards of scholarship and readability were nevertheless good. Valuable as it is, Lynn Lees's book would have been still more so had it included a comparison of the rather different immigrant experience in urban Scotland and in London. Like Handley, she is exclusively concerned with the Irish Catholic immigrant. Not numerically insignificant, Irish Protestants settling in Britain were readily accepted into the native population from which they were then culturally indistinguishable. The author takes Irish to mean the Celtic and Catholic Irish. Nor is she interested in the middle-class Irish Catholic immigrants who very largely became anglicized, identifying, if they remained practising Catholics, with the English minority of their church in London and elsewhere. Those few of the Irish Catholic working-class in this country who climbed into the middle-class similarly distanced themselves from their Irish origins and loyalties.

Exiles of Erin, as the title suggests, is really a study in immigrant cohesiveness, in the reinforcement, that is, of religious and political loyalties by the occupational and residential pressures familiar to students of nineteenth-century Britain. Those pressures, as they operated in the capital, are well set forth in detailed chapters. The problems involved in the transition from rural to urban living are emphasized in the chapters on migration and family structure, which might perhaps have been combined under some such heading as 'The decline of the extended (and Catholic) family', allowing for the author's reservations about that decline. The crucial chapter on 'The reforging of an Irish Catholic culture' is not altogether convincing. For this 'reforging' was, to a greater extent in London than in some English provincial and Scottish centres, a losing, if long drawn out, battle. Conditions of life and work in the metropolis made it very difficult, outside certain neighbourhoods, for the second and third generation Irish to retain the religion which was the preservative of their national identity. Irish priests, and English priests willing to immerse themselves in the ancestral emotions of their alien flocks, sustained the expatriate nationalism which found expression in the ways mentioned in an indifferent chapter on immigrant politics.

E. D. Steele
School of History, University of Leeds

Norman Longmate, *The Hungry Mills. The Story of the Lancashire Cotton Famine 1861–5*. London: Maurice Temple Smith, 1978. 319 pp. £7.00.
In the 1860s writing in prose or verse about the cotton famine became, as Norman Longmate remarks, 'almost a distinctive branch of literature'. Two histories of the event, by Arthur Arnold and John Watts respectively, were in print almost before it was over. Southern visitors like Ellen Barlee and Mary Bayly wrote of their experiences in Lancashire, whilst Edwin Waugh, Samuel Laycock and a host of lesser known local bards graphically depicted the struggles and sufferings of the unemployed operatives.

Mr Longmate makes good use of this wealth of literary material, quoting copiously from it and from the more sober, clear and factual official reports. Indeed, at times, he appears to be 'letting the ball do the work for him' as the soccer pundits have it, and this results in lively accounts of, for example, the Stalybridge riot or of the adventures of blockade running recounted by Thomas Taylor and William Watson.

The author draws wholly on published sources, and his account contains little by way of evidence or interpretation that will seem new to readers of this journal. His work in no way supersedes W. O. Henderson's scholarly *The Lancashire Cotton Famine, 1861–65*, first published in 1934, nor does it claim to do so. Nevertheless the author shows himself to be in touch with recent research in the field, as for example in his laying of the myth that Lancashire millowners and operatives were unanimous in their support for the Northern States during the American Civil War. Whilst the book is without footnotes, a list of references for each chapter show clearly the sources on which it is based. *The Hungry Mills* will be read with interest and enjoyment by the general public as well as by students and teachers of history, and it may stimulate further research at local level into the impact of the cotton famine.

It is too easy for the professional historian to be patronizing about this book. In our search for novelty, in our quantifying and model making, there is always a danger that we may lose sight of the need to communicate the past to people, a need which the old masters, the Trevelyans, the Tawneys or the Taylors, have always met with consummate skill. The popularity of Norman Longmate's works shows that there is a demand for historical writing beyond the narrow confines of our conferences and colloquia.

Michael E. Rose
Department of History, University of Manchester

D. A. Gowland, *Methodist Secessions. The origins of free Methodism in three Lancashire towns: Manchester, Rochdale, Liverpool.* [Chetham Society, 3rd series vol. 26.] Manchester: Manchester University Press, 1979. x + 191 pp. Bibliography. £10.00.

This excellent monograph, the fruit of a good many years' reflection by the author upon his doctoral thesis, is primarily a contribution to the history of Methodism, and especially to the history of Methodist reform; but it is also of first-class interest to students of urban history. It shows in the first place how much can be reconstructed of the history of urban Methodism by a resolute application to local archives, press and libraries in towns which developed a real sense of municipal patriotism in the nineteenth century. Zealous field-work has lately accomplished something similar for Cumbrian Methodism; but in the main, whatever conservative propagandists might say, rural society had not the cohesiveness to stick to its records displayed by the more intensely self-conscious towns, and in the countryside there was less likely to be a new paper for every faction, each casting its own lurid illumination on the contests of the day. The author's footnotes and bibliography are a monument not merely to his own energy and perseverance, but also to the enlightenment still to be derived from the earnest record-keeping and the zealous, even reckless, diffusion of information and ideas which went with municipal patriotism.

In the second place D. Gowland's secessions show clearly how different was the fate even of a relatively centralized movement like Wesleyan Methodism in three towns which, though close together, and all having a substantial stake in the textile trades, were very different. The sheer preposterousness of the Halévy thesis about Methodism and the French Revolution, a thesis first invented by the connectional propagandists in the aftermath of the Napoleonic Wars, is well brought out; so far from Methodism saving the nation from revolution, it could not preserve its own union from being fractured in three different ways, in three adjacent but different towns. There was a good deal of resemblance between the situations in Manchester and Liverpool. In Manchester the early suburban migration of the Methodist social elite left the preachers to appease a restive democracy in decayed town-centre chapels with the doctrine of the pastoral office and little else. Resentment at class separation in Methodism, at connectional pressure on undenominational traditions, at the decay of revivalism combined to wreak havoc. In Liverpool it was a similar story, but the life of the town was so dominated by foreign issues, Irish, Welsh and Scots, that the politics of English Methodism was bound to be a peripheral affair, and those who gave themselves to Methodist reform could hardly have succeeded at anything else. In Rochdale, on the other hand, the centrality of the Church to the Tory interest, and the intensity of the clash between that interest and new forces in the town helped to shape a radical Methodist elite which provided the cash and skill to lead the Wesleyan Methodist Association and to make a major contribution to Rochdale civic life. The author's excellent Rochdale material might indeed have benefited by a succinct exposition of the Rochdale Church question which lies behind the whole story.

The short verdict must be that this is a valuable book, of much more than local or denominational interest, and that its value is barely reduced by three small blemishes: on p. 70, Bernard Slater should read Barnard Slater: on p. 82, forty-shilling freehold appears as 'forties freehold'; and on p. 164, J. S. Simon would be more accurately described as a twentieth- than as a late nineteenth-century writer.

W. R. Ward
Department of Modern History, University of Durham

Derek Linstrum, *West Yorkshire. Architects and Architecture.* London: Lund Humphries, 1978. 399 pp. 298 plates. 1 map. Biographical Appendix. £30.00. Architectural history, like other enthusiasms such as railway history, is long on factual detail but short on concept. As Asa Briggs showed many years ago in his cameo on Leeds Town Hall, the history of architecture can be a fruitful source of insights into much more than the buildings themselves. A great cathedral might tell us much about contemporary values and attitudes, about the social and economic structure, about the distribution of power and wealth: yet it will not do so if we merely wonder at the stained glass and the flying buttresses, impressive though they may be. West Yorkshire, that administrative conurbation created in 1974, is a region of great potential for the architect who knows his history and who can place the man-made environment in its social and economic setting.

Derek Linstrum certainly is an erudite architectural historian and his sumptuous, impressive book is a definitive repository of information on a region's architecture. However, he has not written that work of synthesis which urban historians would so much have welcomed – a marriage of buildings and the society which produced them. Perhaps we should not be surprised at Linstrum's reluctance to meet this challenge for it was he who produced an earlier book on the architecture of Leeds without mentioning that city's most prolific and distinctive architectural form – the back to back. But then, he is more interested in meritorious architectural design than in the social history of housing.

Of course authors have a legitimate complaint when they are pilloried by reviewers for not having written the book they have not claimed to write. Within Linstrum's aim to catalogue the variety of architectural styles and to illustrate the work of architects practising in West Yorkshire, he is impressively successful. The book is essentially an explanation in architectural terms of what existed, lavishly illustrated with some 300 photographs taken especially for this volume. Even here, however, we should not expect any coherent analysis to emerge. There is some logic in treating categories of buildings separately – country houses, churches, markets, etc., but this can wreak havoc with any sense of chronology. The chapter on working-class housing which ends in the 1970s is followed by one on medieval churches; the same page which discusses a Victorian college also deals with a thirteenth-century school. This thematic treatment in fact fragments the architectural analysis. For instance, Saltaire as a projected community is discussed on pp. 139–42, but we have to wait until p. 205 for a description and illustration of the Congregational Chapel and p. 295 for Salt's mill. Yet as Linstrum knows, Saltaire was an integrated architectural experience whose meaning and significance is entirely lost if its component parts are broken up in this way.

The treatment of Saltaire is but one of many examples where architecture alone explains little. Linstrum fails entirely to bring out that desire for order and discipline which was at the very heart of Salt's creation. Similarly he could have explained the Georgian mansions so much better by relating them to the position of the merchants in the cloth trade. Again the rebuilding of Leeds parish church is seen solely in terms of the architectural choices to be made – over chancel, tower, aisles, organ. Yet the whole project was but part of a wider campaign by the great Anglican pastor, W. F. Hook, to rejuvenate Anglicanism in a town dominated by militant dissent.

These and many other topics will frustrate urban historians who will regret that the author's enormous architectural knowledge does not yield a more fruitful analysis. Most would have foregone some of the variety of the architectural judgments on the piles of bricks for an exploration in depth of the circumstances which produced them. This is, perhaps, unfair, for Linstrum's compilation will give great pleasure, though its price will put it beyond most private buyers. It is indeed the veritable academic coffee table book which costs more than the table on which it rests. It is sometimes difficult to identify the correct picture to which the separated captions belong and some of the photographs have produced the most odd angles. The tendency to dizziness because of this is accentuated by the fact that the paper used glares under electric light.

The author has produced a fount of knowledge on architectural design in West Yorkshire and not the least of the merits of his book is the excellent appendix, giving biographical details of some 200 architects. His book will be a quarry for historians and conservationists alike. Within its limitations it is a well-organized and well-produced *tour de force*.

Derek Fraser
School of Social Sciences, University of Bradford

Frances Finnegan and Eric Sigsworth, *Poverty and Social Policy. An Historical Study of Batley*. [Papers in Community Studies, Third Series, No. 19, ed. E. Butterworth and I. Coles.] Tadcaster: DND Business Services, 1978. 127 pp. Illustrations. Tables. £2.80.

This study analyses four aspects of urban development – health, housing, employment and education – in their relation to the poverty of a small West Riding textile town. It is well supplied with statistical data and pictorial illustration and offers a valuable addition to the evidence of social deprivation. The authors modify the traditional explanation for the rise and fall of Batley as a function specifically of the fortunes of a dependent 'shoddy' trade, and see it more generally as the humble product of West Riding textile expansion and decline. As one of the peripheral areas of the region's activities, its opportunities for social amelioration were restricted by the incidence of low wages and by the absence of a paternalist local gentry and of a sufficiency of employers rich enough to countenance the more dramatic experiments occasionally found in the larger towns. Indirectly the study pinpoints as crucial to development the quality of local and central government. It documents the wide cultural gap between a working class struggling to make the best of an inheritance of deprivation and a new bureaucracy of doctors, nurses and teachers trying to implement the precepts of their professions. It is not concerned with the political context. Consequently, the impact on social development, in a working-class town, of a Labour movement led by one of Labour's folk heroes, Ben Turner, is not clarified. In the main, however, it is concerned to establish the facts and it does so effectively.

J. Reynolds
School of Social Sciences, University of Bradford

Martin Bulmer (ed.), *Mining and Social Change. Durham County in the Twentieth Century*. London: Croom Helm, 1978. 318 pp. 4 figures. Tables. Bibliography. £6.95.

This is a curious piece of book-making. It consists of 16 chapters, seven of them – and these the most substantial – written by the editor, Martin Bulmer, who also acts as 'link-man'. Some of the contributions are fragments from earlier works of varying genres – a short excerpt from Mark Benney's *Charity Main* (1946), a series of extracts from Jack Lawson's biography of Peter Lee (1949) and part of a chapter of Graham Turner's *The North Country* (1967). The remaining chapters, other than those written by the editor himself, are summaries of work available in more extensive form elsewhere. The main value of these brief studies is as an indication of wider areas of investigation either completed or in prospect.

The justification for the book, therefore, lies in the contributions of Martin Bulmer himself. These chapters are varied in content and reflect both an extensive research interest and a willingness and ability to pursue enquiry by a wide range of methods. Bulmer proceeds from the general to the particular, introducing his book by a substantial study of social structure and social change in twentieth-century Durham and ending it by examining and evaluating the experience of a small mining community in decline and the parallel experience of a group of miners transferred to factory employment. These final chapters, based on detailed local enquiry, make particularly interesting reading.

The book, as a whole, is indeed better in its parts than in its totality. As a general survey it is patently incomplete and uneven. What is most valuable in it is largely the editor's own work. Had he decided to go it alone he could well have produced an even more rewarding volume.

Arthur J. Taylor
School of History, University of Leeds

W. R. Powell (ed.), *The Victoria History of the County of Essex*, vol. VII. London: Oxford University Press, 1978, xix + 212 pp. 45 plates. 11 figures. £40.00.
Anthony H. Windrum, *Horsham: An Historical Survey*. Chichester: Phillimore, 1978. xi + 212 pp. 17 plates. 14 figures. Bibliography. £5.95.
C. F. Tebbutt, *St Neots: the History of a Huntingdonshire Town*. Chichester: Phillimore, 1978. xi + 363 pp. 32 plates. 10 figures. Bibliography. £5.95.

The V.C.H. already has to its credit several large volumes on the history of individual towns in different parts of the country, and its urban coverage continues to spread with the publication of recent work on the historic, if now much dismembered, counties of Middlesex and Essex. In those areas the writing of urban history presents peculiar problems, thanks to the development of Greater London. It is fashionable to hold that the traditional framework of the V.C.H. is entirely unsuited to the region, and that the History has yet to overcome serious problems of organization and presentation despite recent innovations.

From the standpoint of historians of the last 150 years these strictures may well be reasonable, but as even Greater London was not built in a day there is full justification for the traditional treatment of earlier centuries, whose historians need to know about manorial ownership and jurisdiction, benefices and parish life, fields, pre-urban topography as well as the other familiar features of V.C.H. volumes. Viewed in that light, *V.C.H. Essex*, vol. VII is a splendid addition to the series. It is devoted to the liberty of Havering-atte-Bower and part of Chafford hundred, the area covered coinciding in the main with the London Borough of Havering, formed in 1965.

Earlier centuries afford much of the variety to be found in the volume. The liberty of Havering-atte-Bower enjoyed special privileges and for several centuries formed part of the queen's dower. Hornchurch had an important priory and grew first into an industrial village, later a dormitory suburb. Romford was for long a bustling market town before it became a shopping centre for large housing estates. In Chafford hundred there were moated manor houses and large marsh-land pastures; Rainham was a small port for coastal shipping, and there was an early harbour at Wennington creek; there are still a few farms. On all of this the contributors have much of interest to say before tracing the rise of modern Haver-ing, as the predominantly rural areas were transformed. Along the Thames an im-portant industrial area has grown up including oil and petroleum stores, the manufacture of ferro-alloys, one of the largest cement-producing areas in Europe, and offshoots of Ford's, including its European headquarters. At the same time great housing estates were developed, at Upminster, for example, Gidea Park and Harold Hill.

The volume thus makes a valuable contribution to urban and suburban history. One wishes that rather greater use had been made of census enumerators' returns, directories and other sources which might have permitted a more measured account of the process of urbanization. Moreover the useful introductions to the liberty and the hundred could well have drawn together the strands of economic and social change in the .area. (Perhaps everyone using these topographical volumes should first read W. Ashworth's splendid chapter in *V.C.H. Essex* vol. V, to gain some appreciation of the regional influence of London.) Nevertheless this volume – which is mainly the work of Mr W. R. Powell, Miss G. A. Ward, Miss J. Hasler and Dr D. R. Ransome – displays some of the best characteristics of the V.C.H.: it is a work of considerable scholarship, well organized, lucid and well writ-ten. In short, a work of permanent value and of much more than local interest.

The other two books provide contrasts in several ways. Horsham is an ancient town in the Sussex Weald, which like many another place in the area has changed profoundly under the impact of railways and roads, the growth of population, the spreading influence of London, new habits of shopping and new fashions in com-muting. In 1822 Cobbett described it as 'a very nice, solid, country town'. But, asks Mr Windrum, 'how can we describe it today?' Unfortunately he hardly assembles the skeleton of an answer, much less does he offer the reader a coherent picture. Instead he collects and prints a very great deal of material about ten aspects of the history of the town, including chapters on church life, local government, social life and problems, trade and industry, and communications. (Surprisingly, in a work of this kind, there is little about topographical changes.)

The method adopted has some advantages, of course, but these are outweighed by the drawbacks, of which the most important are two: the absence of any balanced, coherent account of what Horsham was like in any recognized period of history, and the impossibility of imparting to the reader any clear sense of changes in Horsham through time. Each chapter goes back to the earliest evidence of the subject treated and then provides some account of different topics, often very briefly and frequently inconsequentially. The chapter on trade and industry, for example, chronicles the establishment of markets and then describes in turn each of the industries of which there are traces in the town; there is no general survey of the economy at any particular time. Every chapter peters out, and there are no specific or general conclusions. In sum, while the book may provide interest for local readers and a quarry for historians it is set too much in the antiquarian mould to be a successful historical survey.

Disappointingly, much the same conclusion applies to Mr Tebbutt's account of St Neots. Although the town had a Benedictine priory, markets, fairs and a navig-able river during the Middle Ages, and some importance as a market town thereaf-ter, the author has little to say about these earlier periods, for he has chosen to concentrate on the nineteenth century. This decision justifies the organization of material by topic and facilitates the inclusion of much interesting local detail about many aspects of life in St Neots. Here again, unfortunately, the author is content to offer a chronicle and a compilation, with little by way of comment or con-clusion and with no attempt to trace historical change. The book includes a generous allowance of interesting old photographs and is almost doubled in length by the inclusion of a gazetteer of the town, though it is astonishing that changes since 1966 have not been noted: obviously it must be used with care. Although townspeople and visitors may well find these books by Messrs Windrum and Tebbutt respectively useful and interesting, it will surely be clear that Phillimore's series on towns is due for a searching re-appraisal: in that process publisher and authors have much to learn from the urban volumes in the *V.C.H.*

G. C. F. Forster
School of History, University of Leeds

J. S. Moore (ed.), *Avon Local History Handbook*. Chichester: Phillimore, 1979. 188 pp. £2.50.
Judy Middleton, *A History of Hove*. Chichester: Phillimore, 1979. 272 pp. £5.95.
The *Avon Local History Handbook* is intended for students of local history in that region, but it will also be useful to beginners in their areas. Short but valuable essays on 12 major themes in local history outline a summary of the subject under discussion with (in most cases) special reference to the area of the new Avon local authority. These are followed by a second series of bibliographies under the same 12 headings and finally by a section on all the major record repositories and libraries within the region.

Since Avon is centred around Bristol and Bath, urban history is not covered as a separate topic but enters several of the themes discussed – the rural and urban landscape, industry, housing and the standard of living (the works cited in the bibliography do not refer to the current debate on this subject), leisure and recreation and so on. This is a useful regional guide and relatively cheap; it is to be hoped that the binding will stand up to the hard usage it merits.

'Hove' is a work of love by a local resident. Illustrated with many line drawings which reveal a discerning eye for unusual details, the book has collected together a mass of detail, organized into 42 sections. It is not easy to see any order behind the subjects chosen for study, and there is a great concentration on major buildings in the town. Very little of the book concerns the period before 1800 (when the land on which the town now stands was occupied by four small villages), and some aspects of the later history of the town receive scant attention. It concentrates narrowly upon Hove itself, and is descriptive rather than explanatory. This is then not a history of Hove, despite the title, but it contains much of the material from which a history of the emergence of this popular seaside resort, so different in clientele and so fiercely independent from its more successful neighbour of Brighton, can be written.

Alan Rogers
Department of Adult Education, University of Nottingham

3 METHODOLOGY AND SOURCES

Manuel Castells, *The Urban Question: A Marxist Approach*. London: Edward Arnold, 1977. x + 502 pp. 13 diagrams. 62 tables. Bibliography. £12.00 boards, £5.95 paper.
This book has had an odd effect on urban sociologists. It has sent some into paeans of praise, and others into paroxysms of rage. To one, it is 'the harbinger of an important new current in urban sociology', and to another, 'it is a load of humbug'. To suggest that both opinions may be correct may seem even odder, but there is a very real sense in which this book has become important in spite of itself.

The French edition appeared in 1971, although Castells had already given a foretaste in two earlier articles in 1968 and 1969. It is rare for an author to be given the opportunity to confess his 'serious limitations and theoretical errors' within the same covers (a sort of pre-emptive strike against reviewers) but the publication of the English edition in 1977 has afforded him the chance. It is unfortunate that one has to wade through 437 pages before coming to the best bit, the 'afterward', although he warns in the preface to this edition that he has been having second thoughts.

The aim of the book is to help to formulate a 'science' of urban sociology. This use of 'science', it should be said, has a very special meaning, drawn as it is from the French tradition of formalistic and structuralist Marxism as practised by Louis Althusser and Nicos Poulantzas. In this version of reality, men play a part in transforming social systems, but only insofar as 'they are determined by their particular location in the structure thus defined'. The new 'scientific' urban sociology is taken from the 'science' of historical materialism and is to be contrasted with the 'ideological' aspects of knowledge of unreformed urban researchers.

The book opens with a methodological critique of traditional urban studies. Too readily, Castells says, have researchers reified 'the urban' (one has to get used to this adjective-noun: it also appears as 'the urban problematic'), treating social action in urban and rural settlements as if it is to be understood within their confines alone. Castells argues that 'residential space is not a page on which the imprint of social values is laid. It is, on the one hand, historically constituted, and on the other, articulated within the social structure as a whole'. This is a useful critique as urban researchers, including historians, have tended to treat cities and towns as 'things' rather than as arenas within which broader social, economic and political processes are worked out. This is not necessarily a Marxist critique, as Philip Abrams using an explicitly Weberian perspective in *Towns in Societies* has provided a more elegant one.

The core of the book is devoted to an analysis of the urban structure. In answer to his question 'on the basis of the fundamental concepts of historical materialism, how can we grasp the specificity of the forms of social space?', Castells identifies four fundamental elements reflecting the spatial dimension of each. These are: the production of goods, services and information; the consumption, individual and collective, of the product (such as housing and public amenities); exchanges produced between and within production and consumption; and the administration and regulation of relationships between the other elements (such as urban planning and municipal management). There is nothing objectionable in this characterization, but it is not developed in any systematic way.

The later sections on urban politics, focusing upon intervention by the State in the production and distribution of public amenities, and upon 'urban social movements' reflecting new forms of social protest taken by the fundamental class struggle are the most rewarding, perhaps because Castells has been more involved in them as researcher and as a political activist.

So to the 'afterward', written in 1975, which enjoins the reader to judge the book as 'an historically dated product' and which contains a series of 'rectifications' to correct errors and make much plainer what the book was supposed to be about.

It is, then, a curious book. It is badly written, long-winded and often self-indulgent. Stylistically, it is poor. It is full of 'francoisms' such as 'complexification', 'efficacity' and 'planificatory'. The diagrams have to be seen to be disbelieved. Ruth Glass has likened them to 'drawings of some lunatic plumbing system'. Despite his rejection of traditional urban studies (as 'ideological'), he uses them extensively and uncritically, and like some prosecuting barrister, he is partial in his selection and interpretation.

How, then, is one to judge *The Urban Question*? There have been many excellent books attempting to re-orientate a field of study and which, largely because of the intellectual climate, have been less successful. Here is a book which has had an impact well beyond its actual merits. Castells denies that it has been at the root of 'new tendencies in urban research', but since its publication there has been a welter of Marxist writings on urban matters, and traditional academic barriers between sociology, politics, geography and planning have been crossed. The nub of Castells' argument, that so-called urban problems correspond with fundamental structural contradictions in advanced capitalist societies, has given urban studies a new lease of life, and much of the uncritical silliness of the early 1970s has been replaced by a new and more critical analysis of urban affairs. In spite of itself, then, *The Urban Question* is an important book.

David McCrone
Department of Sociology, University of Edinburgh

G. van Herwijnen, *Bibliografie van de Stedengeschiedenis van Nederland*. Acta Collegii Historiae Urbanae Societatis Historicum Internationalis. Leiden: E. J. Brill 1978. Dfls. 80.

The reviewing of a bibliography is in general a rather ungrateful job. Most bibliographies are useful instruments, but they do not offer pleasant reading. With this publication the proof is in the eating of the pudding. The only thing the reviewer can do is identify the criteria the composer of the bibliography has used and to check them. Let me start this review with the remark that the *Bibliografie van de Stedengeschiedenis van Nederland* is indeed a very useful instrument. The publication is part of a general series of bibliographies on the urban history of different European countries. This particular volume contains titles on Dutch pre-war urban history.

One of the problems with the making of a bibliography is the selection criteria. This is particularly true in the case of urban history, because many publications can also be seen not only as urban history, but as more general history. One has to rethink what urban history is. Not only is the boundary between more general (political, social-economic, etc.) history and urban history fluid, but even with a more limited definition of urban history, problems still exist. The author (and his assistants) of this bibliography used two criteria: one legal, the other demographic. Not only titles of publications on towns with municipal rights were selected, but also ones relating to 'villages' with fast-growing populations during the nineteenth century. Titles were arranged in two ways: first, they were classified geographically in order of provinces, and second, within this classification they were organized according to subject (lists of maps, archives; lists of sources; general histories; special periods, topography; economic, social and demographic history; institutions; history of the churches and culture). The bibliography is very well documented and printed, and deserves high praise. Any researcher working on the history of Dutch towns before 1940 will need to have it to hand.

H. van Dijk
University of Rotterdam

Deborah Sutton (ed.), *York Civic Records, Volume IX*. Leeds: W. S. Maney & Son Ltd., 1978, vii + 148 pp. £5.00 per volume, Subscribers 25% discount.

This book, published under the aegis of the Yorkshire Archaeological Society as part of its Record Series, is the ninth volume dedicated to the transcription and publication of the York corporation House Books. The previous eight volumes appeared between 1939 and 1953. After such a long gap one could have hoped for more than the span covered by this volume, which simply completes the unfinished editing of House Book 30, covering the minute period 1588 to 1590. Given the problems that many towns experienced in the 1590s, including dearth and internal divisions among civic elites – the kind of events which corporation Assembly or House Books can be expected to elucidate – it is a pity that more of the House Books could not have been examined. However, one cannot altogether blame the Society in view of the present financial restraints which have restricted the output of so many local history societies.

The volume itself, like its forbears, is well produced with a useful subject index, always a desideratum in a work of this kind, and within its limited scope, indicates the many characteristic forms of civic concern at this time, ranging from regulation of the markets and the administration of corporation property on the traditional side, to the more recent interest in sabbatarianism, poverty and

under-employment. The editor has provided an introduction outlining the institutional structure of the city as it appeared after the 1517 charter, including a
sketch of the 'cursus honorum' (a fashionable concept in the analysis of early
modern towns). Just how much these materials contribute to the understanding of
the city should become apparent with the Pallisers' study of Tudor York, to be
published before this Yearbook itself appears.

W. A. Champion
Department of English Local History, University of Leicester

R. D. Lee (ed.), *Population Patterns in the Past*. New York, San Francisco, London:
  Academic Press, 1977, x + 376 pp. £13.50/$19.00.
The fastest-growing rural pastime of recent years has surely been the subject of
historical demography. Difficulties of analysis, and the predominantly rural cast
of theorization on past populations, conspire to bypass the towns. This book
reflects that bias, and those contributions devoted to urban questions probably fit
least well the objectives of the 1974 conference on behavioural models in historical
demography from which this book derives.

The book's basic premise is that the established forms of analysis within the
subject – description, and the development of verbal models of demographic
change in a broader socio-economic context – 'need to be linked with a more
rigorous approach to the formulation, estimation, and testing of behavioral
models' (p. 2). Lee's volume is thus a partial guide to the variegated forms of historical demography currently being practised, particularly in North America. As
such, despite the attempt at a central impetus provided by Lee's introduction
giving a brief conspectus of hypotheses of population dynamics found here and in
the literature, this collection seems to lack a consistent focus. Although it is perhaps unfair to make such comparisons, Lee's volume compares unfavourably with
a similar conference collection, Charles Tilly's *Historical Studies in Changing Fertility* (Princeton, 1978). The contributors to both books overlap, but Tilly's book
does possess some central direction. Tilly likewise makes the clarion call to explicit
hypothesis-testing, whilst the contributors to his book appear to have been more
successful in focusing upon a common aim, allowing the editor to provide an
extended analytical introduction and a commentary producing an important new
approach to fertility history. Given the separate aims of the two volumes, these differences are not entirely surprising – but that leads one to question the utility of a
collection of disparate articles, all rather loosely connected by the application of
hypothesis-testing techniques of widely varying degrees of complexity.

Two contributors are specifically interested in urban matters. David Herlihy
provides a fairly conventional descriptive paper on sources and results from his
demographic study of Florence and Tuscany 1300–1550, in some ways offending
against the book's canons by addressing himself to Lee's models of demographic behaviour in something of an afterthought. Uncompromisingly setting herself
within the context provided by the modernization literature, Barbara Anderson
considers the determinants of migration to late nineteenth-century Moscow and St
Petersburg. Although she paints a reasonably convincing picture of the positive
selection of migrants, one remains dubious about the guiding catch-all principle of
'modernization', and of the selection and definition criteria for the variables in her
regression analysis.

Peter Lindert, devoting himself to the Easterlin hypothesis, makes much sense
of the U.S. fertility decline since the civil war despite a regression model which
manages to include the kitchen sink. Standard regression and correlation techniques are used in many of the contributions as a guiding tool. With them, Marvin
McInnis tests Easterlin on Canadian farm families, Hermalin and van de Walle
come to no firm conclusion on the effects of the *Code Napoléon* on French nuptia-
lity and inheritance patterns, Susan Hanley investigates the tight controls found
in eighteenth- and nineteenth-century Japanese villages, and Daniel Scott Smith

provides a thought-provoking cross-sectional analysis of (predominantly French) family reconstitution studies suggesting a 'homeostatic demographic regime' in eighteenth-century western Europe. Smith's paper is perhaps the most successful in integrating statistical and descriptive expertise with the behavioural modelling from which, the book assures us, the insights of the future will derive.

That way forward is promised in a group of admittedly technical chapters. Hammell and Wachter introduce simulation techniques in a paper on household structure which implicitly criticizes the work of Lutz Berkner in this volume, and elsewhere, on the stem family, whilst also making some important statements about the stochastic nature of historical evidence. The French school illustrates their new family of stable population schedules. The book's final chapters, by Massimo Livi-Bacci and by Ron Lee, provide early indications of the important, and exciting, results which may be achieved through the statistical investigation of aggregate time series.

This collection illustrates where we have been in historical demography, and provides some clues as to where we may be going. However, its very catholicity of approach, of time and of space, and the 'research in progress' character of many contributions, attenuate the book's message, whilst omissions of other approaches, of which the urban dimension is but one, prevent its use as a guide to the present practice of historical demography. Nevertheless, a book respecting its antecedents sufficiently to feature Henry's Crulai in its first chapter, and Wrigley's Colyton in its last, at least has its heart in the right place.

David Souden
Emmanuel College, Cambridge

Helmut Jäger (ed.), *Probleme des Städtewesens im industriellen Zeitalter.* Cologne and Vienna: Böhlau Verlag, 1978. xviii + 349 pp. 71 illustrations. Tables. DM 82.

This volume, the latest in a series of works published under the auspices of the Institute for Comparative Urban History in Münster, consists of 12 papers delivered at the Institute in 1974. Whereas the papers delivered at two earlier colloquia focused on medieval and early modern cities, the essays in this book deal almost exclusively with the nineteenth century. Given the tendency among German urban historians up until the mid-1960s to devote their energies almost entirely to the pre-industrial centuries, collaborative works on the modern period have become feasible only during the last few years. At the very least, the volume makes a number of useful contributions to the relatively recent history of European cities.

The individual essays are somewhat disparate not only in length but also with regard to the geographical areas on which they focus and to the methodological approaches they employ. Two number fewer than ten pages, whereas several others run to upwards of 40. Most of them treat Germanic Central Europe, but there is one essay on England and another (by Maja Philippi) on the Rumanian city of Kronstadt-Brasow. Finally, one can distinguish between the essays that consider general processes at work in a number of cities and the ones that concentrate on the experiences of individual urban entities.

The authors who range beyond the confines of single cities reflect a pervasive interest in the geography of urban growth. Michael R. G. Conzen, in a synthetic overview of the changing morphology of English cities, shows how transformative processes in old city centres and additive growth on the peripheries resulted in urban physiognomies that were highly varied at the core but increasingly monotonous elsewhere and also more similar to one another nationwide than had heretofore been the case. The most wide-ranging of the essays on Central Europe is the concluding piece by Heinz Stoob, who compares changes in the urban network between 1800 and 1945 with developments in earlier centuries. While showing clearly that major transformations did occur, he also indicates that the establishment of new cities was not as intensive during the industrial revolution as had been the case around 1300 and that in fact there were fewer cities in the area in 1945 than at the end of the Middle Ages. The essays by Hans-Heinrich Blotevogel and Heinrich J. Schwippe employ varying versions of central place theory and quantitative techniques in order to explore the functional significance of universities on the one hand and of manufacturing activity on the other in cities in Westphalia. In contrast, Peter Schöller and Manfred Hommel consider the consequences of urban growth in new cities that sprang up in industrial and mining areas where there was no central core. Here, the spatial dispersion of urban focal points within city boundaries served as a brake on the development both of communal services and of communal solidarity.

For the most part, the papers on individual cities consider one or another of the three main German-speaking capitals, Berlin, Munich, and Vienna. These essays pay considerable attention to the phenomena of urban growth emphasized in the pieces discussed above, but they also include a great deal on other themes as well. Wolfgang Hofmann carefully assesses the interplay between residential patterns and administrative structures in and around Berlin, showing how suburbanization made expansion of the city's boundaries more and more imperative between 1860 and 1920. Peter Breitling provides an extremely useful survey of the development of Munich, which is especially welcome in view of the fact that we still lack a satisfactory history of the city during the modern period. His paper systematically takes up demographic developments, city services, building projects, technical and legal innovations, and major controversies during each of five periods spanning the years between 1800 and 1910. Vienna is the subject of three essays, by Elisabeth Lichtenberger, Alfred Hoffmann, and Felix Czeike. Lichtenberger emphasizes that although the Austrian capital was relatively traditional socially and economically compared with Paris and Berlin, its achievements in the realm of city planning and municipal administration were exemplary. Czeike takes up similar themes but is more specifically concerned with physical infrastructure and the evolution of building patterns. It is regrettable that there are no essays on any of the major industrial cities of western Germany, but the ones on the capitals still offer a great deal to urban historians whether or not they are especially interested in the heavily geographic orientation characteristic of most of the rest of the book.

A. Lees
Department of History, Rutgers University

Bruce M. Stave (ed.), *The Making of Urban History: Historiography Through Oral History*. Beverly Hills: Sage, 1977. 336 pp. $15.95 hardback, $6.95 paperback. Bruce Stave's interviews with American urban historians have been the sheet-anchor of the *Journal of Urban History* since it was launched in 1974. The publishers of the *Journal*, Sage, have now allowed Stave to bring together nine of these interviews and introduce them with a brief essay on the development of urban history in the United States. The result is quite a pantheon, including Blake McKelvey, Bayrd Still, Oscar Handlin, Richard Wade, Sam Bass Warner, Stephan Thernstrom, Eric Lampard, Samuel Hays, and the late Constance McLaughlin Green.

Stave's involvement in this enterprise has sprung from his interest in oral history, from which it is, apparently, but a short step to oral historiography, if the contradiction in terms can be forgiven. As one of Stave's more recent victims, this reviewer is painfully aware of the drawbacks of the method. Two hours of virtual monologue can be expected to produce a fair crop of platitudes. The subject is allowed to polish the transcript but in removing infelicities he may also destroy the spontaneity of the original – yet it is already too late for *esprit d'escalier*. Perhaps the casual approach is the best, but not everyone is a Stephan Thernstrom.

This collection, nevertheless, works well. Stave knows the field, and the thickets of American academe, well enough to stimulate and draw out his subjects. After a few, discreet questions on family background he goes on to enquire about early student days. Most of his subjects graduated in history but few have anything good to say about either their courses or their tutors. If they acquired an interest in urban history it was in spite of this early training, not because of it. Most selected the specialism at graduate school. Some were moved by personal contact with the pioneers of urban history. Others went through an intellectual conversion, recognizing the explanatory potential of the urban factor in any study of the formation and functioning of modern American society. Stave then leads them through their creative careers, asking about the origins of their major books and articles, seeking clarification of their ideas and attitudes to controversies, and, finally, enquiring about their plans for the future and their views on the general state of the art. There is a certain amount of restrained gossip in all of this, together with some good-humoured banter. Altogether, it makes good reading. Stave achieves for urban history what Ved Mehta, using a similar method, did for philosophy in his *Fly and the Fly-Bottle* some years ago. All those engaged in urban history, and graduate students in particular, will greatly profit from this book, whether or not their interests lie in North America.

Anthony Sutcliffe
Department of Economic and Social History, University of Sheffield

Cheryl Parsons, *Schools in an Urban Community. A Study of Carbrook 1870–1965.* London: Routledge & Kegan Paul, 1978. ix + 155 pp. Map. Bibliography. Index. £5.95.

Carbrook, Sheffield, only existed as a community for about 100 years. Like many urban, working-class suburbs, it was created by industrialization and ultimately destroyed by it; built in a former rural beauty spot and transformed again in the 1950s in a programme of slum clearance and redevelopment. In between, four generations lived, worked, raised families and died there, all sharing the common experience of attending one of the elementary schools in the district. Cheryl Parsons, who was one of the pupils herself, views the schools in the context of the community they served, and shows how their history was inextricably bound up with the economic changes in the area. She also plots the changing relationship between the schools and the neighbourhood – from hostility and suspicion to a working partnership for mutual advantage – and shows the growth of corporate loyalty and pride, fostered by the activities of the schools, until their closure in 1960, after public protest.

As in much working-class history, documentary sources are scant. The author uses log books, Education Committee minutes and local newspapers to advantage, but it is oral history that brings her study to life. She interviewed over 50 ex-pupils and ex-teachers, some with memories stretching back to the 1890s. Their information about the 'mucky Natch' (the National School) and the 'draughty Board' corroborates the documentary evidence, with its story of overcrowding and inadequate facilities and equipment, where the school building programme never quite coincided with the number of places required by the fluctuating workforce.

What happened in the steel industry inevitably affected the schools. Morning school had to finish at 11.30 a.m., as local tradition required children to take their fathers' lunches to the factory gate. Poverty placed part-time employment, scavenging for fuel ('Jubilee'), or bread ('leftings') and begging from wealthy Doncaster racegoers, higher in priority than attendance at school. Slumps in the steel industry affected whole families and long-serving teachers, with an intimate knowledge of needy children, were uniquely placed to provide relief that was acceptable. This was not official charity but relief 'that stemmed from and originated within the community itself'. One headmaster, who served the area for 38 years, organized a scheme of his own. He was able to distribute help in kind, Robin Hood fashion, with tact and sympathy, a method which kept three generations of some families above the bread line. No record of his activities however, appear in the log books. These occasionally listed names of pupils eligible for free meals or clothing parcels, but only the oral evidence revealed the contents of the parcels, how they were distributed and what the local families felt about the different kinds of help on offer. Adding this dimension, the author enables the schools and their place in the community to be evaluated from the viewpoint of the pupils, which could not have been done from log books and minutes alone. Another extra-curricular activity which strengthened the links between schools and community was the School Choir in the 1920s. Local tradition maintains it was superior to the Sheffield Philharmonic, advertising Carbrook to a wider audience, when they travelled about winning competitions and broadcasting on the radio.

By documenting the social role and responsibilities of schools in one small, urban area, this book points a new direction for the history of education and for community studies. It is unfortunate that the map, with industries and schools shaded the same colour and one school named differently from the text, is almost useless.

Sallie Purkis
Department of History, Homerton College, Cambridge

Benjamin Ferrey, *Recollections of A. W. N. Pugin and his father Augustus Pugin.* [With an appendix by E. Sheridan Purcell and an introduction and index by Clive and Jane Wainwright.] London: The Scolar Press, 1978. xlii + 473 pp. 15 illus. 4 plates. 11 drawings. £12.50.

Pugin was a phenomenon in an age of phenomenal men. He was designing furniture by the age of 15, was bankrupt a few years later, became an architect at 23, designed and supervised the erection of cathedrals, innumerable churches and houses, as well as all the detail of the Houses of Parliament, wrote, drew and etched three major books, each of which was enough to transform the taste and convictions of the time – *Contrasts*, *The True Principles of Pointed or Christian Architecture*, and *An Apology for the Revival of Christian Architecture in England* – and was working on another major book when he died. He exhausted three wives (who bore him eight children), countless clients and clergymen, and finally himself: he died insane on 14 September 1852, at the age of 40.

His friend and colleague Benjamin Ferrey, almost his contemporary and a fellow pupil in the elder Pugin's studio, published the *Recollections* in 1861, adding to his vigorous and ultimately harrowing account a lengthy appendix by E. Sheridan Purcell in which 'the writings and character of Augustus Welby Northmore Pugin are considered in their catholic aspect' – a valuable essay which Ferrey accepted somewhat reluctantly as an explanation of his tempestuous subject. Clive Wainwright's new edition, dignified and clear, with a sensible introduction and a valuable index, is timely and provocative.

Pugin's typical day at his house in Ramsgate sets the pace of the main story: in his private chapel at six o'clock when the church bell tolled the Angelus; work in his library until 7.30 a.m.: morning prayers in a cassock and surplice; breakfast for seven minutes; Mass at eight o'clock; work until one o'clock; dinner for a quarter of an hour; inspection of buildings and receiving visitors in the afternoon; correspondence until nine o'clock; designing his own buildings until ten o'clock; Compline; and study of historical and theological works for the last hour. To this frightening story Ferrey adds that on his return from town Pugin had invariably finished his letters, having written them in the railway carriage.

From that mind-shattering volume of work came some important architectural results. He introduced polychromy (spectacularly in the Houses of Parliament), provided not only the polemics but also the profound rationale for the use of Gothic, and formulated principles which have had a major effect on all subsequent architecture especially the modern movement. His best buildings were probably small – Ramsgate and Cheadle for example: most of his bigger buildings were flawed by economies and continual haste. His abilities were extraordinary. He could draw and talk at the same time about different subjects. With a steady hand he drew and etched some of his most intricate designs in a boat in rough seas. He was prolific in invention.

Ferrey was observant, not uncritical and ultimately devoted. For Pugin was phenomenal not only in output but also in generosity, 'wholly unselfish in the advancement of true principles and the glory of God'. Everything he did was done to this end and done with a heroic intensity. 'In short he was a *great* man'.

The last words written by Pugin were 'Pax omnibus. Amen'. It was not an unfitting valediction. This new edition should help to give a greater understanding of an extraordinary and admirable man.

Patrick Nuttgens
Leeds Polytechnic

Ian Cooper and J. David Hulchanski, *Canadian Town Planning, 1900–1930: A Historical Bibliography. Volume I: Planning; Volume II: Housing; Volume III: Public Health.* Toronto: Centre for Urban and Community Studies, University of Toronto, 1978 [Bibliographic Series, nos. 7, 8, 9]. 82+21+24 pp. No price stated.

J. David Hulchanski, *Canadian Town Planning and Housing, 1940–1950: A Historical Bibliography.* Toronto: Centre for Urban and Community Studies, University of Toronto, 1979 [Bibliographic Series, no. 12]. 51 pp. No price stated.

In recent years David Hulchanski has published a number of specialized planning history bibliographies through the good offices of the Centre for Urban and Community Studies. These four fascicules contain some of his most recent work. Here, partly in association with Ian Cooper, he has broadened his sights from his original interest in Thomas Adams, the English founder of modern Canadian planning, to take in the development of policies affecting the urban environment throughout Canada. His method is to list, without comment, items of printed primary material drawn mainly from contemporary journals, according to their year of publication. Each fascicule is complemented by a brief historical introduction, a chronology, and a full array of indexes. Some 1800 titles are listed, many of them from obscure public-works periodicals. Students of this first really creative period of Canadian urban control will find these bibliographies very helpful.

Anthony Sutcliffe
Department of Economic and Social History, University of Sheffield

P. J. Aspinall, *Building Applications and the Building Industry in 19th Century Towns: The Scope for Statistical Analysis.* [Research Memorandum 68.] Birmingham: Centre for Urban and Regional Studies, University of Birmingham, 1978. i + 80 pp. 10 figures. 3 tables. 2 appendices. £1.75.

Mr Aspinall writes in the conviction that a new 'grassroots' history of building is needed. Too little is known about the industry's firms. Too much has been attempted by way of hypotheses about regional fluctuations and complex interactions between economies, 'all based upon an assumed knowledge of the firms themselves'. To this end he advocates 'comparative studies employing a standard methodological framework from which can develop a richer and more refined conceptualisation of size structure' (p. 49). This feature, he holds, together with differences in the financial and other resources employed, might explain in part the observed wide differences in the degree of speculative building from place to place in the late nineteenth century (p. 1).

For this purpose he has investigated the usefulness of local authority building plan registers for three towns, Nottingham, Leeds and Sheffield, and here summarizes the results of the analysis of Sheffield, concentrating on housebuilding between 1865 and 1900. The total number of firms varied closely with the building cycle but over the longer period larger firms increased in numbers while the smallest firms gradually declined. There was also a very high level of movement into and out of the industry – the housebuilding industry, that is – but not necessarily out of all sectors of building since the 'firms' identified were unavoidably a somewhat heterogeneous group, some of which had other interests in building, as Aspinall is careful to explain.

It is indeed a general feature of this paper that its analytical methods are detailed clearly and scrupulously criticized. So, too, are the origins, content, and strengths and limitations of the building registers; and one is able to form an impression of the labour involved in their utilization. The appendices provide a list of building plan registers for English towns and a list of towns included in indices of national, regional, and local house-building activity. Another source, tenders for contracts for public and commercial buildings listed in *The Builder*, is also indicated and discussed.

Whether a vigorous response to Mr Aspinall's appeal for more research on these lines would be as fruitful as he hopes must no doubt be uncertain. But organizational change is after all only one aspect even of the supply side of building (as he is of course aware) and demand, arising from general economic and demographic growth and mediated through investment and migration in particular, may in the end be seen to have been of much greater importance in the history of this conservative, slow-changing industry.

E. W. Cooney
Department of Economics, University of York

Helen E. Meller (ed.), *The Ideal City*. Leicester: Leicester University Press, 1979. 183 pp. £3.80.

In her informative introduction to this new edition of Canon Barnett's *The Ideal City* (1893) and Patrick Geddes's *Civics: As applied sociology* (1905–06), Helen E. Meller observes that 'many contemporaries have stated how much they owed to the stimulus Barnett and Geddes provided, but subsequent generations have been puzzled as to why they were once so influential'.

I fear that the reprinting of these two works will do little to clear up the puzzlement. Both are marked by ample idealism and hope for the future, but neither offers much that is either profound or practical.

Barnett, though best known for his work at Toynbee Hall in the East End of London, was also a non-resident Canon of Bristol Cathedral. His *Ideal City* is a fanciful picture of Bristol as it might be, in which he has synthesized many of the fashionable ideas of his day. His ideal city is a place where no-one is very rich or very poor; where the buildings are beautiful and the people are generous; where medieval pageantry and a good sewerage system are somehow conjoined.

It is all very uplifting but, finally, not very edifying. For all his eloquence, Barnett suggests neither priorities nor methods (aside from continued appeals to the ideal). 'Our duty is clear', he concludes. 'We must preach'.

Patrick Geddes's work, originally delivered as two lectures to the British Sociological Society, is far more substantial, for Geddes did possess an original and important insight: that cities cannot grow by formula but must develop organically out of their own relationship to the region around them. The planner, moreover, must guide urban growth according to each city's unique historical tradition. Nineteenth-century urbanism used the new technology at its disposal to ignore both nature and history; and, since Geddes spoke, the twentieth century has developed these aberrations to frightening lengths.

In this particular selection, however, Geddes does little to enrich his basic insight. Instead, he expounds what he calls his 'abstract method for notation and for interpretation'. This is Geddes at his weakest, indulging himself in multiple neologisms and overcomplicated charts. One sympathizes with Charles Booth's comment that Geddes's presentation reminded him of 'a lady of my acquaintance who had a place for everything. The discovery of America was in the left-hand corner; the Papacy was in the middle; and for everything she had some local habi-tation in an imaginary world.'

More serious, perhaps, than this pseudo-scientific abstraction was Geddes's belief – comparable to Barnett's – that the ideal city could be achieved by preach-ing at the citizens. Geddes's form of preaching would take place not from the pulpit but in civics exhibitions at places like Outlook Tower, his 'civic and regional museum' for Edinburgh. There citizens would be brought face-to-face with the history of their community and the ecology of their region; and from this knowledge good planning would follow. This is admirable, but also unrealistic. Geddes's Civics has surprisingly little to do with the hard facts of politics, pro-perty, and power.

The first commentator on Geddes's paper was Ebenezer Howard, who used the occasion – as he used every other occasion – to argue for the Garden City. Howard lacked Barnett's learning, eloquence, and social position, just as he lacked Geddes's brilliance and scientific training. But, as an urbanist, he possessed some-thing more important: a clear and comprehensible goal for action, and a practical method for achieving that goal. As a proponent of the ideal city, therefore, the modest stenographer succeeded far better than his two estimable and once-influential colleagues.

Robert Fishman
Department of History, Rutgers University

Index of books reviewed

Current bibliography of urban history

This bibliography is a continuation of and a complement to those published in *UHY* 1974–9. It aims to provide comprehensive coverage of books published in Britain that have been listed in the *British National Bibliography* between 1 August 1978 and 30 June 1979. This material is supplemented by the scanning of a large number of current periodicals (see the list of Abbreviations pp. 181–3 and by the selections of the *Yearbook's* foreign correspondents. This year we are again extremely grateful to Professor Stuart Blumin (U.S.A.), Mr T. J. Caulton (British periodicals), Monsieur Bernard Lepetit (France) and Dott. Cinzia Sicca (Italy) for their contributions.

The format and arrangement of the bibliography follows the pattern of previous years. However, we have decided to arrange the section entitled History and Fortunes of Individual Towns in one sequence rather than subdividing it by period. An index of towns is provided on pp. 215–18 and cross-references are given wherever relevant.

Outline of the classification

I GENERAL
RESEARCH METHODS, AIDS AND MATERIALS
URBAN HISTORY – DEFINITIONS AND HISTORIOGRAPHY
URBANIZATION AND THE GROWTH AND FORTUNES OF TOWNS
HISTORY AND FORTUNES OF INDIVIDUAL TOWNS
PORTRAITS OF TOWNS – LITERARY, PHOTOGRAPHIC AND GRAPHIC

II POPULATION
RESEARCH METHODS, AIDS AND MATERIALS
GENERAL FEATURES OF URBAN POPULATIONS
NATALITY AND MORTALITY
DISEASE
MEDICINE
MIGRATION TO, FROM AND BETWEEN TOWNS
POPULATION MOVEMENTS WITHIN TOWNS
FAMILY AND HOUSEHOLD STRUCTURE

III PHYSICAL STRUCTURE
RESEARCH METHODS, AIDS AND MATERIALS
PHYSICAL AND STRUCTURAL CHARACTERISTICS OF TOWNS
PHYSICAL AND STRUCTURAL CHARACTERISTICS OF AREAS WITHIN TOWNS
SITES AND BUILDINGS
HOUSING
ENVIRONMENTAL CONDITIONS

IV SOCIAL STRUCTURE
RESEARCH METHODS, AIDS AND MATERIALS
SOCIAL STRUCTURE AND CHARACTERISTICS OF TOWNS
CLASS STRUCTURE, PROTESTS AND DISORDERS
SOCIAL STRUCTURE AND CHARACTERISTICS OF AREAS WITHIN TOWNS
SOCIAL ORGANIZATIONS, CLUBS AND SOCIETIES
SOCIAL LIFE
SOCIAL PROBLEMS AND DEVIANCE
SOCIAL REFORM AND IMPROVEMENT
MINORITY GROUPS

V ECONOMIC ACTIVITY
RESEARCH METHODS, AIDS AND MATERIALS
URBAN ECONOMIC ACTIVITY
AGRICULTURE
INDUSTRY
EXTERNAL TRADE

INTERNAL TRADE AND SERVICES
CONSUMPTION
LABOUR ORGANIZATION

VI COMMUNICATIONS
RESEARCH METHODS, AIDS AND MATERIALS
INTER-URBAN COMMUNICATIONS
MODES OF INTER-URBAN COMMUNICATION
INTRA-URBAN COMMUNICATIONS
MODES OF INTRA-URBAN COMMUNICATION

VII POLITICS AND ADMINISTRATION
RESEARCH METHODS, AIDS AND MATERIALS
URBAN POLITICS AND ADMINISTRATION
URBAN POLITICS AT NATIONAL LEVEL
URBAN POLITICS, LOCAL AND MUNICIPAL
URBAN ADMINISTRATION
PUBLIC UTILITIES

VIII SHAPING THE URBAN ENVIRONMENT
RESEARCH METHODS, AIDS AND MATERIALS
TOWN PLANNING AND ENVIRONMENTAL CONTROL
EXPOSURE OF URBAN CONDITIONS
UTOPIAN PLANNING AND EXPERIMENTS
HOUSING IMPROVEMENT
NEW AND EXPANDED TOWNS
REGIONAL PLANNING

IX URBAN CULTURE
RESEARCH METHODS, AIDS AND MATERIALS
URBAN CULTURE AND ENTERTAINMENT
ENTERTAINMENT
FINE ARTS
EXCHANGE OF INFORMATION
EDUCATION
URBAN INFLUENCE ON RURAL AREAS AND THE WIDER WORLD

X ATTITUDES TO CITIES
RESEARCH METHODS, AIDS AND MATERIALS
ATTITUDES TO CITIES
POPULAR ATTITUDES
ELITE ATTITUDES
VIEWS OF THE CITY IN LITERATURE, GRAPHIC AND DRAMATIC ART

Abbreviations

AA	Archaeologia Aeliana	AR	Architectural Review
AAn	American Antiquity	ASR	American Sociological Review
ABS	American Behavioral Scientist	BAS	Birmingham Archaeological Society Transactions and Proceedings
ACa	Archaeologia Cambrensis		
AdB	Annales de Bretagne		
AdM	Annales du Midi	BSLH	Bulletin for the Study of Labour History
AdN	Annales de Normandie		
ADH	Annales de Demographie Historique	BSLHR	Bourne Society Local History Records
AESC	Annales Economies, Sociétés, Civilisations	BuH	Business History
		BuHR	Business History Review
AHR	American Historical Review	CA	Current Archaeology
AI	Annals of Iowa	CalH	California History
AJA	American Journal of Archaeology	CarmH	Carmarthen Historian
AJS	American Journal of Sociology	CC	Cake and Cockhorse
APSC	Annals of the American Academy of Political and Social Science	ChH	Church History
		CHST	Caernarvonshire Historical Society Transactions
APSR	American Political Science Review	ChesH	Cheshire History
		CinHSB	Cincinnati Historical Society Bulletin
AQ	American Quarterly		

CJ	Classical Journal	JKLH	Journal of Kent Local History
CSSH	Comparative Studies in Society and History	JLAS	Journal of Latin American Studies
CWAAS	Cumberland and Westmorland Archaeological Society Transactions	JMRS	Journal of Medieval and Renaissance Studies
DAJ	Derbyshire Archaeological Journal	JQ	Japan Quarterly
		JReS	Journal of Regional Science
DASP	Devon Archaeological Society Proceedings	JSH	Journal of Southern History
		JSocH	Journal of Social History
DCLHSB	Durham County Local History Society Bulletin	JTH	Journal of Transport History
		JUH	Journal of Urban History
De	Demography	KAR	Kent Archaeological Review
DH	Devon Historian	LabH	Labor Historian
DGNH	Dumfries and Galloway Natural History and Antiquarian Society	LAHS	Leicestershire Archaeological and Historical Society Transactions
DM	Derbyshire Miscellany	LibH	Library History
EcHR	Economic History Review	LJ	London Journal
EJ	Essex Journal	Lla	Llafur
EMG	East Midlands Geographer	LoH	Local Historian
Eth	Ethnicity	LoMAS	London and Middlesex Archaeological Society Transactions
EuSR	European Studies Review		
FHS	French Historical Studies	LonA	London Archaeology
GA	Geografiska Annaler	LPLS	Leeds Philosophical and Literary Society
GaHQ	Georgia Historical Quarterly		
Geo	Geoforum	LPS	Local Population Studies
GlHB	Gloucestershire Community Council Local History Bulletin	LouH	Louisiana History
		MdHM	Maryland Historical Magazine
GlHS	Gloucester Historical Studies	MedH	Medical History
GM	Geographical Magazine	Mid-Amer	Mid-America
GR	Geographical Review	MidH	Midland History
GRBS	Greek Roman and Byzantine Studies	MilH	Milwaukee History
		MisHR	Missouri Historical Review
GUM	Guildhall Studies in London History	MHSB	Missouri Historical Society Bulletin
HerA	Hertfordshire Archaeology	NEQ	New England Quarterly
HFCAS	Hampshire Field Club and Archaeological Society Transactions	NJH	New Jersey History
		NoA	Norfolk Archaeology
		NPP	Northamptonshire Past and Present
HHSB	Hornsey Historical Society Bulletin	NYH	New York History
		NYHSQ	New York Historical Society Quarterly
HJ	Historical Journal		
HSLC	Historic Society of Lancashire and Cheshire	OH	Oral History
		PaP	Past and Present
HT	History Today	PenH	Pennsylvania History
IBG	Institute of British Geographers Transactions	PenMHB	Pennsylvania Magazine of History and Biography
IHR	Institute of Historical Research Bulletin	PH	Provence Historique
		PHR	Pacific Historical Review
IM	International Migration	PMA	Post Medieval Archaeology
InMH	Indiana Magazine of History	Pop	Population
IRSH	International Review of Social History	PP	Policy and Politics
		PS	Population Studies
JAH	Journal of American History	PSQ	Political Science Quarterly
JAS	Journal of American Studies	RBuc	Records of Buckinghamshire
JBlS	Journal of Black Studies	RdN	Revue du Nord
JEcH	Journal of Economic History	RH	Revue Historique
JEEH	Journal of European Economic History	RHMC	Revue d'Histoire Moderne et Contemporaine
JEthS	Journal of Ethnic Studies	RHS	Royal Historical Society Transactions
JFH	Journal of Family History		
JHG	Journal of Historical Geography	RocH	Rochester History
JHI	Journal of the History of Ideas	RQ	Renaissance Quarterly
JInH	Journal of Interdisciplinary History	RSAI	Royal Society of Antiquaries of Ireland

SANHS	Somerset Archaeology and Natural History Society Proceedings	SS	Soviet Studies
		SV	Studi Veneziani
SAUS	South Atlantic Urban Studies	TESG	Tijdschrift voor Economische en Sociale Geografie
SAC	Sussex Archaeological Collections	TPR	Town Planning Review
SCalQ	Southern California Quarterly	UAn	Urban Anthropology
SCHM	South Carolina Historical Magazine	UAQ	Urban Affairs Quarterly
		UPP	Urbanism Past and Present
SCJ	Sixteenth Century Journal	US	Urban Studies
SF	Social Forces	VS	Victorian Studies
SG	Soviet Geography	WANSM	Wiltshire Archaeological and Natural History Society Magazine
SGM	Scottish Geographical Magazine		
SH	Social History		
ShAS	Shropshire Archaeological Society Transactions	WarH	Warwickshire History
		WeHR	Welsh History Review
SHR	Scottish History Review	WHQ	Western Historical Quarterly
SJPE	Scottish Journal of Political Economy	WisMH	Wisconsin Magazine of History
		XVII	Dix-Septième Siècle
Soc&S	Società e Storia	YAJ	Yorkshire Archaeological Journal
Sp	Speculum		

I GENERAL

RESEARCH METHODS, AIDS AND MATERIALS

Research methods see 54

Directories
1   SHAW, G., The content and reliability of 19th century trade directories. *LoH* 13 (1978) 205–8.

Maps and plans see also 102
2   CARTER, H., The map in urban history. *UHY* (1979) 11–31.
3   DUPEUX, G., Maps of the cities of France, 1809–1812. *UPP* 7 (1979) 36–7.
4   HALL T & BORGWIK L, Urban history atlases: a survey of recent publications. *Särtryck ur Historisk Tidskrift* (1978) 305–19.
5   HOWGEGO, J. L., *Printed maps of London circa 1553–1580.* 2nd edn. Folkestone: Dawson 1978. pp 295, il.

Bibliographies
6   DAVIS, L. G., *Urbanization in the Middle East, with some references to North Africa: an introductory survey.* Monticello, Ill: Council of Planning Librarians 1978.
7   SIMMIE, J. M., *A bibliography on the political sociology of urban development.* University College London 1978. pp 44, il.
8   VAN HERWIJNEN, G., *Bibliografie van de stedengeschiedenis van Nederland.* Leiden: E. J. Brill 1978. pp xxi + 355.

Archives
9   BESTALL, J. M. & FOWKES, D. V., *Chesterfield wills and inventories.* Matlock: Derbyshire Record Office 1977. pp xxxiv + 348.
10   DE BERNARDI, A., Una fonte per la storia locale: l'archivo dell' Amministrazione provinciale di Milano. *Soc&S* (1978) 175–9.
11   EMMISON, F. G., Archives and the local historian. *LoH* 13 (1978) 217–26.
12   GRAHAM, N. H., *The genealogists consolidated guide to parish registers in the Outer London area 1538–1837.* Orpington: author 1977. pp 79, il.
13   PARKER, J. C., *City, county, town and township index to the 1850 Federal census schedules.* Detroit: Gale Research Co 1979.
14   RUTLEDGE, E. & P., Kings Lynn and Great Yarmouth, two thirteenth century surveys. *NoA* 37 (1978) 92–114.
15   SAMWAYS, R., The Middlesex section of the Greater London Record Office. Sources for local historians. *HHSB* 18 (1978) 8–9.

Guides to the literature and printed documentary sources

16   GARSIDE, P. L., The development of London: a classified list of theses presented to the universities of Great Britain and Ireland and the CNAA, 1908–1977. *GUM* 3 (1978) 175–94.

URBAN HISTORY – DEFINITIONS AND HISTORIOGRAPHY

Urban history, definitions and aims

17 HERSHBERG, T., The new urban history: toward an interdisciplinary history of the city. *JUH* 5 (1978) 3–40.
18 HOLLINGSWORTH, J. R. & J., *Dimensions in urban history: historical and social science perspectives.* Madison, Wis: Wisconsin UP 1979.
19 THRUPP, S. L., 'The pedigree and prospects of local history' in Grew & Steneck, *Society and history* [521] 256–68. [reprint of 1940 article].

Urban historiography

20 CONZEN, K. N., Approaches to early Milwaukee community history. *MilH* 1 (1978) 4–12.
21 DAVISON, G., Australian urban history: a progress report. *UHY* (1979) 100–9.
22 LANGER, L. N., The historiography of the preindustrial Russian city. *JUH* 5 (1979) 209–240.
23 REEDER, D., H. J. Dyos: an appreciation. *UHY* (1979) 4–10.
24 RHODES, G., Research in London 1952–77. *LJ* 5 (1979) 57–86.
25 VANCE, J. E., Geography and the study of cities. *ABS* 22 (1978) 131–50.
26 WRIGHT, M., *Hornsey, Highgate and the VCH: a progress report.* Owls Publications 1977. pp 25.
27 Entry deleted.

URBANIZATION AND THE GROWTH AND FORTUNE OF TOWNS

Theory of urbanization

28 LOGAN, J. R., Growth, politics and the stratification of places. *AJS* 84 (1978) 404–16.
29 THRUPP, S. L., 'The creating of cities' in Grew & Steneck, *Society and History* [521] 212–15. [reprint of 1961 review article]

Empirical studies of urbanization and town growth

General

30 AALEN, F. H. A., *Man and the landscape in Ireland.* Academic P 1978. pp xii + 344.
31 BARLEY, M. W. ed, *European towns: their archaeology and early history.* Academic P 1977. pp xxvii + 523, il.
32 BRAUDEL, F., et al eds, *Conjoncture, économique, structures sociales: hommage à Ernest Labrousse.* Paris; The Hague: Mouton 1974. pp 547.
33 BROMLEY, R. D. F., The functions and development of 'colonial' towns: urban change in the Central Highlands of Ecuador 1698–1940. *IBG* 4 (1979) 30–43.
34 CLIFTON TAYLOR, A., *Six English towns.* BBC 1978. pp 178, il.
35 FAGAN, B. M., ed, *Civilization: readings from 'Scientific American'.* San Francisco: W. H. Freeman 1979.
36 HERLIHY, D., 'Urbanization and social change' in FLINN, M. ed, *Proceedings of the seventh International Economic History Congress, I.* Edinburgh: Edinburgh UP 1978. pp 55–74.
37 LAMPARD, E. E., 'Urbanization and social change: an overview' in FLINN, M. ed, *Proceedings of the seventh International Economic History Congress II.* Edinburgh: Edinburgh UP 1978. pp 533–40.
38 O'CONNELL, M., *Historic towns in Surrey.* Guildford: Surrey Archaeological Society 1978. pp 56, il.
39 ÖHNGREN, B., 'Urbanization and social change' [mainly Scandinavia] in FLINN, M., ed, *Proceedings of the seventh International Economic History Congress I.* Edinburgh: Edinburgh UP 1978. pp 75–82.
40 PROCTER, M., *Gritty cities: a second look at Allentown, Bethlehem, Bridgeport, Hoboken, Lancaster, Norwich, Paterson, Reading, Trenton, Troy, Waterbury, Wilmington.* Philadelphia: Temple UP 1978.
41 RICHARD, J., ed, *Histoire de la Bourgogne.* Toulouse: Privat 1978. pp 491.
42 WHEATLEY, P. & SEE, T., *From court to capital: a tentative interpretation of the origins of the Japanese urban tradition.* Chicago: Chicago UP 1978. pp xii + 243, il.

Ancient

43 BULLITT, O. H., *Phoenicia and Carthage: a thousand years to oblivion.* Philadelphia: Dorrance 1978.
44 SMITH, M. E., The Aztec marketing system and settlement pattern in the valley of Mexico: a central place analysis. *AAn* 44 (1979) 110–25.
45 SOLES, J. S., The ancient Gournia town. *AJA* 83 (1979) 133–47.

46   SORRELL, A., *Roman towns in Britain*. Batsford 1977. pp 80.

Medieval and early modern
47   BERGERON, L., PERROT, J. C., & RONCAYOLO, M., 'Définition de la ville et profils d'urbanisation en France' in FLINN, M. ed, *Proceedings of the seventh International Economic History Congress*, I. Edinburgh: Edinburgh UP 1978. pp 83–9.
48   BLOM, G. A., ed, Urbaniseringsprosessen i Norden: Middelaldersteder [Scandinavia]. Oslo: Universitetsforlaget 1977. pp 286.
49   DYER, A., Growth and decay in English towns 1500–1700. *UHY* (1979) 60–72.
50   FRANÇOIS, E., De républiques marchandes aux capitales politiques: la hiérarchie urbaine du Saint Empire. *RHMC* 4 (1978) 587–603.
51   GRAHAM, B., The evolution of urbanisation in medieval Ireland. *JHG* 5 (1979) 111–26.
52   GRIFFITHS, R. A., *Boroughs of medieval Wales*. Cardiff: Wales UP 1978. pp xii + 338.
53   GRIFFITHS, R. A., 'The study of the medieval Welsh borough' in Griffiths, *Boroughs of medieval Wales* [52] 1–18.
54   LEPETIT, B., La croissance urbaine dans la France pré-industrielle: quelques méthodes d'analyse. *Institut d'Histoire Economique et Sociale de l'Université de Paris I Bulletin* 7 (1978) 1–19.
55   NELSON, L. H., The foundation of Jaca (1076): urban growth in early Aragon. *Sp* (1978) 688–708.
56   PHYTHIAN-ADAMS, C. V., Dr Dyer's urban undulations. *UHY* (1979) 73–6.
57   PLATT, C., *The English medieval town*. Paladin 1979. pp 272, il.
58   RIGBY, S. H., Urban decline in the later middle ages. *UHY* (1979) 46–59.
59   TODOROV, N., *La ville balkanique sous les Ottomans XV–XIXes*. Variorum 1977. pp 310, il.

Modern
60   ALLISON, G. D., Japanese cities in the industrial era. *JUH* 4 (1978) 443–76.
61   APPELBAUM, R. P. & FOLLETT, R., Size, growth and urban life: a study of medium sized American cities. *UAQ* 14 (1978) 139–68.
62   ARONSON, D. R., Capitalism and culture in Ibadan urban development. *UAn* 7 (1978) 253–70.
63   BAAR, L., 'Zur Industrialisierung, Urbanisierung und zu Veränderungen der städischen Sozialstruktur während der industriellen Revolution in Deutschland' in FLINN, M. ed, *Proceedings of the seventh International Economic History Congress I*. Edinburgh: Edinburgh UP 1978. pp 90–100.
64   BARKIN, D., 'Confronting the separation of town and country in Cuba' in Tabb & Sawers, *Marxism and the metropolis* [848] 317–37.
65   CORNELIUS, W. A. & KEMPER, R. V., *Metropolitan Latin America: the challenge and the response*. Beverly Hills: Sage 1978.
66   CROCKETT, N. L., *The black towns*. Lawrence, Kan: Regents P of Kansas 1979.
67   CROSS, M., *Urbanization and urban growth in the Caribbean: an essay on social change in dependent societies*. Cambridge UP 1979. pp xii + 174.
68   FEAGIN, J. R. comp, *The urban scene: myths and realities*. New York: Random House 1979.
69   FIREBAUGH, G., Structural determinants of urbanization in Asia and Latin America 1950–1970. *ASR* 44 (1979) 199–215.
70   GAUBE, H., *Iranian cities*. New York: New York UP 1978.
71   GLISKMAN, N. J., *The growth and management of the Japanese urban system*. New York: Academic P 1979.
72   GOLDFIELD, D. R. & BROWNELL, B. A., *Urban America from downtown to no town*. Boston: Houghton Mifflin 1979. pp xi + 435.
73   GORDON, D. M., 'Capitalist development and the history of American cities' in Tabb & Sawers, *Marxism and the metropolis* [848] 25–63.
74   GUGLER, J., *Urbanization and social change in West Africa*. New York: Cambridge UP 1978.
75   HOLZNER, L., Urbanism in West Germany: an alternative case of modernization. *UPP* 6 (1978) 22–8.
76   HURST, W. & PULLEN, G., *Urban growth in New South Wales*. Sydney: Dept. of Decentralisation and Development 1978. pp 22, il.
77   LEVINE, H. B. & M. W., *Urbanization in Papua New Guinea: a study of ambivalent townsmen*. Cambridge: Cambridge UP 1979. pp 161.
78   MERCANDINO, *Storia del territorio e delle città d'Italia. Dal 1800 ai giorni nostri*. Milan: Mazzotta 1976. pp 394.
79   ONOKERHORAYE, A. G., The urban system and national integration in Nigeria.

JBIS 9 (1978) 169–80.

80 PERNIA, E. del M., *Urbanization, population growth and economic development in the Philippines*. Westport, Ct: Greenwood P 1977. pp xvi + 213, il.

81 PERRY, D. C. & WATKINS, A. J. eds, *The rise of the sunbelt cities*. Beverly Hills, Cal: Sage 1978.

82 RIFKIND, C., *Main Street: the face of urban America*. New York: Harper & Row 1978.

83 ROBERTS, H., *An urban profile of the Middle East*. New York: St Martins P 1979.

84 ROMANOS, M. C., ed, *Western European cities in crisis*. Lexington, Mass: Lexington Books 1979.

85 TOBIN, G. A., ed, *The changing structure of the city: what happened to the urban crisis?* Beverly Hills, Cal: Sage 1979.

86 VAN DIJK, H., 'Urbanization and social change in the Netherlands during the nineteenth century' in FLINN M ed, *Proceedings of the seventh International Economic History Congress I*. Edinburgh: Edinburgh UP 1978. pp 101–9.

87 WIRTH, J. D. & JONES, R. L., eds, *Manchester and Sao Paolo: problems of rapid urban growth*. Stanford, Cal: Stanford UP 1978.

HISTORY AND FORTUNES OF INDIVIDUAL TOWNS

This section is arranged alphabetically by the name of the town

88 GRIFFITHS, R. A., 'Aberystwyth' in Griffiths, *Boroughs of Medieval Wales* [52] 19–46.

89 VERSCHUER, M., *Echoes of the past* [Albany, WA]. Victoria Park, WA: J. Kohlen 1978. pp 139, il.

90 RAPER, A. C., *Andover, the Civil War and interregnum*. Andover: Andover Local Archives Cttee 1978. pp 56, il.

91 GATES, G. H., *The model city of the new South – Anniston, Alabama 1872–1900*. Huntsville, Ala: Strode Publishers 1978.

92 CARTLAND, J. comp, *Arundel: a picture of the past*. Chichester: Phillimore 1978. pp 79, il.

93 *The history and topography of Ashbourne, the valley of the Dove and the adjacent villages with biographical sketches of eminent natures*. Buxton: Moorland Publishing Co 1978. pp ix + 380, il. [reprint of 1838 edn]

94 PILKINGTON, F., *Ashburton: the Dartmoor town*. Ashburton: author 1978. pp 136, il.

95 JACKSON, A. A., *Ashstead: a village transformed: a history of Ashstead from the earliest times to the present day*. Leatherhead: Leatherhead & District Local History Society 1977. pp 237, il.

96 WILCOXON, G. D., *Athens ascendant*. Ames, Iowa: Iowa State UP 1978.

97 BATE, W. A., *Lucky city: the first generation at Ballarat 1851–1901*. Carlton South, Vic: Melbourne UP 1978. pp xv + 302, il.

98 GOSLING, S., *A changing landscape: Banbury and the Cherwell valley*. Oxford: Oxford County Council Dept. of Museum Services 1978. pp 38, il.

99 FERRAS, R., *Barcelone, croissance d'une métropole*. Paris: Anthropos 1978. pp 616.

100 BARNES, F., *Barrow and district*. Barrow in Furness: Barrow in Furness Corporation 1978. pp 139, il.

101 *Barton on Humber in the 1850s*. Barton on Humber: Barton on Humber WEA Vol 1 Leisure and pleasure 1977 pp 56, il. Vol 2 The town and the people 1978. pp 90, il.

102 HAMILTON, M., *Bath before Beau Nash: a guide based on Gilmore's map of Bath 1692–4*. Bath: Kingsmead 1978. pp 77, il.

103 MILWARD, R. J., *Belper in bygone years*. Belper: author 1978. pp 27, il.

104 PECK, G. C., *Biggleswade: the history of a small market town*. Bedford: Bedfordshire County Library 1977. pp 48, il.

105 BIRD, V., *Portrait of Birmingham*. 3rd edn. Hale 1979. pp 239, il.

106 WILLMOTT, J., *The book of Bodmin: a portrait of the town*. Chesham: Barracuda Books 1977. pp 3–120, il.

107 ACKERMAN, E. B., *Village on the Seine: tradition and change in Bonnières 1815–1914*. Ithaca, NY: Cornell UP 1978.

108 CANTRILL, E., *Centenary history of Boremore*. Boremore, NSW: Boremore School Centenary Celebrations Cttee 1978. pp 58, il.

109 YOUNG, J. A., *The village of Pokesdown* [Bournemouth]. Bournemouth: Bournemouth Local Studies Publications 1978. pp 30, il.

110 YOUNG, J. A., *Southbourne on Sea 1870–1901* [Bournemouth]. Bournemouth: Bournemouth Local Studies Publications 1978. pp 20, il.

111 LANS, S. J., *The growth of Winton* [Bournemouth]. Bournemouth: Bournemouth Local Studies Publications 1978. pp 44, il.

112 LEMON, A. G. F., *Box Hill*. Melbourne: Box Hill City Council 1978. pp xiv + 270, il.

113 DAVIES, R. R., 'Brecon' in Griffiths, *Boroughs of Medieval Wales* [52] 47–72.
114 *Bygone Bridlington*. Bridlington: Augustinian Society 1978. pp 19, il.
115 UNDERWOOD, E., *Brighton*. Batsford 1978. pp 176, il.
116 *Brisbane retrospect: eight aspects of Brisbane history: proceedings of a seminar conducted by the John Oxley library . . . 5–6 June 1976*. Brisbane: Library Board of Queensland 1978. pp 154, il.
117 MCCLURG, J. H. C., *Historical sketches of Brisbane*. Brisbane: Library Board of Queensland 1975. pp xi + 121, il.
118 MARSHALL, P., *Bristol and the American war of independence*. Bristol: Historical Association 1979.
119 MORGAN, C., *Briton Ferry*. Briton Ferry: author 1977. pp 128, il.
120 HALL, B., *Burnley*. Burnley: Burnley and District Historical Society 1977. pp 40, il.
121 STUART, D., *County borough: the history of Burton upon Trent 1901–1974*. Burton: Charter Trustees. Pt 2 1914–1974 1977 pp 8 + 299, il.
122 LONGMAN, G., *Bushey then and now*. Watford: Enstones 1978. pp 16, il.
123 WILLIAMS-JONES, K., 'Caernarvon' in Griffiths, *Boroughs of medieval Wales* [52] 73–102.
124 JONES, G. G., *Chronicl Caerffili: a collection of notes relating to Caerphilly's past*, Beckenham: author. No 6 1979 pp 69, il.
125 WESLEY, A., *An introduction to the history of Caloundra*. Landsborough, Q: Shire of Landsborough Historical Society Museum 1977. pp 40, il.
126 BROOKS, J. A., *Historic Cambridge*. Norwich: Jarrold 1978. pp 35, il.
127 LEWIS, C. R., A stage in the development of an industrial town: a case study of Cardiff 1845–75. *IBG* 4 (1979) 129–52.
128 WALKER, D. G., 'Cardiff' in Griffiths, *Boroughs of medieval Wales* [52] 103–30.
129 GRIFFITHS, R. A., 'Carmarthen' in Griffiths, *Boroughs of medieval Wales* [52] 131–64.
130 POWER, P. C., *Carrick-on-Suir and its people*. Dun Laoghaire: Anna Livia Books 1976. pp 192, il.
131 BRIGHTLING, G. B., *Some particulars relating to the history and antiquities of Carshalton*. Sutton: London Borough of Sutton Libraries & Art Services 1978. pp 144, il.
132 BRADFIELD, R. A., *The north end, Castlemaine: some early history*. Pearcedale, Vic: author 1978. pp 52, il.
133 SQUIRE, C., *Cheadle Hulme: a brief history*. Stockport: Borough of Stockport 1976. pp 32, il.
134 CONCINA, E., *Chioggia. Saggio di storia urbanistica dalla formazione al 1870*. Treviso: Canova 1977. pp 258, il.
135 MARSHALL, J. D., Cleator and Cleator Moor: some aspects of their social and urban development in the mid 19th century. *CWAAS* 78 (1978) 163–76.
136 ROYLE, S. A., The development of Coalville, Leicestershire in the 19th century. *EMG* 7 (1978) 32–42.
137 BERSON, M., *Cockburn: the making of a community*. Cockburn, WA: Town of Cockburn 1978. pp x + 244, il.
138 STEPHENSON, D., *The book of Colchester*. Chesham: Barracuda Books 1978. pp 144, il.
139 *The burning of Cork City by British forces, December 1920*. Cork: South Gate Books 1978. pp xv + 117, il.
140 JAMES, R. M., *Heritage of pines: a history of the town of Cottesloe Western Australia*. Cottesloe, WA: Town of Cottesloe Council 1977. pp ix + 133, il.
141 MARTINEZ, O., *Border boom town: Cuidad Juarez since 1848*. Austin, Tex: Texas UP 1978.
142 PHILLIPS, C. R., *Cuidad Real 1500–1750: growth, crisis and readjustment in Spanish economy*. Cambridge, Mass: Harvard UP 1978.
143 OWEN, D. H., 'Denbigh' in Griffiths, *Boroughs of medieval Wales* [52] 165–88.
144 LINGHAM, B. F. & HALL, M. J., *The changing face of Didcot*. Didcot: Didcot & District Historical Society 1977. pp 32, il.
145 LINGHAM, B. F., *The long years of obscurity: a history of Didcot*. Didcot: Gem Graphic Services, Vol 1 To 1841 1978 pp 148, il.
146 GREEN, I., *The book of Dover: Cinque port, port of the passage, gateway to England*. Chesham: Barracuda Books 1978. pp 3–144, il.
147 HOLYOAKE, A. V., *Dear little Droitwich*. Bromsgrove: Market Place P 1977. pp 61, il.
148 COSGRAVE, D., *North Dublin*. Dublin: Four Courts Press 1977. pp 132, il. [reprint of 1909 edn].
149 MALTON, J., *A picturesque and descriptive view of the city of Dublin*. Dublin: Dolmen P 1978. pp xiv + 18 [55], il. [reprint of 1799 edn].
150 PARKER, R., *Men of Dunwich: the story of a vanished town*. Collins 1978. pp 272, il.
151 MCWILLIAM, C., *New Town guide: the story of Edinburgh's Georgian new town*. Edin-

burgh: Edinburgh New Town Conservation Cttee 1978. pp 30, il.

152 BUSH, R., *The book of Exmouth: portrait of a resort.* Buckingham: Barracuda Books 1978. pp 3–148, il.

153 TALBOT, R., *Fenton: the town Arnold Bennett forgot.* Fenton: Manor Youth and Adult Centre 1977. pp 112, il.

154 TOSHIKIDO, K., The conflicting philosophies of gain and abundance in my hometown [Fuji City]. *JQ* 26 (1979) 188–98.

155 LANE, J. B., *City of the century: a history of Gary. Indiana.* Bloomington, Ind: Indiana UP 1978.

156 COOMBE, E. H., *History of Gawler 1837–1908.* Hampstead Gardens, SA: Austaprint 1978. pp 427, il.

157 LOYAU, G. E., *The Gawler handbook: a record of the rise and progress of that important town, to which are added memoirs of McKinley the explorer and Dr Nott.* Hampstead Gardens, SA: Austaprint 1978. pp 180, il. [reprint of 1880 edn]

158 SEATON, G. D., *The Ashby story: a history of Geelong West.* Geelong, Vic: Geelong West City Council 1978. pp 276, il.

159 PRITCHARD, K. O., *Gilfach Coch in cameo.* Gilfach Goch: author. Vol 3 1978 pp 100, il.

160 FORTESQUE, S. E. D., *People and places, Great and Little Bookham.* Great Bookham: author 1978. pp xiii + 111, il.

161 MONFRIES, J. E., ed, *A history of Gumeracha and district, SA 1839–1939.* Blackwood, SA: Lynton Publications 1978. pp 173. [reprint of 1939 edn]

162 PORRITT, A. & OGDEN, J., *Halifax old and new.* Wakefield: EP Publishing 1978. pp 79, il.

163 FERRIDAY, D. R. P., *Vintage Hartlepool.* Nelson: Hendon Publishing Co 1978. pp 44, il.

164 SHARP, C., *History of Hartlepool.* Hartlepool: Hartlepool Borough Council 1978. pp 207, 138 [68], 28, il. [reprint of 1851 edn]

165 DYER, W. H., *Hastings and district in 900 years of history 1066–1966.* Hastings: Hastings Tourism and Recreation Dept 1978. pp 144, il.

166 STONE, C. R. & TYSON, P., *Old Hobart town and environs 1802–1855.* Lilydale, Vic: Pioneer Design 1978. pp 208, il.

167 HAYES, J., *The Hong Kong region 1850–1911: institutions and leadership in town and countryside.* Hamden: Archon; Folkestone: Dawson 1977. pp 289.

168 WILLY, F., *A short history of Hove.* Brighton: Brighton and Hove Environmental Studies Association 1978. pp 34, il.

169 ABBOTT, C., Indianapolis in the 1850s: popular economic thought and urban growth. *InMH* 74 (1978) 293–315.

170 LONSDALE, J. M., *Gateway to the west: a record of early Inverleigh.* Inverleigh, Vic: Back to Inverleigh Cttee 1978. pp 49, il.

171 BROWN, A. T. & DORSETT, L. W., *K.C.: a history of Kansas City, Missouri.* Boulder, Colo: Pruett Publishing Co 1978.

172 GOODEN, G. W. & MOORE, T., *Fifty years history of the town of Kensington and Norwood, SA July 1853–July 1903.* Hampstead Gardens: Austaprint 1978. pp 245, il.

173 HILLEN, H. J., *History of the borough of Kings Lynn.* Wakefield: EP Publishing 1978. 2 vols pp 965, il. [reprint of 1907 edn]

174 BELLARS, M., *Kingston then and now: a loyal tribute for the silver jubilee of Queen Elizabeth II.* Esher: Michael Lancel 1977. pp 120, il.

175 *Village into town: Royal Leamington Spa.* Leamington Spa: Warwickshire County Libraries 1977. pp 24, il.

176 DREW, J. H., *The book of Royal Leamington Spa: the last great English spa.* Buckingham: Barracuda Books 1978. pp 3–137, il.

177 ACKERS, N., *An outline history of Leigh.* Leigh: Leigh Local History Society 1978. pp 16, il.

178 *Letchworth Garden City 1903–1978: catalogue of exhibits of a commemorative exhibition 22 July–22 December 1978.* Letchworth: North Herts District Council 1978. pp 85, il.

179 HILLINGS, J. B., *Llandaf past and present.* Barry: S Williams 1978. pp 108, il.

180 ASHTON, R., Stow's London. *LoMAS* 29 (1978) 137–43.

181 BIRD, J., et al eds, *Collectanea Londiniensa: studies in London archaeology and history presented to Ralph Merrifield.* London and Middlesex Archaeological Society 1978. pp 479, il.

182 BORER, M. C., *A history of Berkeley Square.* Berkeley Square Jubilee Association 1978. pp 25, il.

183 CHARLTON, J., ed, *The Tower of London: its buildings and institutions.* HMSO 1978. pp 160, il.

184 GRAY, R., *A history of London.* Hutchinson 1978. pp 352, il.

185 HAMMOND, P., *Royal fortress: the Tower of London through nine centuries*. HMSO 1978. pp 62, il.
186 KINGSFORD, C. L. ed, *The chronicles of London*. Dursley: A Sutton 1977. pp xlvii + 368, il. [reprint of 1905 edn]
187 LINDSAY, J., *The monster city: Defoe's London 1688–1730*. Hart Davis MacGibbon 1978. pp viii + 220, il.
188 MILFORD, A., *Ring the bells of London town*. Lavenham: T Dalton 1978. pp x + 154, il.
189 MULGAN, C., *London: an illustrated history*. Arnold 1979. pp 119, il.
190 PEARL, V., Change and stability in 17th century London. *LJ* 5 (1979) 3–35.
191 STUDD, S., *Puddle Dock*. Peat, Marwick, Mitchell Co 1976. pp 14.
192 WILSON, D. A., *The Tower 1078–1978*. Hamilton 1978. pp x + 257, il.
193 BOAST, M., *The story of Bermondsey*. Borough of Southwark 1978. pp 30, il.
194 ROBINSON, A. J., *The Green: a history of the heart of Bethnal Green and the legend of the Blind Beggar*. Borough of Tower Hamlets 1978. pp 43, il.
195 *The island: the life and death of a London community 1870–1970* [Hackney]. Centre-prise 1979. pp 72, il.
196 MACROBERT, S., *Putney: a brief history*. Putney Society 1978. pp 58, il.
197 AUDIN, A., *Lyon miroir de Rome*. Paris: 1979. pp 304.
198 BLACKMAN, G. R. & LARKIN, J., *Australia's first notable town* [Maldon]. Sydney: Hodder & Stoughton 1978. pp 144, il.
199 SMITH, B. S., *A history of Malvern*. 2nd edn. Gloucester: A Sutton 1978. pp ix + 310, il.
200 SHERCLIFF, W. H., *Manchester: a short history of its development*. Manchester: Man-chester Public Relations Office 1977. pp 68, il.
201 KEMPSON, E. G. H. & MURRAY, G. W., *Marlborough: town and countryside*. Ando-versford: Whittington P 1978. pp iii–xv + 84, il.
202 GRANT, J. & SERLE, G. eds, *The Melbourne scene 1803–1956*. Neutral Bay, NSW: Hale & Ironmonger 1978. pp xviii + 308.
203 MCWILLIAM, G. B., *Hawthorn peppercorns* [Melbourne]. Melbourne: B. Atkins 1978. pp 171, il.
204 *Nutshell History of Merton*. Merton Library Service 1979. pp 12, il.
205 CURZON, J. B., Middlewich: a town of the industrial revolution. *ChesH* 3 (1979) 40–4.
206 BURROWS, K., *Mildenhall between the World Wars 1919–39*. Mildenhall: Riverside Middle School 1977. pp 29, il.
207 BURROWS, K., *Mildenhall in modern times 1945–1977*. Mildenhall: Riverside Middle School 1977. pp 27, il.
208 BURROWS, K., *Mildenhall, the Suffolk regiment and the Great War*. Mildenhall: River-side Middle School 1978. pp 69, il.
209 TAVENAUX, R. et al, *Histoire de Nancy*. Toulouse: Privat 1978. pp 480.
210 GARTON, E., *Nantwich in the eighteenth century: a study of 18th century life and affairs*. Chester: Cheshire Libraries and Museums 1978. pp 90, il.
211 COCKS, C. J., *Notes on Fort Perch Rock, New Brighton, Merseyside and of its garrison from 1826–1956*. Wallasey: author 1977. pp 21, il.
212 PATTERSON, J. E., *Unfinished city: a history of New York*. New York: H. N. Abrams 1978.
213 CHARLETON, R. J., *Newcastle town*. Newcastle: F. Graham 1978. pp iv + 443, il. [reprint of 1885 edn]
214 REEVES, A. C., 'Newport' in Griffiths, *Boroughs of medieval Wales* [52] pp 189–218.
215 *Glimpses of old Newtownards*. Newtownards: Ards Historical Society 1977. pp 60, il.
216 *North Shields, working class politics and housing 1900–1977*. North Tyneside CDP 1978. pp 79, il.
217 *Aspects of life and work in North Thoresby in the 19th century*. North Thoresby Local History Group 1978. pp 105.
218 DYER, A., Northampton in 1524. *NPP* 6 (1979) 73–80.
219 BRYSON, E., *Portrait of Nottingham*. 2nd edn. Hale 1978. pp 208, il.
220 SMITH, L. B., 'Oswestry' in Griffiths, *Boroughs of medieval Wales* [52] 219–44.
221 FASNACHT, R., *Summertown since 1820* [Oxford]. Oxford: St Michaels Publications 1977. pp ix + 111, il.
222 GOSLING, N., *The adventurous world of Paris 1900–1914*. New York: W. Morrow 1978.
223 MOUSNIER, R., *Paris, capitale au temps de Richelieu et Mazarin*. Paris: Pedone 1978. pp 310.
224 *Peacehaven*. Lewes: East Sussex County Library 1979. pp 12, il.
225 BUCHANAN, L. D., *Stories from Perth's history*. Perth: Melven P. 1978. pp 104, il.
226 ROBERTS, A., *New roots: a history of Lynwood and Ferndale* [Perth]. Riverton, WA: Canning P 1978. pp 30, il.
227 TEBBS, H. F., *Peterborough*. Cambridge: Oleander P 1978. pp 200, il.
228 HAMMOND, M., *History of Port Adelaide: chronology 1831–1978*. Port Adelaide: Port

Adelaide Central Mission 1978. pp 30, il.

229 FOSTER, D., Poulton-le-Fylde: a 19th century market town. *HSLC* 127 (1978) 91–108.

230 LEVIN, L. L., *Providence: from provincial village to prosperous port 1750–1790*. Providence, RI: Rhode Island Historical Society 1978.

231 LAWSON, J., *Progress in Pudsey*. Firle: Caliban Books 1978. pp 154, il. [reprint of 1887 edn]

232 *Quorn and district centenary 1878–1978*. Blackwood, SA: Lynton 1978. pp 240, il.

233 NORTH, L., *Reading's colourful past*. Peppard Common: Cressrelles 1979. pp 120, il.

234 CUSDEN, P. E., *Coley: portrait of an urban village*. Reading: WEA 1977. pp 94, il.

235 LLOYD, F., *Woodley in the nineteenth century*. Reading: Reading Libraries 1977. pp 96, il.

236 MITCHELL, F., *Annals of an ancient Cornish town: being notes on the history of Redruth*. Redruth: author 1978. pp 247.

237 DESPORTES, P., *Reims et les Rémois au XIIIe et XIVe siècles*. Paris: Picard 1978. pp 746.

238 GARNETT, R., *Richmond on the Thames*. Petersham: Manor House P 1977. pp 108, il. [reprint of 1896 edn]

239 BURCH, C. R. ed, *Rickmansworth: a glimpse of the past*. Rickmansworth: M & R Printing Services 1977. pp 62, il.

240 CRYER, L. R., *A history of Retford*. Phillimore 1978. pp 225, il.

241 WALLACE, A. F. C., *Rockdale: the growth of an American village in the early industrial revolution*. New York: Knopf 1978.

242 GRANT, M., *History of Rome*. New York: Scribners 1978.

243 KRAUTHEIMER, R., *Rome, profile of a city from Constantine to the middle ages*. Princeton, NJ: Princeton UP 1979.

244 MOLLAT, M. et al, *Histoire de Rouen*. Toulouse: Privat 1979. pp 444.

245 JACK, R. I., 'Ruthin' in Griffiths, *Boroughs of medieval Wales* [52] 245–62.

246 RUNCIE, R., *Cathedral and city: St Albans ancient and modern*. St Albans: Martyn Associates 1977. pp 149, il.

247 FOLEY, W. E., St Louis: the first hundred years. *MisHSB* 34 (1978) 187–99.

248 BURNETT, D., *Salisbury: the history of an English cathedral city*. Tisbury: Compton P 1978. pp 94, il.

249 MCGLOIN, J. B., *San Francisco, the story of a city*. San Rafael, Cal: Presido P 1978.

250 WILLIAMS, J. C., Cultural tension: the origins of American Santa Barbara. *SCalQ* 60 (1978) 349–78.

251 *Sao Paulo, growth and poverty: a report from the Sao Paulo Justice and Peace Commission*. Bowerdean P 1978. pp 128.

252 ASTELL, J. A., *An introduction to the history of Seaford with a description of its historic buildings*. Seaford: Seaford Museum of Local History 1977. pp 10, il.

253 *150th anniversary of Seaham*. Burrow 1978. pp 24, il.

254 SYDENHAM, L., *Shaftesbury and its abbey*. Blandford: Oakwood P 1978. pp 138, il.

255 VICKERS, J. E., *A popular history of Sheffield: with a guide to places, buildings and things of interest*. Wakefield: EP Publishing 1978. pp xii + 164, il.

256 TURNBULL, C. M., *A history of Singapore 1819–1975*. New York: Oxford UP 1978.

257 SILAG, W., Sioux City: an Iowa boom town. *AI* 44 (1979) 587–601.

258 JONES, A. D., *Snowtown: the first century 1878–1978*. Snowtown, SA: Snowtown Centenary Cttee 1978. pp 344, il.

259 CURTIS, W., *Southsea: its story*. Alresford: Bay Tree Publishing Co 1978. pp 72, il.

260 SEARLE, A. E., *Springwood notebook 1788–1979: a miscellaneous collection of facts*. Springwood, NSW: Springwood History Society 1978. pp ii + 30, il.

261 PECK, F., *Academia tertia anglicana, or, The antiquarian annals of Stanford*. Wakefield: EP Publishing 1979. pp 708, il. [reprint of 1727 edn]

262 LANON, T., *Stirling's road to mass culture: a local history of social change*. Stirling: author 1979. pp 28, il.

263 BAINES, C., *Stockport: a town on the Mersey*. Stockport: Stockport Metropolitan Borough 1977. pp 66, il.

264 ANDERSON, J. H. A., *The history of Stonehouse*. Gloucester: Gloucestershire County Library 1977. pp 16, il.

265 *Old Sunderland*. Newcastle upon Tyne: Tyne and Wear County Council 1977. pp 30, il.

266 ROBINSON, W. R. B., 'Swansea' in Griffiths, *Boroughs of medieval Wales* [52] 263–88.

267 KELLY, M., *Nineteenth century Sydney: essays in urban history*. Sydney: Sydney UP 1978. pp viii + 135, il.

268 GORDON, G., *Harbord, Queenscliff and South Curl Curl 1788–1975* [Sydney]. 2nd edn. Harbord, NSW: author 1978. pp 116, il.

269 KELLY, M., *Paddock full of houses: Paddington 1840–1890* [Sydney]. Paddington, NSW: Doak P 1978. pp 208, il.

270   JERVIS, J., *The beginnings of the settlement in the parish of Castle Hill*. Sydney Castle Hill, NSW: Hills District Historical Society 1978. pp 44, il.
271   MUIR, L., *A history of Cook's River* [Sydney]. Belmore, NSW: author 1978. pp 9, il.
272   THORNE, L. G., *North Shore Sydney from 1788 to today*. Sydney: Angus & Robertson 1979.
273   MILLER, R. B., *City and hinterland: a case study of urban growth and regional development* [Syracuse, NY]. Westport, Conn: Greenwood P 1979.
274   HOBDEN, J., *Tamworth: a look at bygone days*. Tamworth, NSW: Tamworth Historical Society 1978. pp 56, il.
275   COURT, G. & HOBDEN, J., *Tamworth: the changing scene*. Tamworth, NSW: Tamworth Historical Society 1977. pp 56, il.
276   DAVIES, E. J., Elite migration and urban growth: the rise of Wilkes Barre in the northern anthracite region 1820–1880. *PenH* 45 (1978) 291–314.
277   DUNSTAN, M. B., *Willunga town and district 1837–1900*. Blackwood, SA: Lynton Publications 1977. pp 143, il.
278   DUNSTAN, M. B., *Willunga town and district 1901–1925*. Blackwood, SA: Lynton publications 1978. pp 175, il.
279   *The changing face of Windsor*. Windsor: Windsor Local History Publications Group Pt 1 The beginnings 1977. pp 33, il.
280   STEEL, J., *Early days of Windsor, NSW*. North Sydney NSW: Library of Australian History 1977. pp 268 [reprint of 1916 edn]
281   MARSDEN, N. S., *Chronology 1836–1976* [Woodville 1836–1976]. Woodville, SA: Woodville Council 1977. pp 27, il.
282   MARSDEN, S., *A history of Woodville*. Woodville, SA: City of Woodville Corporation 1977. pp 332, il.
283   LINDLEY, E. S., *Wotton under Edge: men and affairs of a Cotswold wool town*. Dursley: A Sutton 1977. pp 345, il.
284   FEILMAN, M. A., *An historical survey of the York townsite, WA for the Shire of York*. West Perth, WA: author 1977. pp 45, il.
285   BAYLEY, W. A., *Rich earth: a history of Young, NSW*. Young, NSW: Young Municipal Council 1977. pp 231, il.

PORTRAITS OF TOWNS – LITERARY, PHOTOGRAPHIC AND GRAPHIC

This section is arranged alphabetically by the name of the town

Literary portrayals and personal reminiscences see also 636
286   REID, L. D., *Hurry home Wednesday: growing up in a small Missouri town*. Columbia, Mo: Missouri UP 1978.
287   SHAW, C., *When I was a child* [Potteries]. Firle: Caliban Books 1977. pp vii + 258, il.
288   MCKENZIE, H., *No town like Alice*. Adelaide: Rigby 1979.
289   HAREVEN, T. K. & LANGENBACH, R., *Amoskeag: the oral history of a factory city*. New York: Pantheon Books 1978.
290   VEAR L.E.W., *South of the Avon: glimpses of old Bedminster life*. Wotton under Edge: author 1978.
291   MCAUGHTRY, S., *Play it again Sam* [Belfast]. Belfast: Blackstaff P 1978. pp 95, il.
292   MACCOIL, L., *The book of Blackrock, Co. Dublin through the ages*. Blackrock: Carraig Books 1977.
293   *Bristol as we remember it*. Bristol: Bristol Broadsides 1978. pp 28, il.
294   *Looking back on Bristol: Hartcliffe people remember*. Bristol: Bristol Broadsides 1978. pp 34, il.
295   *Up Knowle West* [Bristol]. Bristol: Knowle West TV Workshop Bristol Broadsides 1977. pp 31, il.
296   HARVEY, R. W., *A Bristol childhood*. Bristol: WEA 1978. pp 28, il.
297   YOUNGER, W. L., ed. *Old Brooklyn in early photographs 1865–1929*. New York: Dover Pubs 1978.
298   LOPE, H. J., 'La ville de Bruxelles rue par Don Diego Alejandro de Gálvez'in MORTIER, R. & HASQUIN, H. eds, *Études sur le XVIIIe siècle*. Brussels: Editions de l'Université de Bruxelles 1979. pp 181–98.
299   MARTIN, G., *Episodes of old Canberra*. Canberra: Australian National UP 1978. pp 96, il.
300   JEFFREYS, D. E., *Maritime memories of Cardiff*. Risca: Starling P 1978. pp 89, il.
301   KOHLER, M. K., *Memories of old Dorking*. Dorking: Kohler & Coombs 1977. pp 252, il. [reprint of 1878 edn].
302   *Dundee: an evocation of town life before the War: from memories collected from local residents*. Blairgowrie: Three Cats P 1978. pp 54, il.

303 TWIST, S., *Faversham 1901–1910*. Faversham: Faversham Society 1977. pp 72, il.
304 HANLEY, C., *Dancing in the streets* [Glasgow]. White Lion Publishers 1979. pp 272, il.
305 WEIR, M., *Best foot forward* [Glasgow]. Bath: Chivers 1979. pp 380, il.
306 ROWE, A., *Boy at the Commercial* [Hereford]. Faber 1978. pp 3–134.
307 GADSBY, E., *Black diamonds, yellow apples: a working class Derbyshire childhood between the wars* [Ilkeston]. Ilkeston: Scollins & Tilford 1978. pp 70, il.
308 TOMKINSON, K., *Characters of Kidderminster*. Kidderminster: author 1977. pp 283, il.
309 THOMASON, M., *Selections from 'Warp and Weft'* [Leigh]. Leigh: Leigh Local History Society 1977. pp 51, il.
310 FORRESTER, H., *Minerva's stepchild* [Liverpool]. Bodley Head 1979. pp 224.
311 FORRESTER, H., *Twopence to cross the Mersey* [Liverpool]. Bodley Head 1979. pp 224.
312 'A street door of our own': a short history of life on an LCC estate. Honor Oak Estate Neighbourhood Association 1977. pp 50, il.
313 BLAKE, J., *Memories of old Poplar*. Stepney Books Publications 1977. pp 48, il.
314 ELIAS, E., *On Sundays we wore white* [London] W. H. Allen, 1978. pp 270, il.
315 GISSING, G., *London and the life of literature in late Victorian England: the diary of George Gissing novelist*. Hassocks: Harvester P 1978. pp vii + 617, il.
316 HALL, E., *Country girls and stockpots* [London]. Luton: WEA 1977. pp 55, il.
317 HARTOG, A., *Born to sing* [East End]. Dobson 1978.
318 HARRIS, H., *Under oars: reminiscences of a Thames lighterman 1894–1909*. Centreprise 1978. pp 47, il.
319 HUGHES, M. V., *A London girl of the 1880s*. Oxford: Oxford UP 1978. pp v + 245, il.
320 HUGHES, M. V., *A London home in the 1890s*. Oxford: Oxford UP 1978. pp 208, il.
321 JACOBS, J., *Out of the ghetto: my youth in the East End: communism and fascism 1913–1939*. Janet Simon 1978. pp 319, il.
322 WILLMOTT, P., *Growing up in a London village: family life between the wars* [Lee]. Owen 1978. pp 143.
323 HART, J., *The Nailsea I knew 1910–1918*. Nailsea: Nailsea Local History Society 1977. pp 19, il.
324 CALLAGHAN, T., *A lang way to the pa'nshop* [Newcastle]. Newcastle upon Tyne: F. Graham 1978. pp 112, il.
325 TAYLOR, L. & G. eds, *Within living memory: recollections of old Headington* [Oxford]. Headington: Friends of old Headington 1978. pp 72, il.
326 BAILLIE, P. J., *Port Lincoln and district: a pictorial history*. Blackwood, SA: Lynton Pubs 1978. pp 168, il.
327 RYAN, P. M., *Rochester recollected: a miscellany of eighteenth and nineteenth century descriptions*. *RocH* 41 (1979) 1–48.
328 BRERETON, W., *Salford boy*. Salford: Salford Local History Society 1977. pp 57, il.
329 RADCLIFFE, H. W., *Reminiscences* [Stalybridge]. Romily: author 1978. pp 31, il.
330 FORMAN, C., ed, *Industrial town: self portrait of St Helens in the 1920s*. Cameron & Tayleur 1978. pp 278, il.
331 PURSEY, W., *Reminiscences of life in the parish of Street, Somersetshire from the year 1844*. Bridgwater: Somerset County Library 1977. pp 34, il.
332 WORGAN, G. B., *Journal of a first fleet surgeon* [Sydney settlement]. Sydney: Library Council of NSW 1978. pp xiii + 71, il.
333 STAGG, W., *Stagg of Tarcowie: the diaries of a colonial teenager*. Jamestown, SA: Najuri Australia 1977. pp 125, il.
334 BRAGG, M., *Speak for England: an essay on England 1900–1975 based on interviews with inhabitants of Wigton, Cumbria*. Coronet 1978. pp 464, il.

Photographic portrayals
335 TEMPLETON, J. P., *North Cumberland: life in villages and towns round Carlisle: a photographic recollection*. Clapham: Dalesman 1977. pp 80, il.
336 PRATT BOORMAN, H. R., *Ashford's progress: the development of an important town*. Maidstone: Kent Messenger 1977. pp 203, il.
337 DOW, G., *Audlem then and now*. Audlem: Audlem District Amenities Society 1977. pp 41, il.
338 PETERS, J., et al, *Bournemouth then and now*. Poole: Blandford P 1978. pp 224, il.
339 WILLIAMS, D. E., *Old Bridgend in photographs*. Barry: S. Williams 1978. pp 120, il.
340 MACEFIELD, W. J., *Bridgnorth as it was*. Nelson: Hendon Publishing Co 1978. pp 44, il.
341 JONES, H. C., *Old Caerphilly and district in photographs*. Barry: S. Williams 1979. pp 120, il.
342 TEMPLETON, J., *Old Carlisle: a second photographic recollection*. Clapham: Dalesman 1978. pp 80, il.

343 BURGESS, F., *Old Cheam: a photographic record and commentary.* Sutton: Sutton Libraries and Art Services 1978. pp 62, il.

344 BIRCH, C. & ARMISTEAD, J., *Chesham: a medley of memory and fact in the eye of the past.* Chesham: Barracuda Books 1977. pp 3–132, il.

345 HEYES, J. T., *An album of old Chorley: a collection of photographs and illustrations.* Preston: Lancashire CC 1978. pp 55, il.

346 BUCHANAN, V., *A look at old Darwen.* Preston: Lancashire CC 1978. pp 48, il.

347 BARHAM, F., *Old Cornwall in camera and Falmouth.* Falmouth: Glasney P 1977. pp 96, il.

348 DUNDON, G., *More old Gosford and district in pictures.* Gosford South, NSW: author 1978. pp 100, il.

349 ALEXANDER, M., ed, *Guildford as it was,* Nelson: Hendon Publishing Co 1978. pp 48, il.

350 ASPIN, C. & PILKINGTON, D., *Helmshore.* Helmshore: Helmshore Local History Society 1977. pp 116, il.

351 BUNDOCK, J. F., *Old Leigh: a pictorial history.* Chichester: Phillimore 1978. pp 128, il.

352 WALKER, B. & HINCHCLIFFE, A., *In our Liverpool home.* Belfast: Blackstaff P 1978. pp 104, il.

353 HOWGEGO, J., *London in the 20s and 30s from old photographs.* Batsford 1978. pp 112, il.

354 MAKEPEACE, C., *Manchester as it was.* Nelson: Hendon Publishing Co. Vol 6 War and its aftermath, 1977. pp 44, il.

355 BEVIS, T. A., *Old March picturebook and 19th century retrospect.* March: compiler 1977. pp 46, il.

356 ANDERSON, J., ed, *Bygone Market Harborough.* Blaby: author 1978. pp 36, il.

357 ADAM SMITH, P., *Victorian and Edwardian Melbourne from old photographs.* Sydney: J. Ferguson 1979. pp 116, il.

358 DA COSTA, R., *Blackburn: a picturesque history* [Melbourne]. Lilydale, Vic: Pioneer Design Studio 1978. pp 144, il.

359 FEININGER, A., *New York in the forties.* New York: Dover Publications 1978.

360 HAWKES, A., *Memories of old Poole.* Poole: author Pt 1 1978. pp 39, il. Pt 2 The old town and Hamworthy 1979 pp 39–73, il.

361 WRIGHT, M., ed, *Vintage Richmond.* Nelson: Hendon Publishing Co 1978. pp 47, il.

362 *The changing face of Shrewsbury.* Shrewsbury: Shropshire County Library 1977. pp 105, il.

363 CARR, A. M., *Shrewsbury as it was.* Nelson: Hendon Publishing Co 1978. pp 44, il.

364 WORSENCROFT, K., *Bygone Sleaford.* Grantham: Bygone Grantham Cttee 1978. pp 35, il.

365 TALBOT, R., *Stoke old and new.* Wakefield: EP Publishing 1977. pp 103, il.

366 MARSHALL, W. W., *Streatham and the surrounding villages 1610–1918: a survey in maps and pictures.* Streatham Society 1976. pp 51, il.

367 RAYSKA, U. & CARR, A., *Telford past and present.* Shrewsbury: Shropshire Libraries 1978. pp 95, il.

368 *Pictures of old Thurso and district: shades of the past.* Thurso: H. Munro 1978. pp 80, il.

369 BENSON, J. & RAYBOULD, T., *Walsall as it was.* Nelson: Hendon Publishing Co 1978. pp 44, il.

370 PILE, A. T., *Buildings of old Whitby.* Whitby: Caedman of Whitby 1979. pp 80, il.

371 *Pictures of Wigan 1870–1920.* Wigan: Wigan College of Technology 1978. pp 48, il.

372 STEVENS, P. & DINE, D., *Winchester seen and remembered.* Winchester: Hants County Library 1978. pp 51, il.

373 STAFFORD, T., comp, *Worcester as it was.* Nelson: Hendon Publishing Co 1977. pp 44, il.

Other graphic portrayals

374 BALL, A. W., comp, *Paintings, prints and drawings of Harrow on the Hill 1562–1899.* Harrow: Borough of Harrow 1978. pp 160, il.

375 WAINWRIGHT, A., *Kendal in the nineteenth century: a book of drawings.* Kendal: Westmoreland Gazette 1977. pp 249, il.

376 BAINBRIDGE, N., *Saltburn by the sea: a pictorial history.* Redcar: AA Sotheran 1977. pp 65, il.

II POPULATION

RESEARCH METHODS, AIDS AND MATERIALS

Research methods see 507

Printed documentary sources

377 BRUNET, G., Paroisses et communes de France: Ain: Dictionnaire d'histoire administrative et démographique. Paris: /Editions du CNRS 1979.

378 GARDEN, M., BRONNERT, C., & CHAPPE, B., *Paroisses et communes de France: Rhône: Dictionnaire d'histoire administrative et démographique*. Paris: Editions du CNRS 1978. pp 388.

Archives

379 BRAYSHAY, M., Using American records to study 19th century emigrants from Britain. *Area* 11 (1979) 156–60.

GENERAL FEATURES OF URBAN POPULATIONS see also 80

380 BELLETTINI, A., Ricerche sulle crisi demografiche del Seicento. *Soc&S* (1978) 35–64.

381 COHEN, A., & LEWIS, B., *Population and revenue in the towns of Palestine in the 16th century*. Guildford: Princetown UP 1978. pp xii + 199, il.

382 FINLAY, R. A. P., Population and fertility in London 1580–1650. *JFH* 4 (1979) 26–38.

383 FUGUITT, G. V. & BEALE, C. L., Population trends of nonmetropolitan cities and villages in subregions of the United States. *De* 15 (1978) 605–20.

384 GAUTRY, A., *Some Eastbourne folk of bygone days*. Eastbourne: Eastbourne Local History Society 1978. pp 21.

385 HAREVEN, T. K. & VINOVKIS, M. A., eds, *Family and population in nineteenth-century America*. Princeton: Princeton UP 1978.

386 HERLIHY, P., Death in Odessa: a study of population movements in a nineteenth century city. *JUH* 4 (1978) 417–42.

387 HIGOUNET-NADAL, A., *Périgueux aux XIVe et XIVe siècles. Étude de démographie historique*. Bordeaux: Féderation Historique du Sud-Ouest 1978. pp 460.

388 HOLT, S. B., A note concerning Russell's estimate of the population of Durham City in the 14th century. *DCLHSB* 22 (1978) 43–44.

389 HUMPHREYS, J. S., *The Queensland urban system: population change and functional structure*. Townsville, Q: James Cook University of North Queensland 1977. pp viii + 530.

390 LYDOLPH, P. E., et al, Recent population trends in the USSR. *SG* 19 (1978) 505–39.

391 MARTIN, J. M., The rich, the poor and the migrant in 18th century Stratford-on-Avon. *LPS* 20 (1978) 38–43.

392 PINI, A. I., *La popolazione di Imola edel suo territorio nel XIII e XIV secolo*. Bologna: Patron 1976. pp, 211.

393 SHABAD, T., Some aspects of Central Asian manpower and urbanization 1959–70. *SG* 20 (1979) 113–28.

NATALITY AND MORTALITY

394 COBB, R. C., *Death in Paris: the records of the Basse-Geole de la Seine, October 1795 – September 1801*. New York: Oxford UP 1978.

395 FINLAY, R., Gateways to death? London child mortality experience 1570–1653. *ADH* (1978) 105–34.

396 FRANCOIS, E., La mortalité urbaine en Allemagne au XVIIIe siècle. *ADH* (1978) 135–66.

397 KUPPERMAN, K. O., Apathy and death in early Jamestown. *JAH* 66 (1979) 24–40.

398 MOSK, C., The decline of marital fertility in Japan [1875–1960]. *PS* 33 (1979)

399 PERRENOUD, A., La mortalité à Genève de 1625 à 1825. *ADH* (1978) 209–34.

DISEASE

400 GLOVER, J., Health and disease in Birmingham 1770–1830. *WarH* 4 (1978/9) 40–55.

401 GOTTFRIED, R. S., *Epidemic disease in fifteenth century England: the medical response and the demographic consequences* [includes a comparison of urban and rural mortality]. Leicester: Leicester UP 1978. pp xiii + 262.

402 GUILLAUME, P., La grippe à Bordeaux en 1918. *ADH* (1978) 167–74.

403 LEWIS, M., Sanitation, intestinal infections and infant mortality in late Victorian society. *MedH* 23 (1979) 325–38.

404 SMITH, F. B., *The people's health 1830–1910*. Croom Helm 1979.

MEDICINE see also 855–9

405 ANNING, S. T., The practice of surgery in Leeds 1823–4. *MedH* 23 (1979) 59–95.

406 SHAPIN, S., 'The politics of observation: cerebral anatomy and social interests in the Edinburgh phrenology disputes' in WALLIS, R., ed, *On the margins of science: the social construction of rejected knowledge*. Sociological Review Monograph 27. Keele: University of Keele 1979. pp 139–78.

MIGRATION TO, FROM AND BETWEEN TOWNS see also 391

407 BAINES, D. E., 'Birthplace statistics and the analysis of internal migration' in Lawton ed, *The census* [507] pp 146–64.
408 FRASER, C. M. & EMSLEY, K., Newcastle merchant adventurers from West Yorkshire. *AA* 6 (1978) 117–30.
409 GOTTLIEB, A. Z., Immigration of British coal miners in the Civil War decade. *IRSH* 23 (1978) 357–75.
410 JONES, H. R., Modern emigration from Scotland to Canada 1957–77. *SGM* 95 (1979) 4–12.
411 MCCLURE, P., Patterns of migration in the late Middle Ages: the evidence of English place-name surnames. *EcHR* 32 (1979) 167–82.
412 PERCAL, R. M., The golden cage – Cubans in Miami [1950–73]. *IM* 16 (1978) 160–73.
413 ST JOHN JONES, L. W., Emigration from Canada in the 1960s. *PS* 33 (1979) 115–24.
414 THOMAS, C., Internal migration in Yugoslavia 1961–71. *TESG* 70 (1979) 177–81.

POPULATION MOVEMENTS WITHIN TOWNS

415 POOLEY, C. G., Residential mobility in the Victorian city [Liverpool]. *IBG* 4 (1979) 258–77.

FAMILY AND HOUSEHOLD STRUCTURE

416 ARROM, S. M., Marriage patterns in Mexico City 1811. *JFH* 3 (1978) 376–91.
417 CLARKSON, L. A., Household and family structure in Armagh City 1770. *LPS* 20 (1978) 14–31.
418 FREY, M., Du mariage et du concubinage dans les classes populaires à Paris 1846–1847. *AESC* 4 (1978) 803–29.
419 HERLIHY, D. & KLAPISCH, C., *Les Toscans et leurs familles*. Paris: Presses de la Fondation Nationale des Sciences Politiques 1978. pp 728.
420 KIRSHNER, J. & MOLHO, A., The dowry fund the marriage market in early Quattrocento Florence. *JMH* 50 (1978) 403–38.
421 LOMNITZ, L. A. & LIZAUR, M. P., The history of a Mexican urban family. *JFH* 3 (1978) 392–409.
422 MORGAN, M. & GOLDEN, H. H., Immigrant families in an industrial city: a study of households in Holyoke, 1880. *JFH* 4 (1979) 59–68.
423 RAMOS, D., City and country: the family in Minas Gerais 1804–1838. *JFH* 3 (1978) 361–75.
424 SMITH, R. J., The domestic cycle in selected commoner families in urban Japan 1757–1858. *JFH* 3 (1978) 219–35.

III PHYSICAL STRUCTURE

RESEARCH METHODS, AIDS AND MATERIALS

Research methods see 440

Printed documentary sources
425 HORROX, R., *The changing plan of Hull 1290–1650: a guide to documentary sources for the early topography of Hull*. Kingston upon Hull: Kingston upon Hull City Council 1978. pp 187, il.

Theory
426 DANSEREAU, P., An ecological grading of human settlements. *Geo* 9 (1978) 161–210.

PHYSICAL AND STRUCTURAL CHARACTERISTICS OF TOWNS

General see also 181
427 ATKIN, M. W. & SUTERMEISTER, H., Excavations in Norwich 1977/8. The Norwich survey 7th interim report. *NoA* 37 (1978) 19–55.
428 BLACK, G., *The archaeology of Tower Hamlets*. London Borough of Tower Hamlets 1977. pp 18, il.
429 CLACK, P. A. G., *Darlington: a topographical study*. Durham: Northern Archaeological Survey 1978. pp 83, il.
430 DIXON, P. W., *Excavations at Greenwich Palace 1970–1971: an interim report*. Greenwich and Lewisham Antiquarian Society 1972. pp 25, il.
431 FREKE, D. J., Excavations at Friars Walk, Lewes. *SAC* 116 (1978) 179–197.
432 FREKE, D. J., Excavations in Church St, Seaford 1976. *SAC* 116 (1978) 199–224.
433 GOURLAY, R. & TURNER, A., *Historic Stonehaven: the archaeological implications of development*. Glasgow: Glasgow University 1978. pp 13, il.
434 ROSKAMS, S., The Milk St excavation. *LonA* 3 (1978) 206–12.

Ancient times
435   BESCHAOUCH, A., HANOUNE, R. & THEBERT, Y., *Les ruines de Bulla Regia.* Rome: École Française de Rome 1978. pp 144.
436   DOWN, A., 'Roman Sussex – Chichester and the Chilgrove valley' in Drewett, *Archaeology in Sussex* [437] 52–8.
437   DREWETT, P. L. ed, *Archaeology in Sussex to AD 1500: essays for Eric Holden.* Council for British Archaeology 1978. pp viii + 101.
438   DUVAL, N. & POPOVIC, V., *Sirmium tome VII Horea et Thermes au bords du rempart.* Rome: École Française de Rome 1978. pp 117.
439   HAMMERSOM, M., Excavations under Southwark cathedral. *LonA* 3 (1978) 206–12.
440   MORGAN, M., Excavation and recording techniques used at the cemetery of St Nicholas, Shambles. *LonA* 3 (1978) 213–16.
441   TODD, M., *The walls of Rome.* Totowa, NJ: Rowman & Littlefield 1978.
442   VALLET, G., VILLARD, F. & AUBERSON, P., *Megara Hyblaea. Tome 1, le quartier de l'Agora.* Rome: École Française de Rome 1978. pp 440 + 52.

Medieval and early modern see also 437
443   The demolition of Northampton's walls, July 1662. *NPP* 6 (1979) 83–4.
444   BALESTRACCI, D. & PICCININI, G., *Siena nel Trecento. Assetto urbano e strutture edilisie.* Florence: CLUSF 1977. pp 201.
445   CASTLE, S. A., A late medieval framed building in Watford. *HerA* 5 (1977) 176–85.
446   CLARKE, H. B., The topographical development of early medieval Dublin. *RSAI* 107 (1977) 29–51.
447   CONTAMINE, P., Les fortifications urbaines en France à la fin du Moyen Age: aspects financiels et economiques. *RH* 3 (1978) 23–47.
448   CRESTI, C., ed, *I centristorici della Toscana.* Milan: 1977.
449   FARLEY, M., Saxon and medieval Walton, Aylesbury excavations 1973–4. *RBuc* 20 (1976) 153–290.
450   FREKE, D., 'Medieval urban archaeology in Sussex' in Drewett, *Archaeology in Sussex* [437] 97–92.
451   GRIFFITHS, R. A., The three castles at Aberystwyth. *ACa* 126 (1977) 74–87.
452   MIONI, A. & ROSSI, R., eds, *I centri storici della Lombardia.* Milan: 1975.
453   PETCHEY, M. R., Excavations in Hertford 1973–4. *HerA* 5 (1977) 157–75.
454   PHILP, B., Major Saxon building discovered at Dover. *KAR* 53 (1978) 64–5.
455   RIGDEN, R., *A Tudor building at Well Hall.* London Borough of Greenwich 1978. pp 13, il.
456   WALKER, J. S. F., Excavations in medieval tenements on the Quilters Vault site in Southampton. *HFCAS* 35 (1978) 183–216.
457   WEBSTER, P. V., Excavations in Quay St, Cardiff. *ACa* 126 (1977) 88–115.

Modern see also 545
458   ERICKSEN, E. P. & YANCEY, W. L., Work and residence in industrial Philadelphia. *JUH* 5 (1979) 147–82.
459   FRENCH, R. A. & HAMILTON, F. E., *The socialist city: spatial structures and urban policies.* New York: Wiley 1979.
460   GULVIN, K. R., Fort Clarence, Rochester. *KAR* 53 (1978) 53–7.
461   MOLLENKOPF, J. H., 'The post-war politics of urban development' [USA] in Tabb & Sawers, *Marxism and the metropolis* [848] 117–52.
462   RODGER, R. G., The building cycle and the urban fringe in Victorian cities: another comment. *JHG* 5 (1979) 72–8.

PHYSICAL AND STRUCTURAL CHARACTERISTICS OF AREAS WITHIN TOWNS

The central business district
463   RUCHELMAN, L. I., The New York World Trade Center in perspective. *UPP* 6 (1978) 29–38.
464   WHITEHAND, J. W. R., Long term changes in the form of the city centre: the case of redevelopment [Glasgow 1840–1969]. *GA* 60 (1978) 79–96.

Industrial areas
465   MOLLER, E. K. & GROVES, P. A., The emergence of industrial districts in mid-nineteenth century Baltimore. *GR* 69 (1979) 159–78.

Slums
466   KIRBY, D. A., *Slum housing and residential renewal: the case in urban Britain.* Longman 1979. pp 102, il.

467   LLOYD, P. C., *Slums of hope: shanty towns of the third world.* New York: St Martins P 1979.

Middle class areas
468   LOCKWOOD, C., Rincon Hill was San Francisco's most genteel neighbourhood. *CalH* 58 (1979) 48–61.

Suburbs see also 109–11 747
469   ASHTON, P. J., 'The political economy of suburban development' [historical approach relevant only to USA] in Tabb & Sawers, *Marxism and the metropolis* [848] 64–89.
470   BONNEVILLE, M., *Naissance et métamorphose d'une banlieue ouvriè: Ville-urbanne.* Processes et forme d'urbanisation. Lyons: PUL 1979. pp 280.
471   COFFIN, D. R., *The villa in the life of Renaissance Rome.* Princeton: Princeton UP 1978.
472   MCDONNELL, K. G. T., *Medieval London suburbs.* Phillimore 1978. pp viii + 196, il.
473   MODELL, J., Suburbanization and change in the American family. *JInH* 9 (1979) 621–46.
474   MULLEN, B. & HARKER, G., *Norbury: the story of a London suburb: its geography and history.* Author 1977.

Open space
475   *Forum et plaza mayor dans le monde Hispanique. Collogue interdisciplinaire Casa de Velasquez, Madrid, 28 Octobre 1976.* Collection Publications de la Casa de Velasquez 1979. pp 150.
476   COKE, D., *The muse's bower: Vauxhall Gardens 1728–1786.* Sudbury: Gainsborough's House 1978. pp 38.
477   ELLIOTT, B. et al, *Highgate cemetery.* Friends of Highgate Cemetery 1978. pp 51, il.
478   JOWETT, E. M., *Morden Park, Morden.* Merton Historical Society 1977. pp 18.
479   LANCASTER, R. K., Green Mount: the introduction of the rural cemetery into Baltimore. *MdHM* 74 (1979) 62–79.
480   WILLIAMS, G. R., *The royal parks of London.* Constable 1978. pp 234, il.
481   WROTH, W., *The London pleasure gardens of the eighteenth century.* Basingstoke: Macmillan 1979. pp 511, il.

SITES AND BUILDINGS

Land ownership and estate administration
482   CHERUBINI, G., la proprieta fondiara nei secoli XV-XVI nella storiografia italiana. *Soc&S* (1978) 9–33.

Architecture see also 151 769 770 777 780 785 867 883
483   *An architectural and general description of the Town Hall Manchester to which is added a report of the inaugural proceedings.* Manchester: City of Manchester 1977. pp xi + 98, il. [reprint of 1878 edn]
484   BERTON, K., *Moscow, an architectural history.* Studio Vista 1977. pp 256, il.
485   BOSANQUET, H., *Bridge Street, Cambridge*: Cambridge: Cambridge History Agency 1976. pp 69, il.
486   BOUDON, P., *Richelieu, ville nouvelle.* Paris: Dunod 1978. pp 200.
487   COHEN, J. L., de MICHELIS, M. & TAFURI, M. *La ville, l'architecture URSS 1918–1978.* Paris: 1978. pp 372.
488   DE NEGRI, E., *Ottocento e Rinnovamento urbano: Carlo Barabino.* Genoa: 1977. pp 190 + 144, il.
489   GROS, P., *Aurea Templea: recherches sur l'architecture religieuse de Rome à l'époque d'Auguste.* Rome: École Française de Rome 1978. pp 282.
490   KOPP, A., *L'architecture Stalinienne.* Grenoble: PUG 1978. pp 416.
491   TARABELLI, G. M., *Palazzi pubblici d'Italia. Nascita e trasformazione del palazzo pubblico in Italia fino al XVI secolo.* Busto Arsizio 1978. pp 258.

HOUSING
492   MACLENNAN, D., Information networks in a local housing market [Glasgow 1974–51]. *SJPE* 26 (1979) 73–88.

House building
493   CLAPP, B., 'A note on housebuilding in Exeter 1867–1940' in MINCHINTON, W. ed, *Capital formation in South West England* (Exeter Papers in Economic History 9). Exeter: Exeter University 1978. pp 55–61.

494   DUCLAUD WILLIAMS, R. H., *The politics of housing in Britain and France* [includes historical analysis 1945–72]. Heinemann 1978. pp 280.

495   MARRINER, S., Sir Alfred Mond's octopus: a nationalised house building business [1920s]. *BuH* 21 (1979) 23–44.

496   STONE, M. E., 'Housing, mortgage lending and the contradictions of capitalism' in Tabb & Sawers, *Marxism and the metropolis* [848] 179–207.

House types
497   GOUDINEAU, C., *Les fouilles de la Maison du Dauphin: recherches sur la romanisation de Vaison la Romaine*. Paris: Editions du CNRS 1979. pp 332.

498   GREELEY, A. M., Ethnic domestic architecture in Chicago. *Eth* 6 (1979) 137–46.

499   SPEIGHT, M. E., *Ludlow houses and their residents*. Ludlow: Ludlow History Research Group 1978. pp 24.

House ownership see also 499
500   *The Crescent, Norwich: listing of occupiers 1825–1978*. Norwich: Crescent History Group 1978. pp 27, il.

501   SCHWITZER, J., Some Victorian businessmen and their residence: Winchester Hall, Highgate. *HHSB* 19 (1979) 40–9.

Housing conditions
502   ROBERTS, E., Working class housing in Barrow and Lancaster 1880–1930. *HSLC* 127 (1978) 109–32.

IV SOCIAL STRUCTURE

RESEARCH METHODS, AIDS AND MATERIALS

Research methods
503   ARMSTRONG, W. A., 'The census enumerators' books: a commentary' in Lawton ed, *The census* [507] 28–81.

504   ASHTON, T. S., *Economic and social investigations in Manchester 1833–1933: a centenary history of the Manchester Statistical Society*. Hassocks: Harvester P 1977. pp xi + 179 [reprint of 1934 edn]

505   BANKS, J. A., 'The social structure of nineteenth century England as seen through the census' in Lawton ed, *The census* [507] 179–223.

506   GORDON, G., Rateable assessment as a data source for status area analysis. *UHY* (1979) 92–9.

507   LAWTON. R. ed., *The census and social structure: an interpretative guide to nineteenth century censuses for England and Wales*. Frank Cass 1978. pp 330.

508   LAWTON. R. ed, 'Census data for urban areas' in Lawton ed, *The census* [507] 82–145.

509   WELLS, R., Counting riots in 18th century England. *BSLH* 37 (1978) 68–72.

SOCIAL STRUCTURE AND CHARACTERISTICS OF TOWNS

General
510   *L'espace social de la ville arabe*. Paris: Maisonneuve et Larose 1979. pp 374.

511   ABRAMS, P. & WRIGLEY, E. A., *Towns in societies: essays in economic history and historical sociology*. Cambridge: Cambridge UP 1978. pp viii + 344, il.

512   Entry deleted

Ancient
513   Entry deleted

514   LEPORE, E., 'Grecia: il lavora urbano' in FLINN, M. ed, *Proceedings of the seventh International Economic History Congress* II. Edinburgh: Edinburgh UP 1978. pp 135–8.

515   TREGGIARI, S. M., 'Rome: urban labour' in FLINN, M. ed, *Proceedings of the seventh International Economic History Congress* II. Edinburgh: Edinburgh UP 1978. pp 162–5.

516   WELSKOPF, E. C., 'Free labour in the city of Athens' in FLINN, M. ed, *Proceedings of the seventh International Economic History Congress* II. Edinburgh: Edinburgh UP 1978. pp 131–4.

Medieval and early modern see also 237 391
517   BEIER, A. L., Social problems in Elizabethan London. *JInH* 9 (1978) 203–22.

518   BLANSHEI, S. R., Population, wealth and patronage in medieval and renaissance

Perugia. *JInH* 9 (1979) 597–620.
519 BULLARD, M. M., Marriage politics and the family in Florence: the Strozzi-Medici alliance of 1508. *AHR* 84 (1979) 668–687.
520 FIETIER, R., *La cité de Besançon de la fin du XIIe siècle au milieu du XIVe siècle. Étude d'une société urbaine.* Atelier de reproduction des theses de Lille III. Diffusion champion 1978.
521 GREW R. & STENECK, N. H., eds, *Society and history: essays by Sylvia L. Thrupp.* Ann Arbor: Michigan UP 1977. pp x + 363.
522 JENSEN, D., Catherine de Medici and her Florentine friends. *SCJ* 9 (1978) 57–74.
523 POLITI, G., *Aristocrazia e potere politico nella Cremona di Filippo II.* Milano: SugarCo 1976. pp 507.
524 POWERS, J. F., Frontier municipal baths and social intèraction in thirteenth century Spain. *AHR* 84 (1979) 649–67.
525 SAIVE-LEVER, E., La mobilité sociale chez les artisans parisiens dans la première moitié du XVIIe siècle. *XVII* 1 (1979) 51–60.
526 SCHWARZ, L. D., Income distribution and social structure in London in the late 18th century. *EcHR* 32 (1979) 250–9.
527 THRUPP, S. L., 'Social control in the medieval town' in Grew and Steneck, *Society and history* [521] 9–24.
528 WILKENFELD, B., *The social and economic structure of the city of New York 1695–1796.* New York: Arno P 1978.

Modern see also 680
529 ALLARD, P., La fortune des Arlésiens en 1820. *AdM* 3 (1977) 281–318.
530 CARTER, H. & WHEATLEY, S., Fixation lines and fringe belts, land uses and social areas: 19th century change in the small town [Aberystwyth]. *IBG* 4 (1979) 214–38.
531 COWLARD, K. A., The identification of social (class) areas and their place in 19th century urban development [Wakefield]. *IBG* 24 (1979) 239–57.
532 DOYLE, D. H., *The social order of a frontier community: Jacksonville, Illinois 1825–70.* Urbana, Ill: Illinois UP 1978.
533 FLANNER, J., *Paris was yesterday 1925–1939.* New York: Penguin Books 1979.
534 FLOWERDUE, R., Spatial patterns of residential segregation in a southern city [Memphis] *JAS* 13 (1979) 93–108.
535 FOX, R. C., The morphological sociological and functional districts of Stirling 1798–1881. *IBG* 4 (1979) 153–67.
536 GORDON, G., The status areas of early to mid-Victorian Edinburgh. *IBG* 4 (1979) 168–91.
537 HARDY, M. A., Occupational mobility and nativity-ethnicity in Indianapolis 1850–60. *SF* 57 (1978) 205–21.
538 KAPFERER, B., Structural marginality and the urban social order. *UAn* 7 (1978) 287–320.
539 LEEMING, F., *Street studies in Hong Kong: localities in a Chinese city.* Hong Kong: OUP 1978. pp xix + 182, il.
540 LOCKARD, C. A., Patterns of social development in modern southeast Asian cities. *JUH* 5 (1978) 41–68.
541 MAY, E. T., The pressure to provide: class, consumerism and divorce in urban America 1880–193. *JSocH* 12 (1978) 180–193.
542 MITCHELL, W. R., *Lancashire mill town traditions.* Clapham: Dalesman 1977. pp 80, il.
543 NOBLE, R. A., Paterson's response to the Great Depression. *NJH* 96 (1978) 87–99.
544 SENTOU, J., Les fortunes au décès à Toulouse au debut du XXe siècle. *AdM* 3 (1976) 345–9.
545 SHAW, M., Reconciling social and physical space: Wolverhampton. *IBG* 4 (1979) 192–213.

SOCIAL STRUCTURE AND CHARACTERISTICS OF AREAS WITHIN TOWNS see also 539

546 POWER, M. J., 'The East and west in early modern London' in IVES, E. W., KNECHT R. J. & SCARISBRICK J. J. eds, *Wealth and power in Tudor England· essays presented to S. T. Bindoff.* Athlone P 1978 pp 167–85.

Central business district
547 CHINITZ, B. ed, *Central city economic development.* Cambridge, Mass: ABT Books 1979.

Working class areas
548 BEIRNE, D. R., Residential growth and stability in the Baltimore industrial community of Canton during the late nineteenth century. *MdHM* 74 (1979) 39–51.
549 COBB, T., *Classe ouvrière et pauvreté: les conditions de vie des travailleurs Montrealais 1897–1929*. Montreal: 1979. pp 214.
550 PEMBER REEVES, M., *Round about a pound a week* [Lambeth]. Virago 1979. pp xxi + 237, il. [reprint of 1913 edn]

Suburbs see also 645

SOCIAL ORGANIZATIONS, CLUBS AND SOCIETIES see also 917

551 HUX, R. K., The Ku Klux Klan in Macon 1919–1925. *GaHQ* 62 (1978) 155–68.
552 RAINGER, R., Race, politics and science: the Anthropological Society of London in the 1860s. *VS* 22 (1978) 51–70.
553 STANLEY, S., The Cheyenne Club: an oasis of urban luxury in 19th century Wyoming. *HT* 7 (1979) 471–7.
554 STEELE, E. D., The Leeds Patriciate and the cultivation of learning 1819–1905: a study of the Leeds Philosophical and Literary Society. *LPLS* 16 (1978) 183–202.

CLASS STRUCTURE, PROTESTS AND DISORDERS

Occupational structure see also 832
555 *Essays in Tyneside labour history*. Newcastle: Dept Humanities Newcastle upon Tyne Polytechnic 1977. pp 200, il.
556 BELLAMY, J. M., 'Occupation statistics in the nineteenth century censuses' in Lawton ed, *The census* [507] pp 165–78.
557 GROPPI, A., Sur la structure socio-professionnelle de la section des gravilliers de Paris. *AHRF* 2 (1978) 246–76.
558 HEAVNER, R. O., Indentured servitude: the Philadelphia market 1771–1773. *JEcH* 38 (1978) 701–13.
559 INGHAM, J. N., *The iron barons: a social analysis of an American urban elite 1874–1965*. Westport, Conn: Greenwood P 1978. pp xix + 242, il.
560 LETHUILLIER, J. P., Les structures socio-professionelles à Falaise à la fin du XVIIIe siècle. *RHES* 1–2 (1977) 42–69.
561 PROTHERO, I. J., *Artisans and politics in early 19th century London*. Folkestone: Dawson 1979. pp xi + 418, il.

Class composition and interaction see also 525 832
562 CUMBLER, J. T., *Working class community in industrial America: work, leisure and struggle in two industrial cities 1880–1930*. Westport, Conn: Greenwood P 1979.
563 FAIRCHILDS, C., Masters and servants in eighteenth century Toulouse. *JSocH* 12 (1979) 368–93.
564 GREEN, J. R. & DONAHUE, H. C., *Boston's workers: a labour history*. Boston: Boston Public Library 1978.
565 HIRSCH, S., *Roots of the American working class: the industrialization of crafts in Newark 1800–1860*. Philadelphia: Pennsylvania UP 1978.
566 KIRK, G. W., *The promise of American life: social mobility in a nineteenth century immigrant community, Holland, Michigan 1847–1894*. Philadelphia: American Philosophical Society 1978.
567 ROCK, H. B., *Artisans of the New Republic: the tradesmen of New York City in the age of Jefferson*. New York: New York UP 1979.
568 ROCK, H. B., A delicate balance: the mechanics and the city in the age of Jefferson. *NYHSQ* 63 (1979) 93–114.
569 WALKOWITZ, D. J., *Worker city, company town: iron and cotton worker protest in Troy and Cohoes, New York 1855–84*. Urbana, Ill: Illinois UP 1978.

Social and class attitudes see also 605
570 BOYER, P. S., *Urban masses and moral order in America 1820–1920*. Cambridge, Mass: Harvard UP 1978.
571 DODD, J. S., The working classes and the temperance movement in ante bellum Boston. *LabH* 19 (1978) 510–31.
572 MCDOUGALL, M. L., Consciousness and community: the workers of Lyon 1830–1850. *JSocH* 12 (1978) 129–45.
573 MCKIBBIN, R. I., Social class and social observation in Edwardian England. *RHS* 28 (1978) 175–200.

574 SEWELL, W. H., Corporations républicaines: the revolutionary idiom of Parisian workers in 1848. *CSSH* 21 (1979) 195–203.
575 VOLKOV, S., *The rise of popular anti-modernism in Germany: the urban master artisans 1873–1896*. Princeton, NJ: Princeton UP 1978.

Protests and disorders see also 737
576 CAZALS, R., *Avec les ouvriers de Mazamet. Dans la grève et l'action quotidienne 1909–1914*. Paris: Maspero 1979. pp 352.
577 DINWIDDY, J., Luddism and politics in the northern counties. *SH* 4 (1979) 33–64.
578 EVANS, R. J., 'Red Wednesday' in Hamburg: social democrats, police and lumpenproletariat in the suffrage disturbances of 17 January 1906. *SH* 4 (1979) 1–32.
579 FOURQUIN, G., *The anatomy of popular rebellion in the Middle Ages*. Amsterdam: North-Holland 1978. pp xiv + 181.
580 GRUNSZPAN, R., *The uprising of the death box of Warsaw*. New York: Vantage P 1978.
581 HARRISON, R., New light on the police and the hunger marchers [London 1934]. *BSLH* 37 (1978) 17–50.
582 HENNESSEY, M. M., Race and violence in reconstruction New Orleans 1837–1878. *LouH* 20 (1979) 77–92.
583 LE ROY LADURIE, E., *Le Carnaval de Romans 1579–1580*. Paris: 1979, pp 426.
584 LUCAS, B. K., Banbury – trees or trade [riots 1824]. *CC* 7 (1979) 270–2.
585 MIDLARSKY, M. I., Analyzing diffusion and contagion effects: the urban disorders of the 1960s. *APSR* 72 (1978) 996–1008.

SOCIAL LIFE

Social life, traditions and customs
586 HUELIN, G., Christmas in the City. *GUM* 3 (1978) 164–74.
587 LOTTIN, A., *Chavatte, ouvrier lillois, un contemporaine de Louis XIV*. Paris: 1978. pp 472.
588 PULLAR, P., *Gilded butterflies: the rise and fall of the London season*. H. Hamilton 1978. pp 192, il.

Religious activity see also 489 947
589 DAVIES, J., Persecution and Protestantism: Toulouse 1562–75. *HJ* 22 (1979) 31–52.
590 DAVIES, R. E., GEORGE, A. R., & RUPP, E. G., eds, *A history of the Methodist church in Great Britain*. Epworth P Vol 2 1978 pp 340.
591 ENRIGHT, W. G., Urbanization and the Evangelical pulpit in nineteenth century Scotland. *ChH* 47 (1978) 400–7.
592 GOLDEN, R. M., Religious extremism in the mid 17th century: the Parisian Illuminés. *EuSR* 9 (1979) 195–210.
593 HURWICH, J. J., 'A Fanatick town': the political influence of dissenters in Coventry 1660–1720. *MidH* 4 (1977) 15–47.
594 JOHNSON, P. E., *A shopkeeper's millenium: society and revivals in Rochester, New York 1815–1837*. New York: Hill and Wang 1978.
595 MAHONEY, M., Presbyterianism in the City of London. *HJ* 22 (1979) 93–114.
596 MONTER, E. W., Historical demography and religious history in sixteenth century Geneva. *JInH* 9 (1979) 399–428.
597 PELLEGRINO, B., *Terra e clero nel Mezzogiorno. Il reclutamento sacerdotale a Lecce dalla Restaurazione all Unita*. Lecce: Milella 1976. pp 148.
598 PORUSH, I., *The house of Israel: a study of Sydney jewry from its foundation (1788) and a history of the Great Synagogue of Sydney: the mother congregation of Sydney jewry, compiled on the occasion of its centenary*. Melbourne: Hawthorn P 1977. pp vii + 347, il.
599 RALPH, R. M., The city and the church: Catholic beginnings in Newark 1840–1870. *NJH* 96 (1978) 105–19.
600 RECTOR, W. K., Lewes quakers in the 17th and 18th centuries. *SAC* 116 (1978) 31–40.
601 REYERSON, K. L., Changes in testamentary practices at Montpellier on the eve of the Black Death. *ChH* 47 (1978) 253–69.
602 RYAN, M. P., A woman's awakening: evangelical religion and the families of Utica, NY, 1800–1840. *AQ* (1978) 602–23.
603 SINGLETON, G. H., *Religion in the city of Angers*. Ann Arbor: UMI Research P 1978.
604 SIZER, S. S., Political and apolitical religion: the great urban revivals of the late nineteenth century. *ChH* 48 (1979) 81–98.
605 STRUMINGHER, L. S., 'A bas les prêtres! a bas les couvents!': the church and the workers in nineteenth century Lyon. *JSocH* 11 (1978) 546–53.
606 THOMPSON, D. M., 'The religious census of 1851' in Lawton ed, *The census* [507] pp 241–88.

607 TRINDER, B., The origins of Quakerism in Banbury. *CC* 7 (1979) 263–9.
608 WIGFIELD, F. W. M., Quakers in Chard. *SANHS* 122 (1978) 113–16.

Recreation
609 STARSMORE, I., *English fairs*. Thames & Hudson 1975. pp 128.

Holidays and resorts see also 152 168
610 COLLINS, G., *100 years of holidays at Skegness*. Boston: Lincolnshire Standard Group 1977. pp 34, il.
611 WALTON, J. K., *The Blackpool landlady: a social history*. Manchester: Manchester UP 1978. pp × + 229.
612 WALTON, J. K., 'Holidays and the discipline of industrial labour: a historians view' in SMITH M. A. ed, *Leisure and urban society*. Leisure Studies Association, nd. p 15.

SOCIAL PROBLEMS AND DEVIANCE

613 FORSTER R., & RANUM, O., eds, *Deviants and the abandoned in French society: selections* from *the Annales ESC*. Baltimore: Johns Hopkins UP 1978. pp xii + 245.

Delinquency see also 937.
614 CASTAN, N., 'Summary justice' [includes material on urban crime levels in 18th cent. France] in Forster & Ranum, *Deviants* [613] 111–56.
615 JONES, D., & BAINBRIDGE, A., The 'Conquering of China': crime in an industrial community 1842–64 [Merthyr Tydfil] *Lla* 4 (1979) 7–37.
616 ROSSIAUD, J., 'Prostitution, youth and society in the towns of south-eastern France in the fifteenth century' in Forster & Ranum, *Deviants* [613] pp 1–46.
617 SELVAGGI, G., *The rise of the Mafia in New York*. Indianapolis: Bobbs-Merrill 1978.

Poverty and poor relief see also 549 853
618 DELASSELLE, C., 'Abandoned children in eighteenth century Paris' in Forster & Ranum, *Deviants* [613] 47–82.
619 DONALDSON, J., Mid 19th century poverty in Dumfries. *DGNH* 53 (1977–8) 147–56.
620 FINNEGAN, F., & SIGSWORTH, E., *Poverty and social poverty: an historical study of Batley*. Heslington: University of York Dept of Social Administration and Social Work 1978. pp 130, il.
621 FLECKER, J. A., Poverty and relief in nineteenth century Janesville [Wis]. *WisMH* 61 (1978) 279–99.
622 GAILLARD, L., La misère et l'assistance à Marseille sous le Second Empire et les premières années de la Troisième République. *PH* 4 (1977) 341–64.
623 GONTHIER, N., *Lyon et les pauvres au Moyen Age* (1350–1500). Lyon: 1979. pp 270.
624 LARQUIE, G., Une approche quantitative de la pauvreté – les madrilènes et la mort au XVII. siècle. *ADH* (1978) 175–96.
625 SOUBEYROUX, J., *Paupérisme et rapports sociaux à Madrid au XIe siècle*. Atelier de Reproduction des Theses de Lille III. Diffusion Champion 1979.

Other social problems
626 BLEANDONU, G., & LE GAUFEY, G., 'The creation of the insane asylums of Auxerre and Paris' [19th cent] in Forster & Ranum, *Deviants* [613] 180–212.
627 DALY, S., Cork: a city in crisis: a history of labour conflict and social misery 1870–1872. Cork: Tower Books Vol I pp iii–xviii + 336, il.

SOCIAL REFORM AND IMPROVEMENT

Social reform movements and institutions
628 JACKSON, J. J., Prohibition in New Orleans: the unlikeliest crusade. *LaH* 19 (1978) 261–84.

Charities see also 507 622–3 663
629 BENSON, S. P., Business heads and sympathizing hearts: the women of the Providence Employment Society. *JSocH* 12 (1978) 302–13.
630 HILDRETH, P. B., Early Red Cross: the Howard Association of New Orleans 1837–1878. *LaH* 20 (1979) 49–76.

MINORITY GROUPS

Racial and ethnic minorities see also 321 537 948
631 BERMAN, M., *Richmond's jewry 1769–1976: Shabat in Shockoe*. Charlottesville, Va: Virginia UP 1978.

632 BERROL, S. C., *Immigrants at school, New York City 1898–1914*. New York: Arno P 1978.

633 BRIGGS, J. W., *An Italian passage: immigrants to three American cities 1890–1930* [Utica, Rochester, Kansas City]. New Haven: Yale UP 1978. pp xxv + 348, il.

634 CLAY, P. L., The process of black suburbanization. *UAQ* 14 (1979) 405–24.

635 DELLA FEMINA, J., *An Italian grows in Brooklyn*. Boston: Little, Brown 1978.

636 DINER, H. R., *In the almost promised land: American Jews and blacks 1915–1935*. Westport, Conn: Greenwood P 1977. pp xviii + 271, il.

637 ERNST, R., 'The economic status of New York City negroes, 1850–1863' in Meier & Rudwick, *Making of black America* [659] 250–61.

638 FISHER, M. P., Creative and ethnic identity: Asian Indians in the New York City area. *UAn* 17 (1978) 271–86.

639 FITCHETT, E. H., 'The traditions of the free negro in Charleston, South Carolina' in Meier & Rudwick, *Making of black America* [659] 206–15.

640 FONER, N., *Jamaica farewell: Jamaican immigrants in London*. Berkeley: California UP 1978.

641 FORD, L & GRIFFIN, E., The ghettoization of Paradise [San Diego], *GR* 69 (1979) 140–58.

642 FOX, D. R., 'The negro vote in Old New York' in Meier & Rudwick, *Making of black America* [659] pp 232–49.

643 GOLAB, C., *Immigrant destinations*. Philadelphia: Temple UP 1978.

644 GOLDSZMIT, H., *Ghetto diary* [Warsaw]. New York: Holocaust Library 1978.

645 GUEST, A. M., The changing racial composition of suburbs 1950–1970. *UAQ* 14 (1978) 195–206.

646 HERSHBERG, T., et al, A tale of three cities: blacks and immigrants in Philadelphia 1850–1880, and 1970. *APSC* 441 (1979) 55–81.

647 JANIS, R., Ethnic mixture and the persistence of cultural pluralism in the church communities of Detroit 1880–1940. *Mid-Amer* 61 (1979) 99–116.

648 KANTROWITZ, N., Racial and ethnic residential segregation in Boston 1830–1870. *APSC* 441 (1979) 41–54.

649 KARTMAN, L. L., Jewish occupational roots in Baltimore at the turn of the century. *MdHM* 74 (1979) 52–61.

650 KEMPER, D. J., Catholic integration in St Louis 1935–1947. *MisHR* 73 (1978) 1–22.

651 KUSMER, K. L., *A ghetto takes shape: Black Cleveland 1870–1930*. Urbana, Ill: Illinois UP 1978. pp xiv + 305, il.

652 KUZNIEWSKI, A. J., Milwaukee's Poles 1866–1918: the rise and fall of a model community. *MilH* 1 (1978) 13–24.

653 LAGUERRE, M. S., Internal dependency: the structural position of the black ghetto in American society. *JEthS* 6 (1979) 29–44.

654 LAMET, M. S., French Protestants in a position of strength: the early years of the Reformation in Caen 1558–1568. *SCJ* 9 (1978) 35–56.

655 LEE POH PING, *Chinese society in nineteenth century Singapore*. Kuala Lumpur: OUP 1978. pp xiii + 139, il.

656 LEES, L. H., *Exiles of Erin: Irish migrants in Victorian London*. Ithaca, NY: Cornell UP; Manchester: Manchester UP 1979. pp 264, il.

657 LIESKE, J. A., The conditions of racial violence in American cities: a developmental synthesis. *APSR* 72 (1978) 1324–40.

658 MEER, F., *The ghetto people: a study of the effects of uprooting the Indian people of South Africa*. Beverly Hills, Cal: Sage Pubs 1977. pp 263.

659 MEIER, A., & RUDWICK, E., eds, *The making of black America: essays in negro life and history*. New York: Atheneum Vol I The origins of black Americans 1978 pp xvi + 378.

660 MODELL, J., *The economics and politics of racial accomodation: the Japanese of Los Angeles 1900–1942*. Urbana, Ill: Illinois UP 1977. pp xii + 201.

661 MOORE, D. D., From Kehillah to Federation: the communal functins of federated philanthropy in New York City 1917–1933. *AJH* 68 (1978) 131–46.

662 MOYNIHAN, D. P., Patterns of ethnic succession: blacks and hispanics in New York City. *PSQ* 94 (1979) 1–14.

663 RAPHAEL, M. L., Federated philanthropy in an American Jewish community 1904–1908. *AJH* 68 (1978) 147–62.

664 SILVER, C., A new look at old South urbanization: the Irish worker in Charleston, South Carolina 1840–1860. *SAUS* 3 (1979) 141–72.

665 SORKIN, A. L., *The urban American Indian*. Lexington, Mass: Lexington Books 1978.

666 SPAIN, D., Race relations and residential segregation in New Orleans: centuries of paradox. *APSC* 441 (1979) 82–96.

667 THRUPP, S. L., 'Aliens in and around London in the fifteenth century' in Grew & Ste-

neck, *Society and history* [521] 101–27. [reprint of 1969 article]
668 THRUPP, S. L., 'A surveu of the alien population of England in 1440' in Grew & Steneck, *Society and history* [521] 133–49. [reprint of 1957 article]
669 TOLL, W., Fraternalism and community structure on the urban frontier: the Jews of Portland, Oregon – a case study. *PHR* 47 (1978) 369–404.
670 TOLL, W., Voluntarism and modernization in Portland jewry: the B'Nai B'Rith in the 1920s. *WHQ* 10 (1979) 21–38.
671 WILLIAMS, W., The Jewish immigrant in Manchester: the contribution of oral history. *OH* 7 (1979) 43–53.
672 WROBEL, P., *Our way: family, parish and neighbourhood in a Polish-American community.* Notre Dame, Ind: Notre Dame UP 1979.

Cultural minorities
673 SZPORLUK, R., West Ukraine and west Belorussia: historical tradition, social communication and linguistic assimilation. *SS* 31 (1979) 76–98.

Majority reaction to minorities
674 GREEN, J., & HUNTER, A., 'Racism and busing in Boston' in Tabb & Sawers, *Marxism and the metropolis* [848] 271–96.
675 GRENZ, S. M., The exodusters of 1879: St Louis and Kansas City responses. *MisHR* 73 (1978) 54–70.
676 HARLAN, L. R., 'Desegregation in New Orleans public schools during reconstruction' in Meier & Rudwick, *Making of black America* [659] 345–57.
677 HATA, D. T., *Undesirable: early immigrants and the anti-Japanese movement in San Francisco 1892–1893, prelude to exclusion.* New York: Arno P 1978.
678 JANIS, R., Flirtation and flight: alternatives to ethnic confrontation in white Anglo-American Protestant Detroit 1880–1940. *JEthS* 6 (1978) 1–18.
679 SHELDON, M. B., Black-white relations in Richmond, Virginia 1792–1820. *JSH* 45 (1979) 27–44.

Women
680 DUBLIN, T., Women workers and the study of social mobility. *JInH* 9 (1979) 647–66.
681 KATZMAN, D., *Seven days a week: women and domestic service in industrializing America.* New York: Oxford UP 1978.
682 MCBRIDE, T. M., A woman's world: department stores and the evolution of women's employment 1870–1920. *FHS* 10 (1978) 664–83.
683 NASH, G. B., The failure of female factory labor in colonial Boston. *LabH* 29 (1979) 165–88.

V ECONOMIC ACTIVITY

RESEARCH METHODS AIDS AND MATERIALS

Research methods see also 503

Archives see also 729
684 *Notice to employees: office regulations for a Burnley cotton mill.* Narbulla Agency 1978. pp 16, il.

URBAN ECONOMIC ACTIVITY

Ancient
685 FRIER, B. W., Cicero's management of his urban properties. *CJ* 74 (1978) 1–6.
686 SHIMADA, I., Economy of a prehistoric urban context: commodity and labor flow at Moche v Pampa Grande, Peru. *AAn* 43 (1978) 589–93.

Medieval and early modern see also 237 381 528
687 BRATCHEL, M. E., Italian merchant organisation and business relationships in early Tudor London. *JEEH* 7 (1978) 5–32.
688 CLOUGH, C. H., 'Towards an economic history of the State of Urbino at the time of Federigo da Montefeltro and his son Guidobaldo', in DE ROSA ed, *Studi in memoria di Federigo Melis.* Naples: Giannini. Vol 3 1978. 469–504.
689 KOTEL'NIKOVA, L. A., *Mondo contadino e città in Italia dall' XI al XIV secolo. Dalle*

font dell' Italia centrale e settentrionale. Bologna: Il Mulino 1975. pp xxx + 467.
690 PIUZ, A. M., 'La politique économique et la relance des affaires au XVIIIe siècle: le cas de Genève' in FLINN M. ed, *Proceedings of the seventh International Economic History Congress* II. Edinburgh: Edinburgh UP 1978. 387–94.

Modern see also 877.
691 BERGERON, L., *Banquiers, negociants et manufacturiers parisiens du Directoire à l' Empire.* Paris: Mouton 1979. pp 436.
692 COOKE, A. J., Robert Owen and the Stanley Mills 1802–11. *BuH* 21 (1979) 107–11.
693 FARNIE, D. A., An index of commercial activity: the membership of the Manchester Royal Exchange 1809–1948. *BuH* 21 (1979) 97–106.
694 GLASSBERG, E., Work, wages and the cost of living: ethnic differences and the poverty line, Philadelphia 1880. *PenH* 46 (1979) 17–58.
695 GOLDIN, C., Household and market production of families in a late nineteenth century American city. *JEcH* 16 (1979) 11–31.
696 HILL, B. C., At the cross roads: the political economy of postwar Detroit. *UPP* 6 (1978) 1–21.
697 KRUIJT, B., The changing spatial pattern of firms in Amsterdam: empirical evidence [1966–74]. *TESG* 70 (1979) 144–56.
698 MOORE, J. W., The lowcountry in economic transition: Charleston since 1865. *SCHM* 80 (1979) 156–71.

AGRICULTURE see also 717

INDUSTRY see also 565 765

699 CHAPMAN, S. D., Financial restraints on the growth of firms in the cotton industry 1790–1850. *EcHR* 32 (1979) 50–69.
700 ENGRAND, C., Concurrences et complémentarities des villes et des campagnes: les manufactures picardes de 1780 à 1815. *RdN* 1 (1979) 61–81.
701 GLEN, R., The Milnes of Stockport and the export of English technology during the industrial revolution. *ChesH* 3 (1978) 8–11.
702 HILLIER, R., The origins of engineering in Peterborough: the Queen St ironworks. *NPP* 6 (1979) 101–14.
703 HILLS, R. L., *Beyer, Peacock* [Gorton]. Manchester: North Western Museum of Science and Industry 1977. pp 19, il.
704 SIMON, R. D., Foundations for industrialization [Milwaukee] 1835–1880. *MilH* 1 (1978) 38–56.
705 STEFFEN, C. G., Changes in the organization of artisan production in Baltimore 1790–1820. *WMQ* 36 (1979) 101–17.
706 STOCK, L. A., *The history of John Maden and Son Ltd 1837–1977* [Bacup]. Higherford: author 1978. pp 55, il.
707 STOREY, R., The motor industry in Leamington: an introduction. *WarH* 4 (1978) 28–34.
708 TEISSEYRE, L., L'industrie lainière à Nîmes au XVIIe siècle: crise conjoncturelle ou structurelle? *AdM* 4 (1976) 383–400.
709 WHITE, D. P., The Birmingham button industry. *PMA* 12 (1978) 67–79.

EXTERNAL TRADE

710 BALARD, M., Assurances et commerce maritime à gènes dans la seconde moitié du XIXe siècle. *AdB* 2 (1978) 273–82.
711 DEVINE, T. M., An 18th century business elite: Glasgow West India merchants c. 1740–1815. *SHR* 57 (1978) 40–67.
712 DIETZ, B., 'Antwerp and London: the structure and balance of trade in the 1560s' in IVES, E. W., KNECHT, R. J. & SCARISBRICK, J. J., eds, *Wealth and power in Tudor England: essays presented to S. T. Bindoff.* Athlone P 1978. pp 186–203.
713 KEENE, C. A., American shipping and trade 1798–1820: the evidence from Leghorn. *JEcH* 38 (1978) 681–700.
714 PAGAN, J. R., Growth of the tobacco trade between London and Virginia. *GUM* 3 (1979) 248–62.
715 REBER, V. B., *British mercantile houses in Buenos Aires 1810–1880.* Cambridge, Mass: Harvard UP 1979.
716 VERACHTERT, K., 'An analysis of the growth of the Antwerp port during the 19th century' in FLINN, M. ed, *Proceedings of the seventh International Economic History Congress* II. Edinburgh: Edinburgh UP 1978. pp 95–103.

INTERNAL TRADE AND SERVICES

Food supply

717 ARMITAGE, P., Hertfordshire cattle and London meat markets in the 17th and 18th centuries. *LonA* 3 (1978) 217–23.

718 HERTNER, P., 'L'approvisionnement des villes et la politique des prix alimentaires des administrations municipales au 17e/18e siècles: le cas de Strasbourg et de Marburg an der Lahn' in FLINN, M., *Proceedings of the seventh International Economic History Congress* II. Edinburgh: Edinburgh UP 1978. pp 347–59.

719 SHEPPARD, F. H. W., *Brakspear's Brewery, Henley on Thames, 1779–1979*. Henley: W. H. Brakspear & Sons Ltd. 1979. pp viii + 103, il.

Retailing

720 CONZEN, M. P. & K. N., Geographical structure in 19th century urban retailing: Milwaukee 1836–90. *JHG* 5 (1979) 45–66.

721 HEYWOOD, C., *A History of the first 50 years of the Preston and District Chamber of Commerce*. Preston: Chamber of Commerce 1978. pp 34.

722 JONES, R., Consumer's cooperation in Victorian Edinburgh: the evolution of a pattern. *IBG* 4 (1979) 292–305.

723 KINGMAN, M. J., Markets and marketing in Tudor Warwickshire: the evidence of John Fisher of Warwick and the crisis of 1586–87. *WarH* 4 (1978) 16–28.

724 RIDEN, P., The origin of the new market of Chesterfield. *DAJ* 97 (1977) 5–15.

725 SHAW, G. & WILD, M. T., Retail patterns in the Victorian city. *IBG* 4 (1979) 278–91.

726 WHYTE, I. D., The growth of periodic market centres in Scotland 1600–1707. *SGM* 95 (1979) 13–26.

727 WILD, M. T. & SHAW, G., Trends in urban retailing: the British experience during the 19th century [Yorkshire]. *TESG* 70 (1979) 35–44.

Finance, banking and insurance

728 CLARK, J. G., Marine insurance in eighteenth century La Rochelle. *FHS* 10 (1978) 572–98.

729 READER, W. J., *A house in the City: a study of the City and of the Stock Exchange based on the records of Foster and Braithwaite 1825–1975*. Batsford 1979. pp x + 189.

730 SHERGOLD, P. R., The loan shark: the small loan business in early twentieth century Pittsburgh. *PenH* 45 (1978) 195–224.

Other non-municipal services

731 BLACKBURN, G. M. & RICARDS, S. L., The prostitutes and gamblers of Virginia City, Nevada 1870. *PHR* 48 (1979) 239–58.

732 POWELL, H., *Philadelphia's first fuel crisis: Jacob Cist and the developing market for Pennsylvania anthracite*. University Park, Pa: Penn State UP 1978.

734 STARR, S. Z., Prosit!!!! A non cosmic tour of the Cincinnati saloon. *CinHSB* 36 (1978) 175–91.

LABOUR ORGANIZATION

735 JONES, P. E., *The butchers of London: a history of the Worshipful Company of Butchers of the City of London*. Secker & Warburg 1976. pp x + 246, il.

736 THRUPP, S. L., 'Medieval gilds reconsidered' in Grew & Steneck, *Society and History* [521] 226–36.

Trade unions see also 555 830

737 BARNES, J. C. F., The trade union and radical activities of the Carlisle handloom weavers. *CWAAS* 78 (1978) 149–62.

738 CASSITY, M. J., Modernization and social crisis: the Knights of Labor and a midwest community 1885–1886. *JAH* 66 (1979) 41–61.

739 DAUNTON, M., Jack ashore: seamen in Cardiff before 1914. *WeHR* 9 (1978) 176–203.

740 LEVI, S. C., The battle for the eight hour day in San Francisco. *CalH* 57 (1978) 342–53.

741 PORTER, J. H., The Northampton boot and shoe arbitration board before 1914. *NPP* 6 (1979) 93–9.

Strikes and lockouts see also 577

742 PIOTT, S. L., Modernization and the anti monopoly issue: the St Louis transit strike of 1900. *MisHSB* 35 (1979) 3–16.

743 TOBIN, E. M., Direct action and conscience: the 1913 Paterson strike as example of the relationship between labor radicals and liberals. *LabH* 20 (1979) 73–88.

Labour see also 740

744 STEFFEN, C. G., The pre-industrial iron worker: Northampton iron works 1780–1820. *LabH* 20 (1979) 89–110.

745 TAPLIN, E. L., Dock labour at Liverpool: occupational structure and working conditions in the later 19th century. *HSLC* 127 (1978) 133–54.

VI COMMUNICATIONS

RESEARCH METHODS, AIDS AND MATERIALS

Research methods

746 NEWMAN, A. G., Bus services and local history. *LoH* 13 (1979) 280–91.

INTER-URBAN COMMUNICATIONS

General

747 ROBBINS, M., Transport and suburban development in Middlesex down to 1914. *LoMAS* 29 (1978) 129–36.

Ancient times

748 BURGHARDT, A. F., The origin of the road and city network of Roman Pannonia. *JHG* 5 (1979) 1–20.

749 BARRIE, J. & WOODROW, D., A half century of transport in Hornsey. *HHSB* 19 (1979) 50–6.

750 MORACHIELLO, P., *Ingegneri e territorio nell'età della Destra (1860–1875): Dal Canale Cavour all' Agro Romano*. Rome: Officina 1976.

MODES OF INTER-URBAN COMMUNICATION

Roads

751 ALBERT, W., Popular opposition to turnpike trusts in early 18th century England. *JTH* 5 (1979) 1–17.

752 BERROW, P., *Drawing the map of Romsey*. Romsey: Lower Test Valley 1977. pp 18, il.

Shipping see also 300 318 710

753 BROWN, R. D., *The Port of London*. Lavenham: T. Dalton 1978. pp x + 202, il.

754 CLEERE, H., 'Roman harbours in Britain south of Hadrians Wall' in Taylor & Cleere, *Roman shipping and trade* [759] 36–40.

755 CONWAY JONES, A. H., The development of Gloucester docks. *G1HS* 10 (1979) 56–8.

756 MILNE, C. & G., The making of the London waterfront. *CA* 66 (1979) 198–204.

757 ROBINSON, A., *The maritime history of Maryport*. Clapham: Dalesman Pt 2 1978. pp 40, il.

758 STANIER, P. H., The copper ore trade of south west England in the 19th century. *JTH* 5 (1979) 18–35.

759 TAYLOR, J. du P. & CLEERE, H. eds, *Roman shipping and trade: Britain and the Rhine provinces*. Authors + Council for British Archaeology 1978. pp viii + 86.

Canals and inland navigation see also 751

760 BILLOT, C., Chartres et la navigation sur l'Eure à la fin du Moyen-age. *AdB* 2 (1978) 245–60.

761 BURNBY, J. G. L. & PARKER, M., *The navigation of the River Lee 1190–1970*. Enfield: Edmonton Hundred Historical Society 1978. pp 26, il.

762 CLINKER, C. R., *The Ashby-de-la-Zouch canal and its railways*. Bristol: Avon Anglia Publications 1978. pp 27, il.

763 ELLMERS, D., 'Shipping on the Rhine during the Roman period: the pictorial evidence' in Taylor and Cleere, *Roman shipping and trade* [759] pp 1–14.

764 GREB, G. A., Opening a new frontier: San Francisco, Los Angeles and the Panama canal 1900–1914. *PHR* 47 (1978 405–24.

765 MESSENGER, M. J., *Caradon and Looe – the canal, railways and mines: the history of the Liskeard and Looe railway and the mines and industries they served*. Truro: Twelveheads P 1978. pp 128, il.

766 SPENCER, H., *London's canal: the history of the Regent's canal*. Lund Humphries 1976. pp 96, il.

Railways see also 762 765 802

767 BANNISTER, G. F., Wolverhampton's forgotten station to be preserved. *RM* 124 (1978) 538–9.

768   BAYLISS, D. A., *The Post Office railway*. Sheffield: Turntable Publications 1978. pp 96, il.
769   BETJEMAN, J., *London's historic railway stations*. J. Murray 1978. pp 126, il.
770   CLINKER, C. R., *Paddington 1854–1979: an official history of Brunel's famous station in its 125th year*. Bristol: Avon Anglia Publications 1979. pp 28, il.
771   CONNOR, J. E. & HALFORD, B. L., *Forgotten stations of Greater London*. Bracknell: Forge Books 1978. pp 54, il.
772   DANE, R. A., *Railways of Peterborough*. Peterborough: Greater Peterborough Arts Council 1978. pp 47, il.
773   DEWEY, S. & WILLIAMS, N., *Wolverhampton railway album*. Wolverhampton: Uralia P Vol 1 1978. pp 62, il.
774   GRIFFITHS, R. P., *The Cheshire lines railway*. Blandford: Oakwood P. 1978. pp 92, il.
775   HEAPS, C. G., *London transport railway album*. I Allen 1978. pp 96, il.
776   HILTON, J. A., *A history of the South eastern and Chatham railway*. Hadlow: author Vol 1 1812–1845 1978. pp 54, il.
777   JOHNSTON, C. & HUME, J. R., *Glasgow stations*. Newton Abbot: David & Charles 1979. pp 175, il.
778   KIDNER, R. W., *The Newhaven and Seaford branch*. Tarrant Hinton: Oakwood P. 1979. pp 32, il.
779   KIDNER, R. W., *The South eastern and Chatham railway*. Blandford: Oakwood P 1978. pp 99 [24], il.
780   KINGSTON, P., Paddington 125. *RM* 125 (1979) 286–71.
781   OWEN, N., *The Tattenham corner branch*. Blandford: Oakwood P 1978. pp 33, il.
782   ROBERTSON, C. J. A., Early Scottish railways and the observance of the Sabbath. *SHR* 57 (1978) 143–67.
783   SLOAN, J. & MUIR, M. eds, *Glasgow, Paisley and Greenock railway company*. Glasgow: Jordanhill College of Education 1978. pp 79, il.
784   SOUTH, R., *Crown, college and railways: how the railways came to Windsor*. Buckingham: Barracuda Books 1978. pp 3–136.
785   THORNE, R., *Liverpool St Station*. Academy Editions 1978. pp 88, il.
786   THROWER, W. R., *King's Cross in the twenties*. Tarrant Hinton: Oakwood P 1978. pp 52, il.
787   TREBY, E., Branch to Stanmore. *RM* 125 (1978) 212–15.
788   WOODWARD, G. S., *The Hatfield, Luton and Dunstable railway*. Blandford: Oakwood P 1977. pp 72, il.

Air
789   LEARMOUTH, B., *The first Croydon airport*. Sutton: Sutton Libraries & Arts Services 1977. pp vii + 87, il.
790   PARROTT, E. V., *A pocket history and guide to Heathrow airport, London*. Rickmansworth: E. P. Publications 1977. pp 14, il.

MODES OF INTRA-URBAN COMMUNICATION

Public transport
791   ALTSHULER, A. A., *The urban transportation system: politics and policy innovation*. Cambridge, Mass: MIT P 1979.
792   BLACKER, K. et al, *London's buses*. St Albans: HJ Publications Vol I The independent era 1922–1934. 1977. pp xii + 49, il.
793   BURROWS, V. E., *Tramways in metropolitan Essex*. Upminster: author Vol 2 East Ham Corporation, Ilford Council, Barking Town UDC, West Ham Corporation 1976. pp 220, il.
794   COLLINS, S. G., *The wheels used to talk to us* [London trams]. Sheffield: Tallis Publishing 1977. pp 176, il.
795   CROUCH, M., Problems of Soviet urban transport [1870–1975], *SS* 31 (1979) 231–56.
796   HEARSE, G. S., *Tramways of the City of Carlisle*. Ramsey: author 1978. pp 56, il.
797   HINCHLIFFE, B. ed, *Huddersfield in the tramway era*. Sheffield: Turntable Publications 1978. pp 48, il.
798   JACKSON, A. A., *London's local railways*. Newton Abbot: David & Charles 1978. pp 384, il.
799   LONG, P. D., *One town, two operators: the story of the rise and fall of municipal bus services in Lowestoft*. Omnibus Society 1978. pp 20, il.
800   MACFARLANE WATT, A. K., *Southampton City transport: a history of its motor bus services*. Glossop: Transport Publishing 1977. pp 116, il.
801   MOORE, J. R., *Halifax Corporation tramways*. Halifax: Halifax Central Library Pt 1 1974. pp 26, il.

802 PEACOCK, T. B., *Great Western London suburban services*. Blandford: Oakwood P 1978. pp 109, il.
803 ROBBINS, G. J., *Metropolitan: the story of the tramways (MET) Omnibus Company Ltd 1912–1933*. Omnibus Society 1977. pp 24, il.
804 SEAL, M., *Cambridge buses*. Cambridge: Oleander P. 1978. pp 49, il.

Journey to work
805 BARKE, M., Changing journey to work patterns in Fife 1961–71. *SGM* 94 (1978) 145–58.

VII POLITICS AND ADMINISTRATION

RESEARCH METHODS AIDS AND MATERIALS

Archives
806 KEMPSON, E. G. H., A Marlborough book of statutes. *WANSM* 70/71 (1978) 99–103.
807 PALLISER, D. M., York's earliest administrative record: the Husgabel roll of c. 1284. *YAJ* 50 (1978) 81–91.

Printed documentary sources see 377–8

URBAN POLITICS AND ADMINISTRATION

Ancient times
808 GAGAMIN, M., Self defense in Athenian homicide law. *GRBS* 19 (1978) 111–20.
809 HANSEN, M. H., *Demos, ecclesia* and *dicasterion* in classical Athens. *GRBS* 19 (1978) 127–46.
810 NAGY, B., The Athenian Athlothetai. *GRBS* 19 (1978) 307–14.
811 SHEAR, T. L., *Kallias of Sphettos and the revolt of Athens in 286 BC*. Princeton: American School of Classical Studies at Athens 1978.

Medieval and early modern see also 381
812 BAR-NAVI, E., La ligue Parisienne (1585–94): ancêtre des partis totalitaires modernes? *FWS* 11 (1979) 29–57.
813 CASTELLAN, G., *Une cité provençale dans la Revolution* [Vence]. Paris: Flammarion 1978. pp 320.
814 DANIELS, B. C. ed, *Town and county: essays on the structure of local government in the American colonies*. Middletown, Conn: Wesleyan UP 1978.
815 FINLAY, R., The Venetian republic as a gerontocracy: age and politics in the Renaissance *JMRS* 8 (1978) 157–78.
816 KETTERING, S., *Judicial politics and urban revolt in seventeenth-century France*. Princeton: Princeton UP 1978.
817 LAW, J. E., Venice and the 'closing' of the Veronese constitution in 1404. *SV* 1977 (1978) 69–103.
818 LAW, J. E., Verona and the Venetian state in the 15th century. *IHR* 125 (1979) 9–22.
819 MARTINES, L., *Power and imagination: city states in Renaissance Italy*. New York: Knopf 1979.
820 MILES, T. L., Northleach court leet. *GlHB* 37 (1978) 5–7.
821 NAJEMY, J. M., Guild republicanism in trecento Florence: the successes and ultimate failure of corporate politics. *AHR* 84 (1979) 53–71.
822 NEWTON, R., The Chamber of Exeter in crisis. *DevH* 17 (1978) 7–11.
823 SANDERSON, F. E., The structure of politics in Liverpool 1780–1807. *HSLC* 127 (1978) 65–90.
824 WRIGHT, J., *The life of Cola di Rienzo* [Rome]. Toronto: Pontifical Institute of Medieval Studies 1975. pp 166.

Modern see also 167
825 BONNELL, V. E., Radical politics and organized labor in pre-revolutionary Moscow 1905–1914. *JSocH* 12 (1978) 282–301.
826 CAPECI, D. J., Fiorello H. La Guardia and the Stuyvesant town controversy of 1943. *NYHSQ* 62 (1978) 289–310.
827 CLEMENTS, K. A., Politics and the park: San Francisco's fight for Hetch Hetchy 1908–1913. *PHR* 48 (1979) 189–216.
828 EDWARDS, J. & BATLEY, R., *The politics of positive discrimination: an evaluation of the Urban Programme 1967–77*. Tavistock Publications 1978. pp xiii + 287.
829 FAIRBANKS, R. B., Cincinnati and Greenhills: the response to a federal community

1935–1939. *CinHSB* 76 (1978) 223–42.

830   FINK, L., 'Irrespective of party, color or social standing': the Knights of labor and opposition politics in Richmond, Virginia. *LabH* 19 (1978) 325–49.

831   FRASER, D., Politics and the Victorian city. *UHY* (1979) 32–45.

832   GAFFIELD, C., Big business, the working class and socialism in Schenectady 1911– 1916. *LabH* 19 (1979) 350–72.

833   GIFFORD, B. R., New York city and cosmopolitan liberalism. *PSQ* 93 (1978) 559–84.

834   HAMMACK, D. C., Elite perceptions of power in the cities of the United States 1880– 1900. *JUH* 4 (1978) 363–96.

835   HECKSCHER, A., *Mayor La Guardia and New York's legendary years*. New York: Norton 1978.

836   LEONARD, I. M., The politics of charter revision in New York City 1847–1849. *NYHSQ* 63 (1979) 7–24.

837   LLOYD, T. H., Chartism in Warwick and Leamington. *WarH* 4 (1978) 1–15.

838   LOTCHIN, R. W., The city and the sword: San Francisco and the rise of the metropolitan-military complex 1919–1941. *JAH* 60 (1979) 996–1020.

839   MARCUS, A. I., Professional revolution and reform in the progressive era: Cincinnati physicians and the city elections of 1897 and 1900. *JUH* 5 (1979) 183–208.

840   MARKUSEN, A. R., 'Class and urban social expenditure: a Marxist theory of metropolitan government' in Tabb & Sawers, *Marxism and the metropolis* [848] 90–111.

841   MCKICHAN, F., A burgh's response to the problems of urban growth: Stirling 1780– 1880. *SHR* 57 (1978) 68–86.

842   PATERSON, D., Tory political influence in mid 19th century Warwick. *WarH* 3 (1977/ 8) 197–207.

843   POTTS, J. H., The evolution of municipal accounting in the United States 1900–1935. *BuHR* 52 (1978) 518–36.

844   REICHE, E. G., From 'spontaneous' to legal terror: SA, police and the judiciary in Nurnberg 1933–4. *EuSR* 9 (1979) 237–64.

845   ROSE, M. H. & CLARK, J. G., Light, heat and power: energy choices in Kansas City, Wichita and Denver 1900–1935. *JUH* 5 (1979) 340–64.

846   SEARBY, P., Progress and the parish pump: local government in Coventry 1820–1890. *BAS* 88 (1976) 49–60.

847   STILLMAN, R. J., *The rise of the city manager: a public professional in local government*. Albuquerque: New Mexico UP 1979.

848   TABB, W. K. & SAWERS, L. eds, *Marxism and the metropolis: new perspectives in urban political economy*. New York: OUP 1978. pp viii + 376.

849   WATTS, E. G., *The social bases of city politics, Atlanta 1865–1903*. Westport, Conn: Greenwood P 1978. pp xii + 188.

URBAN POLITICS AT NATIONAL LEVEL

850   FRIEDEN, B. J., *Metropolitan America: challenge to federalism*. New York: Arno P 1978.

851   GOLDSMITH, W. W. & BERIAN, M. J., Is there an urban policy? [USA 1967–79]. *JReS* 19 (1979) 93–108.

852   HIRSCHHORN, L., The urban crisis: a post industrial perspective [USA 1970s]. *JReS* 19 (1979) 109–18.

853   INMAN, R. P., Federal policy and the urban poor [USA 1970s]. *JReS* 19 (1979) 119–30.

854   VINING, D. R., The President's national urban policy report: issues skirted and statistics omitted [USA 1969–75]. *JReS* 19 (1979) 69–78.

URBAN ADMINISTRATION

Public health see also 403 895 898

855   BAKER-JONES, D. L., To supply the sick poor [Carmarthen infirmary]. *CarmH* (1978) 3–28.

856   EVANS, N., 'The first charity in Wales': Cardiff Infirmary and South Wales Society 1837–1914. *WeHR* 9 (1979) 319–46.

857   PELLING, M., *Cholera, fever and English medicine 1825–1865*. Oxford: Oxford UP 1978. pp 342.

858   STORR, F., Nursing in Gloucester infirmary 1755–1865. *GlHS* 10 (1979) 42–9.

859   THOMAS, E. G., Chelmsford and the Board of Health report of 1849. *EJ* 14 (1979) 22–8.

Police

860   GAUTREY, A. J., Early days of Knutsford gaol. *ChesH* 1 (1978) 12–18.

861   JENNINGS, R. W., Northleach prison and the case of Charles Beale. *GlHB* 37 (1978) 3–5.

862   JORDAN, L. W., Police power and public safety in antebellum Charleston: the emergence of a new police 1800–1860. *SAUS* 3 (1979) 122–40.

863   PUGH, R. B., Newgate between two fires. *GUM* 3 (1978/9) 137–63; 199–222.

864   REPPETTO, T. A., *The blue parade*. New York: Free P 1978.

865   WILLIAMS, A., *The police of Paris 1718–1789*. Baton Rouge, La: Louisiana State UP 1979.

PUBLIC UTILITIES

Power see 845

VIII SHAPING THE URBAN ENVIRONMENT

Research methods see 874

Printed documentary sources

866   *Mémoires du baron Haussmann consacrées aux grands travaux de Paris*. Tome I Paris: Durier 1979. pp 268.

867   BERCE, F., *Les premiers travaux de la Commission des Monuments Historiques 1837–1848. Procès verbaux et relevés des architectes*. Paris: Picard 1979. pp 456.

Theory see 875

TOWN PLANNING AND ENVIRONMENTAL CONTROL

General

868   HASWELL, R. F., South African towns on European plans [18th & 19th cents]. *GM* 51 (1979) 686–94.

869   LOCKHART, D. G., The planned villages of Aberdeenshire: the evidence from newspaper advertisements. *SGM* 94 (1978) 95–102.

870   RODGER, R. G., The law and urban change [Scotland] *UHY* (1979) 77–91.

Ancient times

871   KIRK, W., Town and country planning in ancient India according to Kantilya's Arthasastra. *SGM* 94 (1978) 67–75.

Medieval and early modern see also 151 486

872   SZNURA, F., *L'espansione urbana di Firenze nel dugento*. Florence: La Nuova Italia 1975. pp xiv + 186.

873   WHITTINGTON, G., Medieval towns built to plan [Scotland]. *GM* 51 (1979) 541–7.

Modern see also 178 487

874   BLUMENFELD, H., *Metropolis and beyond: selected essays of Hans Blumenfeld*. New York: Wiley 1978.

875   BODDY, M. & GRAY. F., Filtering theory, housing policy and the legitimation of inequality. *PP* 7 (1979) 39–54.

876   BULLOCK, N., Housing in Frankfurt and the new *Wohnkultur*. *AR* 163 (1978) 335–42.

877   CAMPBELL, R. M., The Scottish Office and the Special Areas in the 1930s. *HJ* 22 (1979) 167–84.

878   CHERRY, G. E., The town planning movement and the late Victorian city. *IBG* 4 (1979) 306–19.

879   COOKE, C., Russian responses to the garden city idea *c.* 1902–31]. *AR* 163 (1978) 355–63.

880   FOSTER, M., City planners and urban transportation: the American response, 1900–1940. *JUH* 5 (1979) 365–96.

881   GOTTARELLI, E., *Urbanistica e architettura a Bologna agli esordi dell'Unità d'Italia*. Bologna: Cappelli 1979. pp 150.

882   HALPERN, K., *Downtown USA: urban design in nine American cities*. New York: Whitney Library of Design 1978.

883   HAWKES, D., The architectural partnership of Barry Parker and Raymond Unwin 1896–1914. *AR* 163 (1978) 327–32.

884   JONES, P., *Under the city streets*. New York: Holt, Rinehart and Winston 1979.

885   KAIN, R., Conservation planning in France: policy and practice in the Marais, Paris. *UPP* 7 (1979) 22–35.

886   KAIN, R., First Empire urbanism in the French provinces: a Breton 'Napoleonville':

military expediency and monumental elegance [extension of Pontivy] *Gazette des Beaux-Arts* 93 (1979) 81–94.

887 KAIN, R., Napoleon I and urban planning in Paris. *Connoisseur* (1978) 44–51.

888 KAIN, R., Urban planning and design in Second Empire France. *Connoisseur* (1978) 236–46.

889 MCSHANE, C., Transforming the use of urban space: a look at the revolution in street pavements. *JUH* 5 (1979) 279–307.

890 PEPPER, S., The garden city legacy. *AR* 163 (1978) 321–4.

891 PHILLIPS, P. A., Neo-corporatist praxis in Paris. *JUH* 4 (1978) 397–416.

892 READ, J., The garden city idea and the growth of Paris. *AR* 163 (1978) 345–52.

893 ROMANELLI, G., *Venezia ottocento. Materiali per una storia architettoniea e urbanistica della citta nel secolo XIX.* Rome: Officina Edizioni 1977. pp 622, il.

894 SAWERS, L., 'Cities and countryside in the Soviet Union and China' in Tabb & Sawers, *Marxism and the metropolis* [848] 338–64.

895 SCHULTZ, S. K. & MCSHANE, C., To engineer the metropolis: sewers, sanitation and city planning in late nineteenth century America. *JAH* 65 (1979) 389–411.

896 SICA, P., *Storia dell' urbanistica. Il Novecento.* Bari: Laterza 1978. pp 741.

897 STRUTHERS W. A. K. & WILLIAMSON, C. B., Local economic development: integrated planning and implementation in Merseyside [1947–79]. *TPR* 50 (1979) 164–84.

898 TARR, J. A., The separate vs. combined sewer problem: a case study in urban technology design choice. *JUH* 5 (1979) 308–39.

899 TREBBI, G., *La ricostruzione di una città: Berlino 1945–1975.* Milan: Mazzotta 1978. pp 197.

900 WYNN, M., Barcelona: planning and change 1854–1977. *TPR* 50 (1979) 185–203.

UTOPIAN PLANNING AND EXPERIMENTS

901 GOSI, R., *Il socialismo utopistico. Giovanni Rossi e la colonia anarchia Cecilia.* Milan: Moizzi 1977. pp 179.

902 VEYSEY, L. R., *The communal experience: anarchist and mystical communities in twentieth century America.* Chicago: Chicago UP 1978.

HOUSING IMPROVEMENT

Public housing provision see also 876 892

903 LAMBERT, J., PARIS, C. & BLACKABY, B., *Housing policy and the State: allocation, access and control* [Birmingham 1971–5]. Macmillan 1978. pp x + 178.

904 PEPPER, S. & SWENARTON, M., Home front: garden suburb for munition workers [World War I]. *AR* 163 (1978) 366–75.

905 MILLWARD, S., ed, *Urban harvest: urban renewal in retrospect and prospect.* Berkhamsted: Geographical Publications 1977.

906 HARTMAN, C. & KESSLER, R., 'The illusion of reality of urban renewal: San Francisco's Yerba Buena center' in Tabb & Sawers, *Marxism and the metropolis* [848] pp 153–78.

NEW AND EXPANDED TOWNS

907 OSBORN, F. J. & WHITTICK, A., *New towns: their origins, achievements and progress.* 3rd edn. L. Hill 1977 pp xix + 505, il.

908 RUBENSTEIN, J. M., *The French new towns.* Baltimore: John Hopkins P 1978.

909 TUPPEN, J., New towns in the Paris region: an appraisal [1965–78]. *TPR* 50 (1979) 55–70.

910 WEINER, H. R., New communities in Franco Spain: the rural towns of the Instituto Nacional de Colonizacion. *UPP* 7 (1979) 13–21.

IX URBAN CULTURE

URBAN CULTURE AND ENTERTAINMENT

Medieval and early modern

911 MITCHELL, B., The SPQR festivals of the early and mid cinquecento. *SCJ* 9 (1978) 95–102.

912 MUIR, E., Images of power: art and pageantry in renaissance Venice. *AHR* 84 (1979) 16–52.

913 PHILLIPS, M., Machiavelli, Guicciardini and the tradition of vernacular historiography in Florence. *AHR* 84 (1979) 86–105.

914   QUENIART, J., *Culture et société urbaine dans la France de l'Ouest au XVIIIe siècle.*
      Université de Haute Bretagne, Diffusion Klincksieck 1979. pp 590.
915   ROCHE, D., *Le siècle des lumières en Province. Académies et académiciens provin-*
      ciaux 1680–1789. Paris: Mouton 197. pp 394 + 520.
916   WATKINS, R. N. ed, *Humanism and liberty: writings on freedom from fifteenth century*
      Florence. Columbia, SC: South Carolina UP 1978.

Modern see also 553 554
917   LE BRUN, Y., Les cafés, cabarets et auberges à Rennes de 1849 à 1871. *AdB* 4 (1978)
      595–616.

ENTERTAINMENT

Mass entertainment
918   ALTICK, R. D., *The shows of London.* Cambridge, Mass: Belknap P 1978.
919   KASSON, J. F., *Amusing the million: Coney Island at the turn of the century.* New York:
      Hill & Wang 1978.
920   MCKIBBIN, R., Working class gambling in Britain 1880–1939. *PaP* 82 (1979) 147–78.

Music Hall
921   O'ROURKE, E., *Lambeth and music hall: a treasury of music hall memorabilia.* London
      Borough of Lambeth Directorate of Amenity Services 1977. pp 22.

Theatre
922   ARUNDELL, D., *The story of Sadler's Wells 1683–1977.* Newton Abbot: David &
      Charles 1978. pp xv + 352, il.
923   HAMMOND, N. G. L. & MOON, W. G., Illustrations of early tragedy at Athens. *AJA* 82
      (1978) 371–84.
924   HOWARD, V., *The show must go on: the story of the Theatre Royal, Norwich.* Norwich:
      Wensum Books 1977. pp 48, il.
925   INGRAM, W., *A London life in the brazen age: Francis Langley 1548–1602.* Cambridge,
      Mass: Harvard UP 1978.
926   WARWICK, L., *The Mackenzies called Compton: the story of the Compton Comedy*
      Company incorporated in the history of Northampton Theatre Royal and Opera
      House. Northampton: author 1977. pp 328, il.

Spectator sports
927   BEARMAN, R., Origins of rugby football in Stratford upon Avon. *WarH* 3 (1977/8)
      222–33.

FINE ARTS

Painting
928   ABRAMS, A. U., The Ferrer center: New York's unique meeting of anarchism and the
      arts. *NYH* 59 (1978) 307–25.

Sculpture
929   RIESS, J. B., The civic view of sculpture in Alberti's *De Re Aedificatoria. RQ* 32 (1979)
      1–17.

Other arts
930   *Otto argomenti di archittetura.* Milan: Il Formichiere 1979. pp 135.
931   STURGES, R. P., Harmony and good company: the emergence of musical performance
      in 18th century Derby. *Music Review* 39 (1978) 178–95.
932   TAWA, N., Buckingham's musical commentaries in Boston. *NEQ* 51 (1978) 333–47.

EXCHANGE OF INFORMATION

Newspapers
933   CORRIGAN, J. V., Strikes and the press in the north east 1815–44. *IRSH* 23 (1978)
      376–81.
934   FRASER, G. & PETERS, K., *The northern lights [Aberdeen Press and Journal* and
      Evening Express]. Hamilton 1978. pp 143, il.
935   HOPKIN, D., *The Merthyr Pioneer 1911–22. Lla* 4 (1979) 54–64.
936   Entry deleted

Other publications

937 DUNNE, P. A., Penny dreadfuls: late 19th century boys' literature and crime. *VS* 22 (1979) 133–50.

938 WARD, P., *Cambridge street literature.* Cambridge: Oleander P 1978. pp 64, il.

Radio and television

939 WILBUR, S. K., The history of television in Los Angeles 1931–1952. *SCalQ* 60 (1978) 183–205; 255–85.

EDUCATION see also 674 676

940 *Bell, book and boys: one hundred years of the Whitstable Boys School.* Whitstable: the school 1977. pp xiv + 76, il.

941 COHEN, R. D. & MOHL, R. A., *The paradox of progressive education: the Gary plan and urban schooling 1900–1940.* Port Washington, NY: Kennikat 1979.

942 FISHLANE, R. B., 'The shallow boast of cheapness': public school teaching as a profession in Philadelphia 1865–1890. *PenMHB* 103 (1979) 66–84.

943 GOLDSTROM, J. M., 'Education in England and Wales in 1851: the education census of Great Britain 1851' in Lawton ed, *The census* [507] 224–40.

944 HEATH, J. E., Industrialists and education in Derbyshire in the 19th century. *DM* 8 (1977) 92–4.

945 JONES, G., *The story of Milton Rd School, Gravesend 1884–1976.* Gravesend: author 1978. pp 55, il.

946 LAWES, J., Voluntary schools and basic education in Northampton 1800–1871. *NPP* 6 (1979) 85–91.

947 MEIRING, B. J., *Educational aspects of the legislation of the councils of Baltimore 1829–1884.* New York: Arno P 1978.

948 MOHRAZ, J. J., *The separate problem: case studies of black education in the north 1900–1930.* Westport, Conn: Greenwood P 1979. pp xvi + 165, il.

949 PEARSE, R. N., *The story of the Mary Datchelor School 1877–1977* [Southwark]. Hodder & Stoughton 1977. pp 267, il.

950 PHILIPP, J., *Early days in Bethanga and Springdale: to mark the centenary of the Bethanga State School and the closing of the school at Springdale.* Bethanga, Vic: Bethanga Springdale Schools Centenary Cttee 1977. pp 99, il.

951 REED, W. J., Broadstairs Holy Trinity School 1830–1970. *JKLH* 8 (1979) 8–9.

952 RIMMINGTON, G. T., Leicestershire School Boards 1871–1903. *LAHS* 52 (1976/7) 53–61.

953 SHEARING, D. K., Kettering schoolmasters in the Tudor and Stuart period. *NPP* 6 (1979) 81–2.

954 VIOLAS, P. C., *The training of the urban working class: a history of twentieth century American education.* Chicago: Rand McNally College Publishing Co 1978.

955 WEISS, M., Education, literacy and the community of Los Angeles. *SCalQ* 60 (1978) 117–42.

URBAN INFLUENCE ON RURAL AREAS AND THE WIDER WORLD

956 DANBOM, D. B., *The resisted revolution: urban America and the industrialization of agriculture 1900–1930.* Ames, Iowa: Iowa State UP 1979.

957 FISCHER, C. S., Urban-to-rural diffusion of opinions in contemporary America. *AJS* 84 (1978) 151–59.

958 MCDONALD, A. W., *The urban origins of rural revolution: elites and the masses in Hunan province, China 1911–1927.* Berkeley: California UP 1978.

959 Entry deleted

X ATTITUDES TO CITIES

ATTITUDES TO CITIES

General

960 THRUPP, S. L., 'The city as the idea of social order' in Grew & Steneck, *Society and history* [521] 89–100.

Ancient times

961 SAXONHOUSE, A. W., Comedy in Callipolis: animal imagery in the *Republic*. *APSR* 72 (1978) 888–901.

Medieval and early modern
962   LABROT, G., *Un instrument polémique. L'image de Rome au temps du Schisme 1534–1677*. Atelier de Reproduction des Theses de Lille III. Diffusion Champion 1979. pp 560.

Modern
963   LEES, A., Critics of urban society in Germany [1890–1914]. *JHI* 40 (1979) 61–84.
964   MORSE, R. M., Latin American intellectuals and the city, 1860–1940. *JLAS* 10 (1978) 219–38.
965   PEASE, J. H. & W. H., The bloodthirsty tiger: Charleston and the psychology of fire. *SCHM* 79 (1978) 281–95.

ELITE ATTITUDES

966   DAGNAUD, M., *Le mythe de la qualité de la vie et la politique urbaine en France. Enquête sur l'idéologie urbaine de l'élite technocratique et politique 1945–1975.* Paris: Mouton 1978. pp 326.
967   RICHARDS, P., R. A. Slaney, the industrial town and early Victorian social policy. *SH* 4 (1979) 85–102

Index of places

Register of research in urban history

This list is a continuation of that published in *Urban History Yearbook 1979*. It is based chiefly on replies given to inquiries directed to individual researchers or their supervisors but also draws to some extent on other listings, notably the *Theses Supplement of the Bulletin of the Institute of Historical Research*, and the lists prepared annually under the auspices of the Conference of Heads of Departments of Geography in British Universities, and from two comparable lists prepared by the Institute of British Geographers: Historical Geography Research Group, *Register of Research in Historical Geography*; Urban Geography Study Group, *Register of Members' Research Interest*. The Register given here is not confined to research being conducted for the purpose of obtaining a higher degree nor necessarily limited to work being done in this country or on aspects of its own urban history, though these features predominate. It is not rigidly exclusive in scope but all items included relate explicitly or implicitly to the historical development of particular towns or to broader aspects of urbanization as experienced in the past. The key to abbreviations is given below. The usefulness of the list as a means of promoting effective research depends entirely on the accuracy of the information supplied by individual scholars, and we are glad to be told of new projects or modifications to existing ones at any time. An index to place-names and themes is provided at the end.

Abbreviations

A	Aberdeen	Li	Liverpool
As	Aston	LSE	London School of Economics
Be	Queen's University Belfast		& Political Science
B	Birmingham	Lou	Loughborough
Ba	Bath	M	Manchester
Br	Bristol	N	Nottingham
Bra	Bradford	Ne	Newcastle
Bru	Brunel	O	Oxford
C	Cambridge	OU	Open University
CNAA	Council for National Academic	QMC	Queen Mary College
	Awards		(University of London)
Co	Cork	R	Reading
D	Durham	S	Sheffield
Du	Dundee	Sa	Salford
E	Edinburgh	So	Southampton
EA	East Anglia	SOAS	School of Oriental and African
Es	Essex		Studies (University of London)
Ex	Exeter	Stir	Stirling
G	Glasgow	Str	Strathclyde
Ga	Galway	StA	St Andrews
H	Hull	Sur	Surrey
HATPE	Historical Atlas of the Town	Su	Sussex
	Plans of Europe	TCD	Trinity College Dublin
IHR	Institute of Historical Research	U	Ulster (Coleraine)
K	Kent	UCD	University College Dublin
Ke	Keele	UCL	University College London
L	London	VCH	Victoria County History
La	Lancaster	W	Wales
Le	Leeds	War	Warwick
Lei	Leicester	Y	York

1　ADAMS, Dr I. H., Geog Dept Edinburgh U: Urb gr in Scotland w sp ref to hsg fr 1760
　　Book published [**The Making of Urban Scotland** (Croom Helm, 1978)]
2　AHMED, S. U., (Mr J. B. Harrison): Dacca 1840–84 (MPhil, L)
3　AHMED, Mrs Z., (Mr J. B. Harrison): Dacca c1880–1920 (PhD, L)
4　AIBARA, Miss A., (Prof K. A. Ballhatchet): Bombay City in late 19th c (PhD, L)
5　ALCRAFT, D., (Mr R. M. Y. Shackleton): Jos Chamberlain and pols of cent B'ham

1889–95 (MA, B) *Completed*

6 ALDERTON, D., (Dr K. G. T. McDonnell): Admin of Bury St Edm fr Dissoln to 17th c (MPhil, L)

7 ALEXANDER, Miss (Dr P. R. Thompson): Employment of women in Ldn in 20th c (PhD, Es) *Suspended*

8 ALEXANDRIS, A., (Mr R. R. M. Clogg): Greek minority in Istanbul 1918–56 (PhD, L)

9 ALLANSON, Dr E. W., Geog Dept U of New Eng Armidale NSW: Hist dev of tpt network of N New South Wales *No news*

10 ALLEN, Mrs M. E., (Dr R. F. Walker): Bor of Aldburgh 1547–1660 (MA, W)

11 ALLISON, Dr K. J., 21 Salmon Grove Hull: (1) Hist of Hedon; (2) Ed **VCH** Yorks E Riding; (3) Country houses of townsmen around Hull 1750–1850

12 ALLISON, Dr R., Coll St Mark & St John Plymouth: Hist geog of Plymouth *No news*

13 AL ZAIDAN, A., (Dr M. J. L. Young): Qayrawan: demog/soc composn during first 250 years (PhD, Le) *Completed*

14 ANDERSON, C. D. B., (Dr A. B. Worden): Pol hist of parl bors of Berks Bucks and Oxon 1660–85 (BLitt, O)

15 ANDERSON, Dr M. and COLLINS, Mrs B. E. A., Soc Dept Edinburgh U: Nat sample fr 1851 census of GB

16 APPLETON, M., (Dr G. L. Turnbull): Hist of Cash's of Coventry (MPhil, Le)

17 ARGENT, A., (Prof V. Pearl), The Flat Trinity Congreg Church St Matthews Rd Ldn SW2: Eccles/pol/soc hist of Ldn 1642–62 w sp ref to City parishes (PhD, L)

18 ARNISON, C. J., (Prof D. H. Aldcroft), 26 Telford Ave Leamington Spa: Estate dev in Leamington Spa (MPhil, Lei)

19 ARTHUR, L., (Mr T. H. Lloyd): Counter-culture of Swansea wkg class 1850–1918 (MSc, W) *Presumed abandoned*

20 ASHFORTH, D., (Dr D. Fraser): Poor Law in Bradford c 1834–c1872 (PhD. Bra) *Completed*

21 ASHTON, O. R., (Mrs D. Thompson): Chartism in Cheltenham Spa and Gloucester (PhD, B)

22 ASPINALL, P. J., Centre for Urb & Reg Stud B'ham U: (1) Leasehold estate management in 19th c prov Eng; (2) Size, struct and performance of house bldg ind in Vict Leeds, Sheffield, Nottingham; (3) (Dr A R. Sutcliffe) Leasehold town in 19th c prov Eng: urb land dynamics w sp ref to Grimsby, Sheffield, Southport, Eastbourne, Jarrow (PhD, S)

23 ASPINWALL, B., Hist Dept Glasgow U: (1) Glasgow as mun model for Amer pol 1890–1914 *Book in prospect*; (2) Robert Monteith 1812–84: soc reformer *Article published* [**Downside Review**, 1979]

24 ATKINS, Dr P. J., Geog Dept UC Swansea: Comm directories of 19th c Ldn

25 ATKINSON, Dr B. J., Eliot Coll Kent U: Bristol 1815–1914

26 ATTON, J. K., (Prof I. R. Christie): Loc pol/admin in Ipswich in early 19th c (MPhil, L)

27 AUSTIN, R. S. P., (Dr A. I. Forrest): Educ policies of Vichy govt in Dept of Hérault (PhD, M)

28 AVIV, Mrs A., (Mr A. R. M. Carr): Madrid bourgeoisie 1900–36 (DPhil, O)

29 AXWORTHY, R., (Dr C. Barron): Ldn and Edward III (MPhil, L)

30 BABOOLAL, E. R., Geog Dept King's Coll Ldn: Changes in distribn of black people in S Ldn 1961–71 (PhD, L)

31 BACON, C., (Dr A. R. Sutcliffe/R. A. Darke): Urb form and urb renewal: case study of Park Hill Flats, Sheffield (MA, S)

32 BAER, M. B., Hist Dept Frostburg State Coll Maryland: (1) Soc/pol struct of Vict Ldn; (2) Comp reg modernization [Ldn, Dublin, Edinburgh, Merthyr, Coventry, Liverpool, Preston, Norwich]; (3) Urbanization and the family in 19thc Br

33 BAGGOTT, Mrs C. M., (Dr C. Richmond): Florentine patrician families in 14th c (PhD, Ke)

34 BAILEY, K. A., (Mr P. Fearon) 32 Westhorpe Rd Ldn SW15: Battersea 1830–1900 w sp ref to estate dev and the bldg ind (PhD, Lei) *Abandoned*

35 BAILEY, Mrs S. C., (Prof Lord McGregor) 31 Rochester Sq Ldn NW1: Sweating system, family struct, and the minimum wage: women chainmakers of Cradley Heath [S Staffs] 1850–1930 (PhD, L)

36 BAINES, D. E., LSE: Internal and overseas migr in late 19th c *Book in prospect*

37 BAIRD, Mrs B. H., (Prof J. Gottmann): Urb gr and settlement struct of inter-urban areas w sp ref to Eng midlands (DPhil, D)

38 BAKER, Miss A. M., (Mr A. J. Nicholls): Hamburg in the Third Reich 1933–45 (DPhil, O)

39 BAKER, T. F. T., c/o IHR Senate Ho Ldn U: ed **VCH** Middx, vol VI [Finchley, Friern Barnet, Hornsey] *Published* 1979; vol VII [Acton, Chiswick, Ealing, Willesden]

40 BALDERSON, W. A., (Dr G. J. Lewis): Resid mobility in Gr Leicester (PhD, Lei)

41 BALL, Mrs J. R., (Dr C. P. S. Platt): Southampton in early spa period 1750–75 (MPhil, So)

42 BALLARD, Mrs P., 21 Grange Hill Rd B'ham 30: New rich in B'ham and W Midlands 1850–1914 (MPhil, R)

43 BALMER, P., (Dr A. R. H. Baker), Geog Dept Cambridge U: Populn migr in Surrey villages 1841–71 w sp ref to proximity of Ldn (PhD, C)

44 BANKS, P. J., (Mr M. Todd): Late Rom and early med Barcelona (PhD, N)

45 BARDSLEY, D. J., (Rev D. T. W. Price): Effects of pol/soc/econ reform movemts on workers in M'chester area 1815–30 (MA, W)

46 BARKER, Miss K. D., (Prof G. H. Martin/Mr R. G. Foulkes): Eng prov theatre 1840–70 (PhD, Lei)

47 BARKER, R., (Prof M. W. Beresford/Dr G. L. Turnbull): Poor law hospital provn 1870–1909 (PhD, Le)

48 BARLOW, G. F., (Prof J. F. Arnott): Queen's theatre in the Haymarket 1705–8 and the Duke's theatre Lincoln's Inn Fields Ldn 1658–1732 (PhD, G) *Presumed abandoned*

49 BARNES, Mrs J. C. F., (Dr J. K. Walton): Hand-loom weavers and radical pols in Carlisle 1795–1850 (MLitt, La)

50 BARRON, Dr Caroline, Hist Dept Bedford Coll Ldn: (1) London 1215–1485; (2) Contribns to med vol HATPE *Forthcoming*; (3) Hist of parish of St. Andrew, Holborn *Completed*

51 BARROS, J. L., (Mr M. D. Deas): Pub order and life in Mexico City 1840–50 (DPhil, O)

52 BARROWS, Mrs B. M., (Prof A. J. Taylor): W Riding Health Dept 1889–1974 (MPhil, Le) *Completed*

53 BARTON, D., (Dr J. C. G. Binfield): Noncon in late 19th c Derbs w sp ref to Methodism [Glossop, Matlock, Belper, Ashbourne, Derby] (MA, Le)

54 BASSETT, S. R., Hist Dept B'ham U: Excavations and research in Saffron Walden

55 BAUGH, G. C., The Shirehall Abbey Foregate Shrewsbury: (1) Ed **VCH** Shropshire; (2) Hist of Telford [Dawley, Madeley, Wellington]

56 BEAMISH, D. F., (Mr F. C. Mather): Parl/mun hist of Poole c1740–1840 (MPhil, So)

57 BECHERAND, A., 60 rue Marechal Foch 57321 Sarreguemines Cedex France: Leics Poor Law Unions since 1834

58 BECKWITH, I. S., Bishop Grosseteste Coll Lincoln: (1) Mkt centres in Lincs; (2) Schools in Lincs

59 BÉDARIDA, F., 13 rue Jacob 75006 Paris: Urb devel and life in late-Vict Ldn

60 BEHAGG, C., (Mrs D. Thompson): Masters and men in B'ham 1790–1850 (PhD, B)

61 BENABOUD, M., (Prof W. M. Watt/Dr M. V. McDonald): Pol/soc hist of Seville under Banū 'Abbād (PhD, E) *Completed*

62 BENTHAM, G., Geog Dept UEA: Changes in loc of employment, residence and journey to work in outer Ldn (PhD, L) *Presumed abandoned*

63 BERESFORD, Prof M. W., Sch of Econ Stud Leeds U: Bldg in 18th and 19th c Leeds

64 BERRY, Miss J. A., (Mr G. A. Usher): Chamberlain's a/cs of Rye corp 1448–64 (MA, W) *Abandoned*

65 BETTS, D. C., (Drs C. T. Harvie/J. F. Davis): Infl of tpt on land use between Nine Elms and Surbiton 1801–1931 (MPhil, OU)

66 BIDDLE, Prof M., Director Univ Mus Pennsylvania U 33rd/Spruce St Philadelphia (1) Archaeol and hist of towns; (2) Winchester Studies II-XI *Publication forthcoming No news*

67 BIDELEUX, Mrs A., (Mr U. P. Burke): Devotional cults in 16th c Lucca (DPhil, Su)

68 BIGGIN, Mrs J. R., (Dr W. B. Stephens/Mr A. Laing): Educ in Peebleshire 1872–1918 (MA, Le)

69 BILLINGE, M., Geog Dept Cambridge U: (1) Science, technology and rational culture in urban NW Eng 18th/19th c; (2) Soc geog of Eng spa towns in late 18th/19th c

70 BILSBOROUGH, P., (Dr N. L. Tranter): Sport/phys recreation in 19th c Glasgow (MLitt, Str)

71 BISHOP, G. L., 15 St Gerard's Rd Solihull B91 1TZ: Solihull parish book 1525–1710 *Published*

72 BLACK, Mrs J. N., (Prof N. Rubinstein): Concept of pub authy in works of Ital lawyers and humanists during Renaissance: Florence, Naples, Milan (PhD, L)

73 BLACK, Sister M. A., (Dr R. E. Aldrich): Ind schools in 19th c Ldn area (PhD, L)

74 BLACKMAN, Miss J. M., Ec & Soc Hist Dept Hull U: Loc mkts and dev of new urb centres in 19th c

75 BLAIR, J., Brasenose Coll Oxford: (1) Med and early mod Leatherhead incl survey of bldgs; (2) Religious gilds of Chesterfield

76 BLAKE, S., Cheltenham Art Gallery & Museum: Bldg hist of Regency and early Vict Cheltenham [Cheltenham Museum Research Project] *Publication forthcoming*

77 BLOCH, Ms C., (Dr N. Macmaster): Crime in 18th c Norwich (PhD, EA)

78 BOLTON, P., 43 Warwick Rd Wellesbourne Warwick: Hist of Leamington Spa *No news*
79 BOND, S. P., (Dr D. E. Martin): Trade unions in postwar Sheffield engineering ind (MA, S)
80 BONE, R., (Prof A. M. Everitt): Urb inns of E Midlands 18th/early 19th c (PhD, Lei)
81 BOOTH, A., (Dr E. J. Evans): Radicalism in NW Eng 1789–1803 (PhD, La) *Completed*
82 BOOTH, T., (Dr W. B. Stephens): Educ and soc in Dewsbury and dist 1800–70 (MEd, Le) *Abandoned*
83 BORSAY, P. N., (Prof G. S. Holmes) St David's UC Lampeter: Eng Urb Renaissance: infl of leisure and luxury on urb dev in Eng prov 1660–1760 w sp ref to Preston, Warwick, Bath (PhD, La)
84 BOULTON, J. P., (Dr R. B. Outhwaite) Darwin Coll Cambridge: Southwark in early mod period (PhD, C)
85 BOWERY, M. M., (Mr G. W. Higg): Educ devs in Newcastle u Tyne 1782–1841 (MEd, N)
86 BRADSHAW, J. T., (Dr W. B. Stephens): Educ and stds of literacy in Ilkeston and dist during ind gr (MPhil, Le)
87 BRAMWELL, W. M., (Mr R. A. Butlin): Commun and class struct in the Vict city (PhD, L)
88 BRAYSHAY, Dr M., Geog Dept Plymouth Poly: (1) Emigr from SW mining towns during 19th c; (2) Soc geog of 19th c Plymouth
89 BRECKLES, R. W., (Dr H. E. Meller): Soc struct in Ashfield 1840–1930 (MPhil, N)
90 BRIDGETT, R. W., (Mr J. H. Y. Briggs) 11 Margaret Av Stoke-on-Trent ST4 8EE: Newcastle-u-Lyme 1660–1760 (MA, Ke)
91 BRIGDEN, Miss S. E., (Prof G. R. Elton): Early Reformation in Ldn 1520–47 (PhD, C) *Completed*
92 BRIGGS, J. H. Y., Hist Dept Ke: Newcastle u Lyme in 19th c
93 BRINDLE, G., (Miss A. J. Kettle): Ec/soc hist of Cinque Ports 1450–1550 (PhD, StA)
94 BRISTOW, B. R., Sch of Ed Preston Poly: Resid differentiation in mid-19th c Preston (PhD, La)
95 BRITTAIN, R. R., The Dell Main Rd Ansty CV7 9JA: Coventry council policy and urb hist 1550–1780 *No news*
96 BROADERWICK, R. F., (Dr J. W. R. Whitehand): Urb fringe belts of B'ham 1750–1970 w sp ref to instit land use (PhD, B)
97 BROADHEAD, P. J., Goldsmiths Coll Ldn: Soc/relig/pol in Reformation Augsburg (PhD, K)
98 BROOKE, Prof C. N. L., Hist Fac Cambridge: Studies of med Ldn incl parish churches
99 BROOKER, K., (Mr K. H. Nield/Dr G. J. Crossick): Effects of tech change on soc/cult life of shoemakers in N'hampton in 19th c (PhD, Hu)
100 BROOM, P., (Prof A. E. Musson): Living std of M'chester cotton spinners 1800–50 (MA, M)
101 BROWN, C. G., (Prof S. G. Checkland/Dr R. J. Holton): Soc/pol role of churches in Vict Glasgow (MLitt, G)
102 BROWN, D., (Dr R. Jones): Evoln of resid land use in Newham, London (PhD, L)
103 BROWN, G., (Mr P. Clark): Blackburn marriages in mid 19th c (MPhil, Lei) *Suspended*
104 BROWN, P. W., (Mr J. H. Y. Briggs): Health and admin in 19th c Leek (MA, Ke)
105 BUCHAN, A. R., (Profs J. Butt/B. F. Duckham): Port of Peterhead (MLitt, Str) *Completed*
106 BUCHANAN, Mrs B. J., (Prof W. Ashworth/Dr C. Clay): Capital formation in N Somerset 1750–1830 (PhD, Br)
107 BUCHANAN, Dr R. A., Centre for Study of Technol Hist Bath U: Ind hist of Bristol region in 19th c
108 BUDD, Mrs J. L., (Dr G. J. Lewis): Spatial images and preferences: Leicester (PhD, Lei)
109 BURGESS, C., (Miss B. F. Harvey) Corpus Christi Coll Oxford: Lay relig in Bristol in 15th c (DPhil, O)
110 BURKE, U. P., Hist Dept Sussex U: Urbanization and soc change in e mod Europe *Book forthcoming* [Edward Arnold]
111 BURROUGHS, C. E. N., (Dr D. S. Chambers): Bldg conds in Rome and Papal states in mid 15th c (PhD, L) *Completed*
112 BUSH, Miss J., (Dr J. A. Ramsden): Lab pols and soc E Ldn during First World War (PhD, L) *Completed*
113 BUSH, R. J. E., Somerset Record Office Taunton: Asst Ed **VCH** Somerset: (1) Taunton; (2) Exmouth; (3) Wellington *Book forthcoming*
114 BUTLIN, Prof R. A., Geog Dept Loughborough U: Genesis and gr of towns in Ireland *No news*
115 BYRNE, M., (Dr R. A. Lewis): Loc govt and pols in Shrewsbury 1800–60 (MA, W)
116 CAFFERTY, P., (Mr W. M. Stern): Soc condits of Irish immigrants in mid 19th c Leeds (MSc, L)

117 CALLIGAS, Mrs C., (Prof D. M. Nicol): Evoln of town of Monemvasia (PhD, L)

118 CAMPBELL, J., Worcester Coll Oxford: Acting ed **Historic Towns** (British section HATPE), vol III Lond to 1500 *In preparation* (1978); vol IV-V Lond 1500–1800; vols VI-VII Edinburgh, S'hampton, B'ham, York, Winchester, Canterbury, Bury St Edmunds, Northampton, Lincoln, Plymouth, Windsor *No news*

119 CAMPBELL, Mrs M. E., Geog Dept Birkbeck Coll Ldn: Communications in 19th c Herts and their impact on populn struct of sel urb centres (MPhil, L)

120 CAMPION, W., 59b Mytton Oak Rd Shrewsbury: Urb elite of Shrewsbury 1480–1640 *No news*

121 CAMSELL, Miss M. M., (Prof R. B. Dobson): Durham city c 1250–1500 (DPhil, Y)

122 CANNADINE, Dr D. N., Christ's Coll Cambridge: Aristocracy and the towns in the 19th c *Book forthcoming* [Leicester UP] *No news*

123 CARLIN, Ms M., Wm Goodenough Ho Mecklenburgh Sq Ldn WC1: Topog'of med Southwark (PhD, Toronto)

124 CARR, A., (Dr A. C. Hepburn): Lab and nationalism in Belfast 1885–1949 (DPhil, U)

125 CARR, F., (Dr J. S. Hinton): Soc hist of Coventry 1914–39 (PhD, Wa)

126 CARR, S. P., (Mr A. R. M. Carr): Ind and soc in Barcelona 1914–23 (DPhil, O)

127 CARRÉ, Mrs B. M. E., (Mr M. Mullett): Soc posn and role of women in Quaker communities of NW Eng c1655–1780 (MLitt, La)

128 CARTER, A., Centre E Anglian Stud UEA Norwich: Norwich Survey

129 CARTER, Dr F. W., Geog Dept UCL: (1) Ind gr in 19th c Prague (PhD, L) *Completed*; (2) Hist geog of Split and Dubrovnik *Articles published* [**British-Croatian Review** 1979; **History Today**, 1980]; (3) Hist geog of Cracow

130 CARTER, Prof H. and WHEATLEY, Mrs S., U Coll of Wales Aberystwyth: (1) Merthyr Tydfil in mid-19th c: soc area analysis; (2) Gr of Welsh city system

131 CARVER, M. O. H., Archaeol Dept B'ham U: (1) Archaeol of Durham; (2) Study of 10th c Stafford pottery; (3) Archaeol definition of Stafford (with Miss J. Walker); (4) excavations in Lichfield

132 CAULTON, T., (Dr M. Naslas), 23A Collegiate Cresc Sheffield 10: Hsg and urb struct in Sheffield c1870–1914 (PhD, S)

133 CAVE, L. F., 24 Portland St Leamington Spa: Archit dev of Leamington Spa 1800–50 (MPhil, CNAA)

134 CEZAR, Prof M., Devlet Güzel Sanatlar Akademisi Findikli-Istanbul Turkey: (1) Architecture of the Turkish city; (2) Comm instits of trad Turkish city *No news*

135 CHAINEY, A., (Dr W. Ferguson/Mr J. M. Simpson): Dev of Assoc Football in Edinburgh area 1900–75 (MLitt, E)

136 CHALKLIN, C. W., Hist Dept Reading U: (1) Finance and construct of pub bldgs in Eng towns 1700–1830 w sp ref to bldg by Q sessions; (2) Dev of Tonbridge and Tunbridge Wells 1670–1870

137 CHAMP, Miss J. F., (Dr D. F. Allen) Kings Coll Ldn: Urbanization and renewal: RC commun in the ind W Mids 1650–1850 (PhD, B)

138 CHAMPION, Miss B., (Dr A. R. Bridbury): Soc/econ hist of Beverley in later M Ages (PhD, L) *Abandoned*

139 CHAMPION, W. A., (Mr C. V. Phythian-Adams): Aspects of elites in some marcher towns in 16th/17th c [Shrewsbury] (PhD, Lei)

140 CHAPLIN, R. A., Extramural Studs Dept B'ham U: New towns of early 19th c *No news*

141 CHAPMAN, A., (Dr D. Rubinstein): People's palace for E Ldn: study of Vict philanthropy (MPhil, H) *Completed*

142 CHAPMAN, Dr J., Geog Dept Portsmouth Poly: Evoln of Portsmouth and Portsea Island from M Ages to 1914 *Completed*

143 CHARLTON, A. A., (Drs I. L. Donnachie/A. A. MacLaren): Criminal behaviour in Glasgow 1800–1901 (PhD, OU)

144 CHECKLAND, Mrs E. O. A., Ec Hist Dept Glasgow U: Philanthropy in Scot in 19th c

145 CHECKLAND Prof S. G. Ec Hist Dept Glasgow U: (1) Dev of Glasgow; (2) Pub pol and urb dev in 19th c Britain; (3) Urb health in Scotland

146 CHERRY, Prof G. E., CURS Birmingham U: (1) 20th c town planning; (2) Effects of statutory town planning on urb form since 1918

147 CHINN, C. A., (Mrs D. Thompson): Soc dimension of retail trade in B'ham 1870–1914 (PhD, B)

148 CHRISTMAS, Mrs A. E., (Prof A. M. Everitt): Soc/econ hist of Gloucester 1820–71 (PhD, Lei)

149 CHRISTOPHER, Dr A. J., Geog Dept Port Elizabeth U South Africa: Dev of rural and urb landscapes in S Africa under European colonization 1652–1960 *No news*

150 CLARK, P. A., Ec & Soc Hist Dept Leicester U: (1) Gloucester and its region 1550–1800 w sp ref to soc/econ change; (2) Soc hist of Eng ale house to 1830

151 CLARKE, Dr C. G., Geog Dept Li: Race relats in San Fernando, Trinidad 1930–70

152 CLARKE, Miss P. C., (Prof N. Rubinstein): The Soderini and 15th c Florentine politics (MPhil, L)

153 CLAY-DOVE, G. M. W., (Prof A. M. Everitt): Sutton-in-Ashfield Notts 1740–1871 (MPhil, Lei)

154 CLEARY, A. S., Esmonde (Prof S. S. Frere): Towns and urbanization in Rom Br: evid from outside the defences (DPhil, O) *Completed*

155 CLEARY, P. G., (Dr R. E. Glasscock) St Joseph's Coll of Edn Belfast 11: Exam of processes involved in evoln of resid areas of Belfast c 1860–1920 (PhD, Be)

156 CLIFTON, Mrs G. C., (Prof A. H. John) 35 The Crescent Ldn N11 3HH: Staff and admin of Met Bd of Works 1856–89 (PhD, L)

157 CLOSE, Miss J. (Mr D. Large): Rom Catholicism in 19th c Bristol (MLitt, Br)

158 COCKTON, P., (Prof F. M. L. Thompson): Relns between central and loc govt: Loc Govt Bd and pub health 1871–88 w sp ref to NE Eng (PhD, L)

159 COLEMAN, Mrs M. A., (Dr S. Muthesius), 152 Chediston La Halesworth Suffolk: Planned company villages in EA 1920–39 (MPhil, EA)

160 COLES, A. J., (Prof H. J. Perkin): Health and hsg in W Cumb towns 1889–1939 [Whitehaven, Workington, Maryport] (PhD, La)

161 COLLINS, Mrs B. E. A., (Dr M. Anderson) Hist Dept New Univ Ulster: (1) Aspects of Irish immigr into two mid 19th c towns [Dundee, Paisley] (MPhil, E) *Completed*; (2) Textile labour in Edw Belfast

162 COLLINS, M. P., Bartlett Sch of Arch & Town Planning UCL: Gr and changing function of urb centres in S Ldn 1801–1961 (PhD, L)

163 CONZEN, Prof M. R. G., 2 Oakhurst Dr Newcastle NE3 4JS: (1) Hist geog of Europ towns: (2) Morphology of Br towns during Ind Rev *Published* [in Jäger, **Probleme des Städtewesens in industriellen Zeitalter**, Böhlau (Cologne/Vienna) 1978]

164 COONEY, E. W., Ec Dept York U: Bldg ind in Britain since 1860: changes in contract, techniques, and org

165 COOPER, Miss A., (Prof A. M. Everitt), Trelonydd Llanafan nr Aberystwyth Cards: Newark 1835–1914 (PhD, Lei)

166 COOPER, A. J., (Dr C. A. Bolt): L'pool and Amer econ connexion 1865–90 (PhD, K)

167 COOPER, J. C., Geog Dept Kingston Poly Kingston-u-Thames: Evoln and struct of metropolitan fringe of SW Ldn since 1800

168 CORFIELD, Dr P. J., Bedford Coll Ldn: (1) 17th/19th c Norwich; (2) English urb hist in 18th c

169 COSS, Dr P. G., Humanities Dept Newc-u-Tyne Poly: Coventry charters 12th/13th c *Publication forthcoming* [British Academy]

170 COTTRELL, Dr P. L., Ec & Soc Hist Dept Leicester U: Comm/ind/finan hist of 19th c L'pool

171 COWAN, A. F., (Dr P. Earle) Humanities Dept Newcastle Poly NE1 8ST: The urb patriciate: Lübeck, Venice 1580–1700 (PhD, L)

172 COWAN, I. R., (Prof H. J. Perkin): Educ ind and soc in Bolton 1840–1914 (PhD, La)

173 COWLARD, Dr K. A., Geog Sect City of London Poly: Ldn docklands since 1800

174 COX, J. G., 1A Crown La Theale Reading: SM Peto 1809–89, contractor and spec bldr (MSc, Ba)

175 COX, Mrs P. M., (Mr W. M. Stern): Maldistribn of educ resources in Ldn under the voluntary socs 1839–70 (MSc, L) *Completed*

176 COX, S. C., Mander Coll Bedford: Infl of landownership on Beds towns in 18th/19th c *No news*

177 CRAMPSEY, R. A., (Prof S. G. Checkland): Econ/soc/cult effects of Assoc Football on Scots life and leisure 1873–1973 (MLitt, G)

178 CRANE, M., (Prof J. P. C. Roach): Wkg-class educ in 19th c Derby (MA, S)

179 CREET, R. A., (Prof H. J. Perkin): Aspects of soc hist of pawnbroking w sp ref to Ldn, B'ham, Preston 1850–1960 (PhD, La)

180 CRICKMORE, Miss J., Hist Sch B'ham U: (1) West Mids towns and villages in Roman period; (2) Romano-British town and village defences

181 CROFTS, Mrs J. E., Geog Dept Aberdeen U: Resid segreg in urb communities of NE in rel to function and size (PhD, A)

182 CRONE, P. R., Geog Dept UC Wales Aberystwyth: Substandard wkg class hsg in 19th c (PhD, W)

183 CRONJE, Miss G., (Dr E. H. Hunt): Tuberculosis in Eng & Wales 1850–1910 (MPhil, L)

184 CRONON, W. J., (Prof P. Mathias): Energy and the gr of an Eng town: Coventry since 1860 (DPhil, O)

185 CROOK, Dr M. H., Hist Dept Keele U: Revolutionary Toulon

186 CROSSLEY, A., Clarendon Bldg Broad St Oxford: ed **VCH** Oxon IV, City of Oxford *Published*

187 CULHANE, M., Geog Dept UC Cork: Changing patterns of resid dev in 19th c Limerick

(MA, Co) *Presumed abandoned*

188 CULLEN, A. P., Econs Dept Birkbeck Coll Ldn: Dev of owner-occupied hsg market and bldg soc capital accumulation (PhD, H)

189 CUMMINGS, A. J. G., (Prof J. Butt): The York Bldgs Co (PhD, Str)

190 CUNNINGHAM, P. J., (Prof P. H. J. H. Gosden): Formation of schools of design 1830–50 w sp ref to M'chester, B'ham, Leeds (PhD, Le)

191 CUNNINGHAM, R. G., (Dr J. B. Baird) Geog Dept Glasgow U: Origin and evoln of Kirktouns in Scot (MLitt, G)

192 CUTLER, Mrs J., (Prof G. R. J. Jones): 19th c Morley (MPhil, Le) *Presumed abandoned*

193 DANIELS, S. D., Geog Dept UCL: Urb planning and soc order in 19th c Eng

194 DAUNTON, Dr M. J., Ec Hist Dept Durham U: (1) Wkg-class hsg in Vict cities; (2) Lab mkts in Vict cities

195 DAVIDSON, N. S., Hist Dept Leicester U: Inquisition in 16th c Venice (PhD, C)

196 DAVIES, G., (Prof I. G. Jones): Bethesda, dev of a N Wales slate-quarry town (MA, W)

197 DAVIES, J. R., (Dr C. R. Lewis) Geog Dept UC Wales Aberystwyth: Urb dev of Rhondda in 19th c (PhD, W)

198 DAVIES, S. J., (Mr B. P. Lenman/Dr N. G. Parker): Law and order in 17th c Stirling (PhD, StA)

199 DAVIS, G. P., (Dr R. A. Buchanan): Image and reality in a Vict prov city: a wkg-class area of Bath 1830–1900 (PhD, Ba)

200 DAVIS, M. B., Geog Dept LSE: The emerging supranational cities (MPhil, L)

201 DAVIS, M. T., Geog Dept Portsmouth Poly: Functional relat village/town in 19th c E Yorks (PhD, CNAA)

202 DAVISON, A. J., (Dr R. H. Wilkinson): Educ in NY City 1890–1925 (DPhil, Su)

203 DAVISON, R. S., (Dr A. T. Q. Stewart): Effects of German air raids on Belfast (PhD, Be)

204 DAY, M. G., (Prof P. H. Coles/J. Reynolds): Nonconformity and the urb/ind culture in Bradford textile dist (PhD, Bra)

205 DELANEY, S. T., (Dr J. W. R. Whitehand): Diffusion and urb form w sp ref to GB in 20th c (PhD, B)

206 DELVES, A., (Dr J. R. B. Johnson), Dept of Hist Sheffield Poly: Recreation, soc class and culture in 19th c Derby (PhD, B)

207 DENNIS, Dr R. J., Geog Dept UCL: (1) Hsg and resid mobility in Vict towns; (2) Eng ind cities of 19th c *Book in progress*

208 DERRICK, J. M., (Dr R. J. A. R. Rathbone): Douala under Fr rule 1916–36 (PhD, L) *Completed*

209 DEWS, C. R., (Dr D. Fraser): Methodism in Leeds since 18th c (MSc, Bra)

210 DICKINSON, Mr G. C., Geog Dept Leeds U: Changes in urb land use in Leeds 1954–74

211 DILLON, M. J., (Mr M. B. Stedman): Urb conserv in sel towns in W Midlands (PhD, B)

212 DILS, J., Extramural Dept School of Ed Reading U: Soc and econ dev of Reading 1540–1640

213 DOBSON, Prof R. B., Hist Dept York U: Edn of York Chamberlains' accs 1396–1500

214 DOCHERTY, H. N., (Dr I. B. Cowan/I. A. Muirhead): Churches in the med Scottish burgh 1400–1560 (MLitt, G) *Completed*

215 DOHERTY, A. C., (Prof J. R. Jones/W. Letwin): Ldn merchts and America 1660–90 (PhD, L)

216 DONBAVAND, R. M., Geog Dept N'ham U: Soc geog of Vict N'ham 1841–71 (PhD, N)

217 DOTTIE, R. G., (Mrs J. I. Kermode): 17th/18th c Childwall (MA, Li)

218 DOYLE, P. H., (Dr E. Duffy): Dev of Rom Catholic diocese of L'pool c 1850–70 (MPhil, L) *Presumed abandoned*

219 DRAKE, P., (Mr R. M. Y. Shackleton): Labour and the Spanish Civil War w sp ref to B'ham labour movement (MLitt, B) *Completed*

220 DRESSER, Ms M., (Prof W. Ashworth) Humanities Dept Bristol Poly: Hsg policy in Bristol 1918–29 (MSc, Br)

221 DRUMMOND, Mrs G., (Prof J. K. Davies): Leisured classes in Athens 300 BC–cAD50 (DPhil, O)

222 DUKE, Mrs R. L., (Prof K. W. Swart): Religions between church and state in Leiden 1572–1620 (PhD, L)

223 DUNNING, Dr R. W., County Hall Taunton: ed **VCH** Somerset: Bridgwater, Watchet, Williton, **IV [Crewkerne]** *Published* (1978)

224 DUNSTER, Miss S., (Mr M. B. Cooper): Family struct in a Catalan town [Besalú] in 16/17th c (PhD, EA)

225 DUPREE, Miss M. W., (Prof P. Mathias) Nuffield Coll: Family struct in Staffs potteries 1840–80 (DPhil, O)

226 DURES, A. J., (Prof J. Hurstfield): Recusants in Ldn 1580–1629 (PhD, L)

227 DUREY, Dr M. J., Sch of Soc Inquiry Murdoch U Western Australia 6153: (1) Relat between changing envir condits and fluct death rate, Perth WA 1870–1920; (2) Scien-

tific instits and prov medical men 1790–1850 [Worcester, Northampton] *Publication forthcoming*

228 DYCHKOFF, Mrs C., (Prof Rosalind M. T. Hill): York officials and the diocesan and prov admin of York 1317–40 (BLitt, O) *Suspended*

229 DYER, Dr A. D., Hist Dept Univ Coll of N Wales Bangor: Eng prov towns 1500–1700

230 DYER, Dr C. C., Hist Dept B'ham U: (1) Estates of bishopric of Worcester 680–1540 *Publication forthcoming*; (2) Worcester (HATPE)

231 EASTWOOD, J., (Dr W. B. Stephens): Secondary educ in Sowerby Bridge area in late 19th/early 20th c (MEd, Le)

232 EBERY, M. G., Geog Dept Reading U: Pop/soc struct in Reading in mid 19th c (PhD, R)

233 EDDEN, D. W., (Mr M. B. Stedman): Infl of tenants' and residents' assocs on planning processes w sp ref to B'ham area (MA, B)

234 EDWARDS, Dr J. H., Hist Dept B'ham U: (1) City and region of Córdoba 1450–1520; (2) Communidades revolt in Castile early 16th c

235 EDWARDS, P., Roehampton Coll of Ed Surrey: W Mids towns and horse trade in 16th/17th c

236 ELLIS, Dr J. M., Econs Dept L'borough U: Newcastle u Tyne 1660–1760

237 ELLIS, S. P., (Prof S. S. Frere): Archaeol study of Medit urb dom hsg 400–700AD (DPhil, O)

238 ELLISON, D., (Mr J. Reynolds): Pre-ind Bradford (MSc, Bra) *Abandoned*

239 ELLMERS, C. J., (Dr A. M. Lambert): Clerkenwell 1590–1841 (MPhil, L)

240 ELRINGTON, C. R., IHR Senate Ho Ldn U: (1) Hist of Shoreham *Publication forthcoming* [**VCH** Sussex VI]; (2) ed **VCH**

241 ELTON, E. A., (Dr W. B. Stephens): Educ and soc in Holbeck c1800–80 (MPhil, Le)

242 ENGLANDER, D., (Dr A. Mason): L'lord and tenant in urb Br: pols of hsg reform 1838–1924 (PhD. War) *Completed*

243 ESTEVE-COLL, Miss E., 7 Boyd Close, Kingston u T KT2 7RL: Ldn churches in M Ages (MPhil, L)

244 EVANS, Dr A. K. B. and R. H., Hist Dept Leicester U: Colleg church of St Peter's W'hampton (incl estates to 1848) *No news*

245 EVANS, D. G. (Prof J. G. Williams): Mkt towns of Denbighshire 1640–90 (MA, W) *Completed*

246 EVANS, G. (Prof I. G. Jones): Seaside resorts on N Wales coast in 19th c (PhD, W)

247 EVANS, Mrs L. (Prof A. W. Coats): Econ/soc hist of Hucknall in 19th c (MPhil, N) *Suspended*

248 EVERITT, Prof A. M., Eng Loc Hist Dept Leicester U: (1) N'hampton 1500–1760; (2) Evangelicalism Anatomized: N'hampton and early hist of movement 1700–50; (3) Origins of Eng mkt towns; (4) The mkt town in the Ind Rev

249 FALCONER, K. A., (Dr J. H. Appleton): Hist geog of canal tpt in Br Isles (PhD, H)

250 FARMER, A., (Mr J. Reynolds): Soc change and instit in Bradford 1830–70 (PhD, Bra)

251 FARR, I., (Prof A. Teichova): Urbanism and anti-urbanism in pre-1914 Bavaria (PhD, EA)

252 FARR, R., (B. W. Clapp/Dr M. Hewitt): Church and soc in later 19th c Devon w sp ref to Exeter (PhD, Ex)

253 FARRANT, Dr S. and J. H., Humanities Dept Brighton Poly: Populn, occupations and spatial dev of Brighton 1600–1820 *Publications in progress* [**Sussex U Centre for Continuing Education Occasional Papers**]

254 FEDERER, A. J., (H. Horwitz): Soc/econ in Westminster 1660–1800 (PhD, Univ of Iowa)

255 FERSAN, Mrs N. (Prof D. Kuban): Preservation of hist environt of some small Anatolian towns (PhD, Technical U Istanbul) *Presumed abandoned*

256 FEUILHERADE, P. (Dr S. Marks): Crime, law and soc: Johannesburg 1918–39 (MPhil, L)

257 FIELD, J. L. (Mr M. A. Shepherd): Soc control and charity in Portsmouth 1815–70 (PhD, War) *Completed*

258 FINLAY, Dr R. A. P., NW Reg Studs Centre Lancaster U: (1) Pop of Ldn 1580–1650; (2) Hist demog of NW Eng 1550–1800

259 FINNIGAN, R. E., (Dr D. Fraser): Hsg in W Riding 1918–39 w sp ref to Leeds and Bradford (MSc, Bra)

260 FLEMING, D. (Mr C. V. Phythian-Adams): Soc/ec dev in Leics towns 1500–1700 [Melton Mowbray] (PhD, Lei)

261 FORSTER, G. C. F., Hist Sch Leeds U: (1) York in 17th/early 18th c; (2) York for HATPE; (3) Leeds to 1700 *Book forthcoming* [Manch UP]; (4) N Riding towns and York [Hist of Landscape ser]; (5) Towns and town life in Yorks since 1066 [part of book for Batsford]; (6) Early years of Leeds Corp *In the press* [Thoresby Soc]

262 FORSYTH, W., (Prof S. G. Checkland), Ec Hist Dept Aberdeen U: Econ determinants of

expansion of 19th c Glasgow (PhD, G)

263 FORTY, A., Fac Environ Stud UCL: Changes in practice of architecture

263A FOSTER, Dr A., Hist Dept W Sussex Inst of Higher Ed: Arundel and its region 1500–1835

264 FOSTER, B., (Mr E. Gillett): Pub health in 19th c Hull (MPhil, H) *Completed*

265 FOX, J. R. R., (Prof D. P. Waley): Siena: contado and city relns c1200–1400 (MPhil, L) *Abandoned*

266 FOX, R. C., Geog & Hist Dept Sunderland Poly: Demog of Vict Sunderland

267 FRANKGAKIS, E., (Mr R. M. M. Clogg): Commerce of Smyrna in 18th c (MPhil, L)

268 FRASER, Dr D., Undergrad Sch of S in Soc Sci Bradford U: (1) Urb pol in Vict Eng; (2) Estab of mun authy in 19th c cities *Book published* [**Power and Authority in the Victorian City** (Blackwell, 1979)]; (3) Editor **A History of Modern Leeds** *In the press* [Manch UP]

269 FREEMAN, Dr M. J., Sch of Geog Oxford U: Road tpt dev Lancs-Yorks 1750–1850

270 FRENCH, C. J., (Prof W. E. Minchinton): Ldn's overseas trade in 18th c (PhD, Ex)

271 FRENCH, Dr R. A., Geog Dept UCL: Urb origins/morphol in pre-Revol Russia

272 FYSON, R. C. M., (Prof H. J. Perkin): Chartism in N Staffs (PhD, La)

273 GAFFNEY, R. H., (Dr J. F. McCaffrey/Mr G. B. A. M. Finlayson): Hospital prov in Glasgow 1867–97 (PhD, G)

274 GAITSKELL, D., (Dr S. Marks): African women and white women missionaries on the Witwatersrand 1900–40 (PhD, L)

275 GARDNER, R., SOAS Ldn: Serowe: study in urbanization (MPhil, L)

276 GARGRANE, R., 201 Weddington Rd Nuneaton: Coventry council policy and social probs 1650–1750 *No news*

277 GARNER, R. S., (Prof G. R. J. Jones): Changing uses of common land in sel urb areas of W Yorks (PhD, Le)

278 GARRARD, J. A., Dept of Sociol & Pol Stud Salford U: Leadership and pol in Bolton, Blackburn, Rochdale, c 1830–80

279 GARROD, P., (Dr G. L. Turnbull/F. H. Capie): Bradford woollen ind 1900–39 (PhD, Le)

280 GARSIDE, Ms P. L., North Ldn Poly: (1) Dev of town-planning policy by LCC 1930–61 (PhD, L); (2) Estate dev in Somers Town NW1 1783–1812 *Suspended*; (3) Br town planning and econ change 1900–40; (4) Br post-war hsg pol

281 GERSON, Mrs R., (Prof K. W. Swart): Radical movement in Neths w sp ref to Rotterdam (PhD, L)

282 GILL, Mrs R., (Dr T. Raychauduri): Amritsar in 19th/20th c (DPhil, O) *Presumed abandoned*

283 GILLETT, E., Hist Dept Hull U: (with K. A. MacMahon) **History of Hull** [OUP, 1979]

284 GLEAVE, D. R., (Dr R. Virgoe): Bor of Cambridge in 13th c (PhD, EA)

285 GLEN, R. A., Hist Dept Vermont U Burlington VT 05401 USA; (1) Manch grammar school in early 19th c *Article published*; (2) Milnes of Stockport *Published* [**Cheshire History**]; (3) Urb workers in early ind rev

286 GOFFEE, R., (Dr W. A. Armstrong/Mr R. Scase): Kent miners: stabil and change in work and community [Aylesham] 1927–76 *Completed*

287 GOODALL, Miss H., (Dr B. J. Atkinson), Eliot Coll Kent U: Lab aristoc in Ashford and Burnley c1840–c1870 (MA, K)

288 GOODER, Dr A., and Mrs E. A., Oak Tree Cottage Shaw's Lane Five Ways nr Hatton Warwick: (1) Coventry in 13th/14th c; (2) Nuneaton in 14th/16th c

289 GOODWAY, D. J., (Prof E. J. Hobsbawm): Chartism in Ldn 1838–48 (PhD, L) *Completed*

290 GOODWYN, E. A., Cherry Hill Ashman's Rd Beccles Suffolk: Beccles 1816–60 *No news*

291 GORE, D. A., (Mr M. Todd): Topog of Cologne in Rom and early med periods (PhD, N)

292 GOTEL, J., (Dr T. Zeldin): Aspects of crime in Paris 1880–1914 (BLitt, O) *Presumed abandoned*

293 GRACE, F., (Prof R. A. Church): Econ/soc hist of Ipswich 1780–1840 (PhD, EA)

294 GRACE, R. P., (Dr R. A. Lewis): Poor law admin in Hendon, Pwllheli [1834–71] (MA, W) *Abandoned*

295 GRADY, K., (Prof M. W. Beresford): Prov of pub bldgs in Leeds and W Riding towns c1600–1840 (PhD, Le)

296 GRAHAM, Dr B. J., Geog Dept Ulster Poly Jordanstown: (1) Populn of med Irish towns; (2) Evoln of med Irish urbanization *Published* [**Journal of Hist Geog,** 1979]

297 GRAHAM, Mrs E., (Dr D. C. D. Pocock): Explanation in urb geog w sp ref to spatial struct of Vict Edinburgh (PhD, D)

298 GRAHAM, M., (Prof D. H. Aldcroft), 9 Hill View Rd Oxford: Suburb dev of Oxford 1850–1900 (MPhil, Lei)

299 GRANT, G. R. N., (Dr G. R. Searle): Aspects of pol in Norwich in late 19th/20th c (MPhil, EA)

300 GRASBY, K. D., (Dr F. G. B. Millar), Queen's Coll Oxford: City of Rome AD 70–238; aspects of govt and soc (DPhil, O)
301 GREANY, R. A. H., (Dr H. Willmer): Churches in Hartlepools 1850–1900 (MPhil, Le)
302 GREEN, A. M., (Mr T. M. Slater) Hist Dept Worcester Coll of Higher Ed: Worcester in 19th c (MA, B)
303 GREEN, D. R., (Dr G. Stedman Jones) Geog Dept Cambridge U: Poverty in mid-Vict Ldn 1830–90 (PhD, C)
304 GREEN, P., (Dr M. Naslas/Dr A. R. Sutcliffe): German system of reg capitals w sp ref to Munich (MA, S)
305 GREEN, R. J., (Mr D. W. Crossley): Road tpt and roads in Sheffield and N Derbyshire in 18th c (MA, S)
306 GREENALL, R. L., Adult Ed Dept Leicester U: (1) Pol/econ/soc dev of Salford 1790–1914; (2) Hist of Daventry 1574–1851
307 GREENHALGH, Rev D. M., (Mr D. Large): 19th c Wells (MLitt, Br)
308 GREENSHIELDS, T. H., Geog Dept Durham U: Dev of urb system of Gr Syria (PhD, D)
309 GREENSLADE, M. W., County Bldgs Martin St Stafford: ed **VCH** Staffs; Vol VI (Stafford) *In the press*
310 GREGORY, D. J., Geog Dept Cambridge: (1) (Dr E. A. Wrigley) Transf of reg econ systems; ind change in W Riding in 18th/19th c (PhD, C); (2) Emergence of ind urbanism in 19th c Br *Book forthcoming*; (3) Diffusion of cholera in Vict Ldn (with Dr A. D. Cliff)
311 GREGSON, W. J., c/o Geog Dept Hull U: Phys/soc/demog changes in Preston in mid 19th c (MA, H)
312 GRIBBON, Mrs S. E., (Prof J. C. Beckett) Hist Dept UC N Wales: (1) Soc/ec life of Edw Belfast (PhD, Be); (2) Hist of 16th/20thc Belfast
313 GRIFFITHS, Dr R. A., Hist Dept Univ Coll Swansea: Bors of med Wales *Book published* [U of Wales Press, 1978]
314 GUY, Miss I., (Miss A. J. Kettle): Late med and e mod Perth (BPhil, StA)
315 HALFORD, M., CRO Shirehall Shrewsbury: 18th c Shrewsbury *No news*
316 HALL, A. A., Teeside Poly: Wkg class lvg stds in Middlesborough and Teeside 1870–1914 (PhD, CNAA) *Completed*
317 HALLIDAY, A. L., (Prof F. J. H. Haskell): Impact of Napoleonic Paris on Eng art 1802 (BLitt, O)
318 HALSTEAD, J. L., (Prof S. Pollard) Dept Extra-Mural Stud Sheffield U: Ec struc of Huddersfield 1840–1939 (PhD, S)
319 HALSTEAD, Miss K. A., Geog Dept City of Ldn Poly: Dev of urb fabric of part of Ldn dockland 1796–1909 (PhD, L)
320 HAMILTON, Mrs E. C., (Prof A. A. M. Duncan); Glasgow churches c1800–50 (MLitt, G) *Suspended*
321 HANSON, Mrs A. L., (Prof A. M. Everitt): 18th/19th c Mansfield (PhD, Lei)
322 HANSON, Miss J. K. M., (Dr I. N. R. Davies): Civilian pop and the Warsaw uprising 1944 (PhD, L) *Completed*
323 HARBOUR, A. G. W., (Prof F. J. Fisher): Brewing ind in 17th c Ldn (MPhil, L)
324 HARDING, Miss V., (Dr M. C. Prestwich): Port of Ldn in mid 14th c (PhD, StA)
325 HARLEY, Dr J. B., Geog Dept Exeter U: OS town plans in 19th c
326 HARPER, F., (Dr J. M. Winter): Origins of lower middle classes in a mid-W town in USA 1860–1900 (PhD, War)
327 HARRIES, Miss J. D., (Dr J. F. Matthews): Bishops, aristocrats and their towns: role of churchmen from Gaul from Paulinus of Nola to Sidonius Appolinaris (DPhil, O)
328 HARRIS, P. A., Harrogate Grammar Sch: Gr of Harrogate esp in rel to tpt *No news*
329 HARRIS, T. M., (Dr A. Harris), Geog Dept Portsmouth Poly: RN dockyard towns of Gr Br (PhD, H)
330 HARRISON, B. L., (Dr E. J. Evans): Poor law admin in Kirkby Lonsdale 1790–1841 (MLitt, La)
331 HARRISON, M., Birmingham Poly: (1) T. C. Horsfall a soc reformer in late Vict/Edwardian M'chester (PhD, M); (2) Hsg and town planning in M'chester before 1914 *No news*
332 HARROD, L. M., (Prof V. Pearl/Mr D. E. Baines): Islington from mid-17th to mid-19th c (MPhil, L)
333 HART, A. P., (Dr R. M. Hartwell) 6 Caledonia Pl Clifton Bristol: Bristol riots of 1831 and the mass media (DPhil, O)
334 HART, T., Ec Hist Dept Glasgow U: Comp world urb dev 800–1970
335 HARTLEY, Dr O. A., Pol Dept Leeds U: Hist of Eng loc govt 1689–1902
336 HARVEY, Prof P. D. A., Hist Dept Durham U: Gen ed **Portsmouth Record Series:** Royal Charters of Portsmouth 1194–1682 ed G. H. Martin and further titles in preparation

337 HASTINGS, R. P., 11 North Side Hutton Rugby Yarm TS15 0DA: B'ham lab movemt 1900–45 *No news*
338 HASWELL, R., Geog Dept U of Natal SA: Making of historic S African townscapes
339 HAUGEN, F. E., (Mr D. E. Baines): Migr into S Wales coal ind 1861–1911 (PhD, L) *Abandoned*
340 HAYTER, M., (Prof S. Pollard): Lab aristoc in Sheffield 1880–1914 (MA, S)
341 HAYWOOD, T., (Mrs D. Thompson): Elections in Kidderminster before 1850 (MLitt, B)
342 HAZELTON-SWALES, M., (Prof F. M. L. Thompson): Dev of Belgravia in 19th c (PhD, L)
343 HEMBRY, Dr P., Pleasant Cottage Crockerton Warminster Wilts BA12 8AJ: Devel of English spa towns
344 HENSTOCK, A. J. M., County Records Office Nottingham: Georgian Ashbourne
345 HEPBURN, Dr A. C., Hist Dept New Univ of Ulster Coleraine: Segreg and soc struct in Belfast and sel Ulster towns
346 HERBERT, Dr N. M., Record Office Worcester St Gloucester: (1) Ed **VCH** Gloucestershire Vol VII [Lechlade, Fairford] *Publication forthcoming* (1980): (2) Soc hist of the Stroud reg 1750–1800
347 HEY, Dr D. G., Continuing Ed Div Sheffield U: Sheffield c1660–1800
348 HIBBEN, C. C., (Prof K. W. Swart): Gouda in Revolt of Neths 1572–88 (PhD, L)
349 HIBBERD, Mrs D., Geog Dept L'pool U: Demog and urb segreg in 17th c York (MA, Li)
350 HICK, P., (Dr W. B. Stephens/Dr R. W. Unwin): Critical study of educ in York schools 1870–1974 (MPhil, Le)
351 HIGGINS, P., (Dr J. S. Morrill): Crown and bors 1660–79 (PhD, C)
352 HIGGS, E. J., (Prof P. Mathias): Servants in mid-Vict soc [Bath, Rochdale] (BLitt, O)
353 HIGNETT, Mrs J. I., (Dr R. J. Morris): Funeral trade and cemeteries in Edinburgh 1830–1914 (PhD, E)
354 HILL, R. (Dr S. G. Cherry) Soc Studies Dept UEA: 19th c Gt Yarmouth (MPhil, EA)
355 HILL, Prof Rosalind, Hist Dept Westfield Coll Ldn: (1) Register of Archbishop Melton of York Vol II *Forthcoming* [Canterbury & York Soc] (2) Register of Bishop Sutton of Lincoln Vol VIII [Lincoln Record Soc]
356 HILLABY, J. G., (Prof M. W. Beresford/G. C. F. Forster): Evoln of Herefordshire mkt towns 11th/17th c (MPhil, Le)
357 HILTON, Prof R. H., Med Hist Dept B'ham U: (1) Small towns in M Ages; (2) W Mids towns in M Ages
358 HINDSON, J. C., (R. A. Dodgshon): Fam struct in Shrewsbury 1650–1750 (PhD, W)
359 HIPKIN, S., Balliol Coll Oxford: Rye pols, econ, soc structure in 17th c
360 HOCKING, Miss J. M., (Ext): Dev of IOW as a holiday resort (MPhil, L)
361 HOLDEN, R. A., (Dr C. R. Lewis): Internal struct of Shrewsbury and Worcester in 19th c (PhD, W)
362 HOLDER, Mrs M. P., (Dr C. P. S. Platt): Congreg church in S'hampton 17th/18th c (PhD, So)
363 HOLDSWORTH, D. W., Geog Dept Toronto U Canada: (1) House and home in Vancouver: emergence of a W Coast urb landscape (PhD, Br Columbia); (2) Company hsg in ind Cape Breton
364 HOLLINSHEAD, J. E., (Mrs J. I. Kermode): (1) Early 19th c Merseyside (MA, Li); (2) Early 18th c Hale, Merseyside
365 HOLMAN, J. R., (Dr C. G. A. Clay/Mr B. J. S. Moore): Occup/soc struct and the std of living in Bristol 1675–1725 (PhD, Br) *Abandoned*
366 HOLMAN, J. R., 111 Warren Rd Dartford Kent: (1) Bankrupts in 18th c w sp ref to urb trade and professions; (2) Apprenticeship and urb migr in 18th c *Suspended*
367 HOLMES, J. D., (Prof A. E. Musson): Wkg-class violence in M'chester in early 19th c (MA, M)
368 HOLT, Miss S. B. (Dr B. K. Roberts): Hist geog of Durham City in 19th c (PhD, D)
369 HOMAN, R., Cheltenham Ladies Coll: (1) Infl of landowners and land tenure on resid dev of 19th c Sheffield (PhD, S); (2) Instit land-use dev in 19th c Sheffield (with Dr G. Rowley)
370 HOOKE, Mrs D., Geog Dept B'ham U: (1) Anglo-Saxon Droitwich and salt ind; (2) Anglo-Saxon routeways near Worcester
371 HOOPE, A. F. (Prof J. H. Burns): Mid-Vict radicalism: commun and class in B'ham 1850–80 (PhD, L) *Completed*
372 HOPES, J. (Dr W. A. Speck): Eng theatre 1690–1740 (PhD, N)
373 HOPKINS, Prof A. G., Ec & Soc Hist Dept B'ham U: African entrepreneurs in Lagos 1851–1921 *Book in prospect* [Longmans]
374 HOPKINSON, M. F. (Dr J. F. Davis): Soc-econ and demog patterns in Bedford 1837–71 (PhD, L)
375 HORNER, A. A., Univ Coll Dublin: (1) Replanning of Maynooth and Monasterevan (Co

Kildare) in 18th c; (2) 19th–20th c changes in central place system of cent Leinster
376   HOSKIN, R. J. (Dr W. A. Armstrong): 19th c Gravesend (MPhil, K)
377   HOWE, A. C. (Mr A. F. Thompson): Pol and soc in urb Lancs c1820–60 w sp ref to role of textile masters (DPhil, O)
378   HOWE, Miss C. E. D. (Dr W. A. Armstrong): Fertility decline in 19th c: comparison of urb communities (PhD, K)
379   HOWSON, A. J. (Dr J. W. R. Whitehand): Infl of 20th c planning legisln on urb form w sp ref to Warwicks and Co Durham (PhD, B)
380   HUDSON, J., Fac Environ Stud UCL: Self-help hsg (PhD, L)
381   HUDSON, Dr T. P., CRO County Hall Chichester Sussex: (1) Ed **VCH** Sussex; (2) Hist of Bramber and Steyning *Publication forthcoming* [**VCH** Sussex]; (3) Hist of Worthing *Publication forthcoming*; (4) Hist of Horsham
382   HUFF, W. G. (Prof F. J. Fisher): Ec dev of Singapore 1900–39 (PhD, L)
383   HUGHES, D. A. P. (Mr B. Shaw): Implementation of Newsom Report in Hartlepool (MEd, D)
384   HUGHES, D. G., Geog Dept QMC Ldn: Urb hierarchy in NE Wales 1844–1975 (MPhil, L)
385   HULTON, Mrs M., 8 Oxley Dr Coventry CV3 6FB: Urb medieval craftsmen [Coventry]
386   HUMPHRIES, E. (Prof D. Read): Eng and Welsh civic univs and the state 1850–1914 (MA, K)
387   HUMPHRIES, Mrs H. A. (Prof D. Read): Charity and soc work in SE Ldn (MA, K)
388   HUNTER, F. C. (Ext): Poverty and soc welfare in Swindon 1834–88(PhD, L)
389   HUNTER, I. G. (Prof N. McCord): Workers' participation in loc govt on Tyneside to 1919 (MLitt, N)
390   HURLEY, V. J., Geog Dept UC Galway: Dev of towns in Connaught esp E. Galway *No news*
391   HUSSAIN, A. (Dr J. Casey): Medina del Campo in 16th c (PhD, EA)
392   HUTCHINSON, D. J. S. (Prof N. Gash): Soc comp of Dublin c1891–1913 w sp ref to its importance in cult movement of those years (PhD, StA) *Completed*
393   HUTCHINSON, I. G. C., Hist Dept Stirling U: Pols in later-Vict Glasgow
394   HUTCHINSON, J. A. (Prof T. C. Smout/Mr F. Bechhofer): Dev of commercialized mass leisure in late 19th c w sp ref to football in NE Eng and Scots lowlands (PhD, E) *Abandoned*
395   HUTTON, D. (Prof R. H. Hilton): Med urban workshop and family lab force w sp ref Shrewsbury (PhD, B)
396   HUTTON, T. A. (Prof J. Gottmann): Changing role of office location policy within context of reg dev and planning in SE Eng and Paris region (DPhil, O)
397   HYDE, R. N, Guildhall Lib Ldn EC2P 2EJ: (1) Parish maps of Ldn: (2) Plans and panoramas of Br and Irish towns *Book in prospect*
398   IBBS, K. C. (Prof N. McCord): Hsg in 19th c Newcastle (PhD, Ne) *Presumed abandoned*
399   ION, Mrs M. (Mr J. H. Y. Briggs/Prof R. Dyson): Trade unionism in Bolton 1870–1914 (PhD, Ke)
400   IRISH, Miss S. (Prof H. Carter/Dr C. R. Lewis): Urb change in 19th c Wales (PhD, W)
401   JACKSON, Dr G., Hist Dept Strathclyde U: Hist of Br ports
402   JEFFREY, Miss J. (Dr A. H. Smith): Diss in 17th/18th c (MPhil, EA)
403   JENKINS, B. J. (Mr W. Pickles): Paris riots 6 Feb 1934 (PhD, L)
404   JENKINS, D. (Dr P. E. Rock): Post-war soc control in Winchester (PhD, L)
405   JOHANNSEN, H., 43 Broderick Rd Ldn SW17 7DX: Ldn street mkts *No news*
406   JOHN E. L. T., (Prof R. H. Hilton): Warks hundred rolls 1279–80 w sp ref Coventry, Warwick (PhD, B)
407   JOHNSON, D. J. (Prof V. Pearl): Lands and estates of St Paul's Cath in 17th c (PhD, L)
408   JONES, D. M. (Dr M. E. Rose): Loc govt pol in relat to infant and child welfare w sp ref to NW 1890–1914 (MA, M)
409   JONES, D. W. (Mr W. M. Stern): Suburbanization of SW Islington 1820–50 (MSc, L) *Completed*
410   JONES, Prof E., Geog Dept LSE: Distrib of Welsh in Ldn since 16th c
411   JONES, G. G. (Dr J. A. Yelling): Soc geog of Deptford and Lewisham 1840–1901 (PhD, L)
412   JONES, Prof G. R. T., Geog Dept Leeds U: Effects of land tenure on urb gr in W Yorks in 19th c *No news*
413   JONES, J. D. (Mr A. L. Merson): Isle of Wight, 1558–1640 (PhD, So) *Completed*
414   JONES, Mrs M. J. (Mr F. C. Mather): Poor law admin in IOW 1771–1836 (MPhil, So)
415   JONES, Dr P. J., Brasenose Coll Oxford: Communes and despots in med Italy
416   JONES, P. S. (Mr P. Clark), 21 Highway Rd Leicester: Office holding in Leicester, Peterborough 1860–1930 w sp ref class relats (MPhil, Lei)
417   JONES, Dr R., Geog Dept QMC (1) Locational patterns of shops in Vict Edinburgh *Pub-*

lication forthcoming [**IBG Special publication** on Victorian cities, 1979]; (2) Expansion of Edinburgh since 1900 *Publication forthcoming* [**Royal Scottish Geographical Society,** 1979]

418 JONES, R. H. (Prof G. H. Martin): Med settlement in Lincoln (PhD, Lei)

419 JONSSON, S., Geog Dept Durham U: Urb dev in late-med Europe *No news*

420 JORDAN, Miss R. (Dr J. Langton/P. Laxton): Literacy and soc change in L'pool 1750–1840 (M Phil, Li)

421 KAIN, Dr R. J. P., Geog Dept Exeter U: (1) Hist of city planning in France in 17th/19th c *Article published* [**Gazette des Beaux Arts,** 1979]; (2) Urb conservation in France *Article published* [**Urbanism Past and Present,** 1978–9]

422 KATZ Prof M. B., Graduate School of Ed Pennsylvania U: (1) (with M. J. Stern) Differential fertility and early ind: Erie County NY 1855–1915; (2) Demog of selected inmate pops in 19th c NY State

423 KAZMAOGLU, Mrs M. (Prof B Özer): Pedestrian areas in past and present Turkish cities (PhD, State Academy of Fine Arts Istanbul) *No news*

424 KEATING, Dr P. J., Eng Dept Edinburgh U: Soc hist of Eng novel 1875–1914

425 KEENE, Dr D. J., IHR Senate Ho Ldn, (1) Topog of Winchester (incl HATPE); (2) Soc and econ of med Winchester *Publication forthcoming* [OUP]; (3) Med urb records and topog; (4) Topog/soc/ec survey of med Ldn

426 KEIGHLEY, D. A. (Dr O. A. Hartley): Estab of Eng metrop county authorities 1972–6 (MPhil, Le)

427 KEIL, Dr I., Loughborough U: Loc govt of Loughborough in 18th c

428 KEITH-LUCAS, Prof B., Kent U: Unreformed loc govt system 1800–35 *Book forthcoming* [Croom Helm]

429 KELLAWAY, W., IHR Senate Ho Ldn: Ldn sources

430 KELLETT, B. (Prof W. H. Chaloner): Ec/soc dev of Heaton Moor in 19th c (MA, M)

431 KELLY, J. (Mr M. B. Cooper): Catalanism and Barcelona wkg class 1900–20 (PhD, EA)

432 KELSALL, A. F., 32 Beechhill Rd Ldn SE9: Nicholas Barbon and spec bldg in late-17th c Ldn

433 KENNEDY, D. (Dr J. C. G. Binfield): Aspects of the press in W Riding [w sp ref to Leeds, Sheffield, Huddersfield] 1850–1900 (MA, S)

434 KERVEN, R. (Dr R. Jones): Evoln of status areas in selected medium sized towns of S Eng 1871–1931 (PhD, L)

435 KETTLE, Miss A. J., Med Hist Dept St Andrews U: Edn of 'Book of Remembrance of first mayor of Stafford'

436 KIDD, A. (Dr M. E. Rose): Treatment of unemployment in M'chester 1895–1914 (MA, M)

437 KING, A. D., Soc Dept Brunel U: (1) Soc/cult evon of the bungalow as a house-type: (2) **Buildings and Society** *Books forthcoming* [Routledge & Kegan Paul]

438 KING, Miss S. (Prof E. Jones): Concepts of slums in Ldn since 19th c (MPhil, L)

439 KING, W. (Mr C. V. Phythian-Adams): Econ/demogr dev of Rossendale 1650–c1795 (PhD, Lei) *Completed*

440 KINGSTON, Miss J. S. M. (Dr J. W. R. Whitehand): Renewal of physical fabric of selected town centres in W Mids 1890–1978 (MLitt, B)

441 KINKEAD, R. H. (Prof T. P. Morris): Irish soc problem gps in GB in 19th c (MPhil, L)

442 KIRBY, Mrs J. W. (Mr G. C. F. Forster): Docs rel to Leeds in 15th/16th c (MPhil, Le)

443 KIVELL, Dr P. T., Geog Dept Keele U: Postwar French urb growth *Abandoned*

444 KLOTTRUP, A. C. (Prof J. P. C. Roach): Scientific and tech educ in 19th c N East (PhD, S) *Completed*

445 KNAPTON, M. W. S. (Dr P. J. Jones): Paduan soc and Venetian govt in later 15th c (DPhil, O) *Completed*

446 KNOX, J. R. (Dr D. K. Chakrabahti): Origins of urbanism in N India (PhD, C) *No news*

447 KOHNSTAMM, Miss J. (Mr M. B. Cooper): Jewish community of L'Isle-sur-Sorgues in 18th c (PhD, EA)

448 KONURALP, P. (Prof F. Akozan): M-class hsg in late 19th c Istanbul (PhD, State Academy of Fine Arts Istanbul) *No news*

449 KONVITZ, Prof J., Hist Dept Michigan State U East Lansing Michigan 48824: (1) Architecture and city-building *Completed*; (2) 18th c cartography w sp ref to urb growth and city planning

450 KUZUCULAR, K. (Prof D. Kuban): Evoln of physical form in some Anatolian cities (PhD, Technical U Istanbul) *No news*

451 LAITHWAITE, M., Ec Hist Dept Exeter U: (1) (Mr B. W. Clapp) Houses of Totnes fr 16th/19th c with topog and soc/ec background (PhD,Ex); (2) Houses of Burford fr 14th/19th c with soc/ec background

452 LAMBERT, Dr A. M., Geog Dept LSE: Thame in mid-19th c *No news*

453 LAMMING, J. D. (Dr W. B. Stephens): Educ in 19th c Lincoln (MPhil, Le) *Completed*

454 LANGTON, Dr J., Geog Dept L'pool U: Soc/econ dev of L'pool c1760–1830 (with P. Laxton)
455 LARGE, D., Hist Dept Bristol U: Hist of port of Bristol from 1848 [Bristol Rec Soc]
456 LARGE, P. Wolfson Coll Oxford: (1) Droitwich salt ind and politics in 16th/17th c; (2) Kidderminster ind and politics in 16th/17th c
457 LAWTON, Prof R., Geog Dept L'pool U: (1) Soc geog of 19th c L'pool; (2) Populn of 19th c Staffs; (3) Mobil and populn structure in 19th c Br
458 LAXTON, P., Geog Dept L'pool U: (1) Soc and econ dev of L'pool 1760–1830 (with J. Langton); (2) Intra-urb populn trends in 18th/19th c
459 LEACH, R. F. (Dr O. A. Hartley): Loc govt in Ilkley since 1945 (MPhil, Le)
460 LEAD, P. (Mr J. H. Y. Briggs): Gilbert family of Cotton, Staffs in Ind Rev (MA, Ke)
461 LEBLIQUE, C. J. (Prof N. Hampson): Policing Paris during Rev (DPhil, Y) *Suspended*
462 LEECH, A. (Prof J. P. C. Roach): Decision-mkg in org and planning of educ system in Stockport (PhD, S)
463 LEENERS, R. (Mr W. M. Stern): Govt reguln of Ldn taxi trade 1890–1914 (MSc, L) *Completed*
464 LEES, Prof A., Rutgers U NJ USA: Attitudes to urbanization in 19th/20th c Europe
465 LEES, Prof Lynn, Pennsylvania U Pa USA: (1) Class and community in Eng ind towns 1835–1914; (2) (with Prof P. Hohenberg) Hist of European urbanization
466 LETT, J. (Dr J. Langton): Canal dev in NW Eng (PhD, Li) *Presumed abandoned*
467 LEWIS, Dr C. R., Geog Dept U Coll Aberystwyth: Urb hierarchy in Wales from 19th c
468 LEWIS, Dr G. J., Geog Dept Leicester U: (1) Spatial evoln of soc areas in Leicester; (2) Localities and community: studies in Gr Leicester *No news*
469 LEWIS, J. (Dr G. P. Chapman): Urb gr and under-dev: Kenya 1895–1974 (PhD, C)
470 LEWIS, J. P. (Dr Iliffe): Urb soc and Africaaner nationalism on E. Rand 1918–48 (PhD, C)
471 LEWIS, Dr R. A., Hist Dept U Coll N Wales Bangor: (1) Devel of Poor Law policy 1834–71; (2) Poor Law admin in Ldn 1834–71
472 LIDDINGTON, Miss J., M'chester Studies M'chester Poly: Pol/econ life in a weaving town [Nelson]
473 LIDDLE, J. G. (Dr J. K. Walton): Suburb dev on SW Lancs coast in 19th c (PhD, La)
474 LIDDLE, P. (ext): Vict Walsall 1837–1901 (PhD, L) *Presumed abandoned*
475 LINDEN, Mrs J. (Dr R. A. Buchanan): Origins and gr of Methodism in Bath 1740–1914 (MSc, Ba)
476 LINGARD, S. J. (Prof M. W. Beresford/Mr J. R. Killich): Shop and office bldg in cent Leeds 1790–1914 (MPhil, Le)
477 LINKMAN, A., Manch Studies Manch Poly: Archive rescue in loc urb community *No news*
478 LISTON, W. R. (Dr L. Adrian) Geog Dept Cambridge U: Retailing and wholesaling in Lancs 1770–1850 (PhD, C)
479 LLOYD, J. A. (Prof G. D. B. Jones): Hist dev of early Benghazi (PhD, M) *Completed*
480 LOBEL, Mrs M. D., 16 Merton St Oxford: Medieval Ldn *Publication forthcoming* [HATPE Br section vol III (1980)]
481 LOBELL, B. (Dr M. E. Rose): Pol and soc welfare in Oldham 1870–1914 (MA, M)
482 LOCKHART, Dr D. G., Geog Dept Glasgow U: Gr of towns and estate villages in Ireland 1700–1900 *No news*
483 LOGUE, T. (Dr J. F. McCaffrey): Burgh of Clydebank 1867–1914 (MLitt, G)
484 LONGLEY, C. J. (Mr G. C. Dickinson): Urb road pass tpt in Leeds since 1890 (PhD, Le)
485 LONGMORE, Mrs J. (Mr C. W. Chalklin): L'pool Corporation estate 1780–1840 (PhD, R)
486 LOWENTHAL, Prof D., Geog Dept UCL: Attitudes toward the past and views about the significance of relics and artifacts in the landscape *Book forthcoming* [CUP]
487 LOWN, Miss J. (Miss L. Davidoff): Women in family econ in Halstead 1840–80 (PhD, Essex)
488 LUCKIN, W. E. (Mr W. M. Stern), Bolton Inst of Tech: Water pollution in Ldn 1840–1910 w sp ref to the Thames and Lea (PhD, L)
489 LUFFRUM, J. M. (Dr J. W. R. Whitehand): Infl of econ factors on form of small town centres w sp ref to E Anglia (PhD, B) *Completed*
490 LUKEHURST, Miss C. T., Geog Dept Brighton Coll of Ed: Urb functions and form during M Ages and earlier w sp ref to Canterbury and Lewes *No news*
491 LYNCH, Dr M., Sc Hist Dept Edinburgh U: Edinburg and the Reformation *Publication forthcoming* [John Donald]
492 LYTH, P. (Prof A. Teichova): Comp study of impact of inflation on Hamburg and Lauenburg area in 1920s (PhD, EA)
493 McCAFFREY, Dr J., Scottish Hist Dept Glasgow U: (1) [with Mr B. Aspinwall] Glasgow as mun model for Amer pol 1890–1914; (2) Biog of Thomas Chalmers

494   McCAFFREY, P. (Mr M. A. Simpson): Urb machine in Amer pols w sp ref NY City 1865–76 (MSc, W) *Completed*
495   McCLELLAND, B. (Dr D. Brooke): Devel of port of Bristol 1848–1910 (MSc, Ba) *Completed*
496   McCLELLAND, K. (Mrs D. Thompson): Aristoc of lab in Newcastle u Tyne c1850–80 (PhD, B)
497   McCORD, Prof N., Hist Dept Newcastle u Tyne U: Industrialisation and urb gr in NE Eng *No news*
498   McDERMOTT, M. (Dr B. J. Atkinson): Irish immigrants and Ldn lab movement since 1918 (Ma, K) *Completed*
499   McDIARMID, Miss B. (Dr D. Parker): Huguenots in Fr & Eng in 17th/18th c (PhD, Le) *Abandoned*
500   McDONALD, D. (Prof R. J. Helustadter) Hist Dept Toronto U: The churches and evang revivalism in the Vict city c1855–c1914 (PhD, Toronto) *No news*
501   McDONALD, T. A. (Prof J. R. Vincent): Elect hist of Poole 1832–85 (MLitt, Br)
502   McDOUALL, Miss H. (Prof R. B. Dobson): York crafts 1300–1500 (DPhil, Y)
503   MACFARLANE, S. M. (Dr P. A. Slack) Wadham Coll Oxford: Poverty and poor relief in Ldn 1660–1710 (DPhil, O)
504   McINNES, A., Hist Dept Keele U: Hist of Shrewsbury 1500–1800
505   MACKENNEY, R. S. (Prof B. S. Pullan), Queens Coll Camb: Trade guilds and devot confraternities in Venice to 1620 (PhD, C)
506   MacLAREN, Dr A. A., Soc Dept Strathclyde U: (1) Elites and elite recruitment in 19th c Scot; (2) Capitalism and relig in Br since c1780
507   McLEAN, L. (Prof R. E. H. Mellor/Mr J. C. Stone) Geog Dept Aberdeen U: Town plans of Scotland to 1850 (PhD, A)
508   McLEMAN, Miss J. (Prof P. L. Payne/Mrs A. Mallet): Demog study in 17th c Valletta (PhD, A)
509   McLEOD, Dr D. H. Theol Dept D'ham U: Relig in the city 1870–1910: New York, Ldn, Paris, Berlin
510   MACLEOD, F. J., Geog Dept Kings Coll Ldn: Soc change and urb resid struct w sp ref to middling classes in early/mid 19th c Glasgow (PhD, L)
511   MacMASTER, N., East Anglia U: (1) 1766 Norwich riots; (2) A Norwich parish (Pockthorpe)
512   McMILLAN, Mrs J. K. (Mrs Rosalind Mitchison): Scot ec dev 1600–1700 w sp ref to role of Edinburgh (PhD, E)
513   McMULLAN, J. L. (Dr P. E. Rock): Crime in late 16th/17th c Ldn (MPhil, L)
514   McNULTY, D. (Dr I. J. Prothero): Wkg-class movemts in Som/Wilts 1830–40s (PhD, M)
515   MACPHERSON, Miss S. J. (Prof H. J. Perkin): Quakers and dev of Kendal (MLitt, La) *Abandoned*
516   McWHIRR, A. D., 37 Dovedale Rd Leicester: Evoln of Cirencester from archaeol/hist sources *Published* [**Antiq Journal** 1978]
517   MADEN, A. S. (Mr F. V. Emery): Geog of religion in 19th c Ldn (DPhil, O) *Abandoned*
518   MALCOLMSON, Mrs P. E., 203 Victoria St Kingston Ontario: Laundry workers in Vict/Ed Eng
519   MANDERS, F. (Prof N. McCord): Gateshead Poor law Union (MLitt, N)
520   MANTERFIELD, J. B., Geog Dept Exeter U: Topog dev in med/early mod Lincs towns w sp ref to Grantham (PhD, Ex)
521   MARGRAVE, R. D. (Dr C. J. Erickson): Emigr of silk workers to USA in 19th c w sp ref to Coventry, Macclesfield, Paterson N. J., S Manchester Conn (PhD, L)
522   MARLOW, L. (Dr A. Mason): Clubs and wkg class in Vict Eng (PhD, War)
523   MARSHALL, Miss J. (Mr M. H. Port): Ldn govt and vestry radicalism 1830–55 (MPhil, L)
524   MARSHALL, Dr J. D., N. W. Regional Studies Centre/Lancaster U: Hist of Cumbrian towns in 19th c
525   MARTIN, Miss J. (Dr C. F. Slade): Paroch life in Reading in Tudor/early Stuart per (PhD, R)
526   MARTIN, Miss R. (Prof B. S. Pullan): Witchcraft in Venice mid 16th/17th c (PhD, M)
527   MASON, Dr A., Hist Dept Warwick U: Football and Eng soc 1863–1915 *In publication*
528   MASON, Dr E , Birkbeck Coll Ldn: Cal of Westminster Abbey charters 1066–1216 [London Record Soc]
529   MASON, J. J. (Dr E. J. Evans): Soc/ec change in Stockport area 1780–51 w sp ref to Stockport Sunday School (MLitt, La)
530   MATHERS, Mrs H. E. (Dr J. C. G. Binfield): Soc/pol leadership in Sheffield 1893–1926 (PhD, S) *Completed*
531   MATTHEWS, G. (Mrs D. Thompson): Relief of poverty in Worcestershire 1834–1910 (MLitt, B)

532 MAWSON, P. (Prof A. J. Taylor): Loc govt in Keighley c 1850–1900 (MPhil, Le)
533 MAY, Miss B. (Prof M. W. Beresford): Land and econ dev in Hunslet, suburb of S. Leeds 1770–1800 (PhD, Le)
534 MAY, F. B. (Dr R. A. Lewis): Dev of Ilfracombe as a resort in 19th c (MA, W) *Completed*
535 MAY, T. (Prof F. M. L. Thompson): Ldn cab trade in 19th c (MPhil, L)
536 MAYHO, T. C. (Prof S. Pollard): Hist of bldg societies in Bradford (MA, S)
537 MEEHAN, M. J., Geog Dept Nat Phys Educ Limerick: Geog anal of evol of Blarney (MA, Co) *Completed*
538 MEESON, R. A. (S. R. Bassett): Topog and hist of Tamworth (MA, B)
539 MELLER, Dr H. E., Ec & Soc Hist Dept Nottingham U: Reassessment of Sir Patrick Geddes incl work on early town planning and Indian urbanism
540 MELLOR, A. J. L. (Mr J. G. C. Oxborrow): Dover harbour since 1918 (MPhil, K)
541 MERCER, V. M. (Prof J. P. C. Roach): School prov in Ecclesfield, Rotherham, Sheffield 1480–1833 (PhD, S) *Completed*
542 METCALF, Dr P., 15 Ascalon Ho Thessaly Rd Ldn SW8 4EA: (1) City domestic and comm interiors; (2) biog of James Knowles [Vict architect] *Publication forthcoming* [OUP]; (3) edn of Pevsner's **Cathedrals of England** [Penguin]
543 METTERS, A. (Dr A. H. Smith/Mr V. Morgan) 29 Cintra Rd Norwich: Rulers and merchants of 17th c King's Lynn (PhD, EA)
544 MICHELL, A. R. (Prof Sir Charles Wilson) Ec & Soc Hist Dept Hull U: Yarmouth and its relns on both sides of the seas 1550–1714 (PhD, C) *Completed*
545 MILLS, Miss O. A. *see* WEIDMANN, Mrs O. A.
546 MILLS, S. F., American Studs Dept Keele U: Black resid mobility in 19th c Washington DC
547 MILWARD, R. J., 159 Coombe La Ldn SW20: Wimbledon in 18th/early 19th c
548 MITCHELL, I. (Mr B. D. Clark): Decision-making and the evoln of slums in 19th c Glasgow (PhD, A)
549 MITCHELL, T. (Prof G. A. Williams): Quality of wkg-class life in W Riding towns 1780–1830 (DPhil, Y) *Presumed abandoned*
550 MOFFATT, I., Earth and Environt Sciences Stirling U Spatial dynamics of Br urb system 1801–1971 (PhD, Ne) *Completed*
551 MOIR (Dr J. R. Coull): Improving movemt in N. E. Scot (PhD, A)
552 MOORE, J. S., Ec & Soc Hist Dept Bristol U: Ec/soc hist of Bristol reg
553 MORGAN, C. J. (Prof M. W. Beresford): Burial question in Leeds 1800–1914 (MPhil, Le)
554 MORGAN, D. (Prof S. Pollard): Socialist groupings in Yorks/Lancs ind towns 1880–1950 (MA, S)
555 MORGAN, H. N. B. (Dr E. J. Evans): Soc/pol leadership in Preston 1850–75 (MLitt, La)
556 MORGAN, P. H. (Prof H. Carter): Soc class functional change and bldg construction in inner city [Cardiff 1850–1970] (PhD, W)
557 MORIARTY, B. D. (Dr W. B. Stephens): Pol and educ in Huddersfield in late 19th c (MEd, Le) *Completed*
558 MORRIS, Dr C. J., Geog Dept Exeter U: (1) Townscape images: a study in meaning and classification (PhD, Ex) *Completed*; (2) Urban images *Publication forthcoming* (in R. Kain, ed **Planning for Conservation** [Mansell])
559 MORRIS, Miss J. (Prof T. C. Barker/Dr J. F. Harris): Women's work in tailoring trades in late 19th/20th c Ldn and Leeds (MPhil, L)
560 MORRIS, Dr R. J., Ec Hist Dept Edinburgh U: (1) Dev and soc org of middle class in Leeds, Newcastle, Glasgow, Belfast; (2) Self-help in Leeds; (3) Probs of cross-tabulations and correl with data on urb soc struct w sp ref to Leeds 1830–1851
561 MULHOLLAND, R. (Mr R. M. Y. Shackleton): Trade unions and other wkg class instits in B'ham 1870–1914 (PhD, B)
562 MULREANY, P. V. (Prof S. Pollard): Entrepreneurship and dissenting communities of N Ldn 1750–1850 (MA, S)
563 MUNDEN, A. F. (Dr D. H. McLeod), 21 Windsor Terr N'castle u Tyne 2: C of E in Cheltenham 1824–56 (MA, B)
564 MURNANE, B. P., Geog Dept UC Dublin: 1901 census and the hist geog of Dublin (MA, UCD)
565 MURPHY, Miss M. J. B. (Prof G. H. Martin): The artisan in 19th c Cork (PhD, Lei)
566 MURRELL, Mrs M. (Prof F. M. L. Thompson): Vict Ldn water supply (PhD, L)
567 MURRELL, Miss P. (Dr W. A. Speck): Suffolk parl bors from Excl crisis to 1714 (PhD, Ne)
568 MUTHESIUS, Dr S., Fine Arts Dept E. Anglia U: (1) Architecture of Vict suburb houses; (2) Vict hsg in Sandringham area of Norwich
569 NASLAS, Dr M., Dept Town & Reg Plan Sheffield U: (1) Urb dev and planning of Sheffield since beginning of the ind era; (2) Concepts of art, design, the town and town planning in Wm Morris' writings; (3) Utopian ideas and model settlements

in 19th/20th c

570 NEALE, Mrs Frances A., The Knoll Winscombe Hill Winscombe Avon: (1) New edn of Wm Worcestre's **Description of Bristol** c 1480; (2) Topog of late-med Bristol (PhD, L)

571 NEUBURG, V. E., Sch of Librarianship Poly of N Ldn 207/225 Essex Rd Ldn N1: Urb folklore, pop cult, pop lit, 18th c coffee houses, mug houses, radical clubs, relig sects

572 NEWLAND, G. C., Geog Dept City of Ldn Poly: Spatial evoln of urb fabric of part of Ldn docklands w sp ref to planning legisl from 1800 (MPhil, L)

573 NEWMAN, Miss E. K. (Prof F. J. Fisher): Anglo-Hamburg trade in late 17th/18th c (PhD, L)

574 NICHOLSON, J. R. (Mr J. H. Y. Briggs): Popular imperialism and the prov press to 1914 (PhD, Ke)

575 NOBLE, Miss M. (Dr A. Harris): Small towns in E Yorks c1700–1850 (PhD, H)

576 NOEL, R. P. R. (Dr K. A. Fowler): Urb defence in Fr *Midi* during 100 Years' War 1337–1453 (PhD, E) *Completed*

577 NOLAN, G. M. (Dr H. E. Meller): Interaction betwen phys environment and soc change in Derby 1890–1939 (MPhil, N)

578 NOON, J., (Dr C. P. S. Platt): Socio/demog hist of 17th c Portsmouth (MPhil, So)

579 NORFOLK Archaeol Unit, Union Ho Gressenhall Dereham Norfolk: Archaeol excavations and surveys of Norfolk towns

580 NORRIS Miss H. E., Geog Dept Exeter U: Urb design in 2nd Empire prov France [Lille] (MA, Ex)

581 O'BRIEN, Dr J. V., Hist Dept John Jay Coll of Criminal Justice CUNY 455 W59th St NY 10019: Urb problems in Dublin 1899–1916 *Book forthcoming* [Univ of California Press]

582 O'DRISCOLL, Miss P. (Prof G. R. J. Jones): Urb hist geog of W Yorks towns (MPhil, Le)

583 OFFER, A., Hist Dept York U: (1) Pol econ of urb land and hsg in Eng 1895–1922 (DPhil, O) *Completed*; (2) Property and pols 1870–1914 *Book in prospect*

584 OGDEN, P. E., Geog Dept Queen Mary Coll Ldn: Migr to Paris in 19th c w sp ref to rel between origins and destinations of migrants

585 O GRADA, D. F., Trinity Coll Dublin: Dev of S suburbs of Dublin 1800–1930 *No news*

586 OLSEN, Prof D. J., Hist Dept Vassar Coll Poughkeepsie NY USA: (1) Management of Norfolk est in Sheffield to 1870; (2) Gr and struct of mod cities; (3) Ldn, Paris and Vienna fr 18th c

587 OSMANY, Mrs S. (Mr J. B. Harrison): Dev of Chittagong as a port in later half of 19th c (MPhil, L)

588 OSTERUD, Ms N. (Prof J. A. Banks), Vict Stud Centre Leicester U: Wkg-class family life in 19th c Leicester: domestic ind and the transition to factory work in an urb setting (MPhil, Lei)

589 OWEN, D. H., Welsh Hist Dept UC Cardiff: Welsh towns in later M Ages

590 OWEN, D. W. (Prof R. Lawton/Mr A. Charlesworth): Diffusion of electr generation in Eng & W in late 19th/early 20th c (PhD, Li)

591 OWENS, E. J. (Prof R. J. Hopper): The Greek house and urb dev (PhD, S)

592 PALLISER, Dr D. M., Ec Hist Dept B'ham U: (1) Town plan for York (HATPE); (2) Ed **York Historian**; (3) Eng towns 1547–1603; (4) **Tudor York** *Book published* [OUP, 1979]

593 PALMER, R. (Dr P. J. Laven): Control of plague in Venice and N Italy 1348–1600 (PhD, K) *Completed*

594 PALMER, Miss S. R., QMC London (Prof A. H. John): Character and org of shipping ind in Port of Ldn 1815–49 (PhD, L) *Completed*

595 PAPAGEORGIOU, G. (Mr R. R. M. Clogg): Greek merchant community in Eng in 19th c (MPhil, L)

596 PAPWORTH, J. D., Geog Dept Liverpool U: Irish in L'pool 1835–71 (PhD, Li)

597 PARKER, Dr D., Hist Sch Leeds U: Toulouse in 1640–50s

598 PARRY, J. (Prof I. G. Jones): Lab leaders and loc govt in Aberdare Valley 1896–1933 (PhD, W)

599 PARTINGTON, Mrs A. (Dr A. Lambert): Soc change in Barking in late 19th c (MPhil, L) *Presumed abandoned*

600 PARTON, Dr A., Lanchester Poly Coventry: (1) Urb-rural interaction in 19th c Eng Geog of poverty in mid 19th c Birmingham *Suspended*; (2) (with Dr H. Matthews)

601 PATERSON, D. J., 6 Fox Ave Nuneaton: 1868 Warwick election *Completed*

602 PATTEN, Dr J., Hertford Coll Oxford: Urb landscapes in Eng

603 PATTERSON, H. H. (Mr A. F. Thompson): Lab movement in Belfast 1868–1920 (DPhil, O)

604 PATTRICK, M. (Dr B. J. Atkinson/Dr J. Lovell): Labour in Bolton and Blackburn c 1850–80 (MPhil, K) *Abandoned*

605   PEARL, Prof Valerie, Hist Dept UCL: Ldn in 17th c *No news*
606   PEEL, Rev M. J. (Dr E. Duffy): Ldn episcopate of A. C. Tait, (PhD, L)
607   PENN, R. (Dr M. Mann): Class and marriage in Rochdale 1856–1964 (PhD, C)
608   PENNANT, T. G. E. (Dr I. F. Burton), Sociology Dept Malawi U Zomba: Pub health admin in Eng and Prussia w sp ref to Rhineland c 1830–1901 (PhD, L)
609   PENNY, R. I. (Prof J. A. S. Grenville): Stratford-u-Avon 1835–1901, gr and dev in Vict mkt town (PhD, B)
610   PERKIN, Prof H. J., Lancaster U: Infl of urb gr on struct of soc in 19th/20th c
611   PHILLIPS, J. F. (Dr H. E. Meller): Pop movemts in N'ham/S Notts in 19th c (MPhil, N)
612   PHILLIPS, M. (Prof H. J. Perkin): Cotton operatives in Bolton c 1780–1840 (PhD, La) *Abandoned*
613   PHILLIPS, Miss M. C., Geog Dept Exeter U: Demog change in Tavistock, Devon, in rel to mining dev in 19th c (PhD, Ex)
614   PHILLIPSON, Dr N. T., Hist Dept Edinburgh U: (1) Cult/pol hist of Edinburgh 1650–1850; (2) Cult and soc in 18th and early 19th c Scotland *Book in prospect*
615   PHILIPPONNEAU, S. J. C-P. (Dr Scargill): Changing location of ind premises in Br urb agglomerations: comp with Fr experience (DPhil, O)
616   PHYTHIAN-ADAMS, C. V., Dept Eng Loc Hist Leicester U: (1) Soc and demog study of Coventry 1480–1550 *In the press* [**Desolation of a City** (CUP, 1979)]; (2) Urb culture 1450–1850
617   PICKARD, Miss A. M., 7 Boyd Close Kingston uT KT2 7RL: Admin of Ldn Bridge and its estates in M Ages (MPhil, L)
618   PLATT, Prof D. C. M., St Antony's Coll Oxford OX2 6JF: Financing of city moderniz-ation, Buenos Aires 1880–1910
619   PLATT, Mrs P. A. (Dr W. B. Stephens/Dr P. R. Sharp): Dev of RC elem and second educ in Leeds from 1895 (MEd, Le)
620   POLE, Miss N. C. (Prof G. R. Batho): State educ in Macclesfield 1902–75 (MEd, D)
621   POOLE, R. J. R. (Dr J. K. Walton): Pop pols in Kendal 1835–85 (MLitt, La)
622   POOLEY, C. G. (Prof R. Lawton), Geog Dept Lancaster U: Soc geog of 19th c L'pool w sp ref to migr and mobility (PhD, Li) *Completed*
623   POOLEY, Mrs M. (Prof R. Lawton), Geog Dept Liverpool U: Pop and hsg in mid-19th c M'chester (PhD, Li)
624   PORT, M. H., Hist Dept QMC: Pub bldg in later–19th c Ldn
625   PORTWIN, Mrs B. M. (Dr E. H. Hunt), LSE: Covent Garden in 19th/20th c (MPhil, L)
626   POTTER, Mrs I., 11 Hawkesworth Dr Kenilworth CV8 2GP: Demog study of Kenil-worth 1630–1800
627   POWELL, Miss J., Stanford Ho Upper Ladies Hill Kenilworth: Rev W. Best, a study of 17th/18th c Kenilworth
628   POWELL, K. G. (Prof A. G. Dickens): Reformation in Bristol and dist (PhD, L)
629   POWELL, W. R., 17 Arbour Lane Chelmsford Essex: Ed **VCH** Essex: Vol VIII [Harlow, Havering, Hornchurch, Romford] *In press*
630   POWER, Dr M. J., Mod Hist Dept L'pool U: Ldn city and suburbs 1550–1700
631   PRESCOTT, A. (Dr Barron), 15 Rosenau Rd Ldn SW11: Ldn and the Peasants Revolt (PhD,L)
632   PRESTON, B. T., Geog Dept Reading U: Comp study of loc govt policy, soc groups and accessibility (soc and spatial) in three ind towns 1871–1911 (PhD, R)
633   PRICE, Mrs S. F. (Dr R. J. Morris): Wages and lab mkt in Glasgow reg 1880–1930 (PhD, E)
634   PRICHARD, T. J. (Mr J. H. Y. Briggs): Church and soc in Rhondda 1851–1911 (PhD, Ke)
635   PRINCE, H. C., Geog Dept UCL: (1) Preserv of old bldgs in towns; (2) Hist geog of Ldn
636   PRITCHARD, A. D. (Prof W. Ashworth): Soc impact of railways on cities of SW Eng [Bristol, Exeter, Plymouth] 1840–90
637   PRITCHARD, Miss S. (Dr A. R. Sutcliffe): Soc role of street in 19th c Ldn (MA, S) *Aban-doned*
638   PULLAN, Prof B. S., Hist Dept Manchester U: Inquisition and the Jews in Venice 1550–1670 *No news*
639   RACK, H. D. (Prof W. H. Chaloner): Relig and soc in M'chester 1688–1800 (PhD, M)
640   RAE, A. (Dr D. A. Farnie): Ancoats 1780–1900: ec hist of an urb dist (MA, M) *Suspended*
641   RAE, K. (Prof R. H. Hilton): Pop religion in late med Warks [Knowle] (PhD, B)
642   RAHIMI, K. M., Geog Dept Durham U: Hist dev of cent Iranian cities during Islamic period (MA, D) *Completed*
643   RAHTZ, P. A., Archaeol Dept York U: St Mary-le-Port Bristol
644   RANDALL, Dr H. A., Aarhus U Aarhus Denmark: Impact of industrialization and urb-anization in Denmark 1840–1920 *No news*
645   RANDOLPH, W. G., Geog Dept LSE: Urb hsg mkt and soc area change in Gr Ldn since

1961 (PhD, L)

646 RAVETZ, Dr A., Sch of Architecture Hull Reg Coll of Art Brunswick Ave Hull: Hist of town planning and urb dev 1945–75 *Book forthcoming* [Croom Helm, 1980]

647 REDFERN, J. B. (Prof M. Drake), 25 Norfolk Rd B'ham B15 3PU: Domestic and soc structure in mid 19th c suburban Edgbaston (PhD, OU)

648 REDMAN, J. A. (Prof G. R. Batho): School Board elections in the north east: a study in urb pols (MEd, D)

649 REECE, Mrs S. (Prof J. Youings): Topog of Tudor Exeter 1450–1600 (PhD, Ex)

650 REEDER, Dr D. A., Sch of Edn Leicester U: (1) Suburb dev of Vict cities *Suspended*; (2) Ideology and the urb child *Book in prospect*; (3) Bibliog of 19th c Ldn govt

651 REES, Mrs J. C. M. (Dr D. T. Herbert) Geog Dept U Coll Swansea: Resid struct of 19th c Swansea [PhD, W]

652 REES, Mrs R. A. (Prof A. J. Taylor): Aspects of ec hist of 19th c Selby (PhD, Le) *Completed*

653 REID, A. J. (Dr G. S. Jones): Soc/ec hist of Glasgow, Belfast 1919–29 (PhD, C)

654 REID, D. A. (Mrs D. K. G. Thompson): Patterns of work and leisure in B'ham 1800–1900 (PhD, B)

655 REID, Mrs N., (Prof J. Saville): M'chester & Salford ILP 1890–1933 (PhD, H)

656 REID-SMITH, E. R., (Dr P. H. J. H. Gosden/Dr W. B. Stephens): The pub library as an educative force in Eng in 19th c (PhD, Le)

657 REILLY, M. D., Ec Hist Dept L'pool U: Urban electric railways in Britain and USA 1880–1914

658 REYNOLDS, J., Postgrad Sch of Stud in Soc Sci Bradford U: Life and times of Sir Titus Salt: Bradford and Saltaire 1803–77

659 REYNOLDS, Miss S., Lady Margaret Hall Oxford: Med Ldn before 1300 *Suspended*

660 RICKWOOD, D. L., Willems The Common Crostwick Norwich: Admin hist of stranger community of Norwich in 16th/17th c (PhD, UEA)

661 RIGBY, S., 52 Santley St Ldn SW4: Boston and Grimsby in M Ages (PhD, L)

662 RILEY, Dr R. C., Geog Dept Portsmouth Poly: (1) 19th c manuf ind in Portsmouth (2) Rate books and dating properties in Southsea, Hants *Publication forthcoming*; [**Southern History, Portsmouth Papers**]

663 RIPLEY, P. J. G., (Prof P. V. McGrath): City of Gloucester 1660–1740 (MLitt, Br) *Completed*

664 ROBB, J. G., Geog Dept LSE: Towns of Anglo-Saxon Eng *No news*

665 ROBERTS, Mrs A. R. (Prof G. R. J. Jones) 12 Ajax Close Grimsby: Effects of urb dev on agrarian econ of W Yorks 1801–1901 (MPhil, Le)

666 ROBERTS, B. E., (Prof J. P. C. Roach): Excepted district of Scunthorpe 1961–74 (MA, S)

667 ROBERTS, Prof B. R., Soc Dept M'chester U: Hist patterns of urbanism in Lat Amer *Book published* [**Cities of Peasants** (Edward Arnold, 1978)]

668 ROBERTS, Dr E. A. M., NW Reg Studs Centre Lancaster U: Wkg class soc life in Preston 1890–1940

669 ROBERTS, K. W., (Dr M. E. Rose): Soc change in a M'chester suburb [Rusholme] 1850–1900 (MA, M)

670 ROBERTS, R. W., (Prof D. C. Coleman): South Coast seaside resort w sp ref to Bournemouth c 1860–1940 (PhD, C)

671 ROBERTSON, C. J. A., Hist Dept St Andrews U: Early Scot rlys incl effects on towns

672 ROBINSON, Miss L. M. (Dr H. E. Meller): Women in urb community w sp ref to Nottingham 1890–1925 (MPhil, N)

673 ROBSON, G. (Dr D. H. McLeod), Westhill Coll B'ham 29: Relig and irrelig in B'ham and Black Country 1800–51 (PhD, B)

674 RODGER, R. G., Ec and Soc Hist Dept Leicester U: (1) Scottish hsg and housebldg in 19th/20th c; (2) Hsg and the land mkt; (3) Legal and instit influences on urb change

675 ROE-ELY, (Dr I. Keil): Middle class in Vict Loughborough (MA, Lou)

676 ROGERS, Dr A., Dept Adult Educ Nottingham U: (1) Hist of Stamford (HATPE); (2) Aspects of Nottingham hist *No news*

677 ROOK, K., (Mr J. Reynolds): Pre-ind demog of Bradford 1630–1837 (PhD, Bra)

678 ROSE, D., Geog Dept Sussex U: Soc reproduction and growth of wkg class home ownership 1850–1930 (DPhil, Su)

679 ROSEN, Dr A. B., 4678 Barker Way Long Beach Ca 90814 USA: (1) Soc/ec hist of 16th/17th c Winchester *In the press* (Leicester UP); (2) Urb antiquaries 16th/17th c

680 ROWLANDS, Dr Marie, Hist Dept Newman Coll of Edn B'ham 32: (1) Industrialization and urbanization in Midlands in 18th c; (2) Early mod B'ham

681 ROYLE, S. A., Geog Dept Queen's Belfast: (1) Soc geog of Leics towns 1837–71 *Article published* [**E Midland Geographer**, 1978]; (2) Sources for Irish urb hist geog *Article published* [**Irish Geography**, 1978]; (3) Irish urb hist geog in 18th/19th c

682 RUDD, J., (Mrs D. K. G. Thompson): Soc and pol of Finsbury [Ldn] 1820–1850 (PhD, B)

683 RUSCOE, Miss J., 17 Bushy Park Rd Teddington Middx: Hist of St Andrew Holborn Ldn *Completed*

684 RUSSELL, Mrs A., (Prof H. J. Perkin): Changing conds and status of Br wkg class in 20th c (PhD, La)

685 RYAN, J., (Mrs D. K. G. Thompson): Relig and pol in B'ham 1830–50 (MLitt, B) *Completed*

686 RYAN, Miss P., (Prof E. J. Hobsbawm): 'Poplarism' and the poor law w sp ref to E Ldn (PhD, L)

687 SACHS, Miss M. Y., (Profs N. Rubinstein/J. K. G. Sherman): Patronage of art in 16th c Siena (MPhil, L)

688 SALLNOW, J., Geog Dept Plymouth Poly: Contemp urbanization and problems in Soviet town planning

689 SANDERS, J. R., (Dr I. Prothero): Wkg-class movements in W Riding in 1830s (PhD, M)

690 SARABHAI, (Prof E. R. Leach): Hist of Jain Community in Ahmadabad (PhD, C)

691 SAVILLE, Mrs D., (Prof P. J. Buckland): Irish immigr in Eng 1558–1640 (MA, Li)

692 SCALES, D. C., (Dr R. F. Foster): Sir Jos Bazalgette and 19th c Ldn (MPhil, L)

693 SCHILCHER, Mrs L., (Mr A. H. Hourani): Decline of Syrian localism: the Damascene notables 1785–1870 (D Phil, O) *Completed*

694 SCHILLING, Prof W. A. H., Coll of Wooster Ohio 44691 USA: Gt Yarmouth in 17th c *No news*

695 SCHOFIELD, J., (Dr Barron) 14 Melina Rd Ldn W12: Secular bldg in City of Ldn c1300–1550 (MPhil, L)

696 SCOLA, R., (Dr W. A. Armstrong) Darwin Coll Kent U: Food supply of M'chester in 19th c (PhD, K)

697 SCOTT, Miss R. G., (Dr J. A. Yelling) Geog Dept Birkbeck Coll: Migrant and indigenous communities in W Durham 1841–71 (PhD, L)

698 SCRIBNER, Dr R. W., Kings Coll Ldn: Reformation and soc in Germ cities

699 SEGARS, T., (Dr P. R. Thompson): Soc hist of fire service as uniformed wkg class occup (MPhil, Es)

700 SEIKALY, Miss M., (Mr A. H. Hourani): Dev of city of Haifa 1918–36 (DPhil, O)

701 SHAH, S., (Dr Peach): Aspects of geog analysis of Asian immigrants in Ldn (DPhil, O)

702 SHAW, Dr D. J. B., Geog Dept B'ham U: Frontier urbanism and rural-urb relns in S Europ Russia in 17th/18th c *No news*

703 SHAW, Dr G., Geog Dept Exeter U: 18th/19th c commercial directories

704 SHAW, Miss L., (Dr P. L. Hollis) Sch Eng & Amer Stud E Anglia Univ: Poor relief in 19th c Norwich (DPhil, EA)

705 SHEPPARD, Dr F. H. W., Room 686 County Hall Ldn: (1) **Survey of London** South Ken and Grosvenor Est in Mayfair; (2) Ldn vestries 1855–89; (3) Brakspear's Brewery, Henley on Thames 1779–1979 *Published*; () [with V.Belcher and P. L. Cottrell] bldg flucts in Middx and Yorks in 18th/19th c

706 SHERWEN, P., Nuffield Coll Oxford: Burslem and the Staffs pottery towns in 17th/18th c

707 SHOPO, T., Hist Dept SOAS Ldn: Demog hist in a Ghanaian town

708 SHROUDER, G., (Prof P. E. H. Hair): Nonconformist soc work in mid 19th c Blackburn (MA, Li)

709 SIDDIQI, M., (Dr R. Jones): Urb land use of Aberdeen in last 100 years (PhD, A)

710 SIMMONS, R. T., (Dr M. Naslas) Dept Town & Reg Plann Sheffield U: Tpt, ind loc and the journey to work in Sheffield in 19th c (PhD, S)

711 SIMPSON, E. J., (Prof R. H. Campbell): Tourism and society: gr of resorts on Forth estuary (MLitt, Stir) *Abandoned*

712 SIMPSON, M. A., Hist Dept U Coll Swansea: Life of Dr Thos Adams, founder of Town Planning Inst

713 SIRAUT, Miss M. C., County Hall Taunton: Asst ed **VCH** Somerset: Cambridge

714 SISSONS, J. N., (Prof P. E. H. Hair): L'pool blitz (MA, Li)

715 SLACK, Dr P., Exeter Coll Oxford: (1) Impact of plague in Eng 1500–1700 *Book forthcoming*; (2) Urb poverty and poor relief 1550–1750 *No news*

716 SLATER, G. J., (Dr A. C. Hepburn) PRO N Ireland: Belfast pol 1832–68 (DPhil, U)

717 SLATER, T. R., Geog Dept B'ham U: (1) Infl of parkland on urb morphol and gr in GB (PhD, L); (2) Cirencester in 18th/19th c *Suspended*; (3) Urb dev in E Poland before 1700; (4) Town plans of med Warks and Worcs

718 SLOANE, K., (Dr M. Leo Lohé/Mr J. Reynolds): ILP in Bradford 1900–45 (PhD, Bra) *Abandoned*

719 SMITH, D., Sociol Dept Leicester U: Educ prov and dev of urb soc struct w sp ref to B'ham, Sheffield 1840–1914

720 SMITH, J. R., (Mr C. V. Phythian-Adams): Maldon Essex 1688–1835 (MA, Lei)

721 SMITH, L. D., (Mrs D. K. G. Thompson): Kidderminster weavers 1800–50 (PhD, B)

722 SMITH, Miss L. M., (Prof H. R. Trevor-Roper): Law and order in 17th c Edinburgh (DPhil, O)

723 SMITH, M. H., (Mr N. McKendrick): Conflict and soc in late 18th c B'ham (PhD, C) *Completed*

724 SMOOR, Mrs C., (Dr N. P. Brooks): Dev of urb vernacular architecture in 16th/17th c Scot w sp ref to St Andrews (PhD, StA) *Abandoned*

725 SNEWIN, J. J., (Dr B. T. Robson) Geog Dept Cambridge U: Evoln of hsg pols in Bradford and N'ham 1918–72 (PhD, C) *Abandoned*

726 SOANE, J., Sociol Dept Surrey U: Urb dev/soc struct of Bournemouth c1840–1940 *Book in prospect No news*

727 SOYE-MITCHELL, Mrs B. de (Université de Paris III), Dyrham Pk Chippenham Wilts: Les villes d'eaux et la civilisation anglaise 1660–1760 (Dd'E, Paris)

728 SPARKES, D. C., (Mr J. H. Y. Briggs): Dissent and govt of City of Ldn 1661–1828 (MA, Ke)

729 SPICER, P., (Prof J. A. S. Grenville): Midlands pol in B'ham, Nottingham, Leicester 1868–1914 (PhD, B)

730 SPINK, J., (Prof G. R. J. Jones): Evoln of settlement and land use in 'New Town' area (Castleford-Knottingley-Pontefract) in W Yorks (MPhil, Le)

731 SPONZA, L., (Prof E. J. Hobsbawm) Central Ldn Poly: Ital immigr into UK 1814–1914 (MPhil, L)

732 SPRINGETT, Mrs R. J., (Prof G. R. J. Jones): Effects of land ownership on urb gr in Huddersfield in 19th c (PhD, Le)

733 SPUFFORD, Dr P., Queens Coll Camb: 14th/15th c Florence

734 STAFFORD, Miss F., (Dr W. A. Armstrong/Mr J. Whyman): Late-Vict Margate (MPhil, K)

735 STARKEY, H. F., (Mrs J. I. Kermode): Canal port of Runcorn 1786–1887 (MA. Li) *Completed*

736 STEELE, E. D., Hist Sch Leeds U: Pols of Vict Leeds *Book forthcoming* [Manch UP]

737 STEELE, R. F., (Dr R. M. Blinkhorn): Wkg-class movement in Seville 1931–6 (PhD, La)

738 STEFFEL, Prof R. V., Hist Dept Ohio State U Marion Ohio 43302; (1) A Vict slum: The Nichol, Bethnal Green 1840–75; (2) Wkg-class hsg in E End of Ldn 1889–1914; (3) Demog study of Bethnal Green 1851–71

739 STENHOUSE, D., Geog Dept L'pool U: Location and relationships of port-related offices in L'pool 1875–1970 (PhD, Li)

740 STEPHENS, F. J., (Prof A. W. Coats): Barnes Papers in Chesterfield Pub Lib in context of poverty, popular pol and elites (MPhil, N)

741 STEPHENS, Dr W. B., Educ Dept Leeds U: Loc hist, literacy and hist of educ

742 STEVENSON, S. J., (Mrs J. M. Hart), Exeter Coll Oxford: Criminal class and area in the late Vict city w sp ref to B'ham and Tower Hamlets 1869–76 (DPhil, O)

743 STEWART, Miss P., (Ext): Poor law admin in Abingdon before 1834 (MPhil, L) *Completed*

744 STIFF, P., Geog Dept L'pool U: Rural-urb migr and econ change in Eng w sp ref to Chester, Gloucester, Shrewsbury 1550–1650 (PhD, Li)

745 STOKER, D. L., (Dr F. O'Gorman): Elect pol in 18th/19th c Berwick (PhD, M)

746 STRANGE, K., (Dr D. J. V. Jones): Wkg classes in Merthyr Tydfil c 1840–50 (PhD, W)

747 STYLES, J. A., (Dr J. Brewer), Sidney Sussex Coll Cambridge: Aspects of crime, public order and the magistracy in the W Riding 1750–1830 (PhD, C) *Presumed abandoned*

748 SULLIVAN, D. A. J., (Prof P. Mathias): Role of G. W. R. in ec/soc dev of Swindon (DPhil, O)

749 SUMMERBELL, Mrs M., *see* DRESSER, Ms M.

750 SURRY, N. W., Dept Hist & Lit Stud Portsmouth Poly: John Mann's charity 1688–1760 [Newport IOW]

751 SUTCLIFFE, Dr A. R., Ec Hist Dept Sheffield U: Town planning in Eur and US c1900

752 SYKES, R. A., (Dr I. J. Prothero): Wkg-class movemts in SE Lancs 1828–42 (PhD, M)

753 TAKEI, Prof Y, Shinshu U 2–12–29 Sawamura Matsumoto Japan: Ind relation of 19th c B'ham and Sheffield

754 TALBOT, R. J., (Dr J. W. R., Whitehand): 20th c house types in vicinity of Anglo-Scottish border (PhD, B)

755 TANKUT, Ms G, Middle East Technical U Ankara: Orthogonality and urb environment [Nauplia] *No news*

756 TANN, Dr J., Management Centre Aston U: Cost of philanthropy: a study of model hsg companies in Ldn and provinces 1850–1914

757 TANNER, Dr N. P., Campion Hall Oxford: Church in late med Norwich *Book forthcoming*

758 TANYELI, U. (Prof B Özer): Interrelat between urb form and archit in trad Turkish city (PhD, State Academy of Fine Arts Istanbul) *No news*

759   TARN, Prof J. N., Architect Dept Liverpool U: (1) High density hsg for wkg classes in 19th/20th c; (2) Historic bldg in Sheffield

760   TAYLOR, Ms A., N Ldn Poly 383 Holloway Rd N7; (1) Hist of early road network in Islington *Abandoned* (2) Hist of Holloway Rd; (3) Evoln of retail pattern in reln to urb gr and org of retailing in 19th c w sp ref to Islington (PhD, L); (4) Whittington Stone, Islington

761   TAYLOR, Prof A. J., Hist Sch Leeds U: Vict and Edw Leeds *Book forthcoming* [Manch UP]

762   TAYLOR, Mrs D. (Mr J. A. Garrard): Character and role of the local newspaper in 19th c ind town, w sp ref to Leigh and Wigan (MSc, Sci)

763   TAYLOR, Ms G. (Prof J. A. Banks): Prostitution and rescue work, a case study in Vict respectability (MPhil, Lei)

764   TAYLOR, I., (Dr F. O'Gorman): Lancs constituencies 1832–67 (MA,M)

765   TAYLOR, I. C., Athabasca U Edmonton Canada T5L 2W4: (1) Soc geog of 18th/19th c L'pool; (2) Hsg and planning pols in pre 1914 L'pool; (3) Land spec and planning in Canada

766   TAYLOR, J. R., (Dr C. P. S. Platt): Populn movemts and struct in 16th c Hants w sp ref to towns (MPhil, So)

767   TAYLOR, L. C., (Dr E. Duffy): Evang Non-con in NE Ldn 1850–1914 (MPhil, L)

768   TAYLOR, P. B. (Prof V. Pearl): Propaganda and the Press in Ldn 1675–83 (PhD, L)

769   TAYLOR, S. A. (Dr G. J. Crossick): Urbanization, landownership and resid segreg in N'ham, Bolton 1830–90 (PhD, H)

770   TEANBY, K. (Dr D. E. Martin/Mr P. Seyd): Doncaster Labour Party 1918–39 (MA, S)

771   TEBBUTT, Miss M. (Dr M. E. Rose) M'chester Studies Unit M'chester Poly: (1) Irish in M'chester in second half of 19th c : evoln of ethnic sterotypes (MA, M); (2) Pawnbroker in urb soc

772   THOMAS, Prof D., Geog Dept B'ham U: Urb fringes in UK and US

773   THOMAS, J. H., Dept Hist & Lit Stud Portsmouth Poly: (1) (Prof J. S. Bromley) Thos Neale, a 17th c projector [incl property dev in Ldn, Newcastle, Tunbridge Wells] (PhD, So) *Completed*; (2) 18th c Portsmouth; (3) Petersfield and Winchester 1660–1715

774   THOMPSON, Ms B. (Mr J. Reynolds): Pop and soc change in Bradford 1880–1930 (PhD, Bra)

775   THOMPSON, Prof F. M. L., IHR London: (1) Ldn in 18th c *Part of book in prospect;* (2) Town horses; (3) Rise of suburbia *Book in prospect*

776   THOMPSON, Miss K. M., (Mr R. H. Evans): Poor law admin in 19th c Leicester (PhD, Lei)

777   THOMPSON, I. A. (Dr J. W. R. Whitehand): Changes to bldg fabric of town centres since 1880 (MLitt, B)

778   THORNE, J. K. R., 59 De Beauvoir Rd Ldn N1: The Vict city pub [M'chester, L'pool, B'ham]

779   THORPE, Prof H., Geog Dept B'ham U: (1) Gr and function of Warwick; (2) Urb allotments and leisure gdns since 18th c *No news*

780   THORPE-SMITH, S. A., (Prof J. Saville): Soc hist of Hull 1910–40 w sp ref to Lab Movement (PhD, H)

781   TICHELAR, (Dr D. E. Martin): Ldn Labour Party 1910–26 (PhD, S)

782   TIRATSOO, N. (Dr C. Erickson): Mobil and status in the Coventry wkg class 1851–71 (PhD, L)

783   TITTLER, Prof R., Hist Dept Concordia U 7141 Sherbrooke St. West Montreal: (1) Pol/ec problems of Eng bors in 16th c; (2) Emergence of nat urb pol in 16th c *Book forthcoming* [Macmillans]

784   TOMMIS, S. (Prof J. W. House): Socio-spatial environments in Bradford (DPhil, O)

785   TOPLIS, G., 14 Chepstow Ct Chepstow Cres Ldn W11: Spec hsg in W cent Ldn w sp ref to Tyburnia 1630–c1850 (PhD, M) *Completed*

786   TRAINOR, R. H., (Dr B. H. Harrison), Wolfson Coll Oxford: Authy and soc struct in three Black Country Towns [W Bromwich, Dudley, Bilston] 1840–90 (DPhil, O)

787   TRANTER, Dr N. L., Hist Dept Stir U: Ec/soc/demog impact of Portpatrick

788   TRAVERS, P. (Dr M. G. Bradford) Homerton Coll Cambridge: Patterns of prestige resid w sp ref to Norwich 1850–71 (MA, M)

789   TRAVIS, J. F., (Dr H. E. S. Fisher): Lynton and Lynmouth in 19th c (PhD, Ex)

790   TREBLE, Dr J. H., Hist Dept Strathclyde U: (1) **Urban Poverty in Britain 1830–1914** [Batsford, 1979]; (2) Lab markt and unemployment in Glasgow 1890–1914 *Publications in progress*; (3) Devel of RC educ in Scotland

791   TRICKER, M. J. (Dr J. W. R. Whitehand): Infl of met food mkt on agric in Eng & Wales c1700–1900 (PhD, B)

792   TRINDER, B. S., (Prof A. M. Everitt): Soc/ec hist of Banbury 1830–80 (PhD, Lei)

793 TRIPPE, Mrs H., (Mr. A. J. J. Vinson): Phys educ and recreation in Southampton 1919–39 (MPhil, So)
794 TRODD, N. R. (Dr G. A. Philips): Pol change and the wkg-class in Blackburn and Burnley 1880–1914 (PhD, La) *Completed*
795 TROWELL, F., (Dr J. Taylor) Constructional Studs Sch Leeds Poly: Architect hist and dev of hsg in a Vict suburb w sp ref to Headingley Leeds 1838–1914 (PhD, Y)
796 TUFT, Rev. P. A., Chiswick Vicarage The Mall Ldn W4: Eng cathedral close
797 TURNER, C. J., (Prof G. R. Batho): Sunderland School Board 1874–1903 (MEd, D)
798 TURNER, M., Geog Dept Exeter U: Fire as agent of change in 17th/18th c prov towns (PhD, Ex)
799 TURRELL, R., (Dr S. Marks): Hist of Kimberley 1875–90 (MPhil, L)
800 TYLER, A., (Mr. S. R. Bassett): Hist/topog/archaed of Bridgnorth (MA, B)
801 TYSON, R. E., (Prof M. Gaskin): Failures of City of Glasgow Banks 1857, 78 (PhD, A) *Presumed abandoned*
802 UNWIN, Dr R. W. (Dr W. B. Stephens): Educ and soc in Wetherby 1660–1902 (PhD, Le) *Completed*
803 URRY, Dr. W., St Edmund Hall Oxford: (1) Christopher Marlowe and Elizabethan Canterbury *Book in prospect*; (2) Town plan for Canterbury (HATPE); (3) Topog of Canterbury *Book forthcoming* [**Atlas of Medieval English Maps**, eds Skelton and Harvey (OUP)]; (4) Narrative and topog account of death of Thomas Becket; (5) Hist of Canterbury
804 USER, E., Geog Dept LSE: Urb expansion in Turkey (PhD, L)
805 VAN ONSELLEN, Dr C., Internat Area Studies Centre 15 Woburn Sq Ldn WC1: Early Johannesburg *No news*
806 VEASEY, E. A., 120 Windermere Ave Nuneaton: Hist of Bedworth and Nuneaton *No news*
807 VLAEMINKE, Mrs E. M. M., (Prof P. V. McGrath/Mr. D. Large): Bristol during Revol & Napol wars (MLitt, Br)
808 WADE, K., Planning Dept St. Peter's House Ipswich: Origins and dev of Ipswich
809 WADE, K. R., Suffolk Archaeol Unit Shire Hall Bury St. Ed: Urb devel in Suffolk *Articles forthcoming* [**East Anglian Archaeology**]
810 WAKELING, C., (Dr. S. Muthesius), Adult Educ Dept Keele U: Vict Nonconformist church architecture
811 WALEY, Dr D., MSS Dept British Lib Ldn: 13th c Siena
812 WALKER, D. R., (Dr R. A. Griffiths): Shrewsbury in 15th c (PhD, W)
813 WALKER, G., M'chester Studies M'chester Poly: Study of community living in Trafford Park Ind Estate 1896–1940 using oral and photographic evidence (with D. Russell)
814 WALKER, R. F., Hist Dept Univ Coll Wales: Med Tenby *Published* [**Boroughs of Medieval Wales**] ed R. A. Griffiths U Wales Press, 1978
815 WALL, R., Camb Gp for Hist of Pop & Soc Struct 27 Trumpington St Cambridge: (1) Popln turnover in late-17th c rural and urb areas w sp ref to Swindon, Lyme Regis, London; (2) Urb/rural variations in h'hold structure in early 19th c W Flanders
816 WALLER, R. J., (Mr. A. F. Thompson): Soc stabil and dislocation in coalfields: Notts 1918–57 (DPhil, O)
817 WALTER, Mrs B. M., Cambridge Poly: Geog of Irish migr to Br since 1939 w sp ref to Luton and Bolton (DPhil, O) *Completed*
818 WALTON, Dr J. K., Hist Dept Lancaster U: Eng seaside holiday towns 1750–1914
819 WARD-PERKINS, B. R. (Prof J. M., Wallace-Hadrill): Urb pub bldgs in N Italy in early M Ages (DPhil, O)
820 WASZAK, P. J. D., (Prof W. Ashworth): Cult and leisure facils in Som towns [Taunton, Bridgwater, Street, Yeovil] 1870–1900 (PhD, Br)
821 WATERS, Miss M. J., (Dr. P. R. Thompson): Chatham dockyard workers 1860–1906 (PhD, Essex) *Completed*
822 WATSON, W. C., (Prof A. Slaven): Clydebank in depression of 1930s (MLitt, G)
823 WATT, Miss A. (Mr. R. I. Hodgson): Effects of land ownership patterns on urb dev: case of Egerton estate M'chester (MA, M)
824 WATTS, D. J., (Mr. M. Todd): Town defences in Rom Br (MPhil, N)
825 WATTS, L., Archaeol Dept York U: Hist and archaeol of Birmingham moat *Publication forthcoming*
826 WEBB, J. G., (Dr A. A. Ruddock). Eliz Ipswich (PhD, L)
827 WEIDMANN, Mrs. O. A., (Prof W. A. Cole/Dr. A. J. H. Latham): Soc consequences of inflation in Mainz 1918–25 (PhD, W)
828 WEINSTEIN, Mrs. R., Ldn Museum: Gr and urb dev of N Ldn suburbs 1200–1700
829 WELSH, C., Geog Dept Leeds U: Anal of emerg of soc areas in Leeds and Wakefield 1851–71 (MPhil, Le)

830 WEYMOUTH, Miss M. (Prof C. H. Lawrence): Church in med Northampton (MPhil, L) *Suspended*

831 WHEATLEY, Prof P., Geog Dept Chicago U 5828 S Univ Ave Chicago Illinois 60637: (1) Origins of SE Asia urb traditions; (2) Urb symbolism *In the press* [Edizioni Morcelliana, Brescia, 1979]; (3) [with K. S. Sandhu] Melaka: the transformation of a Malay capital c 1400–1980 *In the press* [OUP]

832 WHEATLEY, Mrs. S. E., Univ Coll of Wales Aberystwyth: [with Prof H. Carter] Soc and resid areas in Merthyr Tydfil in mid-19th c

833 WHEELER, M., (Dr O. A. Hartley): Debate on town planning profession 1900–70 (PhD, Le) *Abandoned*

834 WHITE, Miss, B. M., (Dr A. Crowther/Prof S. G. Checkland): Role of MOHs in W. Scotland 1860–1930s (MLitt, G)

835 WHITEHAND, Dr J. W. R., Geog Dept B'ham U: (1) Bldg cycles and spatial pattern of urb gr and redev; (2) Form of city centres

836 WHITEHEAD, A., (Prof R. J. Harrison): Soc mobil and radicalism in Clerkenwell 1851–81 (PhD, War)

837 WHITFIELD, R. (Mr. D. Large): Lab movement in Bristol 1914–39 (PhD, Br)

838 WHITING, R. C., (Mr. A. F. Thompson): Wkg class in 'new industry' towns between wars w sp ref to Oxford (DPhil, O) *Completed*

839 WHYMAN, J., Rutherford Coll Kent U (Dr. W. A. Armstrong): Gr and dev of Ramsgate, Margate, Broadstairs 1736–1815 (PhD, K)

840 WICKHAM, Dr C. J., Med Hist Dept B'ham U: Town and country in early med Italy

841 WICKHAM, Ms P., (Dr C. P. S. Platt): Pop listings in Southampton 1695–7 (MPhil, So)

842 WILKINSON, Miss A. M. (Prof P. Mathias): Work of medical officers of health in three S Ldn parishes 1856–1900 (DPhil, O)

843 WILLIAMS, B., M'chester Studs M'chester Poly: (1) Oral hist of loc community; (2) Jewish immigrant life 1875–1945

844 WILLIAMS, H., (Mr. D. E. Baines): Soc change in two mining communities 1860–1926 [Aberdare valley/Leen valley Notts] (PhD, L)

845 WILLIAMS, J. D., (Dr N. L. Tranter): Bridge of Allan in 19th c (MLitt, St)

846 WILLIAMS, J. H., (Prof G. H. Martin): Northampton AD 800–1200 (PhD, Lei)

847 WILLIAMS, R., (Dr G. J. Crossick): Lab aristoc in late-19th c Middlesbrough (PhD, Hu)

848 WILLIAMS, S. R., (Prof I. G. Jones): Industrialization and language in ind Monmouthshire (MA, W)

849 WILLIS, J. G. I. (Prof N. McCord): Soc struct of Morpeth in 1851 (MLitt, Ne) *Presumed abandoned*

850 WILSON, C., (Dr J. W. R. Whitehand): Dev of med town plans w sp ref to Hull, Stratford-upon-Avon (PhD, B)

851 WILSON, Mrs. (Dr A. R. Sutcliffe): Soc/ec dev of Seaham Harbour (MA, S)

852 WINCHESTER, A. J. L., (Dr B. K. Roberts): Hist geog of Cockermouth (MPhil, D) *Presumed abandoned*

853 WINCHESTER, Mrs. H. P. M., (Prof J. House): Rural and urb perspectives on pop mobility in France w sp ref to Isère (DPhil, O)

854 WISEMAN, Prof T. P., Classics Dept Exeter U: Topog of city of Rome under the late Republic *In the press* [Duckworth] *No news*

855 WOJCIECHOWSKA-KIBBLE, Ms B. J. M., (Dr. Armstrong): Soc change, structure and migration in Kent 1841–71 (PhD, K)

856 WOOD, C. J. K., (Dr R. Burt): Role of civic auths in adopt tech innovations for ec/soc improvement fr early 19th c (PhD, Ex) *Abandoned*

857 WOODBERRY, R. D. A., (Mr. D. Large): Pols of Bristol 1867–86 (MLitt, B)

858 WOODHEAD, Miss C. (Prof T. C. Barker): B'ham branch of Bank of Eng 1827–50 (PhD, L)

859 WOODHOUSE, T. (Prof A. J. Taylor): Lab movements in Leeds and Bradford 1880–1914 (PhD, Le)

860 WOODS, D. C., Management Centre Aston U: Crime and soc in Black Country 1860–1900

861 WORM, P., (Mr. K. E. Thurley): Workshop solidarity in GB/US engineering ind [Coventry (Warwicks) and Bridgeport (Conn)] 1900–25 (PhD, L)

862 WORTHINGTON, R. A., (Prof H. Carter): Bor towns of Monmouthshire (PhD, W)

863 WRIGHT, Dr A. P. M. IHR Ldn: Sen Asst to gen ed **VCH; Cambridgeshire**

864 WRIGHT, R. A., (Mr. R. M. Y. Shackleton): Lib party org and pols in B'ham, Coventry, W'hampton 1886–1914 w sp ref to indep lab rep (PhD, B) *Completed*

865 WRIGHT, S. J., (Mr. C. V. Phythian-Adams): Posit of women in e mod town [Salisbury, Southampton, Winchester] (PhD, Lei)

866 WRIGLEY, Dr E. A., Peterhouse, Cambridge: Hist demog of Eng 1550–1850

867 WROTHALL, J. E., (Dr P. H. J. H. Gosden): Teacher training in Huddersfield 1900–70 (MEd, Le)

868 WYKES, D. L., (Mr. R. H. Evans): Nonconformists in trade and ind of Leicester 18th/19th c (MPhil, Lei)

869 WYNCOLL, P. H., (Prof J. Saville): Dev of N'ham lab movement (PhD, OU)

870 YEADELL, M. H., (Prof J. Saville): 19th c hsg dev in W Riding w sp ref to bldg socs (PhD, H)

871 YEAMAN, Miss W. J., Geog Dept Keele U: Soc/econ structure of N Staffs ind towns in mid 19th c (PhD, Ke)

872 YELLING, Dr J. A., Geog Dept Birkbeck Coll Ldn: Slums and slum clearance in Ldn 1840–1914

873 YENAL, Dr E., Devlet Güzel Sanatlar Akademisi Findikli Isanbul-Turkey: (1) Planning initiatives in late 19th c Ottoman city; (2) Case-study of evoln urb form [Anatolia]; (3) Trade and commerce in the Ottoman city; (4) Architecture of Anatolian city: residential patterns and reflections

874 YOLDAS, Dr Y., Technical U Istanbul: Istanbul's urb topog in 17th c *No news*

875 YOUNG, Dr K. G., 28 Melcombe Ct Dorset Sq Ldn NW1 [Bristol U]: (1) Pol and governmental dev of Ldn in 19th/20th c *Book forthcoming*; (2) Loc authy pol responses to econ change in Ldn region in 1970s *Book forthcoming*

Index to register of research